...eyes and ...y
...d a fire to warm
...ll and ... — bia...
...this were ...
...left I in excel
...still more they en...
comp... speech — and ~~xxx~~
...of affection A kindnes-
...tears mean? did they
...un? I was at first
...these questions but
...tion and time
...e many of the appear
...at first seemed
...ith Poxim...

MARY
SHELLEY

L. Holst. del.   W. Chevalier sculp

FRANKENSTEIN.

"By the glimmer of the half-extinguished
light, I saw the dull, yellow eye of the
creature open: it breathed hard, and a
convulsive motion agitated its limbs.
* * * I rushed out of the room."

Page 43.

London, Published by H. Colburn and R. Bentley, 1831.

MARY SHELLEY

HER LIFE

HER FICTION

HER MONSTERS

ANNE K. MELLOR

METHUEN • New York & London

Published in 1988 by

Methuen, Inc.
29 West 35 Street
New York, NY 10001

Published in Great Britain by
Methuen & Co. Ltd.
11 New Fetter Lane
London EC4P 4EE

Library of Congress Cataloging-in-Publication Data

Mellor, Anne Kostelanetz.
  Mary Shelley, her life, her fiction, her monsters / by Anne K.
Mellor.
    p. cm.
  Bibliography: p.
  Includes index.
  ISBN 0–416–01761–4
  1. Shelley, Mary Wollstonecraft, 1797–1851. 2. Authors,
English—19th century—Biography. 3. Monsters in literature.
4. Family in literature. I. Title.
PR5398.M4   1988
823'.7—dc19

British Library Cataloguing in Publication Data

Mellor, Anne Kostelanetz
  Mary Shelley : her life, her fiction, her
monsters.
  1. Shelley, Mary Wollstonecraft—Criticism
and interpretation
  I. Title
  823'.7 PR5398

  ISBN 0–416–01761–4

FOR DOROTHY GANNETT AND BLAKE MELLOR

CONTENTS

CONTENTS

FRONTISPIECE

The Frontispiece for *Frankenstein, or The Modern Prometheus* (London: Colburn and Bentley, 1831), British Museum Library

PLATE I

"Mary Wollstonecraft," by John Opie, c. 1797, National Portrait Gallery, London

PLATE II

"William Godwin," by James Northcote, 1802, National Portrait Gallery, London

PLATE III

"Percy Bysshe Shelley," by Amelia Curran, 1819, National Portrait Gallery, London

PLATE IV

"Claire Clairmont," by Amelia Curran, 1819, Newstead Abbey, Nottingham City Council Museums, England

PLATE V

"George Gordon, Lord Byron," by Richard Westall, 1813, National Portrait Gallery, London

PLATES VI AND VII (and END PAPERS)

Manuscript of *Frankenstein*, folio pages 106 and 203. Abinger Shelley Collection: Abinger Dep. c. 534, Bodleian Library, Oxford

For most of this century, Mary Shelley's writings have been explored primarily for the light they can throw on the poetic and intellectual development of her husband, Percy Bysshe Shelley. Jean de Palacio's full-length study of her thought and art, *Mary Shelley dans son oeuvre* (1969), typically assumed that she was in effect the product of Percy Shelley's ideas and explores "bien sûr, son obédience intellectuelle à la pensée de Shelley et la connaissance intime qu'elle avait de son oeuvre" (16). And William Veeder's recent Freudian/Lacanian analysis of androgyny and erotic bifurcation in *Mary Shelley and Frankenstein* (1986) persists in reading Mary Shelley primarily in relation to her husband's personality and ideas.

With the single exception of *Frankenstein*, none of her novels has received extensive critical discussion, and even *Frankenstein* has traditionally been excluded from the established academic canon. George Levine and U. C. Knoepflmacher, editing a distinguished group of essays on *Frankenstein* in 1979, felt compelled to defend the academic legitimacy of their project against both those who crudely believe that *Frankenstein* is nothing more "than an adolescent flight that has somehow managed to cash in clumsily on popular traditions" and those "more serious readers" who dismiss the book as an "unselfconscious and accidental" literary act (*The Endurance of Frankenstein*, xii-xiii).

But in the last fifteen years, feminist and psychoanalytic critics—led by Ellen Moers and Marc Rubenstein and culminating in the work of Sandra Gilbert and Susan Gubar, Mary Poovey, and Margaret Homans—have radically revised both our understanding of the originality and complexity of *Frankenstein* and our critical estimation of its value. *Frankenstein* is rapidly becoming an essential text for our exploration of female consciousness and literary technique.

My book is an attempt to contribute further to this process of critical revision. By examining the entire range of Mary Shelley's life and writings, I hope to create a better understanding of the development of Mary Shelley's career, of her literary strengths and intellectual concerns. By taking into account as yet unpublished archival materials in the Abinger Shelley Collection in the Bodleian Library and by paying more attention to the contemporary cultural influences on her work, I hope to clarify the subtle ways in which Mary Shelley's fictions criticize the dominant romantic and patriarchal ideologies of her day. In their place, Mary Shelley offered a more life-supporting ideology grounded on a new conception of the bourgeois family as ideally egalitarian. However, her commitment to the preservation of the bourgeois family posed problems for women, problems which her fictions acknowledge.

Because of her historical circumstances, Mary Shelley was throughout her childhood deprived of a loving nuclear family. She desperately sought to create such a family, both in her life and in her fiction. In *Frankenstein* she analyzed the disastrous consequences of the absence of a nurturing parent or supportive family. In her subsequent novels she idealized the benevolent and democratically structured bourgeois family. But even as she did so, she registered her contradictory consciousness that the egalitarian family she craved might not be possible, at least not in the world of nineteenth-century middle-class England to which she belonged. I argue that the fundamental tension in Mary Shelley's writing is not so much the "ambivalence with regard to female self-assertion"—or conflict between the desire to be an original romantic writer and the social requirement to be a modest, decorous lady—which Mary Poovey described so powerfully in her path-breaking *The Proper Lady and the Woman Writer* (1984). Rather, it is the more profound contradiction inherent in the very concept of an egalitarian bourgeois family promoted in Mary Shelley's fiction. For the bourgeois family is founded on the legitimate possession and exploitation of property and on an ideology of domination—whether of the male gender over the female or of parents over children—that render it innately hierarchical.

Since Mary Shelley's critique of romantic and patriarchal ideologies is sweeping in its implications, I have found myself drawing on insights and interpretive methods garnered from a wide range of sources: Self-in-Relation psychology (developed in the recent work of Nancy Chodorow, Carol Gilligan, and Jean Baker Miller), feminist critical theory, cultural anthropology, Marxism, and the new historicism. I have tried to weld these disparate but often mutually enriching approaches and disciplines into a coherent reading of Mary Shelley's life and work. In the face of recent deconstructive critical theory, I have continued to assume that it is not "language" that speaks but rather "authors" that speak. But I am thinking of the author in Bakhtinian terms, as the nexus of a "dialogue" of conflicting ideological discourses or allegiances produced by sex, class, nationality, and specific economic, political, and familial conditions. In this book, then, "Mary Wollstonecraft Godwin Shelley" is both a historical person lost in time and a subject constituted by a complex configuration of fictional writing, nonfictional discourse (letters, journals), and intertextual references (to the discourse of her parents, husband, friends, peers, and other authors of literary, political, and scientific texts). Because I believe that language both responds to and structures a pre-existent material reality and that any ideology is a complex and contradictory system of representations which conditions our conscious experience of ourselves both as individual subjects and as participants in various personal relationships and social institutions, I have devoted much of this book to tracking the unique biographical situations that produced the ideology of the bourgeois family so problematically celebrated in Mary Shelley's fiction.

I begin with an account of Mary Shelley's childhood and romance with Percy Shelley, then turn to an examination of her first novel, *Frankenstein*, paying careful attention in my third chapter to the changes that Percy Shelley made to his wife's manuscript. After considering the several ideological issues at stake in this, Mary Shelley's greatest novel, I turn to her later works, identifying the ways in which *Mathilda* and *The Last Man* wrestle with both her personal and political obsessions. My final chapter is devoted to those works—*Mathilda*, *Valperga*, *Lodore*, and *Falkner*—which most strikingly manifest the contradictions inherent in Mary Shelley's idealization of the bourgeois family.

A final note on her name. Before her marriage to Percy Bysshe Shelley on 30 December 1816, Mary always referred to herself as Mary Wollstonecraft Godwin. After her marriage, she dropped Godwin and, in continuing homage to her mother, signed her letters as Mary Wollstonecraft Shelley or MWS. Her father's Diary entries after 1817 also refer to his daughter as MWS (with some significant exceptions discussed in the text). I have therefore adopted the practice initiated by Betty T. Bennett in her authoritative edition of Shelley's letters and referred to the subject of this book, after her marriage at the age of nineteen, as Mary Wollstonecraft Shelley.

All scholars of the Godwin and Shelley families owe an enormous debt to Lord Abinger, who has generously deposited his invaluable collection of Shelley and Godwin manuscripts in the Bodleian Library, Oxford University. I am particularly grateful to Lord Abinger for permission to quote from as yet unpublished materials in the Abinger Shelley Collection. The University of Wisconsin Press and the Indiana University Press have generously granted permission to reprint materials in Chapters 5 and 6, respectively. And I wish once again to thank the John Simon Guggenheim Foundation for the support that enabled me to undertake this book.

In my effort to understand Mary Shelley's life and work, I have been greatly helped by several scholars who gave generously of their time and knowledge: Nina Auerbach, Margaret Homans, George Levine, Don Locke, Morton Paley, Donald H. Reiman, Patsy Stoneman, Alexander Welsh, and especially William Veeder, Susan Wolfson, and Ruth Bernard Yeazell. Amy Gustafson has been an invaluable research assistant. For his continuing support and affection, I once again thank Ron Mellor. To the two people who taught me most about motherhood, my mother and my son, I dedicate this book with love and gratitude.

1797

March 29: Mary Wollstonecraft, age 38, marries William Godwin, age 41, at St Pancras church in London.

August 30: Mary Wollstonecraft Godwin gives birth to Mary Godwin.

September 10: Mary Wollstonecraft Godwin dies of puerperal fever.

1801

December 21: William Godwin marries the widow Mrs. Mary Jane Clairmont. She and her two children, Charles and Jane, join William, Mary and Fanny Godwin, the daughter of Mary Wollstonecraft and Gilbert Imlay, at Godwin's home in the Polygon, Somers Town, a suburb of London.

1805

William and Mary Jane Godwin open a publishing firm (M. Godwin and Co.) and bookshop for children's books.

1810

The Godwin Juvenile Library publishes Mary Godwin's verse poem, "Mounseer Nongtongpaw."

1812

January: Percy Bysshe Shelley writes a self-introductory letter to Godwin, assuming the role of disciple to the philosopher.

June: Mary travels to Scotland to stay with the Baxter family, acquaintances of William Godwin.

October: Percy Shelley and his wife, Harriet, meet and dine with the Godwins at Skinner Street.

November 10: Mary returns to London with Christy Baxter.

November 11: First meeting between Percy and Mary when the Shelleys dine with the Godwins.

1813

Mary again lives in Dundee, Scotland, with the Baxters.

1814

March 30: Mary returns to London.

May 5: Percy Shelley dines at Skinner Street, and sees Mary for the second time. They begin spending nearly every day together.

June 26: Mary declares her love for Percy Shelley at her mother's grave in St Pancras churchyard.

July 28: Mary and Percy flee to France, Mary's stepsister Jane (later called Claire) accompanies them. Godwin denounces his daughter.

August: Percy, Mary, and Jane travel through France from Calais to Switzerland. Financial troubles force the trio to return to England.

September 13: Percy, Mary, and Jane arrive in London where they are plagued by financial troubles. When Sir Bysshe, Percy's grandfather, dies, Percy begins negotiations concerning his inheritance which continue throughout his life.

1815

February 22: Mary gives birth prematurely to a baby girl called Clara.

March 6: Mary's baby dies.

August: Percy and Mary send Claire to stay with friends and set up house alone in Bishopsgate.

1816

January 24: Mary's son William is born.

April: Claire is successful in her pursuit of Lord Byron, and becomes his mistress.

May 3–14: Mary, baby William, Percy, and Claire travel to Switzerland to join Lord Byron on Lake Geneva, where Byron and Shelley meet for the first time.

June: Lord Byron leases the Villa Diodati at Coligny, and the Shelley entourage moves into a nearby cottage.

June 15–17: The group engages in discussions about philosophy and the principle of life, and the ghost stories are proposed. On June 16 Mary has her "waking dream" which becomes the germ of *Frankenstein*, and she begins to write her story.

September 8: Mary, William, Percy, and Claire return to England.

October 9: Fanny Godwin commits suicide and is buried anonymously, Godwin having refused to identify or claim the body.

December 10: Harriet Shelley's body, advanced in pregnancy, is found in the Serpentine river, where she had drowned herself.

December 30: Mary Godwin marries Percy Shelley at St Mildred's church in London.

1817

January 12: Claire gives birth to a baby girl, called Alba (later christened Allegra Alba).

March 17: Percy is denied custody of his and Harriet's two children. There is no evidence that Percy ever saw them again.

March 18: Percy, Mary, William, Claire, and Alba move into Albion House at Marlow.

May 14: Mary finishes *Frankenstein*.

September 1: Mary gives birth to a daughter, Clara Everina.

December: Mary publishes *History of a Six Weeks Tour*.

1818

March: *Frankenstein* is published.

March 12: The Shelley entourage departs for Italy, to aid Percy's health and to deliver Allegra Alba to Byron.

April–June: The group finally settles in Bagni di Lucca. Alba is sent to Byron in Venice. Mary begins researching her novel on Castruccio, the Prince of Lucca (later published as *Valperga*).

August 17: Percy accompanies Claire to Venice to see Byron and her ill daughter.

August 31: Mary hastily departs from Bagni di Lucca at Percy's demand to join him in Venice.

September 24: Clara dies from a fever exacerbated by the rushed journey across Italy.

December 28: Elena Adelaide Shelley, the possible daughter of Percy Shelley and their Swiss nursemaid Elise, is born in Naples.

1819

June 7: Mary's son William dies of malaria and is buried in the Protestant cemetery at Rome.

August: At Leghorn, Mary writes *Mathilda*, which is not published in her lifetime.

October: Mary and Percy move to Florence.

November 12: Birth of Percy Florence, the only one of their children to survive.

1820

January 27: The Shelleys arrive in Pisa.

September: Mary begins writing *Valperga*.

1821

January 16: Edward and Jane Williams arrive in Pisa and soon become close friends of the Shelleys. During the following year, Percy becomes especially fond of Jane.

January–February: Percy befriends Emilia Viviani, for whom he writes *Epipsychidion*.

June: Mary completes the second volume of *Valperga*.

1822

April: Allegra Alba dies of typhus fever.

May: The Shelleys and Claire move to the Casa Magni in La Spezia. Percy's boat, the *Don Juan*, arrives.

June 16: Mary miscarries during her fifth pregnancy. Percy saves her from bleeding to death by putting her in an ice bath.

July 8: Percy Shelley and Edward Williams set sail in a storm in the *Don Juan* and are found drowned ten days later.

September: Mary moves to Genoa. Claire joins her brother, Charles, in Vienna and spends most of the remainder of her life on the continent in various posts as a governess and companion. Jane Williams returns to London.

1823

August: Mary and Percy Florence arrive in England and move into lodgings in Brunswick Square. Mary sees Jane Williams frequently.

August 29: Mary sees H. M. Milner's *Frankenstein, or, The Demon of Switzerland* at the Royal Coburg Theatre.

September–December: *Valperga* is published. Mary collects and edits Percy's unpublished poems into a volume, *Posthumous Poems of Percy Bysshe Shelley*, then recalls the unsold copies at the insistence of Sir Timothy Shelley.

1824

February: Mary begins writing *The Last Man*.

April 19: Byron dies at Missolonghi in Greece.
June 21: Mary moves to Kentish Town to be close to Jane Williams.

1825

June: Mary refuses an offer of marriage from John Howard Payne, an American actor-manager and friend of Washington Irving.

1826

February: *The Last Man* is published.
September: Harriet's son Charles dies and Percy Florence becomes heir to the family estates. Mary's allowance from Sir Timothy Shelley is doubled to 200 pounds per year.

1827

April–July: Jane Williams moves in with Thomas Jefferson Hogg. Their daughter, Mary Prudentia, is born in November.
July 13: Mary discovers Jane Williams's betrayal of her trust.

1828

January: Mary begins researching and writing *The Fortunes of Perkin Warbeck*.
March: Mary writes "The Sisters of Albano" for *The Keepsake*, the first of fourteen stories that she will publish in this annual between 1828 and 1838. Percy Florence begins his formal education at Edward Slater's Gentleman's Academy in Kensington.
April: Mary visits friends in Paris and contracts smallpox.
June–July: Mary recovers by the sea at Dover and Hastings.

1829

May: Mary settles at Portman Square, where she remains until April 1833.

1830

May: *Perkin Warbeck* is published by Colburn and Bentley.

1831

January–February: Mary begins writing *Lodore*.
June: Mary refuses a partially jesting offer of marriage from Edward Trelawny, a friend from her days in Italy with Percy.
November: 1831 revised edition of *Frankenstein* is published by Bentley and Colburn in their Standard Novels series.

1832

September 29: Percy Florence enters Harrow.

1833

April: Mary moves to Harrow to limit the expenses of boarding Percy at school and allow him to continue his education.

1834

May: Mary rewrites part of *Lodore*, a section of the manuscript having been lost in the mail or by the publishers.

1835

February: Volume I of the *Lives of . . . Eminent Literary . . . Men of Italy, Spain and Portugal* for Lardner's Cabinet Cyclopedia series is published. Mary contributed the lives of Petrarch, Boccaccio, and Machiavelli.

March: *Lodore* is published.

October: Volume II of the *Lives* is published. Mary wrote the lives of Metastasio, Goldoni, Alfieri, Monti, and Foscolo.

1836

April: Mary engages a tutor for Percy and moves back to London.

April 7: William Godwin dies of catarrhal fever and is buried with Mary Wollstonecraft in St Pancras churchyard.

1837

Falkner is published by Saunders and Otley. Volume III of the *Lives* is published, including essays by Mary on Cervantes, Lope de Vega, and Calderón.

October 10: Percy enters Trinity College, Cambridge.

1838

July: *Lives of the most Eminent . . . Men of France* (1838–39), Volume I, is published, with Mary's essays on Montaigne, Rabelais, Corneille, Rouchefoucauld, Molière, La Fontaine, Pascal, Mme de Sévigné, Racine, Boileau, and Fénelon.

1839

January–May: Volumes I through IV (final volume) of Percy Shelley's *Poetical Works* with notes by Mary are published at monthly intervals. Volume II of *Lives of . . . Men of France* is published, with Mary's essays on Voltaire, Rousseau, Condorcet, Mirabeau, Mme Roland and Mme de Staël.

November: Mary's edition of Percy Shelley's *Essays, Letters* is published.

1840

June–September: Mary spends two months at Lake Como with Percy and his friends.

1841

January: Percy Florence graduates from Cambridge University.

1842

June: Mary and Percy spend the summer in Germany and the winter and spring in Italy.

1843

July 10: Mary returns to England with Percy, stopping to visit Claire in Paris.

1844

Rambles in Germany and Italy is published. Sir Timothy Shelley dies and the heavily indebted estate passes to Percy Florence.

1848

June: Percy Florence marries Jane St John.

1849

Mary moves into Field Place, the Shelley country home in Bournemouth, Sussex, with Percy and Jane.

1850

Mary spends the winter in Chester Square, suffering from nervous attacks and partial paralysis. Percy and Jane attend her diligently and affectionately.

1851

February 1: Mary Shelley dies at age 53. She is buried between the transferred remains of her mother and father in St Peter's churchyard, Bournemouth.

CHAPTER ONE

In Search of a Family

When Mary Wollstonecraft died of puerperal fever on September 10, 1797, she left her newborn daughter with a double burden: a powerful and ever-to-be-frustrated need to be mothered, together with a name, Mary Wollstonecraft Godwin, that proclaimed this small child as the fruit of the most famous radical literary marriage of eighteenth-century England. Watching the growth of this baby girl into the author of one of the most famous novels ever written, *Frankenstein, or The Modern Prometheus*, we can never forget how much her desperate desire for a loving and supportive parent defined her character, shaped her fantasies, and produced her fictional idealizations of the bourgeois family—idealizations whose very fictiveness, as we shall see, is transparent.

Mary Wollstonecraft's death in childbirth was unexpected, although not unusual within the context of eighteenth-century medical practices. She was in excellent health and had three years earlier borne without complications a first daughter, Fanny, the offspring of her passionate affair with the American businessman and gambler, Gilbert Imlay. She chose to give birth to this second baby at home, attended only by a midwife, Mrs. Blenkinsop. But when Mary Wollstonecraft failed to expel the placenta, Mrs. Blenkinsop hastily summoned Doctor Poignard who, without washing his hands (as was common at the time), pulled out the fragmented placenta piece by piece. In the process, he introduced the infection of the uterus that ten days later killed Mary Wollstonecraft Godwin, the author of *A Vindication of the Rights of Woman* and the most ardent advocate of her times for the education and development of female capacities.

William Godwin, the author of *Political Justice*, was an austere intellectual who prided himself on his philosophical rigor and revolutionary principles. Having tasted the intense joy of a passionate love for a woman for the first time only thirteen months before at the age of forty, Godwin was shocked and deeply grieved by his wife's death. His diary, in which he conscientiously recorded every day his reading, his visits and visitors, his activities and, rarely and usually in French, the emotional crises of his life, found no words to articulate her death. Poignantly, it reads only

Sep. 10. Su   20 minutes before 8 ....

....

....

Married only five months earlier, despite both his own and Mary Wollstonecraft's principled opposition to the institution of marriage, in order to give their child social respectability, William Godwin was now left with two infant girls to care for alone. He dealt with his grief in the way most natural to him, by reasoned reflection and writing. The day after her funeral, he began to sort through Mary Wollstonecraft's papers. By September 24 he had begun writing the story of her life, and by the end of the year he had finished his loving celebration, *Memoirs of the Author of the Vindication of the Rights of Woman* (published in January 1798).

Despite the genuine feeling and sensitively distanced rhetoric of Godwin's account of his dead wife's history and writings, qualities that render this book one of his most compelling works, despite his noble intention of memorializing his wife's literary reputation, despite his deep admiration for her political wisdom and personal courage, Godwin completely misjudged his audience. Public outrage followed his published account of Mary Wollstonecraft's thwarted affair with the painter Henry Fuseli (during which she had offered to join Fuseli and his new wife Sophia in a platonic ménage à trois), of her passionate love affair with Gilbert Imlay and the birth of her illegitimate daughter, followed by her two suicide attempts when Imlay deserted her, and of Godwin's unabashed admission that he had been sexually intimate with Mary Wollstonecraft well before their marriage. The *Monthly Review* declared that

blushes would suffuse the cheeks of most husbands, if they were *forced* to relate those anecdotes of their wives which Mr. Godwin voluntarily proclaims to the world. The extreme eccentricity of Mr. G.'s sentiments will account for this conduct. Virtue and vice are weighed by him in a balance of his own. He neither looks to marriage with respect, nor to suicide with horror.[1]

The novelist Charles Lucas called the book *Godwin's History of the Intrigues of his own Wife* while Thomas Mathias considered it

> "a convenient Manual of speculative debauchery, with the most select arguments for reducing it into practice;" for the amusement, initiation, and instruction of young ladies from sixteen to twenty-five years of age, who wish to figure in life, and afterwards in Doctor's Commons and the King's Bench; or ultimately in the notorious receptacles of *patrician* prostitution.[2]

Many readers were more shocked by Mary Wollstonecraft's suicide attempts—and the lack of religious conviction that they implied—than by her love affairs. On this score, Godwin was unfair to Wollstonecraft. Being an atheist himself, he had concealed her faith in a benevolent deity and an afterlife and had instead declared at the end of the *Memoirs* that "during her whole illness, not one word of a religious cast fell from her lips."[3]

The end result of the publication of Godwin's devoted but injudicious *Memoirs*, coupled with the publication later that year of *The Posthumous Works of Mary Wollstonecraft* which included not only her unfinished novel *Maria, or The Wrongs of Woman* but also all of Mary Wollstonecraft's infatuated and overtly sexual love letters to Gilbert Imlay—letters which Godwin asserted were superior in "the language of sentiment and passion" to Goethe's *Werther*[4]—was to undermine Mary Wollstonecraft's influence as an advocate of women's rights for almost a hundred years. Immediately after the original publication of *A Vindication of the Rights of Woman*, many upper-class women had rallied behind Wollstonecraft's claim that state-supported education for females as well as males would render women better fitted to serve as sensible mothers, more interesting companions to men, and more useful citizens of the nation. The bluestocking Anna Seward thought *A Vindication* a "wonderful book. . . . It has, by turns, pleased and displeased, startled and half-convinced me that its author is oftener right than wrong."[5] The young Dissenter Mary Hays, who was to become Mary Wollstonecraft's most ardent disciple, wrote that the book was "a work full of truth and genius."[6] And even Lady Palmerston, the meekest of wives, warned her husband that "I have been reading the Rights of Woman, so you must in future expect me to be very tenacious of my rights and privileges."[7] But Godwin's revelations made it impossible for a respectable English woman openly to associate herself with Mary Wollstonecraft's feminist views. And they further increased the burden upon his and Wollstonecraft's daughter, who grew up both idolizing her dead mother and at the same time keenly aware of the social opprobrium and personal costs suffered by any woman who openly espoused the causes of sexual freedom, radical democracy, or women's rights.

Domestically, Godwin struggled valiantly to care for his two infant charges. He assumed full responsibility for Fanny, now aged three, whom he called Fanny Godwin, as well as for the newborn Mary Godwin. He immediately hired Louisa Jones, a friend of his sister Harriet, to serve as housekeeper and governess at the Polygon where Godwin now resided. When the baby Mary became ill on December 20, 1797, he arranged for a wet-nurse for Mary who fed her between December 31 and April 30, 1798. Judging from Louisa's letters, Mary Godwin's earliest years seem to have been happy. Louisa was devoted to the two little girls, and Fanny was delighted with her baby sister. When Godwin went to Bath in March, 1798, Louisa sent a vivid account of the girls' activities:

> Fanny has a great many things to tell *Somebody* but I very much fear they will be all forgotten we have been most gloriously happy this morning, such a game of romps as would frighten you and we have been to Mr Marshals garden and told him to come and put the seeds in the Garden and we have been playing in the pretty place besides twenty other *ands* all conducive to the harmony of the mental and bodily faculties. . . . Fanny's progress in reading astonishes as much as it pleases me. all the little words come as freely from her as from a much older child & she spells pig, boy, cat, box, boy, without seeing them when asked. . . .

Louisa wrote again to Godwin when he went to Bristol in June:

> Sister Mary goes on very well indeed, has left off her cap today and looks like a little cherub. . . . I cant get Fanny to send you a kiss only one to my Sister she says. Farewell return soon and make us happy.[8]

But this idyll was not to last. During that spring, the impressionable Louisa fell in love with Godwin's young Scots disciple, John Arnot.[9] After Arnot went to Russia that summer, she became increasingly involved with one of Godwin's more tempestuous and irresponsible protégés, George Dyson. Godwin objected strongly to this relationship and for two years Louisa tried to repress her attraction to Dyson, but failed. "I have felt for a very long time that I ought to have told you my feelings," she wrote to Godwin in the spring of 1808, "but I have lived in the hope of overcoming them the struggle I have had with myself has been very severe indeed and it would be impossible to convey to you the emotions that have by turn oppressed and agitated me." Godwin had told her that if she went off with Dyson, she could never see the girls again, which clearly distressed her enormously and delayed her departure. But after Dyson appeared at Godwin's house in a fit of drunken despair in July, 1800, while Godwin was on holiday in Ireland, Louisa capitulated and agreed to go to live at Bath with him. Before she left, she begged Godwin to let her visit the girls, claiming that she could yet be of service to Fanny: "As a visitor a frequent one if it meets approbation I can produce double the effect I could ever hope to do by living with her—for I am sure at present I should be the ruin of her temper and her habits in general." She justified her decision to leave on the grounds that it would have happened eventually anyway, that someone else would have more authority with the servants than she had, and most importantly, that she left the children in good hands, for Cooper, the nursemaid, was *extraordinarily attached* to Mary." Louisa insisted that Cooper could take adequate care of the girls: "Where she knows what she has to do, she would do it to the minutest particular. You will have only to say to her what you require & I am certain she will be more ready & willing than she has ever shewn herself to me. . . . Cooper told me this morning that she would lay down her life for the child if it were required of her." Louisa was deeply attached to the girls and found it very hard to leave them, especially Mary, "whom I feel I should love better than ever I did human being."[10] Her departure, when Mary was just three years old, deprived the little girl of the only mother she had ever known.

Godwin had long realized that the situation was untenable. Within a year of Mary Wollstonecraft's death, he had begun looking for a wife who could be a mother to Fanny and Mary. He courted Harriet Lee, whom he had met in Bath in March 1798 throughout the winter of 1798–99, but she was too proper a lady to accept the irreligious philosopher. He pursued Mrs. S. Elwes, a widow, vigorously through the spring and summer of 1799; but when the husband of Maria Reveley, a woman he had long admired, died on July 6, Godwin interrupted this pursuit to propose to Maria, with indecent haste, within the month. Turned down by Maria Reveley (who nonetheless remained fond of Godwin and many years later, after her marriage to John Gisborne, became a close friend of Mary Godwin and Percy Shelley in Italy), Godwin proposed to Mrs. Elwes. She continued to see Godwin through the coming winter, but did not accept his proposal.

In the meantime, Godwin became quite close to the children. He took them with him on excursions to Pope's Grotto at Twickenham, to theatrical pantomimes (they saw "Deaf and Dumb" on March 23, 1800) and to dinners with his friends James Marshall and Charles and Mary Lamb. When he went to Ireland for six weeks during the summer of 1800, he sent them frequent and fond messages in his letters to James Marshall, who had assumed responsibility for them:

Their talking about me, as you say, they do, makes me wish to be with them, and will probably have some effect in inducing me to shorten my visit. It is the first time I have been seriously separated from them since they lost their mother, and I feel as if it was very naughty in me to have come away so far. . . . Tell Mary I will not give her away, and she shall be nobody's little girl but papa's. Papa is gone way, but papa will very soon come back again, and see the Polygon across two fields from the trunks of the trees at Camden Town. Will Mary and Fanny come to meet me? . . . [11 July 1800]

I depute to Fanny and Mr Collins, the gardener, the care of the garden. Tell her I wish to find it spruce, cropped, weeded, and mowed at my return; and if she can save me a few strawberries and a few beans without spoiling, I will give her six kisses for them. But then Mary must have six kisses too, because Fanny has six. [2 August 1800]

And now what shall I say for my poor little girls? I hope they have not forgot me. I think of them every day, and should be glad, if the wind was more favourable, to blow them a kiss a-piece from Dublin to the Polygon. I have seen Mr. Grattan's little girls and Lady Mountcashel's little girls, and they are very nice children, but I have seen none that I love half so well or think half so good as my own. [2 August 1800]

My visit to Ireland is almost done. Perhaps I shall be on the sea in a ship, the very moment Marshall is reading this letter to you. There is about going in a ship in Mrs. Barbauld's book. . . . And in a day or two . . . I shall hope to see Fanny and Mary and Marshall sitting on the trunks of the trees. [14 August 1800][11]

Already we can see Mary's anxiety lest her father abandon her ("Tell Mary I will not give her away"). During her first four years, Mary became intensely attached to her father, her only parent, whom she worshipped.

But Godwin's search for a wife continued and on May 5, 1801, his Diary, in a rare burst of enthusiasm, underlines the entry, "Meet Mrs. Clairmont." According to legend, this encounter took place while Godwin was sitting reading on his balcony at the Polygon. A maturely attractive woman appeared at a neighbouring window. "Is it possible," she exclaimed, "that I behold the immortal Godwin?" Godwin was always very susceptible to flattery and immediately saw in Mary Jane Clairmont, a "widow" with a six-year-old son Charles and a four-year-old daughter Jane, the ideal mate and mother. He promptly fell in love, courted her assiduously, and married her on December 21st. His friends, however, did not share Godwin's enthusiasm for this "Widow with green spectacles." Charles Lamb found her "a damn'd disagreeable woman, so much so as to drive me and some more old cronies [including Marshall] from his house"; and James Marshall, who came to know her better than most, summed her up as "a clever, bustling, second-rate woman, glib of tongue and pen, with a temper undisciplined and uncontrolled; not bad-hearted, but with a complete absence of all the finer sensibilities."[12] Even Godwin was disheartened by her frequent temper tantrums. Before their marriage, he wrote urging her to "manage and economize" her temper, and during one of their marital quarrels in 1803 when she spoke of separating, Godwin wrote opposing her wish

> because I know that here you have every ingredient of happiness in your possession, & that, in order to be happy, you have nothing to do, but to suppress in part the excesses of that baby-sullenness for every trifle, & to be brought out every day (the attribute of the mother of Jane), which I saw you suppress with great ease, & in repeated instances, in the months of July & August last. . . . You part from the best of husbands, the most anxious to console you, the best qualified to bear & be patient toward one of the worst of tempers.[13]

The marriage survived, primarily because Godwin genuinely loved Mary Jane Clairmont and found her a supportive companion and satisfactory mother. Whenever he left this "sympathizing & matured partner of my fire-side," he wrote her passionate love letters which on more than one occasion compared her favorably to his first wife. In response to her letter of April 4, 1805, for instance, Godwin enthused

> the whole reminded me strongly of an epistolary style that never was written but by one person before, in the world. You cannot misunderstand me, since, alas! the compositions which I allude to were not confined to me, but before my time were addressed with no less fervour to others. But yet, whether they were superscribed to a fusty old pedant of a painter [Fuseli], or to an imprudent & unprincipled debaucher [Imlay], the same susceptibility irradiated them, the same warmth of feeling, the same strength of affection, the same agonising alarm, the same ardent hope, as I trace with such unspeakable delight in the letter before me.[14]

Their quarrels continued, much exacerbated by Godwin's incurable habit of living beyond his means and borrowing against non-existent capital, leading finally to his bankruptcy in 1825. Yet Godwin became increasingly dependent upon his wife, both for her skills in managing their children's book-publishing business (M. Godwin & Co.) and for her emotional consolation. When his mother died in 1809, Godwin confessed to his wife

> while my mother lived, I always felt to a certain degree as if I had somebody who was my superior, & who exercised a mysterious

protection over me. I belonged to something; I hung to something; there is nothing that has so much reverence & religion in it as affection to parents. The knot is now severed, & I am for the first time, at more than fifty years of age, alone. You shall now be my mother.[15]

His sense of powerful bonding with Mary Jane Clairmont Godwin was further sealed, after the death of a stillborn son, christened William I in Godwin's Diary entry for June 4, 1802, by the birth of their son William on March 28, 1803; this son quickly became Mrs. Godwin's favorite child.

What sort of a mother was Mrs. Godwin to her newly acquired step-daughters? Mary Godwin clearly found her very difficult. Mrs. Godwin resented Mary's intense affection for Godwin. As Mary much later confessed to Maria Reveley Gisborne, her sensibility by the age of twelve was "covert—except that Mrs Godwin had discovered long before my excessive & romantic attachment to my Father."[16] Visitors to the Godwin household intensified Mrs. Godwin's jealousy by showing a special interest in Mary, the daughter of both of the most celebrated radical political thinkers of the day. Mrs. Godwin constantly encroached on Mary's privacy, demanding that she do household chores, opening her letters (even as late as 1823, Mary had to warn Leigh Hunt not to write to her at Godwin's home "unless you write for Mrs G's most certain and attentive perusal"[17]), and limiting her access to her father.

Nor did Mrs. Godwin encourage Mary's intellectual curiosity and love of reading. Although Godwin recognized that Mary was "considerably superior in capacity" to Fanny or Mrs. Godwin's children and acknowledged her active mind, her great desire for knowledge, and her "almost invincible" perseverance in everything she undertook,[18] he agreed with his wife that she required no formal education. When asked in 1812 whether he had educated his daughters according to Mary Wollstonecraft's principles, Godwin responded:

> Your enquiries relate principally to the two daughters of Mary Wollstonecraft. They are neither of them brought up with an exclusive attention to the system and ideas of their mother. I lost her in 1797, and in 1801 I married a second time. One among the motives which led me to chuse this was the feeling I had in myself of an incompetence for the education of daughters. The present Mrs. Godwin has great strength and activity of mind, but is not exclusively a follower of the notions of their mother; and indeed, having formed a family establishment without having a previous provision for the support of a family, neither Mrs. Godwin nor I have leisure enough for reducing novel theories of education to

practice, while we both of us honestly endeavour, as far as our opportunities will permit, to improve the minds and characters of the younger branches of our family.[19]

So far as I can determine, Mary never went to school. She was taught to read and write at home, first by Louisa Jones, who used Mary Wollstonecraft's *Ten Lessons* (the little reading book that Mary Wollstonecraft originally prepared for "my unfortunate girl," Fanny, and that Godwin published with her *Posthumous Works* in 1798), and then by Godwin and his new wife. Presumably, Mary's earliest education, received directly from Godwin, followed the lines recommended by Godwin to William Cole in 1802:

You enquire respecting the books I think best adapted for the education of female children from the age of two to twelve. I can answer you best on the early part of the subject, because in that I have made the most experiments; and in that part I should make no difference between children male and female.

I have no difficulty in the initiatory part of the business. I think Mrs Barbauld's little books, four in number, admirably adapted, upon the whole, to the capacity and amusement of young children. I have another little book in two volumes, printed for Newbury, entitled "The Infants' Friend, by Mrs. Lovechild," which I think might, without impropriety, accompany or follow Mrs Barbauld's books.

I am most peremptorily of opinion against putting children extremely forward. If they desire it themselves, I would not baulk them, for I love to attend to these unsophisticated indications. But otherwise, *Festina lente* is my maxim in education. I think the worst consequences flow from overloading the faculties of children, and a forced maturity.

. . . the imagination, the faculty . . . [which I] aim at cultivating . . . if cultivated at all, must be begun within youth. Without imagination there can be no genuine ardour in any pursuit, or for any acquisition, and without imagination there can be no genuine morality, no profound feeling of other men's sorrow, no ardent and persevering anxiety for their interests. This is the faculty which makes the man, and not the miserable minutenesses of detail about which the present age is so uneasy. . . .

I will put down the names of a few books, calculated to excite the imagination, and at the same time quicken the apprehensions of children. The best I know is a little French book, entitled "Contes de ma Mère, or Tales of Mother Goose." I should also recommend "Beauty and the Beast," "Fortunatus," and a story of a Queen and a Country Maid in Fénelon's "Dialogues of the Dead." Your own memory will easily suggest to you others which would carry on this train, such as "Valentine and Orson," "The Seven Champions of Christendom," "Les Contes de Madame Darmon," "Robinson Crusoe," if weeded of its methodism, and the "Arabian Nights." I would undoubtedly introduce before twelve years of age some smattering of geography, history, and the other sciences; but it is the train of reading I have here mentioned which I should principally depend upon for generating an active mind and a warm heart.[20]

Mary clearly profited by these pedagogical principles. Years later she recalled that "as a child I scribbled; and my favorite pastime, during the hours given me of recreation, was to 'write stories'." She was encouraged to write specifically for the Godwin Company's Juvenile Library. One of her first literary efforts, a thirty-nine quatrain expansion of Charles Dibdin's five stanza song, "Mounseer Nongtongpaw," was published early in 1808 when she was only eleven.[21] Her version became so popular that it was reissued in 1830 in an edition illustrated by Robert Cruikshank. This lengthy ballad in iambic tetrameter humorously recounts John Bull's trip to Paris, where his questions in English concerning the ownership of everything he sees—houses, palaces, servants, feasts, pretty girls, and babies—all receive the same response, "Je vous n'entends pas." John Bull greatly envies the man whom he assumes is their proud possessor, "Mounseer Nongtongpaw," until he sees the funeral of that same Nongtongpaw. Here are some early lines from Mary Godwin's skillful revision of Dibdin's rather awkward verse satire on English linguistic provincialism, lines that reveal a remarkable linguistic fluency for so young a girl:

> He asked who gave so fine a feast,
>   As fine as e'er he saw;
> The landlord, shrugging at his guest,
>   Said, "Je vous n'entends pas."

> "Oh, Mounseer Nongtongpaw!" said he,
>   "Well, he's a wealthy man,
> And seems disposed, from all I see,
>   To do what good he can." (11, 20–27)

Dibdin's song ends with the apparent death of Nongtongpaw, to which Mary Godwin adds both a moral

> Then, pondering o'er th' untimely fall
>   Of one so rich and great,
> Reflections deep his mind appall
>   On man's uncertain state.

and a characterization of her protagonist

> For, though in manners he was rough,
> John had a feeling heart.

Moreover, she goes significantly beyond Dibdin's song in her final image of John Bull recounting his adventures to his friends:

> They hear it all with silent awe,
>   Of admiration full,
>   And think that next to Nongtongpaw
>   Is the great traveller Bull. (11. 200–4)

These closing lines contain a pointed verbal irony (in the pun on bull as a ludicrous jest) that suggests an exceptional literary maturity in the young Mary Godwin. She also wrote weekly lectures, on such subjects as "The Influence of Government on the Character of the People", for the eight-year-old William to deliver, in the pontifical style of Coleridge, to Godwin's guests.[22]

Mary Godwin was, moreover, given access to her father's excellent library of old English authors. Godwin taught her that the proper way to study was to read two or three books simultaneously, a habit of reading that both he and she kept up throughout their lives. She was particularly fortunate in having access as well to her father's friends. Mary would often listen quietly in a corner while Godwin carried on political, philosophical, scientific, or literary conversations with such visitors as William Wordsworth, Charles Lamb, Samuel Coleridge, Thomas Holcroft, John Johnson, Humphrey Davy, Horne Tooke, and William Hazlitt. And on Sunday, August 24, 1806, when Coleridge and Charles and Mary Lamb came to tea and supper, she heard Coleridge himself recite "The Rime of the Ancient Mariner," an event she never forgot. The image of the isolated, tormented old Mariner would haunt her own fiction, even as Coleridge's verses reverberate through *Frankenstein* and *Falkner*.

Such powerful intellectual and imaginative stimulation strongly roused Mary's own imagination. Even more than writing, she enjoyed day-dreaming, "the formation of castles in the air—the indulging in waking dreams—the following up trains of thought, which had for their subject the formation of a succession of imaginary incidents. My dreams were at once more fantastic and agreeable than my writings. In the latter I was a close imitator—rather doing as others had done, than putting down the suggestions of my own mind . . . . but my dreams were all my own; I accounted for them to nobody; they were my refuge when annoyed—my dearest pleasure when free."[23] The only formal teaching she received, however, was from Mr. Benson the music master who gave the children weekly half-hour lessons in singing and reading music.[24] The boys in the family, on the other hand, were sent to excellent schools, Charles to Charterhouse School (at least until May

1811), and William both to Charterhouse and to Dr. Burney's School at Greenwich.[25] In this, as well as in the adolescent reading he permitted her (when Godwin sent Anthony Collins's book on rationalism to Charles Clairmont in May 1811, he expressly forbade Mary to read it[26]), Godwin followed the sexist educational practices of the day.

To be fair to Mrs. Godwin, she did take good care of Mary's physical needs. The children were well fed and clothed, even on a wildly fluctuating income. And when at the age of thirteen, Mary's health deteriorated and her arm and hand became infected with a skin disease, Mrs. Godwin took her to Ramsgate as Doctor Cline recommended and nursed her assiduously. After three weeks at Ramsgate, Mrs. Godwin could report that

> Mary is decisively better today, has had her dip today, but no Mr. Slater. So far, she has had but one *fresh* water poultice which I put on last night, seeing her a little spent with pain. The pustules when pricked, die away, and others succeed. In the bathing machine today, she made I observed involuntary efforts to assist herself with the sick hand, in particular, she raised it to her sling with somewhat of a nimble motion and without help. I indulge the hope of all being yet well, and that our poor girl will escape the dreadful evil we apprehended.[27]

Mary remained for six months at Ramsgate in the care of Miss Petman, who "almost kills us with kindness." Miss Petman ran a "Ladies School" at No. 92 High Street, Ramsgate, Kent, but there is no record that Mary received lessons from her—only room, board, and kindness.

Despite Mrs. Godwin's attentions, Mary grew up hating her stepmother, whom she blamed for having taken her father away from her. She later described her to Marianne Hunt as "odious" and to Maria Gisborne as a "filthy woman", she told Shelley that "I detest Mrs G. she plagues my father out of his life." She held Mrs. Godwin responsible for all her "girlish troubles," and even after Shelley's death she was reluctant to return to her father's house because "I know the person I have to deal with; all at first will be velvet—then thorns will come up."[28] Reading Mary Godwin's diatribes against Mrs. Godwin, one can see that she construed Mrs. Godwin as the opposite of everything that she had learned to worship in her own dead mother—as conservative where Mary Wollstonecraft was a free thinker, as philistine where Mary Wollstonecraft was intellectual, as devious and manipulative where Mary Wollstonecraft was open and generous. Mary Godwin cast herself in the role of Cinderella, deprived by her wicked stepmother of both motherly love and fatherly understanding. And her fairy-tale has some basis in fact. Mrs. Godwin contrived to give her own daughter more education than Mary received. Jane Clairmont attended a boarding school at Margate for six months when she was ten and was later sent to another boarding school kept by a French woman at Walham Green on and off for two years, that she might learn French and prepare herself to earn a living as a French teacher.[29] Lady Jane Shelley later remembered Mary saying that her "troubles began early; the jealousy of her stepmother hurt her much at times, for Mrs. G[odwin] was jealous of M[ary] W[ollstonecraft]'s child. 'Jane might be well educated,' she said . . . 'but Mary could stay at home and mend the stockings.' "[30]

Moreover, Godwin had deliberately distanced himself from his daughter. Once married, Godwin gratefully withdrew into his study and left the care of the children and the running of the household almost entirely to Mrs. Godwin. Percy Shelley's friend Elizabeth Hitchener reported in 1812 that Godwin was "different to what he seems, he lives so much from his family, only seeing them at stated hours."[31] As Don Locke, Godwin's most perceptive biographer, concludes

> Godwin had found it easy to express his obvious affection when his daughters were small, but as they all grew older together he became remote and awkward, more dutiful than sensitive, unable to show what he really felt for them. They, too, had to be fitted into his methodical timetable, with periods alloted when they might interrupt his writing or listen to his latest story. He would take them with him sometimes, to a lecture or the theatre or some other public occasion, but they were all very much in awe of him, a famous figure so they were told.[32]

Although Godwin admired Mary, he does not seem to have favored or felt any special affection for his only biological daughter. He described her as "singularly bold, somewhat imperious, and active of mind,"[33] qualities which were so like his own that they may have rubbed him the wrong way. Certainly they caused endless friction with Mrs. Godwin and disrupted domestic harmony in the Godwin household. When Mary went to Ramsgate, Godwin asked his wife to "tell Mary that in spite of unfavourable appearances, I have still faith that she will become a wise, & what is more a good & a happy woman."[34] Regardless of Mary's devotion to him, Godwin kept her at arm's length, declining to write directly to her at Ramsgate while Mrs. Godwin was with her because it would be "most natural and come most easily" to write after Mrs. Godwin had gone. He then wrote her but four times in the six months she spent at Miss Petman's, and not at all in her last eleven weeks there.

Godwin's favorite child, oddly enough, was Fanny Imlay Godwin. In deference to Mrs. Godwin who doted on the baby William, he always took a particular interest in William's development, but Fanny alone among his children emerges in Godwin's Diary as a person whose opinions merit recording. On May 3, 1812, he records a conversation with Fanny "on justice" and when Fanny, Jane, and William all went to Somers Town for a holiday on August 9, 1809, it is Fanny upon whom Godwin calls the following day and to whom he writes. This special concern for Fanny probably derived from Godwin's appreciation of her anomalous position in the household: she was the only child who had no living parent and who might therefore feel insecure about her right to Godwin's protection. Godwin would have been aware of her anxieties ever since he had his *explanation with Fanny* concerning her true parentage on February 8, 1806, when she was eleven (the rare underlining in the Diary emphasizes the importance of the event). But it was Fanny's temperament that pleased Godwin and drew forth his affection and protective impulses toward her. When she was only five, he had perceptively described her in the character of Julia in his novel *St. Leon* (1799) as

> uncommonly mild and affectionate, alive to the slightest variations of treatment, profoundly depressed by every mark of unkindness, but exquisitely sensible to demonstrations of sympathy and attachment. She appeared little formed to struggle with the difficulties of life and frowns of the world; but in periods of quietness and tranquillity nothing could exceed the sweetness of her character and the fascination of her manners.[35]

The plain, unassuming, serious Fanny was the peacemaker in the family. And as the oldest child, she took on a special responsibility for caring for Godwin's needs. When the rest of the family went with Mary to Ramsgate in 1811, she insisted on staying in London to help Godwin. As he wrote to his wife:

> Fanny is quite ferocious & impassioned against the journey to Margate. Her motive is a kind one. She says, This cook is very silly, but very willing; you cannot imagine how many things I have to do. She adds, Mamma talks of going to Ramsgate in the autumn: why cannot I go then?[36]

And Christy Baxter, who observed the Godwin household two years later, recalled that Jane was lively and quick-witted, and probably rather unmanageable. Fanny was more reflective, less sanguine, more alive to the prosaic obligations of life, and with a keen sense of domestic duty, early developed in her by necessity and by her position as the eldest of this somewhat anomalous family. Godwin, by nature as undemonstrative as possible, showed more affection to Fanny than to anyone else. He always turned to her for any little service he might require.[37]

But Fanny's surface sweetness and pliability masked a profound lack of self-esteem, a deep-rooted, melancholic conviction of her innate worthlessness that finally took its toll on her life.

When Mary returned from Ramsgate at Christmas, the tension between her and Mrs. Godwin was so great that by spring Godwin was seeking a way to get Mary out of the house. On May 25, 1812, he wrote to a mere acquaintance, William Baxter, who lived in Dundee, Scotland, proposing that Mary board with his family for several months. Having received an invitation for Mary to join the Baxters, Godwin promptly sent her off on June 7. Written to Baxter the next day, Godwin's description of Mary reveals his sense of distance from her, the character she had developed in his eyes, and his anxiety about both her physical and emotional well-being:

> I have shipped off to you by yesterday's packet, the Osnaburgh, Captain Wishart, my only daughter.... I cannot help feeling a thousand anxieties in parting with her, for the first time for so great a distance; & these anxieties were increased by the manner of sending her, on board a ship, with not a single face around her that she had ever seen till that morning. She is four months short of fifteen years of age ...
>
> I dare say she will arrive more dead than alive, as she is extremely subject to sea-sickness, & the voyage will not improbably last nearly a week. Mr. Cline, the surgeon, however decided that a sea-voyage would probably be of more service to her than any thing.
>
> I am quite confounded to think how much trouble I am bringing on you & your family, & to what a degree I may be said to have taken you in, when I took you at your word in your invitation upon so slight an acquaintance. The old proverb says, "He is a wise father who knows his own child;" & I feel the justness of the apothegm on the present occasion. There never can be a perfect equality between father & child, & if he has other objects & avocations to fill up the greater part of his time, the ordinary resource is for him to proclaim his wishes & commands in a way somewhat sententious & authoritative, & occasionally to utter his censures with seriousness & emphasis. It can therefore seldom happen that he is the confidant of his child, or that the child does not feel some degree of awe & restraint in intercourse with him. I am not therefore a perfect judge of Mary's character. I believe she has nothing of what is commonly called vices, & that she has considerable talent. But I tremble for the

trouble I may be bringing on you in this visit. In my last I desired that you would consider the first two or three weeks as a trial . . . I do not desire that she should be treated with extraordinary attention, or that any one of your family should put themselves in the smallest degree out of their way on her account. I am anxious that she should be brought up (in that respect) like a philosopher, even like a Cynic. It will add greatly to the strength & worth of her character. I should observe that she has no love of dissipation, & will be perfectly satisfied with your woods & your mountains.—I wish too that she should be *excited* to industry. She has occasionally great perseverance; but occasionally too she stands in great need to be roused.

You are aware that she comes to the sea-side for the purpose of bathing. . . . She will want also some treatment for her arm. . . . In all other respects except her arm, she has admirable health, has an excellent appetite, & is capable of enduring fatigue.[38]

At "The Cottage" on the Broughty Ferry Road overlooking the Tay estuary where the Baxter family lived, Mary experienced an unalloyed happiness she had rarely known before. The Baxter family were a large, loving, closely knit group[39] who provided Mary with both intimate companionship—she quickly became very close to the two daughters, Christina and Isabella—and an example of domestic affection and harmony that would heavily influence her fantasy life and fiction. Observing the Baxters from the outside, as a stranger in their midst, Mary Godwin came to idealize the bourgeois family as the source both of emotional sustenance and of ethical value. They inspired her later fictional representations of the nuclear family as a community of mutually dependent, equally respected, and equally self-sacrificing individuals.

As Mary wandered along the beach and surrounding hills and bathed in the sea, both her physical and mental health improved. Her bad arm seems to have been cured, which suggests that her illness was at least psychosomatic, brought on by her discomfort within the querulous Godwin household. She spent her days with the Baxter girls studying, taking long walks, and writing stories and essays which she eagerly shared with Christy or Isabel. Years later Mary would invoke these halcyon days in the Scottish episodes of *Mathilda*, where Mathilda remembers

how dear to me were the waters, and mountains, and woods of Loch Lomond now that I had so beloved a companion for my rambles. I visited . . . every delightful spot, either on the islands, or by the side of tree-sheltered waterfalls; every shady path, or dingle entangled with underwood and fern.[40]

And in the Preface to the 1831 Standard Novels edition of *Frankenstein* she recalled these times more precisely:

> I lived principally in the country as a girl, and passed a considerable
> time in Scotland. I made occasional visits to the more picturesque
> parts; but my habitual residence was on the blank and dreary
> northern shores of the Tay, near Dundee. Blank and dreary on
> retrospection I call them; they were not so to me then. They were the
> eyry of freedom, and the pleasant region where unheeded I could
> commune with the creatures of my fancy. I wrote then—but in a
> most common-place style. . . . What I wrote was intended at least for
> one other eye—my childhood's companion and friend; but my
> dreams were all my own. . . . It was beneath the trees of the grounds
> belonging to our house, or on the bleak sides of the woodless
> mountains near, that my true compositions, the airy flights of my
> imagination, were born and fostered. I did not make myself the
> heroine of my tales. Life appeared to me too common-place an affair
> as regarded myself. I could not figure to myself that romantic woes
> or wonderful events would ever be my lot; but I was not confined to
> my own identity, and I could people the hours with creations far
> more interesting to me at that age, than my own sensations.[41]

When Mary returned to London with Christy Baxter on
November 10, 1812, for a seven month visit, the Godwin household
was abuzz with talk of a new, young, and very wealthy disciple of the
impecunious philosopher whom they had met for the first time a
month earlier. Percy Bysshe Shelley had introduced himself to Godwin
almost a year before in a letter that immediately aroused the aging and
no longer celebrated philosopher's intense interest:

> You will be surprised at hearing from a stranger. . . . The name of
> Godwin has been used to excite in me feelings of reverence and
> admiration, I have been assustomed to consider him a luminary too
> dazzling for the darkness which surrounds him, and from the earliest
> period of my knowledge of his principles I have ardently desired to
> share on the footing of intimacy that intellect which I have delighted
> to contemplate in its emanations. . . . I had enrolled your name on
> the list of the honourable dead, I had felt regret that the glory of your
> being had passed from this earth of ours.—It is not so—you still live,
> and I firmly believe are still planning the welfare of humankind. I
> have just entered on the scene of human operations, yet my feelings
> and my reasonings correspond with what yours were. . . . I am
> convinced I could represent myse{lf} to you in such terms as not to
> be thought wholly unworthy of your friendship.[42]

Godwin responded immediately, on January 6, 1812, with a lecture on
the principles of political justice which in no way deterred the
enthusiastic Shelley. Throughout that spring before she left for Dundee,
Mary must have heard more and more of this young man as Godwin's

correspondence with Shelley continued apace, stimulated not only by Shelley's sincere flattery but also by the information contained in Shelley's second letter that he was "the Son of a man of fortune in Sussex ... heir by entail to an estate of 6000£ per an."[43] Godwin repeatedly urged Shelley to visit him. On March 14, 1812, he wrote to Shelley in Ireland, "I wish to my heart you would come immediately to London. ... You cannot imagine how much all the females of my family, Mrs Godwin and three daughters, are interested in your letters and your history."[44]

Gradually Godwin and his family learned Shelley's history. He had received a superior education at Syon House, Eton and, briefly, at Oxford, where his "earliest passion for the wildest and most extravagant romances: ancient books of Chemistry and Magic" and his taste for writing Gothic romances (*St. Irvyne* and *Zastrozzi* were published before he was seventeen) had given way, under the influence of Godwin's *Political Justice* which he read in December, 1810, to a desire to benefit humanity more directly. Shelley had then tried to educate deluded Christians by publishing a pamphlet on *The Necessity of Atheism*, which had resulted in the immediate expulsion of himself and his best friend Thomas Jefferson Hogg from Oxford on March 25, 1811. Five months later, rejected by his cousin Harriet Grove who shared the Shelley family's horror at Percy's blasphemous opinions, Shelley, barely nineteen years old, had married on the rebound Harriet Westbrook, a girl whom he did not passionately love but whom he felt obliged to rescue from a tyrannical father. Shelley had taken Harriet and her sister Eliza with him on his travels. In Ireland he made a futile attempt to undermine the control of the Roman Catholic Church through the dissemination of copies of *The Necessity of Atheism*; in Wales he lent support to William Madocks's socialist community development and landfill scheme at Tremadoc and Portmadoc. Shelley had fled Madocks's house, Tan-yr-allt, which he had rented, on February 26, 1813, convinced that one of the locals had tried to murder him.[45] He had then written the poem *Queen Mab*, whose lengthy prose notes remain one of the natal texts in the history of English socialism. At first, Shelley's marriage to the naively affectionate and eagerly studious Harriet had gone well, despite the occasionally overbearing presence of her older sister. Shelley had genuinely rejoiced in the birth of his daughter Eliza Ianthe on June 23, 1813. But after Ianthe's birth Harriet gave up her efforts to share Shelley's intellectual and poetic interests and abandoned both her habit of reading aloud to him and her former devotion to study.[46] Since childhood, Shelley had felt a powerful psychological need to be surrounded by sympathetic and supportive women, a need fully met during his favored youth as the oldest son of a wealthy baronet by his young mother and four adoring younger sisters. He therefore sought the female companionship and intellectual sympathy he missed in Harriet elsewhere, first in an ill-fated friendship with Elizabeth Hitchener whom he wooed by mail as "the sister of my soul"[47] but found unendurable when she finally joined his household in Lynmouth in July 1812, and then in the older and more gracious company of Mrs. Boinville and her daughter Cornelia Turner during the winter of 1814.

Percy Shelley, then twenty, first met the fifteen-year-old Mary Godwin on November 11, 1812, when he, his wife, and sister-in-law dined at the Godwins' the day after Mary's return from Dundee. Three days later the Shelleys abruptly left London. This initial meeting did little more than further pique Mary's interest in the handsome young man who shared her adoration of her father. Godwin's next encounter with Shelley took place at tea on June 8, 1813, five days after Mary and Christy had gone back to Dundee. By the time Mary again returned to London, nine months later, on March 30, 1814, Godwin had become not only emotionally dependent on Shelley's sympathy and intellectual stimulation, but financially dependent on him as well. Shelley shared Godwin's belief that the greatest justice is done when he who possesses money gives it to whoever has greatest need of it. As a consequence, Godwin had no compunction about taking as much money as Shelley would give him, even insisting that Shelley assume post-obit bonds at ruinous interest rates in his favor.[48]

When Mary Godwin next met Shelley, on May 5, 1814, she had come to share the Godwin family's obsessive concern with this generous young idealist. Since her return to London two months before, her father and sisters had spoken of little else, while Mrs. Godwin repeatedly recorded the niceties of Harriet Shelley's wardrobe even as she resented her stuck-up airs. Shelley, by now deeply dissatisfied with his marriage and ever more alienated from a home dominated by his sister-in-law Eliza Westbrook, was half-consciously seeking an alternative, spending ever longer hours in the company of the Boinville women. When he saw Mary Godwin again, her beauty, intellectual interests, evident sympathy for him, and perhaps above all her name immediately attracted him. Shelley called frequently on Godwin that May and early June and dined with Mary at the Godwins at least twice, on May 26 and June 7. The next day, June 8, he took Thomas Jefferson Hogg with him to call. Hogg described the brief meeting thus:

> When we reached Skinner Street, he said "I must speak with Godwin; come in, I will not detain you long."

I followed him through the shop, which was the only entrance, and upstairs. We entered a room on the first floor; it was shaped like a quadrant. In the arc were windows; in one radius a fire place, and in the other a door, and shelves with many old books. William Godwin was not at home. Bysshe strode about the room, causing the crazy floor of the ill-built, unowned dwelling-house to shake and tremble under his impatient footsteps. . . . "Where is Godwin?" he asked me several times, as if I knew. I did not know, and, to say the truth, I did not care. He continued his uneasy promenade; and I stood reading the names of old English authors on the backs of the venerable volumes, when the door was partially and softly opened: a thrilling voice called "Shelley!" A thrilling voice answered, "Mary!" And he darted out of the room, like an arrow from the bow of the far-shooting king. A very young female, fair and fair-haired, pale indeed, and with a piercing look, wearing a frock of tartan, an unusual dress in London at that time, had called him out of the room. He was absent a very short time—a minute or two; and then returned. "Godwin is out; there is no use in waiting." So we continued our walk along Holborn.

"Who was that, pray?" I asked; "a daughter?"

"Yes."

"A daughter of William Godwin?"

"*The daughter of William and Mary.*"[49]

By the end of June, 1814, Percy Shelley was dining with the Godwins every day.

During her lonely childhood, Mary frequently visited her mother's grave in St. Pancras Churchyard, where she read her mother's works and sought solace from nature and her mother's spirit. Percy began to go on daily walks with Mary to the grave of Mary Wollstonecraft. They took Jane along as a chaperone, but as Jane later recalled

they always sent me to walk some distance from them, alleging that they wished to talk on philosophical subjects and that I did not like or know anything about those subjects—I willingly left. I did not hear what they talked about.[50]

On June 26 they declared their love for each other, a declaration initiated by Mary Godwin who saw in Percy Shelley everything she had ever desired: a poet, young, handsome, and enthusiastic, who shared her passion for both her parents and who offered her the opportunity to replicate her parents' love and to create the supportive family she craved. For Mary, Percy was a youthful version of her father, a revolutionary and a philosopher, but one who, in contrast to Godwin, might fully reciprocate her love and embrace her as his companion. To Percy, Mary Wollstonecraft Godwin embodied the soulmate and intellectual beauty he had been seeking. As the daughter of Godwin and Wollstonecraft, she must possess extraordinary intelligence, poetic sensibility, and a commitment to revolutionary principles. In addition, she was at sixteen extremely pretty, with very fair skin, light brown hair, and a wide brow and clear gaze. Shelley recorded this early perception of Mary Godwin in his dedicatory stanza for *The Revolt of Islam* (1818):

> They say that thou wert lovely from thy birth,
> Of glorious parents, thou aspiring Child.
> I wonder not for One then left this Earth
>   Whose life was like a setting planet mild,
>   Which clothed thee in the radiance undefiled
> Of its departing glory; still her fame
>   Shines on thee, through the tempests dark and wild
> Which shake these latter days; and thou canst claim
> The shelter, from thy Sire, of an immortal name.

Their emotional and sexual passion for each other was explosive and overwhelming. When Godwin discovered their relationship on July 8, he immediately wrote to Shelley and remonstrated with Mary, forbidding them to meet again. Mary tried to obey her father, although she found his strictures against seeing a married man less forceful than she might have, given both Godwin's and Wollstonecraft's personal histories and, especially, Shelley's own assurances that his marriage was over (Shelley even went so far as to accuse Harriet of being pregnant by another man, a lie which he may actually, in his desperate desire for Mary, have persuaded himself was true). But when Percy threatened to commit suicide in a violent scene witnessed by both Jane and Mrs. Godwin, Mary knew that she could never give him up. At five in the morning on July 18, 1814, she fled with Percy to France.

Mary and Percy took Jane Clairmont with them, a decision that was to have profound repercussions on their relationship. Probably it was made on the spur of the moment, with no forethought. Jane wished to escape from her mother's watchful eye; her adolescent reading of romances and ghost stories made her eager for adventure; her own future, as a governess or French teacher, rightly seemed grim; and as the Godwins later claimed, she was probably half in love with Shelley herself and reluctant to let her sister take him entirely away. Whatever reservations Mary may have had, she was caught up in the exhilaration of first love and ready to embrace the world. Besides, Jane's presence would soften the blow of a violent separation from her father and provide continuity with her former life. And Jane could speak French and thus help them to settle more easily into a home in France. Moreover, Percy, with his "harem psychology," his perennial desire to be surrounded by several adoring women,[51] was eager to have Jane's company. Above all, the three had entered into a kind of esprit de corps through the preceding weeks, as Jane cooperated in arranging Mary's and Percy's secret meetings. At the moment of their elopement, Jane's presence seemed natural, and the lovers welcomed her with gleeful high spirits and genuine affection.

Mrs. Godwin caught up with the runaways in Calais and, after an hour's interview with Jane, thought she had persuaded her to return to London. But Jane then spoke to Percy who convinced her to stay with him and Mary; Percy's desire to keep Jane by him was sincere and strong. Forced to admit defeat, Mrs. Godwin never forgave Mary whom she blamed as the primary cause of this disaster. When Maria Gisborne called on the Godwins in 1820, after having befriended Mary and Percy Shelley in Italy, Mrs. Godwin refused to see or converse with "any person who should be attached to Mrs S the author of all her misery," while Godwin

> expatiated much on the tender maternal affection of Mrs G. for her daughter, and the bitter disappointment of all her hopes in the person to whom alone she looked for comfort and happiness in the decline of her life; he described her as a being of the most irritable disposition possible, and therefore suffering the keenest anguish on account of this misfortune, of which M[ary] is the sole cause, as she pretends; she regards M as the greatest enemy she has in the world.[52]

Godwin shared his wife's view. Although he continued to demand that Shelley give him money, he refused to see or write to Mary for the next three-and-a-half years. As he wrote to his bill-discounter, John Taylor, on August 27, 1814, "Jane has been guilty of indiscretion only, & has shown a want of those filial sentiments, which it would have been most desirable to us to have discovered in her: Mary has been guilty of a crime."[53] Godwin could see Mary only as a home-wrecker who broke up Shelley's marriage with Harriet, and as a disobedient daughter who flouted his explicit injunction against their dishonorable and "licentious" love.

Heedless of parental anger, Mary, Percy, and Jane proceeded to Paris. Seeing themselves as characters in a sentimental novel, Mary recorded the exhilaration they felt on touching French soil during the peace of Amiens that summer of 1814:

> Every inconvenience was hailed as a new chapter in the romance of our travels; the worst annoyance of all, the Custom-house, was amusing as a novelty; we saw with extasy the strange costume of the French women, read with delight our own descriptions in the

passport, looked with curiosity on every *plât*, fancying that the fried-leaves of artichokes were frogs; we saw shepherds in opera-hats, and post-boys in jack-boots; and (*pour comble de merveille*) heard little boys and girls talk French: it was acting a novel, being an incarnate romance.[54]

Settled in cheap lodgings at the Hôtel de Vienne in Paris, Percy and Jane set out to borrow money and arrange passports for their journey to Switzerland, while Mary rested and recovered from her severe sea-sickness and the fatigue of her journey. During the week they waited for funds, they visited the Tuileries, Notre Dame, and the Louvre where the only picture that captured their attention was Poussin's "Deluge." Passionately in love, Mary could hardly eat and seemed, Percy noted in her journal, "insensible to all future evil. She feels as if our love would alone suffice to resist the invasions of calamity."[55]

Mary immediately showed Percy her treasured collection of papers which she had brought with her from Skinner Street in a box: her own writings (adolescent stories and journals) and letters from her father, friends, and Percy. Percy had intended to claim her promise to let him read and study "these productions of her mind that preceded our intercourse"[56] at their journey's destination at Uri; but when they left Paris a week later, taking only what they could carry on a sickly ass they had bought, Mary's box was left behind at the hotel with instructions for forwarding it. Mary never saw it again. The incident has a peculiar symbolic resonance. Mary's first impulse in her new life with the poet Shelley was to establish her own literary credentials, to assert her own voice, and to assume a role as his intellectual companion and equal—the role her mother had advocated for women in *A Vindication of the Rights of Woman*. No sooner is that voice uttered than it is lost, considered not worth taking along, even though Percy carefully carried with him the books he wished to read, including Mary's copies of her mother's works. Percy always encouraged Mary to write. Indeed, he *expected* it of her as the daughter of two such literary geniuses. But neither Percy nor Mary ever considered her literary talent or efforts as equal to his, a fact that would have significant repercussions on the revisions of *Frankenstein*. Percy, as the older published poet, quickly assumed the role of mentor-teacher to his young student-mistress, setting Mary to work on a rigorous program of reading and study that she followed dutifully for years to come. The tone of this hierarchical relationship is caught in a love-note Mary scribbled to Percy three months after their elopement:

> Goodnight my love—tomorrow I will seal this blessing on your lips dear good creature press me to you and hug your own Mary to your

heart perhaps she will one day have a father till then be everything to
me love—& indeed I will be a good girl and never vex you any more
I will learn Greek and—[57]

Nonetheless, it was Mary who was the more literarily productive
during the first weeks of their life together. Her journal entries and
long letters home to Fanny became the basis of a published account of
their travels, *History of A Six Weeks Tour through a part of France,
Switzerland, Germany, and Holland, with Letters descriptive of a Sail
round the Lake of Geneva, and of the Glaciers of Chamouni* (1817).
Mary's account of their tour, on foot, by ass-back, voiturier, and
finally riverboat, from Paris through the wartorn French countryside to
Lake Lucerne, reveals an eye trained in Burke's and Gilpin's categories
of the sublime, the beautiful, and the picturesque. She singles out the
"magnificent" alpine landscape of Brunnen where the "high mountains
encompassed us, darkening the waters"; a "beautiful scene" just
beyond Besançon where they saw "a castle built high on a rock; hills
covered with pine, with a lovely plain in the middle, through which ran
a silent river"; as well as the picturesque "irregularities" of the
countryside of Provence and the ruined citadel on the hill above. She
further develops a romantic aesthetic, justifying her decision to publish
these letters and journals on the grounds that they record the
"enthusiasm" of youth and are the responses of travellers who looked
upon nature and humanity with particular "sympathy."

In composing her letters and journal, Mary Godwin looked for a
literary model to her mother's *Letters written during a short residence
in Sweden, Norway, and Denmark* (1796); that work had so moved
William Godwin when he read it between January 25 and February 3,
1796 that he called on Mary Wollstonecraft on February 13 (she was
not at home). When she returned his call on April 14, the two were
intensely drawn to each other, an attraction that blossomed into a full-
blown, consummated love affair by July 16. Godwin later enthused, "If
ever there was a book calculated to make a man in love with its
author, this appears to me to be the book. She speaks of her sorrows,
in a way that fills us with melancholy, and dissolves us in tenderness, at
the same time that she displays a genius which commands all our
admiration."[58]

As they travelled down the Rhine, Percy read Wollstonecraft's
Letters from Norway aloud to Mary and Jane.[59] Like her mother,
Mary Godwin enthusiastically records the glorious natural scenery she
visits. But in contrast to Wollstonecraft's perceptive and judicious
discriminations among the cultural attitudes and behavior of the

different national groups she encounters in Scandinavia, Mary Godwin typically sees the people she passes by at a distance. Her reserve occasionally verges on snobbish superiority. She feels entirely alien to the starving peasants and more prosperous burghers of France, Switzerland, and Germany. She complains of the heat, the insects, the dirty inns, the sour stinking food; the voiturier is "disobliging, sullen and stupid," and the French villagers are "squalid with dirt, their countenances expressing every thing that is disgusting and brutal."[60] The Swiss peasants seem to her "a people slow of comprehension and of action," although she acknowledges that "habit has made them unfit for slavery." The Germans who travelled with them on their return boat trip along the Rhine are the worst of all: "Our companions in this voyage were of the meanest class, smoked prodigiously, and were exceedingly disgusting"; "they swaggered and talked, and what was hideous to English eyes, kissed one another."[61] Mary's journal entries are even more vitriolic. At Mettingen on August 28, she surveys "the horrid and slimy faces of our companions in voyage; our only wish was to absolutely annihilate such uncleanly animals, to which we might have addressed the Boatman's speech to Pope—' 'Twere easier for God to make entirely new men than attempt to purify such monsters as these'."[62] Here we must recognize Mary Shelley's deep aversion to the lower classes and the racist chauvinism implicit in her condemnations. For as we shall see, her commitment to the preservation of a class-system informs both her own later attempts to gain a place in "society" and her fictional idealizations of the bourgeois family.

Characteristically, Mary can find beauty in a natural scene only by *removing* people from it:

> "We heard the songs of the vintagers, and if surrounded by disgusting Germans, the sight was not so replete with enjoyment as I now fancy it to have been; yet memory, taking all the dark shades from the picture, presents this part of the Rhine to my remembrance as the loveliest paradise on earth." (*Six Weeks Tour*, 69)

Mary's excessive hostility to the foreigners she encounters (her only positive response is to a fragile young German woman weakened by disease which gives her countenance, "expressive of uncommon sweetness and frankness," an "appearance of extreme delicacy"[63]), also betrays a deep anxiety about her elopement and what it portends for her future place in the world. Rather than feeling "at home" among strangers, Mary is already withdrawing into an isolated, self-constructed world of literary fantasy. As she sails down the Rhine, her perceptions of the environment are mediated by poetry. Together she and Percy read Byron's descriptions of the Rhine banks in the second canto of *Childe Harold*:

> We read these verses with delight, as they conjured before us these lovely scenes with the truth and vividness of painting, and with the exquisite addition of glowing language and a warm imagination. (*Six Weeks Tour*, 68)

Perhaps more significant is the characteristic movement, in her descriptions of the landscape, from images of turbulence to images of calm. On the boatride from Mumph to Mayence, when there were "no fellow-passengers to disturb our tranquillity by their vulgarity and rudeness," the river suddenly narrowed and

> the boat dashed with inconceivable rapidity round the base of a rocky hill covered with pines; a ruined tower, with its desolated windows, stood on the summit of another hill that jutted into the river; beyond, the sunset was illuminating the distant mountains and clouds, casting the reflection of its rich and purple hues on the agitated river. . . . the shades grew darker as the sun descended below the horizon, and after we had landed, as we walked to our inn round a beautiful bay, the full moon arose with divine splendour. (*Six Weeks Tour*, 62–63)

Mary concludes this passage, not at a moment of excitement, but at a moment of relaxed peace. In striking contrast, Percy Shelley's first description of the Alps in their journal emphasizes their sublime and overwhelming grandeur:

> Two leagues from Neufchâtel we see the Alps; hill after hill is seen extending its craggy outline before the other, and far behind all, towering above every feature of the scene, the snowy Alps; they are 100 miles distant; they look like those accumulated clouds of dazzling white that arrange themselves on the horizon in summer. This immensity staggers the imagination, and so far surpasses all conception that it requires an effort of the understanding to believe that they are indeed mountains. (*Mary Shelley's Journal*, 10)

In her encounters with nature, Mary seeks out experiences, not of sublime exhilaration but rather of beautiful tranquillity. At Besançon, she delighted in the peace of the "hills covered with pine with a lovely plain in the middle through which ran a silent river."[64] Such serene harmony becomes a metaphor in Mary Shelley's early writing for the highest human pleasure, a peaceful interdependence between the self and nature. For the next decade, she typically depicts nature as Dame Kind, a sacred life-force that sustains those human beings who treat her with respect—an ecological vision that she owed in part to what she read as Wordsworth's celebration of a maternally nurturant Nature "that never did betray / The heart that loved her." Again we sense in the young Mary Godwin a profound need for security, for assured calm and domestic harmony, that is at variance with Percy Shelley's restless seeking after intellectual beauty, for participation in a divine energy—the One, the True, the Good—that he perceived constantly in motion around him.

Certainly this six-week tour did nothing to satisfy Mary Godwin's need for tranquillity, although in her passionate new love and the excitement of Percy's presence she hardly cared. The three young people tramped and rode across southern France to Lake Lucerne. When they arrived at Brunnen, opposite Uri, they rented lodgings in an ugly house called the Château for six months only to find that, as Jane put it, "the stove don't suit" and "there were too many Cottages."[65] What was more to the point, they had but £38 left. They turned back at once to London by the cheapest possible route, water conveyances along the Rhine. En route, they read together several of Mary Wollstonecraft's books (not only the *Letters* but also *Mary, a Fiction* and Godwin's *Memoirs*) as well as L'Abbé Barruel's *L'Histoire du Jacobinisme* and Rousseau's *Emile*.[66] When they reached Marsluys on the coast of Holland, a bad wind prevented their crossing to England for another three days.

At rest for the first time in six weeks, Mary and Percy immediately set up the daily routine they would follow during their life together: reading and writing separately in the morning, sightseeing, visiting or doing errands and housework (Mary's responsibility) after midday dinner, reading together in the evening. Percy continued writing his romance, *The Assassins*, a story of a utopian sect of communists, modelled on the Druze of southern Lebanon and influenced by Tacitus's account of the siege of Jerusalem, which he had begun at Brunnen; Mary began writing a story suggestively titled "Hate." Since this story has been lost, we can never know whether its title in any way reflects Mary's hostility towards the people she had passed on her journey or towards her immediate companions. Mary's Journal had noted the interruption caused on August 27 by "Jane's horrors"—nightmares, sleepwalking, or hysterical shrieking fits brought on by Jane's excessively emotional response to the literature she preferred: ghost-stories, Gothic novels, or dramatic tragedies. In this case, it was *King Lear* to which Jane, thinking perhaps of her recent betrayal of her stepfather, responded with an "almost stupendous despair."[67] Significantly, the writing of "Hate," Percy noted in their Journal, "gives Shelley the greater pleasure."[68] Mary was already keenly aware of Percy's literary expectations for her. Even Jane, not to be outdone, began a story called "Ideot" about a girl "full of noble affections and sympathies" who acted entirely upon impulse and thereby committed "every violence against received opinion."[69]

Back in London by September 13, Mary and Percy faced a host of problems. Harriet Shelley, now six months pregnant, refused to take seriously Shelley's suggestion that she join his new menage as a "sister" and eventually turned to a lawyer to secure financial support and legal guardianship of her children. Godwin, implacable in his opposition to the liaison (rather hypocritically, given his principled opposition to marriage in *Political Justice* and his own willingness to live with or marry women who had carried on illicit sexual relationships) refused to see Mary and Percy, although he continued to try to persuade Jane to return to Skinner Street and to insist that Percy pay his debts. Percy's father had cut off his allowance and his finances were in desperate straits. For the next eight months he engaged in a constant struggle to escape bailiffs, pawning and selling his possessions and borrowing money from his friends. There were frequent changes of lodgings, and for a fortnight in early November Percy was forced to hide out in Peacock's home and to see Mary only on Sunday when the bailiffs could not arrest him in London. The tension of these times is vividly captured in Mary's novel *Lodore* where the young lovers, Edward Villiers and Ethel Lodore, frantically flee their creditors only to end finally in debtors' prison. Mary and Percy remained passionately in love; by October Mary was pregnant. They tried hard to sustain the rhythm of their lives together, writing and reading together every day. Percy continued his romance, while Mary began to learn Greek and to reread, as a kind of substitute for Godwin's presence, his *Political Justice* and Wollstonecraft's *Posthumous Works*. On November 6 she recorded contentedly, "this is a day devoted to Love in idleness."[70]

Caught up in his own excited passions, Percy wanted to intensify the emotional life of his entire household. To Mary's disgust, he encouraged Jane's "horrors," staying up late at night alone with her, talking of witches and ghosts. At one in the morning of October 7, Jane burst into Mary and Percy's bedroom in a state of hysterical terror, skin deathly white and eyes starting from their sockets. Significantly, when Percy informed her of Mary's pregnancy, "this seemed to check her violence."[71] One suspects an attempt by Jane to intervene in Mary and Percy's sexual life, an attempt which during the coming months Percy did nothing to discourage. On the contrary, he developed a habit of taking long walks alone with Jane, which made Mary increasingly uneasy as her pregnancy developed. It is probable that Jane and Percy became lovers during the winter of 1814–15. Shelley's oft-proclaimed free-love ethic (summed up in the lines he wrote for "Epipsychidion" in 1821, "True Love in this differs from gold and clay, / That to divide is not to take away") encouraged this; and his powerful concern for Jane's welfare ever after suggests a sexual as well as emotional bonding between them. The Godwins thought Jane was in love with Shelley, and her Journal entry concerning Cordelia during their trip that past summer suggests the same: " 'What shall poor Cordelia do—Love & be silent'—Oh [th]is is true—Real Love will never [sh]ew itself to the eye of broad day—[i]t courts the secret glades."[72] Jane was more than ready to flout convention and become Percy's lover. Her later letters to Byron in which she describes Shelley as "the man whom I have loved" and compares her history to that of the raped Maria Eleanora Schöning in Coleridge's *The Friend* suggest that she did.[73]

On his return to London, Shelley quickly renewed his friendship with Thomas Hogg; it had been broken off three years before at Harriet Shelley's insistence after Hogg made unwelcome sexual overtures to her. Ever since their days at Oxford together, Hogg had been extremely emotionally dependent on Shelley. As Richard Holmes has suggested, their relationship was more that of lovers than of friends.[74] Hogg had repeatedly tried to strengthen the bond between himself and Shelley by making love to Shelley's women. Immediately after their expulsion from Oxford, he had sent passionate love letters to Percy's favorite sister Elizabeth Shelley, a complete stranger whom he fantasized as a female Percy.[75] After Shelley's marriage to Harriet Westbrook, Hogg had, with Shelley's explicit encouragement and approval, tried to make love to her. Shelley had always insisted on his allegiance to an ideal of free and communal love; he was eager to share his wife sexually with others, and especially with his best friend Hogg. I believe that Shelley's renewed offer of friendship to Hogg was identified in Shelley's mind with the creation of a sexual union between Hogg and Mary. As Shelley noted in their Journal, "Perhaps he still may be my friend . . . he was pleased with Mary; this was the test by which I had previously determined to judge his character."[76] Once Mary's approval of Hogg was gained, Shelley rapidly encouraged Hogg to make love to Mary and even persuaded Mary to accept Hogg's attentions, although her pregnancy and consequent ill health made a sexual liaison impossible. By January 1, Mary was writing to Hogg:

> You love me you say—I wish I could return it with the passion you deserve—but you are very good to me and tell me that you are quite

happy with the affection which from the bottom of my heart I feel for you—you are so generous so disinterested that no one can help loving you. . . . But you know Hogg that we have known each other for so short a time and I did not think about love—so that I think that *that* also will come in time & then we shall be happier I do think than the angels who sing for ever or even the lovers of Janes world of perfection. There is a bright prospect before us my dear friend— lovely—and—which renders it certain—wholly dependent on our selves—for Shelley & myself I need promise nothing—nor to you either for I know that you are persuaded that I will use every effort to promote your happiness & such is my affection for you that it will be no hard task—[77]

From March 10, 1815, Hogg lived for six weeks in the house with Mary, Percy, and Jane (who was now in the process of changing her name to the more poetic Clara/Claire). Percy's urgent desire to link Mary and Hogg, despite Mary's initial feeling that she was quite satisfied with Percy alone, lends further support to the suggestion that Percy was here trying to negotiate a sexual quid pro quo with Mary, her affair with Hogg for his affair with Claire. Significantly, nine separate sections have been removed from Mary Shelley's Journal for the period January to May, 1814; Claire's journal for this period has not survived; Hogg's second volume of his unfinished *Life of Shelley* breaks off in the middle of the spring of 1815; and Percy Shelley's only surviving letters from this period are brief notes to his solicitors. Richard Holmes persuasively concludes that the destruction of the journal evidence

> was intended to obliterate the best documented of Shelley's attempts at setting up a radical community of friends, in which everything was shared in common. Around the central relationship between himself and Mary, he tried to encourage secondary intimacies between Mary and Hogg, and himself and Claire. While Hogg adopted a slightly chivalric role of confidant and lover towards Mary, Shelley in turn adopted the tutorial one of philosophic friend and lover towards Claire.[78]

Percy's effort, grounded on Godwin's socialist principles, no longer seems, as it has done to his earlier biographers, so outrageous as to be unbelievable. Similar attempts in both America and Britain since the 1960s have taught us that Percy Shelley's utopian scheme for a commune based on shared property and sexuality is physically and psychologically possible, however fraught with tension and exploitative of women it may be.

Mary was not entirely pleased with this psychosexual exchange. She displayed increasing annoyance at Claire's continued presence in the household. Claire and Mary, almost the same age, had been both friends and sibling rivals within the Godwin family household, where Mrs. Godwin had persistently favored her own daughter. Mary was genuinely fond of Claire. She had initially welcomed her company on their tour, and would all her life feel a profound concern for Claire's happiness and even a financial responsibility for her welfare. But Claire's "horrors" and difficult personality were getting on her nerves; Percy had already begun lecturing Claire on her childish bad temper, moodiness, selfishness, and irresponsibility.[79] More and more Mary would jealously resent the time and emotional energy that Percy devoted to Claire.

Mary's irritation with Claire was doubtless intensified by her pregnancy. Her nesting instincts were growing stronger, even as her fatigue and swollen body made her a less active companion in Percy's daily walks and business trips across town, on which Claire frequently accompanied him. Their financial problems were gradually eased after Shelley's grandfather, Sir Bysshe Shelley, died on January 6, 1815, leaving his considerable estate entailed on Percy Bysshe Shelley and his oldest male heirs, after the death of his father Sir Timothy. Shelley was finally able to negotiate an annual allowance from his father of £1000 per year in return for his renunciation of a second landed estate valued at £140,000 (which would then pass to his younger brother John). He was also able to pay off £2,900 of bills, and to arrange for Harriet to receive one-fifth of his annual allowance. At this point Godwin, hearing of Shelley's financial solvency, broke his outraged silence to write to Shelley, demanding that he make good his earlier promises to pay Godwin's debts. Shelley, urged on by Mary who continued to feel a powerful loyalty to Godwin, continued to help Godwin with a loan of £1000, even though he knew Godwin's financial situation was hopeless. By the time he died in 1822, Shelley had lent Godwin over £4000, none of which Godwin repaid.[80]

Mary's first child, a daughter, was born two months prematurely on February 22, 1815. Mary named the baby Clara, out of loyalty to Claire. Mary recovered quickly, but as Percy noted in their Journal, "the child not expected to live." Surprisingly, even without medical care the child seemed to thrive, nursed regularly by Mary. Percy and Claire frequently left Mary at home with the baby while they went shopping for a cradle, visited Dr. Pemberton not about the baby but about Percy's health which seemed to be getting worse (he was diagnosed as having a weak heart and needing rest and a warm climate), and did numerous errands which kept them away from home for the entire day. In the meantime, Mary was diverted by Hogg who came every evening. He spent Sunday, March 5, with her while Percy and Claire went to town. But the next morning, as Mary recorded in her Journal, "Find my baby dead. Send for Hogg. Talk. a miserable day."[81] The very next day, Percy and Claire were gone again, despite Mary's depression.

We see already a pattern that would recur. Percy Shelley seems to have been singularly unconcerned with the welfare of his female children, and unmoved by their deaths. He clearly did not share Mary's grief at the death of this baby girl and was glad to leave the work of consoling Mary to Hogg, who now joined the household. Mary's growing resentment of Claire was sharpened by her perception that Claire was distracting Percy, not just from Mary herself, but from his primary family relationships, from his commitment to the maintenance of the nuclear family that Mary valued so highly. She would later represent Percy Shelley's lack of parental concern for his offspring in the fictional form of Victor Frankenstein's abandonment of his creature. But we must recognize here that Shelley's indifference was confined to his daughters; for his son William he felt a strong—if narcissistic—affection.

Mary's emotional involvement with her baby daughter was intense. For days after its death, she brooded. As she recorded in her Journal for March 9, "Still think about my little baby—'tis hard, indeed, for a mother to lose a child." A week later, she was still depressed: "Stay at home; net, and think of my little dead baby. This is foolish, I suppose; yet, whenever I am left alone to my own thoughts, and do not read to divert them, they always come back to the same point—that I was a mother, and am so no longer." A week later, she dreamed two nights in a row about her dead daughter: "Dream that my little baby came to life again; that it had only been cold, and that we rubbed it before the fire, and it lived. Awake and find no baby. I think about the little thing all day. Not in good spirits."[82] The death of her first child aroused deep anxieties in Mary Godwin, anxieties that were only partially alleviated by her dream-work. Could she be a mother? Could she create life or only death? Her anxieties were rendered more acute by the memory that Harriet Shelley, Percy's legal wife, had "been brought to bed of a son and heir," just three months earlier. As Mary had then sardonically noted in her Journal, "Shelley writes a number of circular letters of this event, which ought to be ushered in with ringing of bells, etc., for it is the son of his *wife*."[83] No longer a mother, Mary more than ever needed reassurance from Percy of his primary commitment to her, to their love, and to the family unit she represented—this at just the point when Percy seems to have been most intensely involved with Claire. While Hogg flattered her with his attentions, he did not replace Percy as the object of Mary's passionate devotion; it is not accidental that Mary first expresses her desire for Claire's departure in her Journal five days after the loss of her baby.

At this time, Mary was hoping to persuade Claire either to return to the Godwins' house or to take up a position as a governess with a family. Her exasperation at Percy's continued insistence that they provide a home for Claire surfaces in her Journal entry for March 11:

> "Talk about Clara's going away; nothing settled; I fear it is hopeless. She will not go to Skinner Street; then our house is the only remaining place, I see plainly. What is to be done?"[84]

Three days later, Mary pressed harder for Claire's departure, but without success; as she recorded in her Journal, "the prospect [of Clara's going] appears to me more dismal than ever; not the least hope. This is, indeed, hard to bear."[85] Mary's increasing resentment erupted as sarcasm in her Journal two months later, on May 12: "Shelley goes out with his friend [Claire]; he returns first. . . . Shelley and the lady [Claire] walk out."[86] The next day Claire did leave for an eight-month stay alone in a village near Lynmouth, financed by Shelley; Mary thankfully noted, "Clara goes . . . the business is finished . . . I begin a new Journal with our regeneration."[87]

Mary's liberation from Claire was short-lived, however. At first Claire was delighted with her solitary rural retreat at Lynmouth. As she wrote to Fanny Godwin, "I am perfectly happy—After so much discontent, such violent scenes, such a turmoil of passion & hatred you will hardly believe how enraptured I am with this dear little quiet spot."[88] But the gregarious Claire could not long be satisfied by only "a few Cottages with little long faced children, scolding wives and drunken husbands;"[89] by January 5 she was back in London and in frequent contact with Percy.

Convinced that she could not continue her affair with Percy, Claire had determined to capture her own poet. She had set her cap at Lord Byron, the most famous writer of the day. She introduced herself to Byron that winter. By the time Byron left for Switzerland at the end of April, 1816, Claire had become his lover, despite Byron's obvious lack of affection for her. Claire than persuaded Percy and Mary to accompany her to Geneva to meet the famous Byron. As she wrote to Byron, "you bid me not come without protection—'the whole tribe of Otaheite philosophers have come'—Shelley's Chancery suit was decided against him, he had therefore nothing to detain him & yielded to my pressing solicitations."[90] In a complicated settlement of his grandfather's will, Shelley had hoped to sell his rights to a second landed estate valued at £140,000 to his father in return for an annual income of £1000 and the settlement of his debts; the Court of Chancery decided, however, that this arrangement would violate the original entail. Nonetheless, Sir Timothy agreed to continue Shelley's allowance, thus making possible his departure from England.

The decision to go with Claire meant that Claire had effectively rejoined Mary and Percy's household for another five years, to Mary's ever increasing dismay. When they returned to England in December, she begged Percy for

> a house with a lawn a river or lake—noble trees & divine mountains that should be our little mousehole to retire to—But never mind this—give me a garden & *absentia Clariae* and I will thank my love for many favours.[91]

A year later she was still protesting to Percy that "Claire is forever wearying with her idle & childish complaints."[92] Despite her protests, Percy remained deeply attached to Claire, an attachment that he passionately recorded in the "Constantia" poems of 1817. Claire did not leave the Shelleys until October, 1820, after a period in which, according to Claire's Journal entry for July 4, 1820, "The Clare, & the Ma / Find something to fight about every day—,"[93] and fully two years after the death of Mary's second daughter for which Mary held both Claire and Percy responsible.

Mary never forgave Claire for the damage she caused during these years. On May 4, 1836, she wrote to Trelawny, enclosing a recent letter from Claire:

> Claire always harps upon my desertion of her—as if I could desert one I never clung to—we were never friends—Now, I would not go to Paradise with her for a companion—she poisoned my life when young—that is over now—but as we never loved each other, why these eternal complaints to me of me. I respect her now much—& pity her deeply—but years ago my idea of Heaven was a world without a Claire—of course these feelings are altered—but she has still the faculty of making me more uncomfortable than any human being—a faculty she, unconsciously perhaps, never fails to exert whenever I see her—[94]

When Claire came to visit Mary in 1849, her daughter-in-law, disliking Claire, wanted to leave the room. According to Lady Jane Shelley, Mary "burst out in a vehement manner, not usual to her, 'Don't go, dear; don't leave me alone with her. She has been the bane of my life ever since I was two! [sic].'"[95]

Claire felt equally ambivalent toward Mary, whom she described as "a mixture of vanity and good nature." Her hostility to Mary, her jealousy and envy, surfaced powerfully in her journal of "Reminiscences and Anecdotes," probably written in the 1870s. There Claire accused Mary of callousness, of betraying Shelley's memory, and—in an extended piece of malicious fantasy—of watching the execution of a child in Pisa coolly, rejoicing in her comfortable place, chatting with her neighbors, never once wincing, and even shaking the executioner's hand afterwards. Claire then insisted that she "never saw her afterwards without feeling as if the sickening crawling motion of a Death Worm had replaced the usual flow of my Blood in my veins."[96] This image of Mary coolly shaking an executioner's hand is probably a metaphor for Mary's continued friendship with Byron even after the death of Claire's daughter Allegra from typhoid in the convent to which Byron had consigned her. Despite what Claire recognized as "the imposing beauty" of Mary's mind, she condemned Mary vitriolically in a passage that reveals her own enduring passion for Percy Shelley:

> She has given up every hope of imaginary excellence, and has compromised all the nobler parts of her nature and has sneaked in upon any terms she could get into society although she full well knew she could meet with nothing there but depravity. Others still cling round the image and memory of Shelley—his ardent worth, his exalted being, his simplicity and enthusiasm are the sole thought of their being, but she has forsaken even their memory for the pitiful pleasure of trifling with trifles, and has exchanged the whole thought of his being for a share in the corruptions of society. Would to God she could perish without note or remembrance, so the brightness of his name might not be darkened by the corruptions she sheds upon it.[97]

For eight months in 1814–15, however, Mary and Percy were free of Claire's company. They took a trip into the country, to Torquay, where Percy left Mary at Clifton for three weeks in June and July while he visited Peacock at Marlow and looked for a house in that neighborhood. Percy's obvious restlessness and reluctance to settle unnerved Mary. Alone at Clifton, she wrote plaintively, "we ought not to be absent any longer indeed we ought not—I am not happy at it—when I retire to my room no sweet Love—after dinner no Shelley—though I have heaps of things *very particular* to say—in fine either you must come back, or I must come to you directly." Her real source of anxiety surfaced in the next paragraph, "Pray is Clary with you? for I have enquired several times & no letters—but seriously it would not in the least surprise me if you have written to her from London & let her know that you are there without me that she should have taken some such freak."[98]

By August 4, Percy's birthday, Mary and Percy moved into a house near Peacock at Bishopsgate, the eastern entrance to Windsor Park, where they remained for the next nine months. Early in September, together with Peacock and Charles Clairmont, they made a ten-day boating excursion up the Thames, stopping at Oxford where Shelley showed Mary the rooms where he had lived and made his early scientific experiments. Back at Bishopsgate, Mary and Percy settled into a regular routine of reading and writing. Percy began "Alastor," while Mary, who was pregnant again, studied Latin and read Locke's *Essay Concerning Human Understanding* and Bacon's *Essays*. On January 24, 1916, after an easy labor, she gave birth to a son whom she named after her father. Although Godwin was still not speaking to Mary, he recorded this event in his Diary: "William, nepos, born." The birth of a healthy son did much to restore Mary's self-confidence, first as a mother and a creative woman, and secondly as a companion who could give Percy the son he desired.

When Shelley proposed that they accompany Claire to Switzerland in pursuit of Byron, Mary, happy with her child, intrigued by the thought of meeting the famous Byron, and recalling their ecstatic times on the Continent the year before, was willing to leave England for the summer. By June, the Shelley entourage had settled into the chalet Chappuis (or Mont Alègre) on the banks of Lake Geneva at Maison near Byron, his physician Dr. William Polidori, and his servants who had leased a larger house, the Villa Diodati, a short walk away. Byron and Shelley immediately became close friends, sailing together on the lake and meeting almost every evening for literary and philosophical discussions.

It was an exhilarated but anxiety-prone girl who joined Byron, Shelley, Polidori and Claire in these evening talks. Mary Godwin was fascinated by the mad, bad—and extremely handsome—Byron, as well as by the range of topics covered in their conversations. But her troubled girlhood had left her with a deep need to belong to a stable family, to be passionately and unconditionally loved, with a love that would substitute for the nurturant parental love she had never received. This need was rendered acute by Mary's recent estrangement from the father whom she had idolized and who had now abandoned her. Desperately, she turned to Percy Shelley as his replacement: "hug your own Mary to your heart perhaps she will one day have a father till then be everything to me love."[99] The absence of adequate mothering had also left Mary with remarkably low self-esteem: in her rich fantasy life, she never allowd herself to play the heroine, for she could never believe that in her own "common-place" life, "romantic woes or wonderful events would ever be my lot."[100] Her two pregnancies had drained her both physically and emotionally. And Percy's continuing allegiance to Claire undermined her confidence in the success and permanence of her own relationship with Percy. The intellectual and erotic stimulation of Shelley's and Byron's combined presence, together with her deep-seated anxieties and insecurities, once again erupted into Mary's consciousness as a waking dream or nightmare, much like the recurrent dream of her dead baby a year before. But this dream became, even more than Coleridge's reverie of "Kubla Khan," the most famous dream in literary history.

CHAPTER TWO

Making a Monster

Mary Shelley's waking nightmare on June 16, 1816, inspired one of the most powerful horror stories of Western civilization. It can claim the status of a myth, so profoundly resonant in its implications for our comprehension of our selves and our place in the world that it has become, at least in its barest outline, a trope of everyday life. Of course, both the media and the average person in the street have mistakenly assigned the name of Frankenstein not to the maker of the monster but to his creature. But as we shall see, this "mistake" actually derives from an intuitively correct reading of the novel. *Frankenstein* is our culture's most penetrating literary analysis of the psychology of modern "scientific" man, of the dangers inherent in scientific research, and of the exploitation of nature and of the female implicit in a technological society. So deeply does it probe the collective cultural psyche of the modern era that it deserves to be called a myth, on a par with the most telling stories of Greek and Norse gods and goddesses.

But Mary Shelley's myth is unique, both in content and in origin. *Frankenstein* invents the story of a man's single-handed creation of a living being from dead matter. All other creation myths, even that of the Jewish *golem*,[1] depend on female participation or some form of divine intervention (either directly or instrumentally through magical rituals or the utterance of holy names or sacred letters). The idea of an entirely man-made monster is Mary Shelley's own. And this myth of a man-made monster can be derived from a single, datable event: the waking dream of a specific eighteen-year-old girl on June 16, 1816.[2] Moreover, Mary Shelley created her myth single-handedly. All other myths of the western or eastern worlds, whether of Dracula, Tarzan,

Superman or more traditional religious systems, derive from folklore or communal ritual practices.

As myth, Mary Shelley's *Frankenstein*, for all its resonance, has hardly been well explored. While the film industry has exploited and popularized the more salient dimensions of the story, it has ignored the complexity of Mary Shelley's invention—in particular, it has over-looked the significance of the making and unmaking of the female monster. Before Ellen Moers's ground-breaking discussion of *Frankenstein* in *The New York Review of Books* in 1973, literary scholars and critics had for the most part discussed Mary Shelley's career merely as an appendage to her husband's, dismissing *Frankenstein* as a badly written children's book even though far more people were familiar with her novel than with Percy Shelley's poetry. Feminist critics have, of course, noted the injustice of this; in the last fifteen years they have begun to explore the multi-layered significance of *Frankenstein*.[3] In the discussion that follows, I shall look at the novel from several different perspectives—feminist, biographical, psychological, textual, historical, and philosophical. I wish to assess the many ways in which *Frankenstein* portrays the consequences of the failure of the family, the damage wrought when the mother—or a nurturant parental love—is absent.

I have throughout referred to the manuscript and to the first (1818) edition of *Frankenstein*, since these present a more coherent literary vision generated from the most immediate psychological and social experiences of the author. The most often reprinted second edition of 1831 was substantively revised by Mary Shelley in an attempt to interpolate a later and in some ways contradictory concept of nature and the human will, a concept produced by the traumatic deaths of her husband and children. The three versions of *Frankenstein*—manu-script, 1818 edition, and 1831 edition—constitute a text-in-process whose stages differ as much as do the various texts of Wordsworth's *Prelude*, albeit for different reasons.

Perhaps I should explain why *Frankenstein* receives a more extended discussion in this book than do Mary Shelley's other novels. Not only is this novel Shelley's most famous, most complex, and most culturally resonant, but it was also written at a time in her life—before the deaths of her children, Clara Everina and William, and her husband—when her imagination was free to explore and articulate the profound ambivalences in her relationship with Percy Shelley. Her later novels suffer from her obsessive need to idealize her husband and the bourgeois family, the results of which are overly sentimental rhetoric and implausible plot-resolutions. Nonetheless, as I shall try to show, these later novels are fascinating for the ways in which they reveal the development of Mary Shelley's thought and undermine the very ideals they purport to affirm.

From a feminist viewpoint, *Frankenstein* is a book about what happens when a man tries to have a baby without a woman. As such, the novel is profoundly concerned with natural as opposed to unnatural modes of production and reproduction. Ellen Moers first drew our attention to the novel's emphasis on birth and "the trauma of the after-birth."[4] Since this is a novel about giving birth, let us begin with the question of origins, "the question," as Mary Shelley acknowledged in her Introduction to the revised edition of *Frankenstein* of 1831, "so very frequently asked me—'How I, then a young girl, came to think of, and to dilate upon, so very hideous an idea?' " Mary Shelley then tells a story almost as well-known as the novel itself, of how she and Byron and Percy Shelley and Dr. Polidori, after reading ghost stories together one rainy evening near Geneva in June, 1816, agreed each to write an equally thrilling horror story; how she tried for days to think of a story, but failed; and finally, how one night after a discussion among Byron, Polidori, and Percy Shelley concerning galvanism and Erasmus Darwin's success in causing a piece of vermicelli to move voluntarily, she fell into a reverie or waking dream in which she saw "the pale student of unhallowed arts kneeling beside the thing he had put together" and felt the terror he felt as the hideous corpse he had renanimated with a "spark of life" stood beside his bed, "looking on him with yellow, watery, but speculative eyes."[5]

Why did Mary Shelley have such a dream at this point in her life? Affectively, the dream evoked a powerful anxiety in her. Over fifteen years later, she claimed she could still see vividly the room to which she woke and feel "the thrill of fear" that ran through her. Why was she so frightened? Remember that Mary Shelley had given birth to a baby girl eighteen months earlier, a baby whose death two weeks later produced a recurrent dream: "Dream that my little baby came to life again; that it had only been cold, and that we rubbed it before the fire, and it lived. Awake and find no baby." Once again she was dreaming of reanimating a corpse by warming it with a "spark of life." And only six months before, Mary Shelley had given birth a second time, to William. She doubtless expected to be pregnant again in the near future; and indeed, she conceived her third child, Clara Everina, only six months later in December. Mary Shelley's reverie unleashed her deepest subconscious anxieties, the natural but no less powerful anxieties of a very young, frequently pregnant woman. Clearly, in her dream, Mary Shelley lost her distanced, safely external view of "the pale student"—she initially "saw" him kneeling beside his creation, just as she "saw" the "hideous phantasm" stir into life. Gradually her dream-work drew her into a closer identification with the student. Even as she watched him rush out of the room, she knew how he felt, shared his "terror" at his success and his "hope" that the thing would subside back into dead matter. At the end of her dream, nothing separates the dreamer from the student of unhallowed arts. Even though she continues to use the third person—"he sleeps; he opens his eyes"—she has become the student; she is looking up at the "yellow, watery, but speculative eyes" of the "horrid thing." For only from *inside* the student's drawn bed-curtains could she see those eyes.

This dream economically fuses Mary Shelley's myriad anxieties about the processes of pregnancy, giving birth, and mothering. It gives shape to her deepest fears. What if my child is born deformed, a freak, a moron, a "hideous" thing? Could I still love it, or would I be horrified and wish it were dead again? What will happen if I can't love my child? Am I capable of raising a healthy, normal child? Will my child die (as my first baby did)? Could I *wish* my own child to die, to destroy itself? Could I kill it? Could it kill *me* (as I killed my mother, Mary Wollstonecraft)?

One reason Mary Shelley's story reverberates so strongly is because it articulates, perhaps for the first time in Western literature, the most powerfully felt anxieties of pregnancy. The experience of pregnancy is one that male writers have by necessity avoided; and before Mary Shelley, female writers had considered the experiences of pregnancy and childbirth as improper, even taboo, subjects to be discussed before a male or mixed audience. Mary Shelley's focus on the birth-process illuminates for a male readership hitherto unpublished female anxieties, fears, and concerns about the birth-process and its consequences. At the same time, her story reassures a female audience that such fears are shared by other women.

Mary Shelley's dream thus generates that dimension of the novel's plot which has been much discussed by feminist critics, Victor Frankenstein's total failure at parenting. For roughly nine months, while "winter, spring, and summer, passed away," he labours to give life to his child until, finally, on a dreary night in November, he observes its birth: "I saw the dull yellow eye of the creature open; it breathed hard, and a convulsive motion agitated its limbs."[6] But rather than clasping his newborn child to his breast in a nurturing maternal gesture, he rushes out of the room, repulsed by the abnormality of his creation. And when his child follows him to his bedroom, uttering inarticulate sounds of desire and affection, smiling at him, reaching out to embrace him, Victor Frankenstein again flees in horror, abandoning his child completely.

Frankenstein's failure to mother his child results from an earlier failure of empathy. Throughout his experiment, Frankenstein never considers the possibility that his creature might not wish the existence he is about to receive. On the contrary, he blithely assumes that the creature will "bless" him and be filled with "gratitude" (49). Frankenstein's lack of imaginative identification with his creation, his lack of what Keats would have called "negative capability," causes him to make a critical mistake. In his rush to complete his experiment, and because "the minuteness of the parts formed a great hindrance," he resolves to make his creature "of a gigantic stature; that is to say, about eight feet in height, and proportionably large" (49). He never once considers how such a giant will survive among normal human beings. Nor does he carefully contemplate the features of the creature he is making. "I had selected his features as beautiful. Beautiful!— Great God! His yellow skin scarcely covered the work of muscles and arteries beneath; his hair was of a lustrous black, and flowing; his teeth of a pearly whiteness; but these luxuriances only formed a more horrid contrast with his watery eyes, that seemed almost of the same colour as the dun white sockets in which they were set, his shrivelled complexion, and straight black lips" (52). Frankenstein's inability to sympathize with his child, to care for or even to comprehend its basic needs, soon takes the extreme form of putative infanticide. After his next glimpse of his child, he confesses, "I gnashed my teeth, my eyes became inflamed, and I ardently wished to extinguish that life which I had so thoughtlessly bestowed" (87).

Even after the creature reminds Frankenstein of his parental obligation to provide for his child—"I ought to be thy Adam" (95)—Frankenstein still fails to give him the human companionship, the Eve, the female creature, that he needs to achieve some sort of a normal life. The creature's consequent despair is registered in the epigraph which appears on the title page of each of the three volumes of the first edition. It is Adam's cry of misery at being punished for his freely chosen sin, a cry which—given the creature's innocence—reverberates more poignantly, and ironically, with each reappearance:

> Did I request thee, Maker, from my clay
> To mold me man? Did I solicit thee
> From darkness to promote me?
> (*Paradise Lost*, X, 743–45)

Read rhetorically, these questions sharpen our sense of Frankenstein's responsibility to his creature, and his culpable denial of that responsibility. They articulate the cry of an unfairly punished child: "I never asked to be born!"

Frankenstein's refusal to parent his child is both an impulsive emotional reaction and a deliberate decision. Even on his death-bed Frankenstein stubbornly insists that he has acted correctly. As he confesses to Walton:

> During these last days I have been occupied in examining my past conduct; nor do I find it blameable. In a fit of enthusiastic madness I created a rational creature, and was bound towards him, to assure, as far as was in my power, his happiness and well-being. This was my duty; but there was another still paramount to that. My duties towards my fellow-creatures had greater claims to my attention, because they included a greater proportion of happiness or misery. Urged by this view, I refused, and I did right in refusing, to create a companion for the first creature. He shewed unparalleled malignity and selfishness, in evil: he destroyed my friends; he devoted to destruction beings who possessed exquisite sensations, happiness, and wisdom; nor do I know where this thirst for vengeance may end. Miserable himself, that he may render no other wretched, he ought to die. (215)

Frankenstein's statement is a tissue of self-deception and rationalization. He never once considers whether the creature's "malignity" might have been prevented, as the creature himself repeatedly insists, by loving care in infancy; he never asks whether he was in any way responsible for the creature's development. He relies on a Benthamite utilitarian ethical calculus, the greatest good for the greatest number, without first demonstrating that the creature could not have benefited from the companionship of a female, and without proving that the female creature would have been more malignant than the male (as he claimed when he destroyed her partially finished form). And it never occurs to him that he might have created a female incapable of reproduction. Instead he assumes that the two creatures would share his egotistical desire to produce offspring who would bless and revere them. From the moment of the creature's birth, Frankenstein has rejected it as "demoniacal" (53) and heaped abuse upon it. Frankenstein represents a classic case of a battering parent who produces a battered child who in turn becomes a battering parent: the creature's first murder victim, we must remember, is a small child whom he wished to adopt.

Throughout the novel, Frankenstein's callous disregard of his responsibility as the sole parent of his only child is contrasted to the examples of two loving fathers: Alphonse Frankenstein and Father De

Lacey. Both these fathers assiduously care for their motherless children, providing them with loving homes and moral guidance. "My father . . . watched me as a bird does its nestling," remarks Victor Frankenstein, in a passage deleted from the manuscript of the novel (at 183:33). No "More indulgent and less dictatorial parent" than Alphonse Frankenstein exists upon earth, acknowledges Victor (150). And Father De Lacey has a "countenance beaming with benevolence and love" (104). They construct what Lawrence Stone has described as the closed domestic nuclear family of the eighteenth century, which is organized around the principle of personal autonomy and bound together by strong affective ties.[7] Such loving fathers as Alphonse Frankenstein and Father De Lacey are rewarded with the genuine gratitude of their children; Felix and Agatha even starve themselves that their father may eat. Mary Shelley promoted this ideal of the loving family in one of the creature's comments upon his reading:

> Other lessons were impressed upon me even more deeply. I heard of the difference of sexes; of the birth and growth of children; how the father doated on the smiles of the infant, and the lively sallies of the older child; how all the life and cares of the mother were wrapt up in the previous charge; how the mind of youth expanded and gained knowledge; of brother, sister, and all the various relationships which bind one human being to another in mutual bonds. (116–17)

Shelley both anticipates and goes beyond Stone's model of the closed domestic nuclear family, however, by introducing a new element, an egalitarian definition of gender-roles within the bourgeois family. Notice that both the father and the mother are equally devoted to their children; that both boys and girls ("youth") are expected to receive an education; that the same bonds mutually bind persons of opposite gender. Shelley's ideological commitment to a mutually supportive, gender-free family functions in the novel as the ethical touchstone by which the behavior of Victor Frankenstein is found wanting.

As she wrote out her novel, Mary Shelley distanced herself from her originating dream-identification with the anxious and rejecting parent and focused instead on the plight of the abandoned child. Increasingly she identified with the orphaned creature. The heart of this three-volume novel is the creature's account of his own development, which occupies all but thirty pages of the second volume of the first edition. And in this volume, Mary Shelley spoke most directly in her own voice: Percy Shelley's manuscript revisions are far less numerous in

Volume II than in Volumes I or III. As she described the creature's first experiences in the world and his desperate attempts to establish a bond of affection with the De Lacey family, Mary Shelley was clearly drawing on her own experiences of emotional isolation in the Godwin household. Specific links join the creature's life to Mary Shelley's own. The creature reads about his conception in the journal of lab reports he grabbed up as he fled from Victor Frankenstein's laboratory (125–26); Mary Shelley could have read about her own conception in Godwin's Diary (where he noted the nights on which he and Mary Wollstonecraft had sexual intercourse during their courtship with a "Chez moi" or a "Chez elle", including every night but two between December 20, 1796, and January 3, 1797). Both the creature and Mary Shelley read the same books. In the years before and during the composition of *Frankenstein*, Mary Shelley read or reread the books found by the creature in an abandoned portmanteau—Goethe's *Werther*, Plutarch's *Lives of the Noble Romans*, Volney's *Ruins or, . . . the Revolutions of Empire*, and Milton's *Paradise Lost*, as well as the poets the creature occasionally quotes, Coleridge and Byron.[8] Moreover, as a motherless child and a woman in a patriarchal culture, Mary Shelley shared the creature's powerful sense of being born without an identity, without role-models to emulate, without a history.[9] The creature utters a *cri de coeur* that was Mary Shelley's own: "Who was I? What was I? Whence did I come? What was my destination? These questions continually recurred, but I was unable to solve them" (124).

What the creature does know is that a child deprived of a loving family becomes a monster. Again and again he insists that he was born good but compelled by others into evil: "I was benevolent and good; misery made me a fiend" (95). Granted a mate, he will become good again: "My vices are the children of a forced solitude that I abhor; and my virtues will necessarily arise when I live in communion with an equal" (143). Even after the destruction of all his hopes has condemned him to unremitting vengeance, the creature still insists, "I had feelings of affection, they were requited by detestation and scorn" (165).

The creature's argument is derived in part from Rousseau's *Emile*, which Mary Shelley read in 1816.[10] Rousseau claimed that "God makes all things good; man meddles with them and they become evil."[11] He blamed the moral failings of children specifically upon the absence of a mother's love. Attacking mothers who refuse to nurse or care for their own children in early infancy, Rousseau insists, in a comment that self-servingly ignores a father's parental responsibilities (Rousseau abandoned his own children at the local orphanage):

> Would you restore all men to their primal duties, begin with the
> mothers; the results will surprise you. Every evil follows in the train
> of this first sin; the whole moral order is disturbed, nature is
> quenched in every breast, the home becomes gloomy, the spectacle of
> a young family no longer stirs the husband's love and the stranger's
> reverence. (13)

Without mothering, without an early experience of a loving education,
writes Rousseau in a statement that the creature's experience vividly
confirms, "a man left to himself from birth would be more of a
monster than the rest" (5).

Mary Shelley powerfully evoked the creature's psychic response to
the conviction that he is destined to be forever an outcast, as alone as
the Ancient Mariner on his wide, wide sea—a horrifying spectacle that
had haunted Mary Shelley's imagination since she heard Coleridge
recite the poem in 1806. Again and again the creature cries out:

> Every where I see bliss, from which I alone am irrevocably excluded.
> (95)
> I had never yet seen a being resembling me, or who claimed any
> intercourse with me. What was I? (117)
> Increase of knowledge only discovered to me more clearly what a
> wretched outcast I was. . . . no Eve soothed my sorrows, or shared
> my thoughts; I was alone. (127)

Here Mary Shelley unearthed her own buried feelings of parental
abandonment and forced exile from her father. Her creature,
disappointed in his long-cherished desire for a welcome from the De
Lacey family, feels anger, then a desire for revenge, and finally a violent
severing from all that is human, civilized, cultural. "I was like a wild
beast that had broken the toils; destroying the objects that obstructed
me, and ranging through the wood with a stag-like swiftness . . . All,
save I, were at rest or in enjoyment: I, like the arch-fiend, bore a hell
within me" (132). Both the allusion to Milton's Satan and the image of
a beast breaking out of harness focus her argument that a human being
deprived of companionship, of nurturing, of mothering, is driven
beyond the pale of humanity. The creature has crossed the barrier that
separates the human from the bestial, the domesticated from the wild,
the cooked from the raw. Symbolically, the creature turns his
acculturated love-gifts of firewood back into raw fire by burning the
De Lacey cottage to the ground while dancing round it, himself
consumed in a frenzy of pure hatred and revenge.

Searching for his only legitimate parent, the creature encounters
outside Geneva the five-year-old William Frankenstein. Once more
thwarted in his desire for a family when the child refuses to accompany

him, his anger claims—perhaps unintentionally—its first human sacrifice. Here, as U. C. Knoepflmacher has suggested, Mary Shelley is uncovering her own repressed aggression.[12] For it can be no accident that the creature's first victim is the exact image of her son William, named after his grandfather Godwin. Having felt rejected by her father, emotionally when he married Mary Jane Clairmont and overtly when she eloped with Percy Shelley, Mary had long repressed a hostility to Godwin that erupted in the murder of his namesake. It is actually his double namesake, since Godwin had given the name William to his own son, who was the favored child in the Godwin-Clairmont household, tenderly nicknamed Love-will by his doting mother. This murder thus raises to consciousness one of the most deeply buried fears energizing Mary Shelley's original dream: *might I be capable of murdering my own flesh and blood?* For William Frankenstein is a deliberate portrait of William Shelley: he has the same "lively blue eyes, dimpled cheeks, and endearing manners" (37), the same "dark eyelashes and curling hair" and propensity to take little *wives* (62), Louisa Biron being William Frankenstein's favorite playmate, where Allegra Byron was William Shelley's choice. The creature's calculated strangling of the blue-eyed, blond-haired, manly boy articulates both Mary Shelley's horrified recognition that she is capable of imagining the murder of her own child—capable of infanticide itself—and her instinctive revulsion against that act. As she suggests, a rejected and unmothered child can become a killer, especially the killer of its own parents, siblings, children. When the nuclear family fails to mother its offspring, it engenders homicidal monsters.

And yet, even without mothering, the creature manages to gain an education. Mary Shelley's allusion to Rousseau's theory of the natural man as a noble savage, born free but everywhere in chains and inevitably corrupted by society, focuses one of the minor concerns of the novel, its theory of education. In the great debate on the relative importance of nature versus nurture, on whether learning achievements should be attributed primarily to innate intelligence or to social environment, Mary Shelley was convinced that nurture is crucial. Her reading of Rousseau's *Second Discourse* had given her insight into the limitations of the natural man as well as the potential evils of civilization.[13] Her creature *is* Rousseau's natural man, a creature no different from the animals, responding unconsciously to the needs of his flesh and the changing conditions of his environment. He feels pleasure at the sight of the moon, the warmth of the sun, the sounds of bird-song, the light and heat of fire; pain at the coldness of snow, the burning sensation of fire, the pangs of hunger and thirst. In the state of nature, man is free and unselfconscious; insofar as he can gratify his primal desires easily, he is happy. For Frankenstein's creature, a dry hovel is "paradise, compared to the bleak forest, my former residence, the rain-dropping branches, and dank earth" (102). But as Rousseau also emphasized, especially in *The Social Contract*, the natural man lacks much: language, the capacity to think rationally, companionship and the affections that flow from it, a moral consciousness. Peering through the chinks of his hovel, Mary Shelley's creature rapidly discovers the limitations of the state of nature and the positive benefits of a civilization grounded on family life.

Even though she depicts Frankenstein's creature as Rousseau's natural man, even though she echoes Rousseau's *Emile* at critical points, she does not endorse Rousseau's view that the simple gratification of human passions will lead to virtuous behavior. Her account of the creature's mental and moral development is more closely allied to the epistemological and pedagogical theories of David Hartley and John Locke. The associationist David Hartley argued that early sensative experiences determine adult behavior, and the rationalist John Locke concurred that natural man is neither innately good nor innately evil, but rather a white paper or blank slate upon which sensations write impressions that then become ideas or conscious experience. The creature's moral development closely parallels the paradigm that Hartley laid out in his *Observations of Man, His Frame, His Duty, and His Expectations* (1749)[14] and follows the theories that Locke propounded first in 1690 in his *Essay Concerning Human Understanding* (which Mary Shelley read in 1816) and later in the more pragmatically oriented *Some Thoughts Concerning Education* (1693). The creature first experiences purely physical and undifferentiated sensations of light, darkness, heat, cold, hunger, pain and pleasure; this is the earliest period of infancy when "no distinct ideas occupied my mind; all was confused" (98). Gradually, the creature learns to distinguish his sensations and thus his "mind received every day additional ideas" (99). At the same time he learns the causes of his feelings of pain or pleasure and how to produce the effects he desires by obtaining clothing, shelter, food and fire.

The creature's education is completed in just the way Locke advocates, by providing him with examples of moral and intellectual virtue. As Locke insisted:

> Of all the ways whereby children are to be instructed, and their manners formed, the plainest, easiest, and most efficacious, is to set before their eyes the examples of those things that you would have them do or avoid. . . . Virtues and vices can by no words be so

plainly set before their understandings as the actions of other men will show them.[15]

When the creature stares through the chink in the wall of his hovel into the adjoining cottage, he sees before him a living illustration of benevolence, affection, industry, thrift, and natural justice in the actions of the De Lacey family. The De Laceys embody Mary Shelley's ideal of the egalitarian family—with one important exception: they lack a mother. The De Laceys not only stimulate the creature's emotions and arouse his desire to do good to others (which takes the form of gathering firewood for them), but also introduce him to the concept and function of a spoken and written language. Here adopting a referential theory of language, in which sounds or words are conceived as pointing to objects or mental states, Mary Shelley traces the creature's linguistic development from his earliest acquisition of nouns and proper names through his grasp of abstractions to his ability to speak, read, and finally write, the latter processes enabled by his overhearing Safie's French lessons in the next room and by his acquisition of a private library. While Locke's insistence that children learn best from examples now seems commonplace, Peter Gay has rightly reminded us that Locke was the first educator to recognize that human rationality and the capacity for self-discipline evolve gradually in the growing child and that the subject-matter to be learned must be adapted to the differential capacities of children at different stages of development.[16]

The creature learns from sensations and examples; what he learns is determined by his environment. The De Lacey family provides a lesson in almost perfect virtue, grounded in the private domestic affections, together with a treatise on social and human injustice as practiced in the public realm by the law courts of France and Safie's ungrateful Turkish father. The creature's knowledge of human vice and virtue is further enlarged by his reading. From Plutarch's *Lives of the Noble Romans* he learns the nature of heroism and public virtue and civic justice; from Volney's *Ruins, or A Survey of the Revolutions of Empires* he learns the contrasting nature of political corruption and the causes of the decline of civilizations; from Milton's *Paradise Lost* he learns the origins of human good and evil and the roles of the sexes; and from Goethe's *Werther* he learns the range of human emotions, from domestic love to suicidal despair, as well as the rhetoric in which to articulate not only ideas but feelings.

The creature's excellent education, which includes moral lessons garnered from the two books Locke thought essential, Aesop's Fables and the Bible, is implicitly contrasted to the faulty education received by Victor Frankenstein. While Alphonse Frankenstein initially followed Godwin's pedagogical precepts—he inspired his children to learn in a noncompetitive atmosphere by encouraging their voluntary desire to please others and by giving them practical goals (one learns a foreign language in order to read the interesting books in that tongue)—he failed to monitor sufficiently closely the books that Victor Frankenstein actual read. Instead of the Bible, Aesop, and *Robinson Crusoe* recommended by Godwin, Locke, and Rousseau, Victor devoured the misleading alchemical treatises of Cornelius Agrippa, Paracelsus, and Albertus Magnus, books which encouraged, not an awareness of human folly and injustice, but rather a hubristic desire for human omnipotence, for the gaining of the philosopher's stone and the elixir of life.

Mary Shelley's pedagogy, derived in large part from her father's espousal of Locke, emphasizes the role of the affections in the education of young children. Victor learns because he wishes to please his father, Elizabeth because she wishes to delight her aunt, the creature because he wishes to emulate and be accepted by the De Lacey family. Clearly an unloved child will not learn well—the creature's education is effectively ended when the De Laceys abandon him. But how well does even a much-loved child learn? Victor Frankenstein was such, but his father's indulgence only encouraged his son's egotistical dreams of omnipotence. In this Mary Shelley reveals her nagging doubt whether even a supportive family can produce a virtuous adult. In the successes and failures of both the creature's and Frankenstein's education, Mary Shelley registered a pervasive maternal anxiety: *even if I love and nurture my child, even if I provide the best education of which I am capable, I may still produce a monster—and who is responsible for that?*

Behind Mary Shelley's maternal anxieties lies a more general problem, the problem posed for her by Rousseau's writings. For Rousseau had made it clear that the movement away from the state of nature into the condition of civilization entails a loss of freedom, a frustration of desire, and an enclosure within the prisonhouse of language or what Lacan has called the symbolic order. Civilization produces as much discontent as content. In place of the natural man's instinctive harmony with his surroundings, society substitutes a system of conflicting economic interests and a struggle for individual mastery, an aggressive competition restrained by but not eliminated from Rousseau's favored constitutional democracy. For once the creature has left the state of nature and learned the language and laws of society, he has gained a self-consciousness that he can never lose, the consciousness of his own isolation:

> I learned that the possessions most esteemed by your fellow-creatures were, high and unsullied descent united with riches. . . . but . . . I possessed no money, no friends, no kind of property. I was, besides, endowed with a figure hideously deformed and loathsome; . . . When I looked around, I saw and heard of none like me. . . .
>
> I cannot describe to you the agony that these reflections inflicted upon me; I tried to dispel them, but sorrow only increased with knowledge. Oh, that I had for ever remained in my native wood, nor known or felt beyond the sensations of hunger, thirst, and heat! (115–16)

Deprived of all human companionship, the creature can never recover from the disease of self-consciousness; for him, no escape, save death, is possible. In this context, the novel points up the irony implicit in Locke's most famous pedagogical maxim: "A sound mind in a sound body is a short but full description of a happy state in this world" (19). Exercise and good diet can produce the healthy body Locke found so conducive to the development of mental and moral capacities; but can the creature, born with a grotesquely oversized and unsound body, ever develop a sound mind? Or, in the terms posed for Shelley by David Hartley, can an unmothered child whose formative experiences are of pain rather than pleasure ever develop a rational intellect, a healthy moral sense, or a normal personality?

CHAPTER THREE

My Hideous Progeny

Mary Shelley's anxiety about her capacity to give birth to a normal, healthy, loving child manifests itself in *Frankenstein* in forms other than the plot. Mary Shelley thought of her ghost story as her baby: the metaphor is overtly articulated at the end of her Introduction to the 1831, Standard Novels edition of *Frankenstein* where she bids her novel, "my hideous progeny," to go forth and prosper. Her metaphor is hardly original: Plato long ago said that men write books to gain the immortality women achieve by having children, while Jean Rhys recently confessed that when she finished her masterpiece *Wide Sargasso Sea*:

> I've dreamt several times that I was going to have a baby—then I woke with relief.
>
> Finally I dreamt that I was looking at the baby in a cradle—such a puny weak thing.
>
> So the book must be finished, and that must be what I think about it really. I don't dream about it any more.[1]

But for Jean Rhys as for Mary Shelley, the metaphor of book as baby fused a double anxiety, an insecurity about both her authorship and her female identity. In giving birth to a full-fledged novel, Mary Shelley was giving birth to her self-as-author. Unlike those women writers who have experienced what Sandra Gilbert and Susan Gubar have described as the female's "anxiety of authorship"[2]—a difficulty in finding a precursor or public voice in which to speak within a culture that has historically suppressed the female voice and denied the means of literary production to women—Mary Shelley did have female role-models to emulate: most notably her mother Mary Wollstonecraft, such eighteenth century writers of sentimental and satiric fiction as Fanny Burney, Charlotte Ramsay Lennox, Sarah Fielding, Elizabeth Inchbald, and Amelia Alderson Opie (to whom her father had once proposed marriage), and most directly, given her commitment to a ghost story, Ann Radcliffe and the other female authors of Gothic fiction (Clara Reeve, Charlotte Dacre, Sarah Wilkinson, Sophia Lee). Yet despite this tradition of female authorship, Mary Shelley doubted the legitimacy of her own literary voice, a doubt that determined her decision to speak through three *male* narrators (Walton, Frankenstein, the creature), the structure of her novel, and the revisions of her text.

Mary Shelley's anxiety about her authorship did not derive from the fear that her desire to publish would be blocked by a patriarchal literary establishment. On the contrary, Mary Shelley grew up *expecting* that she would write for publication. She felt a *compulsion* to write, a compulsion that was as much external as internal. When Byron proposed that they each write a ghost story for their common amusement, no one but Mary Shelley took him terribly seriously. Percy Shelley scribbled a few lines of doggerel verse; Byron himself began a story which he abandoned after a few pages, publishing the fragment at the end of "Mazeppa"; Dr. Polidori may have written either the absurd tale concerning a skull-headed lady that Mary Shelley remembered or, more likely, the tale of "The Vampyr" that afterwards achieved a certain success when it was erroneously published under Byron's name. But fifteen years later, Mary Shelley vividly recalled her mortification at being forced to admit that she had not yet thought of a story.

The intensity of her embarrassment caused her, in 1831, to make a significant error. In her description of the ghost story competition, Mary Shelley stated that several mornings had passed during which "dull Nothing" replied to her anxious invocations: " '*Have you thought of a story?*' I was asked each morning, and each morning I was forced to reply with a mortifying negative" (226). Then, she says, came the evening discussion between Byron and Percy Shelley concerning "the nature of the principle of life, and whether there was any probability of its ever being discovered and communicated," at the end of which she had her famous waking dream of the pale student and his hideous phantasm. But as James Rieger has noted, the only other surviving record of these events suggests a different chronology. John William Polidori recorded in his Diary that a conversation took place on the evening of June 15, 1816 between himself and Percy Shelley "about principles,—whether man was to be thought merely an instrument;" that Byron, Polidori, and the entire Shelley entourage dined and slept at Villa Diodati on June 16 (this is presumably the evening in which they read and agreed to write ghost stories); and that on June 17 "the ghost-stories are begun by all but me."[3] By lengthening the lapse of time between Byron's proposal and her dream-invention of a plot for her ghost story from a few hours to several days, Mary Shelley inadvertently revealed the extreme anxiety she felt lest she not be able to meet Byron's expectations.

Why did she care so much whether she wrote a story or not? Mary Shelley was compelled by two feelings of inadequacy. She identified her inability to conceive a story with a woman's inability to conceive a child: "that blank incapability of invention which is the greatest misery of authorship, when dull Nothing replies to our anxious invocations." Her mortification was intensified by the anxieties roused by her mother's death in childbirth and the death of her own two-week-old daughter two years before. It is out of this doubled fear, the fear of a woman that she may not be able to bear a healthy, normal child and the fear of a putative author that she may not be able to write, that Mary Shelley's nightmarish reverie was born. As Barbara Johnson has trenchantly observed, *Frankenstein* is "the story of the experience of writing *Frankenstein*."[4] Significantly, Mary Shelley dedicated the novel to Godwin, even though he had disowned her after her elopement, rather than to Percy Shelley who helped her with its composition. She wanted to give the book to its father, *her* father, for the book is her created self as well as her child.

The dating of the plot sharpens the identification of the novel as Mary Shelley's self-image. *Frankenstein* is narrated in a series of letters written by Walton to his sister Margaret Walton Saville (whose initials, M. W. S., are those Mary Wollstonecraft Godwin coveted—and gained when she and Percy Shelley were married on December 30, 1816). In this sense, the novel is written by the author to an audience of one, herself. The first letter is dated December 11, 17—; the last is dated September 12, 17—. Exactly nine months enwomb the telling of the history of Frankenstein, bringing Mary Shelley's literary pregnancy to full term. Moreover, these nine months correspond almost exactly with Mary Shelley's third pregnancy, conceived and carried during the actual writing of *Frankenstein*: her daughter Clara Everina, named for her dead daughter and her aunt Everina Wollstonecraft, was born three days after Mary Shelley's own birthday, on September 2, 1817. We can further speculate, on the basis of (not always consistent) internal evidence, as to the calendar year in which Walton is writing.[5] The creature first appears before Walton's startled eyes on Monday, July 31, 17—; later we learn that the creature read a copy of Volney's *Ruins*, which was not published until 1791 (and not translated into English until 1795). The only year in the last decade of the eighteenth century when July 31 falls on a Monday is 1797, the year in which Mary Shelley herself was born. The novel's final entry is dated two days after Mary Wollstonecraft Godwin's death. Mary Shelley thus symbolically fused her book's beginning and ending with her own—Victor Frankenstein's death, the Monster's promised suicide, and her mother's death from puerperal fever can all be seen as the consequences of the same creation, the birth of Mary Godwin-the-author.

Mary Shelley felt intensely ambivalent toward her creation: it was a "hideous progeny," all the more horrible for having been produced by so young a girl. Her Introduction to the Standard Novels edition, even fifteen years after the event and when her fame was secure, is strikingly defensive: "I am very averse to bringing myself forward in print"; "Shelley urged me to develope the idea at greater length"; "once again, I bid my hideous progeny go forth and prosper. I have an affection for it" (222, 229). The intensity of her apology goes well beyond the conventional topoi of either literary or female modesty. Why did Mary Shelley feel so apologetic? In giving birth to her self-as-author, Mary Shelley is here able to conceive only a monster: she is the author-of-horror, perhaps even what Percy Shelley called Victor Frankenstein, "the author of unalterable evils" (87).

In creating her famous monster, Mary Shelley powerfully reinforced the tradition of the Gothic novel as a peculiarly female domain. *Frankenstein* surpasses its male-authored contenders, whether Walpole's *The Castle of Otranto*, Beckford's *Vathek*, Lewis's *The Monk*, Maturin's *Melmoth the Wanderer*, or Bram Stoker's *Dracula*, as our most culturally resonant and disturbing Gothic novel. Women writers have been drawn to the Gothic novel because, as Cynthia Griffin Wolff has argued, its conventions permit them to explore one of the most deeply repressed experiences in a patriarchal culture, female sexual desire.[6] Ann Radcliffe, Charlotte Dacre, and Sophia Lee typically used the medieval ruined castle or abbey as a metaphor for the female body, penetrated by a sexually attractive villain. Within the ruined walls hides a chaste young woman, who is both terrified and hypnotically fascinated by the villain. Thus Radcliffe, Dacre, and Lee articulated the deep sexual ambivalence experienced by their young female readers who intensely desired the passionate erotic experience that a patriarchal culture adamantly forbids to unmarried girls. The conclusion of these novels, in which the heroine is narrowly saved from seduction or death by a chaste knight whom she then marries, enables the female reader, like Keats's dreaming Madeline in "The Eve of St. Agnes," to have her cake and eat it too, to participate imaginatively in an intensely erotic seduction but to wake "warm in the virgin morn, no weeping Magdalen." The real "evil" encountered in the Gothic novel, then, is the female's overwhelming desire for uninhibited and all-consuming sexual experience in a society which, even in the late twentieth century, is for the most part uncomfortable with the aggressive, sexually liberated woman. Hence the enormous popularity of the Mills and Boon novels in England and the Harlequin Romances in America, Gothic romances which continue to provide an "acceptable" form of sexual passion to women whose own lives do not permit it. But as Tania Modleski has shown us, this sexual passion is often directed toward aggressive, dominating, virile men, men whose egotism—like Victor Frankenstein's—can lead them to manipulate, exploit, and even rape the women whose desire they arouse.[7]

Mary Shelley's novel swerves from this female Gothic tradition in that its central protagonist is not a woman. But the death of Elizabeth Lavenza Frankenstein on her wedding night draws our attention to the fact that female sexuality is at issue here. The denial of all overt sexuality in the surface texture of the novel—Walton is alone, writing to his beloved . . . sister; Victor Frankenstein regards his bride-to-be as his cousin/sister; Victor's mother marries her father's best friend, to whom she becomes a devoted and dutiful daughter/wife; even Felix and Safie meet only in an entirely public, chaste, domesticated space—forces the more powerful erotic desires in the novel to erupt as violence. The repression of sexual desire, in the male as well as the female, generates monstrous fantasies.

In another way as well, the genre of the Gothic novel or horror story uncovers and satisfies a repressed female desire. In a patriarchal culture which assigns linguistic and social authority to men, the very act of a woman's speaking in public is a trespass on male domains. As Mary Poovey has emphasized, women who wrote for publication in the eighteenth century defied the decorum of the proper lady, a decorum so long established that it was considered a law of nature.[8] Hence the very act of female authorship could be seen as an unnatural act, a perversion that arouses both anxiety and hostility in the male reader. While the England of Mary Shelley's day admitted a legitimate line of female authorship, from the Duchess of Winchelsea to her contemporary Jane Austen, this tradition was sufficiently fragile to arouse Mary Shelley's insecurities. Mary Shelley's youthful fantasy-life never featured her self as heroine. She insisted that she was "very averse to bringing myself forward in print" and had become "infinitely indifferent" to the acquisition of "literary reputation" (222–23). While her words conform to the modesty topos of the conventional literary prologue, they also express a deep-seated conviction of literary inadequacy. And this shame contributed to the generation of her fictional images of abnormality, perversion, and destruction, to her obsession with monsters and father-daughter incest and plagues that annihilate mankind.

Finally, as Margaret Homans has suggested in her provocative essay on the Brontës in *The Female Gothic*, the portrayal of the supernatural in this literary tradition functions as a literalization of the metaphorical. Female writers may well feel a closer affinity with nature, defined in Western culture as female or the mother, and hence with the nonfigural or what Julia Kristeva has called the semiotic. In their fiction, the figural may often take the form of the literal, whether it be Jane Eyre and Rochester's mental telepathy or Cathy and Heathcliff's ghostly figures on the moor. In *Frankenstein*, the repressed semiotic may return in the form of a monster who enacts his maker's desire for domination and at the same time literalizes the death that is, as Nancy Hartsock has argued in her recent study of *Money, Sex and Power* (1986), at the heart of Western practices of eros.

Because she was frightened by what she had dreamt, by her "hideous" idea, Mary Shelley systematically censored her own speech in *Frankenstein*. The structure of the novel builds a series of screens around her authentic voice. The monster's autobiographical account of a benevolent disposition perverted by social neglect drew most directly on Mary Shelley's own experience of childhood abandonment and emotional deprivation in the Godwin household after her father's remarriage to the unsympathetic Mrs. Clairmont. Mary Shelley's decision to enclose that narrative within not one but two other narratives (Frankenstein's account of his own history as recorded in Walton's journal of his voyage towards the North Pole) has the effect of twice distancing her private voice from public speech. Moreover, Mary Shelley claimed in her Introduction to the 1831 *Frankenstein* that she began her story with the words "*It was on a dreary night of November,*" but in the first edition these words do not occur until the beginning of the seventh chapter. Even her originating dream of giving birth to a monster has been repressed, hidden behind the intervening narratives of Walton's mission and Frankenstein's autobiography. This double suppression of her personal anxieties may help to explain the relative lack of characterization that some readers have found in Walton, who seems to function primarily as a mirror for Victor Frankenstein.[9] Walton's mission is the one part of the story Mary Shelley had to tell that drew on an intellectual rather than psychological dimension of her consciousness.

Mary Shelley's self-censoring took an even more overt form. As she wrote her manuscript of *Frankenstein*, she gave it to her husband to edit. She later claimed that she "certainly did not owe the suggestion of one incident, nor scarcely of one train of feeling" to Percy Shelley (229). In this she was quite correct, with one minor exception: it was Percy who suggested that Frankenstein's trip to England be proposed by Victor himself, rather than by his father. And yet Percy made numerous revisions, which Mary almost invariably accepted.

The editor of the 1818 edition of *Frankenstein*, James Rieger, presents an account of these changes so biased in Percy Shelley's favor that it must be read as a tissue of facts, half-truths, and pure speculation. Rieger credits Percy Shelley with wording the contrasts between the personalities of Frankenstein and Elizabeth and between the governments of the Swiss republic and less fortunate nations; with coining the metaphoric description of the power within Mont Blanc; with conceiving the "idea that Frankenstein journey to England for the purpose of creating a female Monster;" with revising the ending; and with correcting Mary Shelley's "frequent grammatical solecisms, her spelling, and her awkward phrasing." He then concludes that Percy Shelley's "assistance at every point in the book's manufacture was so extensive that one hardly knows whether to regard him as editor or minor collaborator" (xviii). The only other person to examine the manuscript evidence closely, Eugene Murray, provides an accurate account of the text but also suggests that Percy Shelley's contributions to *Frankenstein*, although always "in keeping with Mary's conception and with her implicit sanction," were "substantial enough to require Mary's editorial carte blanche, whenever first given, and original enough to suggest that at times his creative impulse added its own initiative to the novel's effect."[10] Murray thus concurs that Percy Shelley's considerable contribution to *Frankenstein* was entirely positive.

Careful examination of the manuscript in the Abinger Collection in the Bodleian Library shows that Percy made numerous revisions on Mary's original manuscript, changes which both improved and damaged the text and which must be analyzed with care. To dispose of Rieger's misinformation first, Percy did expand, although he did not initiate, the comparison of Elizabeth's character to Victor Frankenstein's; and he did interpolate a favorable comparison of Switzerland's republicanism with the tyranny of other nations. But the descriptions of Mont Blanc in the novel are based on Mary Shelley's own observations made in July 1816 and recorded both in her Journal and in her letters to Fanny Imlay; these letters were later published in her *History of a Six Weeks Tour* (1817). As we have already noted, Percy suggested merely that Victor rather than Alphonse Frankenstein propose the trip to England. We might pass over Rieger's annoying habit (which Murray shares) of referring to Percy Shelley only by his last name and to Mary Shelley only by her first, or his failure to acknowledge, in his assertion that Percy corrected "her frequent grammatical solecisms, her spelling, and her awkward phrasing," that Mary made relatively few grammatical errors or misspellings in the manuscript of *Frankenstein*, while her phrasings were often more graceful than her husband's revised versions. But Rieger's concluding suggestion, which Murray tentatively endorses, that Percy Shelley can be regarded as a "minor collaborator" does a disservice to Mary Shelley's unique genius.

The manuscript of *Frankenstein* in the Abinger Collection in the Bodleian Library survives in two sections (Abinger Dep.c.477/1 and Dep.c.534), constituting in the Rieger edition pages 30:12–97:16 and 97:17–109:8 plus 117:17–end. We need to look at this manuscript closely in order to distinguish Mary Shelley's language from her husband's. As Mary wrote her novel, she gave the finished chapters to Percy to edit and augment, just as Walton gave his journal to Frankenstein to correct. Percy's revisions usually amount to some five or six changes per manuscript page (Murray estimates about one thousand words in all), although they are less numerous in the creature's narrative than elsewhere.

Percy Shelley's editorial revisions can be roughly grouped under two headings: those that improve the novel and those that do not. He made many technical corrections and several times clarified the narrative and thematic continuity of the text; on other occasions he misunderstood his wife's intentions and distorted her ideas. Throughout he tried to elevate her prose style into a more Latinate idiom. Mary Shelley's willingness to accept virtually all of these revisions strikingly reveals her own authorial insecurity, her deference to what she saw as Percy's more legitimate literary voice (he had by this time published novels, essays, and poems, including *Queen Mab*), and above all the hierarchical relationship that existed between her husband and herself.

Percy genuinely helped his wife's manuscript in many small ways. He corrected three minor factual errors, eliminated a few obvious grammatical mistakes, occasionally clarified the text, and frequently substituted more precise technical terms for Mary Shelley's cruder ones. He occasionally improved the narrative continuity and coherence of the text, smoothed out some of his wife's paragraph transitions, and enriched the thematic resonance of certain passages. He emphasized the psychological complexity of the monster in a few places and underlined Victor Frankenstein's responsibility for his creature. (For a detailed discussion of these positive changes, see the Appendix.)

By far the greatest number of Percy Shelley's revisions of his wife's manuscript fall into one category. He typically changed her simple,

Anglo-Saxon diction and straightforward or colloquial sentence structures into their more refined, complex, and Latinate equivalents. He is thus in large part responsible for the stilted, ornate, putatively Ciceronian prose style about which many readers have complained. George Levine, for instance, has condemned *Frankenstein* to the ranks of the "minor" novels primarily because of "the inflexibly public and oratorical nature of even its most intimate passages,"[11] passages almost invariably overwritten by Percy. Mary's voice tended to utter a sentimental, rather abstract, and generalized rhetoric, but typically energized this with a brisk stylistic rhythm. Here is Mary on Frankenstein's fascination with supernatural phenomena:

> Nor were these my only visions. The raising of ghosts or devils was also a favorite pursuit and if I never saw any I attributed it rather to my own inexperience and mistakes than want of skill in my instructors.

And here is Percy's revision:

> Nor were these my only visions. The raising of ghosts or devils was a promise liberally accorded by my favorite authors, the fulfillment of which I most eagerly sought; and if my incantations were always unsuccessful, I attributed the failure rather to my own inexperience and mistake, than to a want of skill or fidelity in my instructors (34:14–19)

Percy's preference for more learned, polysyllabic terms was obsessive. In addition, he rigorously eliminated Mary's colloquial phrases, as the following lists indicate.

Mary Shelley's manuscript	Percy Shelley's revision
have	possess
wish	desire, purpose
caused	derive their origin from
a painting	a representation
place	station
plenty of	sufficient
time	period
felt	endured
hope	confidence
had	experienced
stay	remain
took away	extinguish
talked	conversed

hot	inflamed
smallness	minuteness
end	extinction
inside	within
tired	fatigued
die	perish
leave out	omit
add to	augment
poverty	penury
mind	understanding
ghost-story	a tale of superstition
about on a par	of nearly equal interest and utility
we were all equal	neither of us possessed the slightest pre-eminence over the other
it was safe	the danger of infection was past
bear to part	be persuaded to part
the use I should make of it	the manner in which I should employ it
eyes were shut to	eyes were insensible to
do not wish to hate you	will not be tempted to set myself in opposition to thee
wrapping the rest	depositing the remains
it was a long time	a considerable period elapsed
had a means	possessed a method
how my disposition and habits were altered	the alteration perceptible in my disposition and habits
whatever I should afterwards think it right to do	whatever course of conduct I might hereafter think it right to pursue
what to say	what manner to commence the interview

Percy is clearly responsible for much of the most inflated rhetoric in the text. When Clerval's father "said he did not see of what use learning could be to a merchant," Percy elevated it to "in compliance with his favourite theory, that learning was superfluous in the commerce of ordinary life" (39:12–14). When Frankenstein swore that he would "not die until my adversary lay at my feet," Percy rhetorically proclaimed that he would "not relax the impending conflict until my own life, or that of my adversary, were extinguished" (192:20–21).

When Mary rather breathlessly described Frankenstein's enthusiasm for his project:

> When I looked around for my materials they hardly appeared adequate to so arduous an undertaking, but I did not despair. I allowed that my first attempts might be futile, my operations fail or my work be imperfect, but I looked around on the improvement that every day takes place in science and mechanics and although I could not hope that my attempts would be in every way perfect, yet I did not think that the magnitude and grandeur of my plan was any argument of its impracticability.

Percy elaborated thus:

> The materials at present within my command hardly appeared adequate to so arduous an undertaking; but I doubted not that I should ultimately succeed. I prepared myself for a multitude of reverses; my operations might be incessantly baffled, and at last my work be imperfect: yet, when I considered the improvement which every day takes place in science and mechanics, I was encouraged to hope my present attempts would at least lay the foundations of future success. Nor could I consider the magnitude and complexity of my plan as any argument of its impracticability. (48:28–49:4)

Perhaps someday an editor will give us the manuscript Mary Shelley actually wrote, cleansed of such elaborations (for further examples, see Appendix). Percy Shelley's linguistic talents were more suited to poetry than to prose, as Mary herself asserted in her Introduction to *Frankenstein*. I do not wish to claim that Mary Shelley was a great prose stylist, but only that her own prose, despite its tendency toward the abstract, sentimental, and even banal, is more direct and forceful than her husband's revisions.

More important, Percy Shelley on several occasions actually distorted the meaning of the text. He was not always sensitive to the complexity of character created by the author. He tended, for instance, to see the creature as more monstrous and less human than did Mary. When Frankenstein destroyed the female creature, and Mary had the creature withdraw "with a howl of devilish despair," Percy added "and revenge," thus blunting our sympathy for the forever forsaken creature and destroying the author's more perceptive understanding of the monster. When Mary wished to stress the creature's identification with Frankenstein by assigning the word "wretch" to them both within four lines, Percy changed the second wretch to "devil," thus implying that the creature is more reprehensible than Frankenstein (200:24, cf. 200:21). And it was Percy Shelley who introduced the oft-quoted description of the monster as "an abortion" (219:26), a term he again

applied to the creature in his unpublished review of *Frankenstein*.[12]
Mary Shelley saw the creature as potentially monstrous, but she never
suggested that he was other than fully human.

Percy underestimated, too, the subtlety with which his wife
portrayed the limitations of Victor Frankenstein's personality. When
Frankenstein neglects his family in order to work on his experiment,
Mary gave his self-justification in these terms: "I wished, as it were, to
procrastinate my feelings of affection, until the great object of my
affections was completed." Percy, eager to avoid the repetition of
"affection," revised this to "I wished, as it were, to procrastinate all
that related to my feelings of affections until the great object, which
swallowed up every habit of my nature, should be completed"
(50:31–33). But this revision removes Mary's powerful dramatic irony:
Frankenstein will of course feel no affection whatsoever for his
creature. Moreover, Mary's calculated repetition underlined the degree
to which Frankenstein had substituted work for love; instead of
developing his heterosexual relationship with Elizabeth, he has engaged
in a homoerotic fantasy of omnipotence, devoting all his attention to a
male object in a parody of God's creation of his only begotten Son
through the agency of the Holy Spirit, resulting in what Mary Daly has
called the masturbatory Trinity.[13] Similarly, when Mary wished to
reveal the contradiction inherent in Frankenstein's project (his desire to
create what he did not wish to have) by describing his frantic morning-
after pacing in the streets of Inglostadt "as if I sought the wretch whom
I feared every turning of the street would present to my view," Percy
eliminated this complexity by inserting "to avoid" after "sought"
(54:13).

Percy Shelley consistently read Victor Frankenstein sympathetically.
As his review of the novel concludes, Frankenstein was not a
perpetrator but only "the victim" of evil. Throughout the original text,
Mary Shelley stressed Frankenstein's capacity for self-deception, while
Percy, sometimes as blind as Frankenstein himself, softened or
eliminated his errors. When Mary described Frankenstein's mingled
dread and relief, on the eve of his departure to England, at the thought
that at least he would lure the monster away from his family and
friends, Percy disastrously persuaded her to introduce into
Frankenstein's meditations the possibility "of the reverse," of the
creature's staying behind in Geneva (151:8–14). He thus undercut her
otherwise consistent portrayal of Frankenstein as an egotist who
perceives only his own feelings and dangers. Mary's original idea, that
Frankenstein would inevitably assume that the creature would follow
him, powerfully prefigures Frankenstein's later assumption that the

creature would be with him alone on his wedding night. When Frankenstein glimpses the creature peering through his laboratory window in Scotland, he immediately concludes that "his face expressed the utmost extent of malice and barbarity." Percy altered this to "his countenance *appeared to* express the utmost extent of malice and treachery" (my italics), thus introducing the impossibility that Frankenstein might be aware that the creature's countenance is merely an appearance and not a revelation of his moral character. So opposed was this to Mary's idea of how Frankenstein interprets faces and the general role of physiognomy in the novel that it was one of the rare occasions when she refused to accept her husband's emendation. The final text preserves "his countenance expressed the utmost extent of malice and treachery" (164:6–7).

Moreover, Percy imposed his own favorite philosophical, political, and poetic theories on a text which either contradicted them or to which they were irrelevant. For instance, Mary throughout assumes the existence of a sacred animating principle, call it Nature or Life or God, which Frankenstein usurps at his peril. During Frankenstein's final pursuit of his creature across the polar wastes, at times inspired not so much by vengeance as by the conviction that it was "a task enjoined by heaven," Percy tried to undermine this notion of a functioning "heaven" by adding his own atheistic concept of a universe created and controlled by pure Power or energy, "as the mechanical impulse of some power of which I was unconscious" (202:16–17).

At other times, his interpolations do not change the meaning of the text so much as they sidetrack it from the issue at hand. His revolutionary hostility to hierarchical institutions erupted in the lengthy discussion of the differences between the treatment of servants in France or England as opposed to Switzerland, where the condition of servitude uniquely "does not include the idea of ignorance, and a sacrifice of the dignity of a human being" (60:14–23). And his dislike of the legal system led him to add a rather exaggerated image of judges as "executioners, their hands yet reeking with the blood of innocence" (83:4), to Elizabeth's denunciation of the court that convicted Justine.

Despite Mary Shelley's belief in the existence of a material reality determined by the laws of nature, Percy's idealist concept of the poetic imagination as a creative participation in the universal mind that is reality invaded the text. Percy struck out the rather trite description of Elizabeth's amusements as "drawing and music" and added this:

> I [Victor Frankenstein] delighted in investigating the facts relative to the actual world; she busied herself in following the aërial creations of the poets. The world was to me a secret, which I desired to

discover; to her it was a vacancy, which she sought to people with
imaginations of her own. (30:20–24)

The last line is of course an echo of the concluding question of his
"Mont Blanc," composed in July, 1816:

> And what were thou, and earth, and stars, and sea,
> If to the human mind's imaginings
> Silence and solitude were vacancy?

At least one of Percy Shelley's revisions carries significant interpretive weight in the novel. He introduced all the references to Victor
Frankenstein as the "author" of the creature (see, for examples, 87:16,
96:18, 96:35). Several critics have claimed that the identification of
Frankenstein as an author highlights Mary Shelley's anxiety of
authorship. But since it is Percy rather than Mary who sees
Frankenstein as an "author," these references actually work more to
associate Frankenstein with the already published author Percy Shelley
than with the unpublished Mary Shelley. Perhaps because he felt an
intuitive sympathy for Victor Frankenstein and his goals, Percy Shelley
here inadvertently sharpened his wife's identification of him with her
protagonist.

Two other dimensions of the 1818 text of *Frankenstein* remain to be
considered. The printed text of the first edition differs in significant
respects from the corrected rough draft manuscript in the Abinger
Collection. We do not have the complete fair copy of the manuscript
that Mary Shelley sent to the printers. We do know that the proofs
were sent directly to Percy Shelley, either in London or at Marlow.
Percy had assured Lackington, Allen & Company that he felt
"authorized to amend . . . any mere inaccuracies of language" while
proofreading.[14] On Octobert 23, 1817, he returned proofs in which he
claimed he had "paid considerable attention to the correction of such
few instances of baldness of style as necessarily occur in the production
of a very young writer";[15] five days later, he sent back two proof-
sheets with "considerable alterations" which were "of the last
importance to the interest of the tale."[16] However, we also know that
Mary herself corrected the proofs of *Frankenstein*. On September 24,
1817, she sent some of the proofs to Percy with the comment, "in
looking it over there appeared to me some abruptnesses which I have
endeavoured to supply—but I am tired and not very clear headed so I
give you carte blanche to make what alterations you please."[17] We
must assume therefore that the changes that occur in the text between
the surviving manuscripts and the printed first edition are the product
of both Mary and Percy Shelley, a point of some importance since

previous editors have assumed that all such changes were introduced by Percy alone.

Certain revisions more plausibly originated from Mary. Since she introduced the term "species" in the draft manuscript to refer to the human race (124:34), it seems likely that she, in revising, changed Frankenstein's desire that "a new creation would bless me as its creator," which Percy had revised to "a new existence would bless me," to its final "a new species would bless me" (49:16). The word has great resonance, particularly in terms of the novel's response to Erasmus Darwin's concept of evolution. The extensive analysis of Clerval's character in the printed text (153:28–154:31) seems likely to come from Mary's hand, relying as it does on quotations from both Wordsworth and Leigh Hunt and describing Clerval's "imaginations fanciful and magnificent, which formed a world, whose existence depended on the life of its creator" (124:17–18), in terms more general than Percy would have used on such an occasion.

On the other hand, Percy Shelley's characteristic imagery and ideas seem to have informed the passage added to the creature's question why Frankenstein formed a being so hideous that even he could not bear to look at it. Where Mary had written, "God in pity made man beautiful and alluring—I am more hateful to the sight than the bitter apples of Hell to the taste," the printed text reads, "God in pity made man beautiful and alluring, after his own image; but my form is a filthy type of your's, more horrid from its very resemblance" (sic, 126:15–17). Percy Shelley's essay "On Love" (dated by David Lee Clark to 1814–15[18]) develops careful distinctions between prototype and antitype, thus anticipating the use of "type" in this context.

The lengthy deletions from the manuscript, all marked improvements, could have been struck out by either Mary or Percy Shelley, but perhaps Percy would have been more likely to see their irrelevance (even though he did not excise them on his first reading of the manuscript). They include a short description of Alphonse Frankenstein's concern for his son's spirits after Clerval's death ("even my father who watched me as the bird does its nestling was deceived . . .", omitted at 183:33) and a much more extensive and trivial description of the roads of Holland (too often blocked by windmills, or so narrow as they pass along canals that carriages meeting each other have to back up as much as a mile, or lined by a mud-soaked, drying flax whose stench "is not very esily endured"). By far the longest deletion, amounting to some four pages of manuscript, described in greater detail the scenery surrounding Oxford, sarcastically recounted the university controversy concerning the expulsion of two students who had worn light-colored rather than dark-colored pantaloons to class, and concluded with Frankenstein's and Clerval's visit to the room of "the Lord Chancellor Bacon" which "was predicted, would fall in when a man wiser than the philosopher should enter it." All this was replaced by the text that now appears on pages 157:11–158:22, almost certainly written by Mary Shelley herself.

Finally, the fair copy of roughly sixty pages of the revised manuscript of *Frankenstein* that survives in the Abinger Collection (Dep.c.534) contains a final thirteen pages written in Percy Shelley's hand which revise over a quarter of the ending of the novel. Percy significantly changed the style—but, with one notable exception, not the content—of the novel's conclusion. He dramatically revised Mary's breathless rhythms and simple sentence structures. Here for instance is her original manuscript version of the monster's feelings after he murders Clerval:

> When Clerval died I returned to Switzerland heart-broken and overcome—I pitied Frankenstein and his bitter sufferings—My pity amounted to horror—I abhorred myself—But when I saw that he again dared hope for happiness—that while he heaped wretchedness and despair on me he sought his own enjoyment in feelings & passions from the indulgence of which I was forever barred—I was again roused to indignation and revenge. I remembered my threat and resolved to execute it—Yet when she died—Nay then I was not miserable—I cast off all feeling & all anguish. I rioted in the extent of my despair & being urged thus far—I resolved to finish my demoniacal design. And it is now ended—There is my last victim.

And here is Percy's version:

> After the murder of Clerval, I returned to Switzerland, heart-broken and overcome. I pitied Frankenstein; my pity amounted to horror: I abhorred myself. But when I discovered that he, the author at once of my existence and of its unspeakable torments, dared to hope for happiness; that while he accumulated wretchedness and despair upon me, he sought his own enjoyment in feelings and passions from the indulgence of which I was for ever barred, then impotent envy and bitter indignation filled me with an insatiable thirst for vengeance. I recollected my threat, and resolved that it should be accomplished. I knew that I was preparing for myself a deadly torture; but I was the slave, not the master of an impulse, which I detested, yet could not disobey. Yet when she died!—nay, then I was not miserable. I had cast off all feeling, subdued all anguish to riot in the excess of my despair. Evil henceforth became my good. Urged thus far, I had no choice but to adapt my nature to an element which I had willingly chosen. The completion of my demoniacal design became an insatiable passion. And now it is ended; there is my last victim!
> (217:30–218:12)

Critics may dispute whether this second version, which has manifestly eliminated what Percy Shelley would have considered a "baldness of style," is a genuine improvement, even granting that its repetitions of the master/slave image and the Satanic allusion are more thematically resonant.

More important, Percy changed the last line of the novel in a way that potentially alters its meaning. Mary penned Walton's final vision of the creature thus: "He sprung from the cabin window as he said this upon an ice raft that lay close to the vessel & pushing himself off he was carried away by the waves and I soon lost sight of him in the darkness and distance." Percy changed this to "He sprung from the cabin-window, as he said this, upon the ice-raft which lay close to the vessel. He was soon borne away by the waves, and lost in darkness and distance." Mary's version, by suggesting that Walton has only lost "sight of" the creature, preserves the possibility that the creature may still be alive, a threatening reminder of the potential danger released when men egotistically transgress nature and "read" the unknown as evil. Percy's revision, by flatly asserting that the creature was "lost in darkness and distance," provides a comforting reassurance to the reader that the creature is gone into the darkness and distance. We might go so far as to say that Percy's reading of the novel's conclusion is a defensive maneuver to ward off anxiety and assert final authorial control over his wife's subversive creation.

The psychological significance of these final revisions cannot be overstressed. With the one exception I have just discussed, they do not radically alter the plot or the emotional nuances of the novel's conclusion, but they do change its diction and tone. In effect, Mary Shelley has substituted Percy's style for her own. She has thus enveloped her novel in a protective covering of borrowed speech, allowing Percy not only to write the Preface but also to dominate the conclusion. Defensively, she has hidden her own voice behind his more public and impersonal linguistic persona. She has in effect swaddled her hideous progeny within her husband's prefatory claim that the novel's chief concern is "the exhibition of the amiableness of domestic affection, and the excellence of universal virtue" (7).

That Percy Shelley thought he had the *right* to speak for his wife is clear from his comment to Lackington, Allen & Co. that he was "authorized to amend" her text,[19] with the play on "authority" and "authorial" fully operative here. Two marginal comments further demonstrate that Percy regarded this "production of a very young writer" with both affectionate approval and an ever-so-slight contempt. Coming upon the draft as Mary was writing it and noting one of the rare misspellings in the manuscript, "igmmatic," Percy scribbled in pencil in the margin: "enigmatic o you pretty Pecksie!" (106:18). And when Mary referred, in a passage subsequently deleted, to "Lord Chancellor Bacon," Percy fondly corrected her, "No sweet Pecksie—'twas *Friar* Bacon, the discoverer of gunpowder." Percy's endearments may be charming, but they also demonstrate that he did not regard his wife altogether seriously as an author, but rather as a lovable, teasable, and not yet fully educated schoolgirl. He expressed his opinion more directly in a postscript to her letter to Maria Gisborne in 1820: "I wonder what makes Mary think her letter worth the trouble of opening—except indeed she conceives it to be a delight to decypher a difficult scrawl."[20] Unfortunately, Mary shared Percy's opinion of her inferior literary abilities. Her deference to his superior mind was intrinsic to the dynamics of their marriage, a marriage in which the husband played the dominant role.

Percy Shelley once again assumed the role of final judge of his wife's manuscript when he decided to review the novel for a critical journal. His unpublished review is extremely laudatory, passing quickly over "some points of subordinate importance, which prove that it is the author's first attempt," to hail its accelerating interest, its exposing of "powerful and profound emotion," the truth of its argument that if we treat a person ill, he will become wicked, and its scenes of "extraordinary pathos." Percy notes the author's indebtedness to Godwin's *Caleb Williams*, especially in the incident of Frankenstein's landing in Ireland. He concludes enthusiastically that the final scene in Walton's cabin—"the more than mortal enthusiasm and grandeur of the Being's speech over the dead body of his victim—is an exhibition of intellectual and imaginative power, which we think the reader will acknowledge has seldom been surpassed."[21] This review clearly reveals how Percy interpreted (or misinterpreted) *Frankenstein*—as a story of original goodness turned to misanthropy and revenge by social ostracism and scorn, a story in which *both* Frankenstein and his creature are innocent victims. (This is the same story that Percy Shelley would tell in *Adonais* of both Keats and himself at the hands of the critics.) Even more important, the review signals the way in which Percy interpreted his wife, as a writer of talent whose work nonetheless depended on the guidance of others, whether her father or her husband. In his review Percy is both promoting Mary and protecting her from possible adverse criticism. He deliberately defines the gender of the author of *Frankenstein* as male, a gesture that might increase the public respect for the novel but which simultaneously denies its actual authorship; indeed, there were some who thought that Percy Shelley had written the novel. His review is thus an act of appropriation as well as of tribute.

CHAPTER FOUR

Promethean Politics

When Mary Shelley subtitled her novel "The Modern Prometheus," she forcefully directed our attention to the book's critique both of the promethean poets she knew best, Byron and Percy Shelley, and of the entire Romantic ideology as she understood it. Victor Frankenstein's failure to mother his child has both political and aesthetic ramifications. The father who neglects his children can be seen as the archetype of the irresponsible political leader who puts his own interests ahead of those of his fellow citizens. Victor Frankenstein's quest is nothing less than the conquest of death itself. By acquiring the ability to "bestow animation upon lifeless matter" and thus "renew life where death had apparently devoted the body to corruption" (49), Frankenstein in effect hopes to become God, the creator of life and the gratefully worshipped father of a new race of immortal beings. In his attempt to transform human beings into deities by eliminating mortality, Victor Frankenstein is himself participating in the mythopoeic vision that inspired the first generation of Romantic poets and thinkers. William Blake had insisted that the human form could become divine through the exercise of mercy, pity, love, and imagination; Coleridge had stated that human perception or the primary imagination is an "echo of the Infinite I AM;" Wordsworth had argued that the "higher minds" of poets are "truly from the Deity;" while both Godwin and his disciple Percy Shelley had proclaimed that man was perfectible. In their view, the right use of reason and imagination could annihilate not only social injustice and human evil but even, through participation in symbolic thinking or what Blake called the "divine analogy," the consciousness of human finitude and death itself.[1] Victor Frankenstein's goal can be identified with the radical desire that energized some of the best known

English Romantic poems, the desire to elevate human beings into living gods.

In identifying Victor Frankenstein with Prometheus, Mary Shelley was alluding to both versions of the Prometheus myth: Prometheus *plasticator* and Prometheus *pyrphoros*. In the first version, known to Mary Shelley through Ovid's *Metamorphoses* which she read in 1815, Prometheus created man from clay:

> *Whether with particles of Heav'nly fire*
> *The God of Nature did his Soul inspire,*
> *Or Earth, but new divided from the Skie,*
> *And, pliant, still, retain'd the Aethereal Energy;*
> *Which Wise* Prometheus *temper'd into paste,*
> *And mix't with living Streams, the Godlike Image caste* . . .
> *From such rude Principles our Form began;*
> *And Earth was Metamophos'd into Man.* (I:101–6, 111–12)

In the alternate, more famous version of the myth, Prometheus is the fire-stealer, the god who defied Jupiter's tyrannical oppression of humanity by giving fire to man and was then punished by having his liver eaten by vultures until he divulged his secret foreknowledge of Jupiter's downfall. By the third century A.D., these two versions had fused; the fire stolen by Prometheus became the fire of life with which he animated his man of clay.[2] As both the creator and/or savior of man and the long-suffering rebel against tyranny, Prometheus was an often invoked self-image among the Romantic poets. Blake visually identified his heroic rebel and spokeswoman Oothoon with the tortured Prometheus in his design for Plate 6 of "Visions of the Daughters of Albion," while Coleridge's Ancient Mariner echoes Prometheus both in his transgression of an established moral order and in his perpetual suffering that he may teach mankind to be both sadder and wiser. Even more directly, Goethe in both his verse drama *Prometheus* and his monologue "Bedecke deinen Himmel, Zeus" portrayed Prometheus as a self-portrait of the artist who has liberated himself from serving dull, idle gods and who rejoices instead in his own creative powers.

Mary Shelley specifically associated her modern Prometheus with the Romantic poets she knew personally. During the summer in which she began writing *Frankenstein*, Byron composed his poem "Prometheus," a celebration of the god's defiance of Jupiter which emphasizes Prometheus' unyielding will, noble suffering, and concern for mankind —qualities with which Byron clearly identified himself.[3] Mary Shelley copied this poem and carried it to Byron's publisher John Murray when she returned to England in August 1816. Byron's Promethean persona appeared again in *Manfred*, which Mary Shelley read soon after its publication on June 16, 1817. Manfred's Faustian thirst for unbounded experience, knowledge, and freedom leads him, like Victor Frankenstein, to steal the secrets of nature. As Manfred confesses:

> [I] dived,
> In my lone wanderings, to the caves of death,
> Searching its cause in its effect; and drew
> From wither'd bones, and skulls, and heap'd up dust,
> Conclusions most forbidden.
>
> (Manfred II.ii.173–77)

Manfred's quest also enchained him in a Promethean suffering for his lost sister Astarte, a painful remorse that articulates Byron's guilty conscience over his incestuous affair with his half-sister Augusta Leigh. In his defiance of Ahrimanes and all other deities, Manfred proclaims Byron's personal belief in the ultimate creative power and integrity of the human imagination, using phrases that Mary Shelley condensed into that single "spark of being" infused by her modern Prometheus into the lifeless creature at his feet:

> The mind, the spirit, the Promethean spark,
> The lightning of my being, is as bright,
> Pervading, and far darting as your own,
> And shall not yield to yours, though coop'd in clay!
>
> (Manfred I, i,154–57)

In England, Mary Shelley met another poet who became a close friend and associate of both Byron and the Shelleys, Leigh Hunt, who intensified the identification of the Romantic poet with the Prometheus myth. Hunt commented in 1819 after the publication of *Frankenstein* that he too had thought of writing a poem entitled *Prometheus Throned* in which Prometheus would successfully defy the gods and be depicted as "having lately taken possession of Jupiter's seat."[4]

Above all, Mary Shelley associated her modern Prometheus with Percy Shelley, who had already announced his desire to compose an epic rebuttal to Aeschylus' *Prometheus Bound* when he reread the play in 1816, although he did not begin writing *Prometheus Unbound* until September 1818, after *Frankenstein* was published.[5] As William Veeder has most recently reminded us, several dimensions of Victor Frankenstein are modelled directly from Percy Shelley.[6] Victor was Percy Shelley's pen-name for his first publication, *Original Poetry; by Victor and Cazire* (1810). Victor Frankenstein's family resembles Percy Shelley's: in both, the father is married to a woman young enough to be his daughter; in both the oldest son has a favorite sister (adopted sister, or cousin, in Frankenstein's case) named Elizabeth. Frankenstein's education is based on Percy Shelley's: both were avid students of Albertus Magnus, Paracelsus, Pliny, and Buffon; both were fascinated by alchemy and chemistry; both were excellent linguists, acquiring fluency in Latin, Greek, German, French, English, and Italian.[7] By sending Victor Frankenstein to the University of Ingolstadt, Mary Shelley further signalled his association with the radical politics advocated by Percy Shelley in *Queen Mab* (1813), "Feelings of a Republican on the Fall of Bonapart" (1816), and *Laon and Cythna* (1817). Ingolstadt was famous as the home of the Illuminati, a secret revolutionary society founded in 1776 by Ingolstadt's Professor of Law, Adam Weishaupt, that advocated the perfection of mankind through the overthrow of established religious and political institutions. Percy Shelley had eagerly endorsed Weishaupt's goals—namely, "to secure to merit its just rewards; to the weak support, to the wicked the fetters they deserve; and to man his dignity" by freeing all men from the slavery imposed by "society, governments, the sciences, and false religion"—when he read Abbé Barruel's vitriolic attack on the Illuminati, *Mémoires, pour servir à L'Histoire du Jacobinisme* (1797), during his honeymoon journey with Mary in 1814. He had even used Barruel's account of the Illuminati, reading white where Barruel wrote black, as the basis of the utopian society depicted in the novel entitled *The Assassins* that he began during the summer of 1814.[8]

More important, Victor Frankenstein embodies certain elements of Percy Shelley's temperament and character that had begun to trouble Mary Shelley. She perceived in Percy an intellectual hubris or belief in the supreme importance of mental abstractions that led him to be insensitive to the feelings of those who did not share his ideas and enthusiasms. The Percy Shelley that Mary knew and loved lived in a world of abstract ideas; his actions were primarily motivated by theoretical principles, the quest for perfect beauty, love, freedom, goodness. While Mary endorsed and shared these goals, she had come to suspect that in Percy's case they sometimes masked an emotional narcissism, an unwillingness to confront the origins of his own desires or the impact of his demands on those most dependent upon him. Percy's pressure on Mary, during the winter and spring of 1814–15, to take Hogg as a lover despite her sexual indifference to Hogg; his indifference to the death of Mary's first baby on March 7, 1815; his insistence on Claire's continuing presence in his household despite Mary's stated opposition—all this had alerted Mary to a worrisome strain of selfishness in Percy's character, an egotism that too often rendered him an insensitive husband and an uncaring, irresponsible parent.

Percy Shelley's self-serving "harem psychology" may have originated as some Freudian critics have suggested, in an unresolved Oedipal desire to possess the mother. This desire emerges in his poem "Alastor" (1816) as a wish to return to the gravelike womb of Mother Earth. Mary Shelley's insight into this dimension of Percy's psyche informs the dream she assigns to Victor Frankenstein immediately after the creation of the monster:

> I thought I saw Elizabeth, in the bloom of health, walking in the streets of Ingolstadt. Delighted and surprised, I embraced her; but as I imprinted the first kiss on her lips, they became livid with the hue of death; her features appeared to change, and I thought that I held the corpse of my dead mother in my arms; a shroud enveloped her form, and I saw the grave-worms crawling in the folds of the flannel. (53)

Like Percy Shelley's, Victor Frankenstein's strongest erotic desires are not so much for his putative lover as for his lost mother. Percy unwittingly revealed this incestuous desire during the troubled period after his expulsion from Oxford. Barred from his mother's and sisters' company, he violently accused his mother of having an affair with his sister Elizabeth's "music master" and of trying to conceal the affair by marrying Elizabeth to him.[9] Percy seems here to have projected onto his innocent friend Edward Fergus Graham his own erotic fantasy: to be the lover of both mother and favorite sister. His efforts to marry Elizabeth to his best friend Hogg can be seen as yet another attempt to close the sexual circle between himself and his sister. Percy Shelley's persistent desire to be the sexual partner of every woman he admired was not only self-indulgent. It also revealed a fundamental inability to separate his ego from his mother's and to function normally without the unquestioning emotional and sexual support of a devoted woman.[10] Mary Shelley projected her irritation with this facet of Percy's character into her portrait of Victor Frankenstein.

But even as Mary Shelley modelled Victor Frankenstein upon Percy Shelley, she introduced into her novel an entirely flattering portrait of her beloved mate. Henry Clerval is both an alter-ego of Victor Frankenstein and the embodiment of all the qualities of Percy Shelley that Mary most loved. By splitting her husband into two characters, Mary Shelley registered her perception of a profound contradiction in Percy's personality as well as her intense ambivalence toward the man she loved. Clerval, in whom Victor Frankenstein recognizes "the image of my former self; . . . inquisitive, and anxious to gain experience and instruction" (155–6), possesses a "refined mind" (39), a passionate love of natural beauty, a fascination with languages and literature, and above all a capacity for empathy. He is a poet. As a child he studied books of chivalry and romance and wrote fairy tales, plays, and verse. In the novel he becomes a positive archetype for the Romantic poet, with a mind "replete with ideas, imaginations fanciful and magnificent, which formed a world, whose existence depended on the life of its creator" (154). As Frankenstein eulogizes him, Clerval

> was a being formed in the "very poetry of nature." His wild and enthusiastic imagination was chastened by the sensibility of his heart. His soul overflowed with ardent affections, and his friendship was of that devoted and wondrous nature that the worldly-minded teach us to look for only in the imagination. But even human sympathies were not sufficient to satisfy his eager mind. The scenery of external nature, which others regard only with admiration, he loved with ardour: . . . "The sounding cataract haunted *him* like a passion." (153–54)

Identified with both Leigh Hunt and Wordsworth in this passage, Clerval embodies Mary Shelley's heroic ideal, the imaginative man who is capable of deep and abiding love and who takes responsibility for those dependent upon him. Clerval both embarks on "a voyage of discovery to the land of knowledge" and also immediately delays that voyage to nurse his sick friend back to health. He thus combines intellectual curiosity with a capacity for nurturing others. Unlike Percy Shelley, Clerval does not openly defy his provincial father's injunctions. Instead, he uses his powers of persuasion to convince his affectionate father to let him attend university. Clerval and Victor Frankenstein together comprise the Percy Shelley with whom Mary Godwin had fallen in love. But the murder of Clerval annihilates the most positive dimensions of Percy Shelley in the novel, leaving Frankenstein as the image of all that Mary Shelley most feared in both her husband and in the Romantic project he served.

For Victor Frankenstein is above all a creator. In a replica of Percy's editorial control over Mary's manuscript, Victor Frankenstein exerts final authority over Walton's journal account of his experiences. As Walton tells us:

> Frankenstein discovered that I made notes concerning his history: he asked to see them, and then himself corrected and augmented them in many places; but principally in giving the life and spirit to the conversations he held with his enemy. "Since you have preserved my narration," said he, "I would not that a mutilated one should go down to posterity." (207)[11]

Victor Frankenstein thus becomes an author, and like Percy Shelley, justifies his defiance of convention (scientific, social, and literary) as the quest for a new and deeper truth. Frankenstein's goal, to discover "whence . . . did the principle of life proceed" (46), specifically echoes the goal of the Narrator of Percy Shelley's poem "Alastor, or The Spirit of Solitude," composed at Marlow during the previous autumn of 1815. At the beginning of "Alastor," the Narrator expresses ambitions identical to Frankenstein's:

> Mother of this unfathomable world!
> Favour my solemn song, for I have loved
> Thee ever, and thee only; I have watched
> Thy shadow, and the darkness of thy steps,
> And my heart ever gazes on the depth
> Of thy deep mysteries. I have made my bed
> In charnels and on coffins, where black death
> Keeps record of the trophies won from thee,
> Hoping to still these obstinate questionings
> Of thee and thine, by forcing some lone ghost
> Thy messenger, to render up the tale
> Of what we are. In lone and silent hours,
> When night makes a wierd sound of its own stillness,
> Like an inspired and desperate alchymist
> Staking his very life on some dark hope,
> Have I mixed awful talk and asking looks
> With my most innocent love, until strange tears
> Uniting with those breathless kisses, made
> Such magic as compels the charmed night
> To render up thy charge. (11. 18–37)

Mary Shelley's Note on "Alastor," which she describes as "the outpouring of his [the author's] own emotion," suggests that she did not see the ironic distance charted between Percy Shelley and the Narrator by such modern critics as Earl Wasserman and Lisa Steinman.[12] In her view, both the Narrator and Victor Frankenstein desire to penetrate Mother Earth, to discover the secret of "what we are," of life and death.[13] By so doing, Frankenstein becomes "the author of unalterable evils" (87).

Mary Shelley sharpens her identification of Frankenstein's scientific quest with Percy Shelley's poetic quest by specifying that *both* of Frankenstein's alter-egos in the novel, Clerval and Walton, are aspiring poets.[14] Walton shares Frankenstein's desire to "break through" boundaries. Where Frankenstein seeks to eliminate the "ideal bounds" between life and death (49), Walton seeks to "tread a land never before imprinted by the foot of man" (10). Walton would, moreover, wrest Frankenstein's own secret from him if he could: "I endeavoured to gain from Frankenstein the particulars of his creature's formation; but on this point he was impenetrable" (207). Above all, Walton desires to create or discover a perfect world. As a youth, he reminds his sister, "I also became a poet, and for one year lived in a Paradise of my own creation" (11). Blocked in his ambition to become a second Homer or Shakespeare, he redirects this desire to the discovery of the North Pole, a land "surpassing in wonders and in beauty every region hitherto discovered on the habitable globe" (10), a land where in his imagination "snow and frost are banished" and Eden is regained. To fulfill this desire to bring to mankind a land of perpetual fire and light, radiant with the Aurora Borealis, Walton like Prometheus has defied his father's final injunction. On his deathbed, Walton's father proscribed a "sea-faring life" for his son. Walton is thus another Promethean poet, seeking to create a more perfect humanity by revealing a new land of fire and light to man.

Once she has carefully excluded Clerval, the poet who brings no fire and defies no one, but seeks only to please others and to become his father's partner, a "very good trader" yet with "a cultivated understanding" (39), Mary Shelley offers a critique of this Romantic project through her calculated identification of Frankenstein, Walton, and Percy Shelley with the "modern Prometheus." For both Prometheus plasticator and Prometheus pyrphoros transgressed the boundaries of the established order in their desire to create a better world. In *Frankenstein*, the modern Prometheus who seeks to know and bestow life itself is explicitly identified with the two greatest overreachers and usurpers of God's divine prerogatives within the Judeao-Christian tradition, Faust and Satan. In his attempt to create a homunculus, Frankenstein, like Faust, has sold his soul to gain forbidden knowledge. As Frankenstein admits, "I seemed to have lost all soul or sensation but for this one pursuit" (50). Walton too has allowed his "senseless curiosity" (207) to lead him into a "mad" search both for Frankenstein's secret and for a nonexistent tropical paradise at the North Pole, a search that first separates him from his beloved sister and finally alienates him from his crew. Rewriting *Paradise Lost*, Mary Shelley insistently links Victor Frankenstein with Satan. Having usurped God's creative power, Frankenstein is forever cursed: "like the archangel who aspired to omnipotence, I am chained in an eternal hell" (208). Walton's voyage to paradise, departing from Archangel, is similarly cursed by his willingness to sacrifice the lives of his crew to his own ambition, a point underlined in a passage inserted in the 1831 edition of *Frankenstein* in which Walton proclaims:

> I was easily led by the sympathy which he evinced to use the language of my heart, to give utterance to the burning ardour of my soul, and to say with all the fervour that warmed me, how gladly I would sacrifice my fortune, my existence, my every hope, to the furtherance of my enterprise. One man's life or death were but a small price to pay for the acquirement of the knowledge which I sought, for the dominion I should acquire and transmit over the elemental foes of our race. (231–32)

Both Walton and Frankenstein are thus numbered among the damned. Both are associated with Coleridge's Ancient Mariner, whom Mary Shelley saw as a type of the wandering Jew, forever ostracized from the human community for killing an innocent creature (14, 54)—Victor finds himself unable to enter the marriage festival "with this deadly weight yet hanging round my neck" (149). Frankenstein is further identified with Cain, the original murderer. "Blasted and miserable" (187), he laments that "I had turned loose into the world a depraved wretch, whose delight was in carnage and misery; had he not murdered my brother?" (72).

Mary Shelley's modern Prometheus is also a fire-bringer. Lévi-Strauss emphasized the anthropological significance of fire as the separator of the cooked from the raw, of culture from nature, of that which human beings organize and domesticate from that which is free of human control. Fire thus becomes the instrument of civilization and political power. When Prometheus pyrophoros stole fire from Jupiter and gave it to man, he violated the divine order and thereby created a world where men might defy the gods. When Victor Frankenstein steals "a spark of being" from nature to infuse into the lifeless thing lying before him, he creates a being who need not die, a creature who has the capacity to do great good or great evil. But to appreciate the subtlety of Mary Shelley's criticism of the modern Prometheus pyrophorus, we must track the crossing paths of fire in this novel.

The creature raised from the dead by Victor Frankenstein's stolen "spark," after having gradually learned to distinguish between differing sensations and ideas, encounters a fire left by some wandering beggars. His first reaction to Prometheus' gift is intense delight at its warmth; his second reaction, after having thrust his hand into the live embers, is intense pain. His judgment, "How strange, I thought, that the same cause should produce such opposite effects!" (99), focuses the moral dilemma of the novel: was the cause that Frankenstein served, the creation of life from death, good or evil or both? The creature's use of fire thus becomes emblematic. Initially, the creature tries to achieve a reunion with both the natural and the human order by domesticating fire. He learns to tame his fire to his own purposes, using it to provide warmth, light during the night, and heat for cooking his raw nuts and roots. More important, he attempts to ingratiate himself with the De Lacey family by bringing them love-gifts of firewood. But finally, this "tamed" fire and what it represents—the possibility of including the creature around the family hearth or within the circle of civilization—is refused by the De Laceys. In his despair, the creature reverts to raw nature: "I gave vent to my anguish in fearful howlings. I was like a wild beast that had broken the toils; destroying the objects that obstructed me, and ranging through the wood with a stag-like swiftness." (132)

Fire now becomes the agency of destruction. The creature, learning that the De Laceys will never return to their cottage and filled with "feelings of revenge and hatred," burns down the only home he has ever known.

> I lighted the dry branch of a tree, and danced with fury around the devoted cottage. . . . I waved my brand; [the moon] sunk, and, with a loud scream, I fired the straw, and heath, and bushes, which I had collected. The wind fanned the fire, and the cottage was quickly enveloped by the flames, which clung to it, and licked it with their forked and destroying tongues. (135)

Fire, with its forked tongue, is now the instrument of Satan. As such, it recurs in the last moments of the novel, when the creature promises Walton (perhaps falsely) that he shall "consume to ashes this miserable frame" in his funeral pyre at the North Pole.

As Andrew Griffin has observed, Mary Shelley thus denies the romantic dream of fusing the contraries of fire and ice, life and death, in a triumph of the divine poetic imagination. Despite Kubla Khan's "miracle of rare device, / A sunny pleasure-dome with caves of ice," despite Walton's image of a tropical paradise at the North Pole where "snow and frost are banished," Mary Shelley's Mariner discovers only mutinous betrayal and destruction at the North Pole while her creature sees only death in the coming together of snow and fire.[15] The romantic attempt to marry opposites, to unite the mortal and the immortal in a transcendental dialectic, to create the human form divine, is seen by Mary Shelley as pure fantasy, no more real than Walton's dream.

Worse, as *Frankenstein* suggests, it is a very dangerous fantasy. Hidden behind Godwin's and Percy Shelley's dream of human perfectibility and immortality is a rampant egoism, the cardinal sin of the Satanic Prometheus. For Godwin and Percy Shelley, as for Coleridge and Blake, it was the mission of the philosopher-poet to guide mankind toward salvation, to participate in the Infinite I AM, and to destroy the mind-forged manacles of society. Mary Shelley had seen just how self-indulgent this self-image of the poet-savior could be. Her father had withdrawn from his children in order to pursue his increasingly unsuccessful writing career and had remorselessly scrounged money from every passing acquaintance in order to pay his growing debts; her father's friend Coleridge had become a parasite on his admirers, unable to complete his Magnum Opus; Byron had callously compromised numerous women, including her stepsister

Claire; Percy Shelley had abandoned his first wife and daughter in his quest for intellectual beauty and the perfect soul-mate, and might do the same again to Mary; and even the amiable Leigh Hunt tormented his wife with his obvious preference for her more intellectual sister Bessy Kent. Mary Shelley perceived that the Romantic ideology, grounded as it is on a never-ending, perhaps never successful, effort to marry the finite and the infinite through the agency of the poetic imagination,[16] too frequently entailed a sublime indifference to the progeny of that marriage. Even before Percy Shelley in his *Defense of Poetry* dismissed the composed poem as a "fading coal" of its originary inspiration, Mary Shelley understood that the romantic affirmation of the creative process over its finite products could justify a profound moral irresponsibility on the part of the poet. When Percy Shelley's dream of a utopian community or free love and intellectual creativity foundered on Harriet Shelley's ignorance of Mary Godwin's and Claire Clairmont's mutual jealousy, Percy Shelley seemed oblivious to the pain he caused; so too Victor Frankenstein callously fled from the outstretched arms of his loving, needful, freakish son.

A Romantic ideology that represented its own poems as self-consuming artifacts within a never-ending dialectical process, that valued the creative act above the created product, and that allowed the poet to attack the past in the name of an unrealizable future, was not in Mary Shelley's eyes a moral ideology. She believed that a poet must take responsibility for his actions, for the predictable consequences of his poems, as well as for the abstract ideals he serves. Percy Shelley's inability to satisfy fully the emotional and financial needs of his first wife, her children, Mary Godwin, Claire Clairmont, and Mary's own children is represented in his second wife's novel in Victor Frankenstein's inability to love and care for his monster. However much she shared her husband's desire for a better world, Mary Shelley conveyed in *Frankenstein* her conviction that it could not be achieved by simply ignoring or destroying past relationships. Instead one must take full and lasting responsibility for *all* one's offspring and continue to care for the family one engenders.

Mary Shelley's critique of romantic Prometheanism thus has direct social and political ramifications. Encoded in the Romantic poets' use of the Promethean myth is an affirmation of revolution, of rebellion against the established social order. Prometheus defied Jupiter's will in order to liberate humanity from tyranny. For Byron, Leigh Hunt, and Percy Shelley, the figure of Prometheus connoted a radical democratic stance, a defiance of the existing monarchy and inegalitarian class system, and a recognition of the equal rights and freedoms of all individuals. Mary Shelley's "modern Prometheus" embraces the political principles of Locke, Rousseau, and Godwin. Not only does he seek his education at the University of Ingolstadt where Illuminism or Jacobinism flourished, but his effort to create a perfect, immortal being entails a profound revolution in the concept of human nature itself. As Lee Sterrenburg has suggested, Victor Frankenstein is a latter-day Godwinian and his creation can be seen as the force of Jacobinism let loose in the land.[17] For Frankenstein's creature articulates one of the fundamental tenets of Jacobin ideology, a belief in every individual's innate capacity for reason, benevolence, and justice. As the creature insists to Walton:

> Once my fancy was soothed with dreams of virtue, of fame, and of enjoyment. Once I falsely hoped to meet with beings, who, pardoning my outward form, would love me for the excellent qualities which I was capable of bringing forth. I was nourished with high thoughts of honour and devotion. . . . my own desires . . . were for ever ardent and craving; still I desired love and fellowship, and I was still spurned. Was there no injustice in this? (219)

One can see Victor Frankenstein's creation as an attempt to achieve the final perfecting of Rousseau's natural man, to produce an immortal being of great physical strength and powerful passions who transcends the chains of social oppression and death.[18] And indeed, Frankenstein's creature might even be invoking Rousseau's *Social Contract* when he claims that social injustice has corrupted his natural affection for others—"I was benevolent and good; misery made me a fiend" (95)—and that, given the sympathy of other human beings, and especially of a like-minded female companion, he would again be virtuous.

But the creature cannot obtain the human sympathy he craves and is driven to violence by the constant suspicion, fear, and hostility he encounters. He thus becomes an emblem for the French Revolution itself. Originating in the democratic vision of liberty, equality, and fraternity disseminated by the idealistic and benevolent Girondists— Condorcet, Mirabeau, Lafayette, Talleyrand—the Revolution failed to find the parental guidance, control, and nurturance it required to develop into a rational and benevolent state. Unable to accommodate their historical resentments toward the aristocracy and the clergy, the Girondists could not create a state which recognized the rights and freedoms of *all* its citizens or find a legitimate place in the revolutionary social order for the dispossessed aristocrats and clergy- men. Unable to reconcile the old order to the new, the Girondists unleashed a political movement that—spurned by the King and his ministers—resorted to brute force to attain its ends, climaxing in the violence of the September massacres and the executions of Louis XVI and Marie Antoinette.

Mary Shelley conceived of Victor Frankenstein's creature as an embodiment of the revolutionary French nation, a gigantic body politic originating in a desire to benefit all mankind but abandoned by its rightful guardians and so abused by its King, Church, and the corrupt leaders of the ancien régime that it is driven into an uncontrollable rage—manifested in the blood-thirsty leadership of the Montagnards— Marat, St. Just, Robespierre—and the Terror. Frankenstein's creature invokes the already existing identification of the French Revolution with a gigantic monster troped in the writings of both Abbé Barruel and Edmund Burke. Barruel warned the readers of his final volume:

> Meanwhile, before Satan shall exultingly enjoy this triumphant spectacle [of complete anarchy] which the Illuminizing Code is preparing, let us examine how ... it engendered that disastrous monster called Jacobin, raging uncontrolled, and almost unopposed, in these days of horror and devastation.[19]

And Edmund Burke, in his widely distributed *Letters on a Regicide Peace* (1796), proclaimed:

> ... Out of the tomb of the murdered monarchy in France has arisen a vast, tremendous, unformed spectre, in a far more terrific guise than any which ever yet have overpowered the imagination, and subdued the fortitude of man. Going straight forward to its end, unappalled by peril, unchecked by remorse, despising all common maxims and all common means, that hideous phantom overpowered those who would not believe it was possible *she* could at all exist. (my italics)[20]

(Note that for Burke, as for Victor Frankenstein, the most hideous monster of all is female). That Mary Shelley had intended to associate her creature with the French Revolution is suggested by the account of Godwin's radical politics in 1789 that she gave after his death in 1836:

> The giant now awoke. The mind, never torpid, but never rouzed to its full energies, received the spark which lit it into an unextinguishable flame. Who can now tell the feelings of liberal men on the first outbreak of the French Revolution. In but too short a time afterwards it became tarnished by the vices of Orléans—dimmed by the want of talent of the Girondists—deformed & blood-stained by the Jacobins. But in 1789 & 1790 it was impossible for any but a courtier not to be warmed by the glowing influence.[21]

In fact, the representation of the French Revolution as a male giant was initiated by the National Convention itself. In November 1793, one year after Victor Frankenstein gave birth to his creature "on a drear night in November" in the year 1792[22] (midway between the September Massacres and the execution of Louis XVI on January 21, 1793), the National Convention in Paris publically denounced the Catholic Church (on November 7, 1793 several priests and bishops among the deputies to the Convention abjured their clerical offices), held the first Festival of Reason in Notre Dame Cathedral, and proclaimed a new symbolic image for the radical Republic. That image, proposed by the painter David, was a colossal statue of Hercules to be erected on the Pont-Neuf and depicted on the new seal of the Convention: "This image of the people *standing* should carry in his other hand the terrible club with which the Ancients armed their Hercules!"[23] Hercules was thus intended to represent, as transparently as possible, the strength, courage, labors, and unity of the common man (or sans-culottes) as he destroyed the many-headed Hydra of monarchical, aristocratic, and clerical tyranny.[24] The Herculean metaphor had already appeared in radical discourse, in Fouché's description in June 1793 of the victory of the people of Paris over the Girondists:

> The excess of oppression broke through the restraints on the people's indignation. A terrible cry made itself heard in the midst of this great city. The tocsin and the cannon of alarm awakened their patriotism, announcing that liberty was in danger, that there wasn't a moment to spare. Suddenly the forty-eight sections armed themselves and were transformed into an army. This formidable colossus is standing, he marches, he advances, he moves like Hercules, traversing the Republic to exterminate this ferocious crusade that swore death to the people.[25]

As Lynn Hunt comments, we can see in this passage how the power of the people has become to the very men who released it both a gigantic liberating energy and a potential monster, the Terror incarnate in the strength and irrational fury of a sublime Hercules.[26] This ambivalent image received perhaps its most vivid graphic representation in an engraving for the journal *Révolutions de Paris* in 1793 entitled "Le Peuple Mangeur de Rois" (see Plate VIII, top) in which the giant Hercules, clad "sans-culottes" in rolled-up trousers and Phrygian cap, bare-chested, club in hand, cooks the child-sized figure of the king over an open Regency pyre. This engraving powerfully prefigures Mary Shelley's images of the gigantic creature firing the De Lacey cottage and strangling the child William Frankenstein by the throat; it thus points up the novel's encoded representation of the French Revolution and the Terror as a monstrous male giant.

By representing in her creature both the originating ideals and the brutal consequences of the French Revolution, Mary Shelley offered a powerful critique of the ideology of revolution. An abstract idea or cause (e.g. the perfecting of mankind), if not carefully developed within a supportive environment, can become an end that justifies any means, however cruel. As he worked to restore life where death had been, Victor Frankenstein never considered what suffering his freakish child might later endure. By 1816, Mary Shelley could see that the Girondists, in their eagerness to end monarchical tyranny and social injustice, had given insufficient thought to the fates of the aristocrats, clergymen, and peasants who would necessarily be hurt, even killed, during the process of social upheaval. She had seen at first hand the suffering inflicted on the French villagers by fifteen years of warfare when she travelled through France with Percy Shelley on her elopement journey to Switzerland in the summer of 1814. She had then found the village of Echemine "a wretched place . . . [which] had been once large and populous, but now the houses were roofless, and the ruins that lay scattered about, the gardens covered with the white dust of the torn cottages, the black burnt beams, and squalid looks of the inhabitants, presents in every direction the melancholy aspect of devastation."[27] Two years later, in 1816, she perceived a further deterioration in the manners of the Parisians as a result of the recent foreign invasion: "the discontent and sullenness of their minds perpetually betrays itself."[28] While correcting the proofs of Percy Shelley's *Prometheus Unbound* for publication in 1839, she commented that her husband "had indulged in an exaggerated view of the evils of restored despotism; which, however injurious and degrading, were less openly sanguinary than the triumph of anarchy, such as it appeared in France at the close of the last century."[29] And that same year she criticized Condorcet, in her *Lives of the most Eminent Literary and Scientific Men of France*, for his failure to recognize the probable consequences of the political enactment of his beliefs:

> Condorcet . . . showed his attachment to all that should ameliorate the social condition, and enlarge the sphere of intellect among his fellow-creatures. He did not, in his reasonings, give sufficient force to the influence of passion, especially when exerted over masses, nor the vast power which the many have when they assert themselves, nor the facility with which the interested few can lead assembled numbers into error and crime.[30]

What Mary Shelley realized, looking back in 1816 at the Terror and Napoleon's restoration of the monarchy after the coup d'état of 18th Brumaire, was that means become ends: no political ideology can be detached from its modes of production. At every step one must balance the abstract ideal one serves against a moral obligation to preserve the welfare of living individuals, especially those family members most dependent upon one.

For Mary Shelley, this ethical position was powerfully reinforced by her rereading of Godwin's *Political Justice* in the year before composing *Frankenstein*. In the most famous passage of the first edition of *Political Justice* (1793), Godwin had insisted on utilitarian grounds that in the case of a fire, one had an obligation to rescue first the person most likely to benefit humanity (in his example, the Archbishop Fénelon, radical humanist and author of *Telemachus*) rather than an immediate relative (e.g. Fénelon's chambermaid—or valet in the second edition of *Political Justice* (1795)—who just happened to be one's mother, or brother). Godwin had insisted upon this logical conclusion to his utilitarian theory of justice until he fell in love with Mary Wollstonecraft in the spring of 1796. He then revised his position to acknowledge that the "private affections" were a virtue in themselves. In a passage first published in his *Memoirs* of Wollstonecraft in 1798 and regarded by Godwin as so crucial to his developing political theory that he reprinted it verbatim both in *St. Leon* (1799) and in his *Reply to Parr* (1801), Godwin announced

a sound morality requires that "nothing human should be regarded by us as indifferent;" but it is impossible we should not feel the strongest interest for those persons whom we know must intimately, and whose welfare and sympathies are united to our own. True wisdom will recommend to us individual attachments; for with them our minds are more thoroughly maintained in activity and life than they can be under the privation of them, and it is better that man should be a living being, than a stock or a stone. True virtue will sanction this recommendation; since it is the object of virtue to produce happiness, and since the man who lives in the midst of domestic relations, will have many opportunities of conferring pleasure, minute in the detail, yet not trivial in the amount, without interfering with the purposes of general benevolence. Nay, by kindling his sensibility, and harmonising his soul, they may be expected, if he is endowed with a liberal and manly spirit, to render him more prompt in the service of strangers and the public.[31]

Mary Shelley clearly endorsed Godwin's later position, which she may well have attributed to her mother's superior understanding of human nature.

From Mary Shelley's ethical perspective, we can see that if Victor Frankenstein had been able to love and care for his creature, he might have created a race of immortal beings that would in future times have blessed him. And if the Girondists had been able to reconcile the King, the nobility, and the clergy to their new republic and to control the suspicion, hostility, and fears of the people, the French Revolution they engendered might have become the just and benevolent democracy they envisioned. As Victor Frankenstein finally acknowledges, in a passage that functions in the novel as both authorial credo and moral touchstone:

> A human being in perfection ought always to preserve a calm and peaceful mind, and never to allow passion or a transitory desire to disturb his tranquillity. I do not think that the pursuit of knowledge is an exception to this rule. If the study to which you apply yourself has a tendency to weaken your affections, and to destroy your taste for those simple pleasures in which no alloy can possibly mix, then that study is certainly unlawful, that is to say, not befitting the human mind. If this rule were always observed; if no man allowed any pursuit whatsoever to interfere with the tranquillity of his domestic affections, Greece had not been enslaved; Caesar would have spared his country; America would have been discovered more gradually; and the empires of Mexico and Peru had not been destroyed. (51)

No revolutionary herself,[32] Mary Shelley clearly perceived the inherent danger in a Promethean, revolutionary ideology: commitment to an abstract good can justify an emotional detachment from present human relationships and family obligations, a willingness to sacrifice the living to a cause whose final consequences cannot be fully controlled, and an obsession with realizing a dream that too often masks an egotistical wish for personal power. As she later observed of Condorcet

> like all French politicians of that day, he wished to treat mankind like puppets, and fancied that it was only necessary to pull particular strings to draw them within the circle of order and reason. We none of us know the laws of our nature; and there can be little doubt that, if philosophers like Condorcet did educate their fellows into some approximation to their rule of right, the ardent feelings and burning imaginations of man would create something now unthought of, but not less different from the results he expected, than the series of sin and sorrow which now desolates the world.[33]

Mary Shelley grounded her alternative political ideology on the metaphor of the peaceful, loving, bourgeois family. She thereby implicitly endorsed a conservative vision of gradual evolutionary reform, a position articulated most forcefully during her times by Edmund Burke. In her view, if political decisions are based on the "domestic affections"—or on what Carol Gilligan has recently described as an "ethic of care"—on a genuine concern to protect the legitimate interests and welfare of every member of the family politic, then tyranny, war, and cultural imperialism can be prevented and the historical examples of national enslavement and military destruction which Shelley cites—Greece, Rome, native America, Mexico, Peru—will not recur. By unveiling the pattern of psychological desire, self-delusion, and egotism that informed Frankenstein's revolutionary goals, Mary Shelley drew our attention to the extent to which a political ideology serves the psychic as well as the economic interests of a specific class: in the case of Frankenstein, the class of the male bourgeois capitalists who would profit from the overthrow of the aristocracy and monarchy. She thus subverts any claim a political ideology might make to serve the universal interests of humanity.

Mary Shelley's own political ideology would serve instead the interests of the family; she thus encourages the active participation of women in the body politic. However, her conservative program of gradual reform, grounded on the preservation of the loving family-politic, necessarily replicates the inequalities inherent in the hierarchical structure of the bourgeois family, whether based on gender or on age. These inequalities were clearly manifested in the nineteenth-century British class system, a social hierarchy which Mary Shelley found acceptable. We must recognize that Shelley's commitment to political reform modelled on bourgeois family relationships, in which no activity interferes with the tranquillity of the domestic affections, entails the acceptance of the domination of parents over children even in an egalitarian family in which husband and wife are regarded as equals. In other words, implicit in Shelley's ideology of the polis-as-family is the constitution of certain political groups as "children" who must be governed. Her endorsement of this hierarchy is tellingly revealed both in her revulsion from the lower classes, particularly those of foreign nations—the German peasants whose "horrid and slimy faces" she found "exceedingly disgusting" during her honeymoon voyage along the Rhine in 1814—and in her unquestioned assumption that she belonged to "society," the upper-middle-class world of her husband's gentry ancestors, rather than to the artisan and dissenting lower-middle classes of her own parents.

Since the personal is the political, it is not surprising that Mary Shelley's political ideology embodies the same contradiction between caring and controlling, between equality and domination, manifested in the dream that engendered Frankenstein. Mary Shelley there identified both with the abandoned monster and with the student of unhallowed arts who abandons him. This dream, together with the murder of little William Frankenstein in the novel, articulates her horrified recognition that she was capable of asserting the final domination of a parent over a child, infanticide; just as her Journal comments on her German boat companions articulate her unself-conscious willingness to destroy other human beings whom she finds distasteful: "our only wish was to absolutely annihilate such uncleanly animals."

Inherent in Mary Shelley's ideology of the bourgeois family politic is an affirmation of the power of parents over children, an affirmation that endorses the preservation of a class system. In her view, parents have the right, even the obligation, to punish as well as to nurture and protect their children. When she voices through Frankenstein her belief that America should "have been discovered more gradually," (51) she implicitly casts America in the role of a newborn child-continent that should have been cautiously developed under the loving parental care of its new explorer-rulers. She does *not* say that America should have been left undiscovered, uncolonized, unexploited, but only that this process of imperial conquest should have occurred more slowly, perhaps less painfully.

Mary Shelley's celebration of the loving and egalitarian bourgeois family as the basis of political justice—embodied in *Frankenstein* by the De Laceys[34]—fails to take into account the innate injustice of the hierarchical structure of the bourgeois family. From the ideological perspective provided by modern socialist-feminist theory, we can posit an alternative model of family and class relationships to that presented in Mary Shelley's fiction. This is the model of the working-class family in which children are raised to pass into adult responsibility and to contribute to the financial resources of the household as quickly as possible. In contrast to the bourgeois family in which paternal authority based on property ownership and legal rights creates a static hierarchy in which fathers govern their children (and even their wives), the nineteenth-century British working-class family provides an alternative paradigm for political relationships, namely, a dynamic evolution of cooperation among shifting social groups or classes working together for the good of the entire society. This socialist alternative is powerfully represented in the industrial novels of Elizabeth Gaskell, most notably *Mary Barton* (1848). From this perspective, we can vividly see the glaring contradiction in Mary Shelley's political ideology: the conflict between an ethic of care and an ethic of control, between a system of justice grounded on mutual rights and responsibilities and a system of justice grounded on the authority of the elders.

CHAPTER FIVE

A Feminist Critique of Science

From a feminist perspective, the most significant dimension of the relationship between literature and science is the degree to which both enterprises are grounded on the use of metaphor and image. The explanatory models of science, like the plots of literary works, depend on linguistic structures which are shaped by metaphor and metonymy. When Francis Bacon announced, "I am come in very truth leading to you Nature with all her children to bind her to your service and make her your slave,"[1] he identified the pursuit of modern science with the practice of sexual politics: the aggressive, virile male scientist legitimately captures and enslaves a fertile but passive female nature. Mary Shelley was one of the first to comprehend and illustrate the dangers inherent in the use of such gendered metaphors in the seventeenth-century scientific revolution.

Mary Shelley grounded her fiction of the scientist who creates a monster he cannot control upon an extensive understanding of the most recent scientific developments of her day. She thereby initiated a new literary genre, what we now call science fiction. More important, she used this knowledge both to analyze and to criticize the more dangerous implications of the scientific method and its practical results. Implicitly, she contrasted what she considered to be "good" science—the detailed and reverent description of the workings of nature—to what she considered "bad" science, the hubristic manipulation of the elemental forces of nature to serve man's private ends. In *Frankenstein, or the Modern Prometheus*, she illustrated the potential evils of scientific hubris and at the same time challenged the cultural biases inherent in any conception of science and the scientific method that rested on a gendered definition of nature as female. To appreciate the full significance of Mary Shelley's feminist critique of modern science, we must look first at the particular scientific research upon which her novel is based.

The works of three of the most famous scientists of the late eighteenth and early nineteenth century—Humphry Davy, Erasmus Darwin, and Luigi Galvani—together with the teachings of two of their ardent disciples, Adam Walker and Percy Shelley, were crucial to Mary Shelley's understanding of science and the scientific enterprise. While no scientist herself (her description of Victor Frankenstein's laboratory is both vague and naive; apparently Victor does all his experiments in a small attic room by the light of a single candle), Mary Shelley nonetheless had a sound grasp of the concepts and implications of some of the most important scientific work of her day. In her novel, she distinguishes between that scientific research which attempts to describe accurately the functionings of the physical universe and that which attempts to *control* or *change* the universe through human intervention. Implicitly she celebrates the former, which she associates most closely with the work of Erasmus Darwin, while she calls attention to the dangers inherent in the latter, found in the work of Davy and Galvani.

Victor Frankenstein chooses to work within the newly established field of chemical physiology. He must thus become familiar with recent experiments in the disparate fields of biology, chemistry, mechanics, physics, and medicine. The need to span the entire range of science is stressed by Victor's chemistry professor, M. Waldman, who observes that "a man would make but a very sorry chemist, if he attended to that department of human knowledge alone" and therefore advises Victor "to apply to every branch of natural philosophy, including mathematics" (43).

After his misguided and self-taught education in the theories of the medieval and renaissance alchemists, Cornelis Agrippa, Paracelsus, and Albertus Magnus, Victor Frankenstein at the age of fifteen was suddenly forced to acknowledge the ignorance of these pseudo-scientists when, during a storm in the Jura, lightning struck a nearby tree:

> As I stood at the door, on a sudden I beheld a stream of fire issue from an old and beautiful oak, which stood about twenty yards from our house; and so soon as the dazzling light vanished, the oak had disappeared, and nothing remained but a blasted stump. When we visited it the next morning, we found the tree shattered in a singular manner. It was not splintered by the shock, but entirely reduced to thin ribbands of wood. I never beheld any thing so utterly destroyed.
> The catastrophe of this tree excited my extreme astonishment; and

> I eagerly inquired of my father the nature and origin of thunder and
> lightning. He replied, "Electricity;" describing at the same time the
> various effects of that power. He constructed a small electrical
> machine, and exhibited a few experiments; he made also a kite, with
> a wire and string, which drew down that fluid from the clouds.
>
> This last stroke completed the overthrow of Cornelius Agrippa,
> Albertus Magnus, and Paracelsus, who had so long reigned the lords
> of my imagination. (35)

In the first edition of *Frankenstein*, Victor is introduced to the recent
discoveries of Benjamin Franklin by his father, but in her later edition,
Mary Shelley remembered that she had described the Frankenstein
family as not interested in science.[2] In 1831, she therefore attributed
Victor Frankenstein's initiation into legitimate science to an unnamed
"man of great research in natural philosophy" who happened to join
them and who then "entered on the explanation of a theory which he
had formed on the subject of electricity and galvanism" which Victor
found at once "new and astonishing" (238–39).

At the University of Ingolstadt, Victor enrolls in courses in chemistry
and natural philosophy, inspired by the charismatic M. Waldman.
Both Victor's and Professor Waldman's concept of the nature and
utility of chemistry is based upon Humphry Davy's famous intro-
ductory lecture to a course in chemistry given at the newly founded
Royal Institution on January 21, 1802.[3] Immediately published as *A
Discourse, Introductory to a Course of Lectures on Chemistry* in 1802,
this pamphlet is probably the work that Mary Shelley read on
Monday, October 28, 1816, just before working on her story of
Frankenstein. Her Journal entry for that day notes: "Read the
Introduction to Sir H. Davy's 'Chemistry'; write."[4] Waldman's
enthusiasm for and description of the benefits to be derived from the
study of chemistry seem to be based on Davy's remarks, as does Victor
Frankenstein's belief that chemistry might discover the secret of life
itself.

Davy probably also supplied Mary Shelley's description of the first
parts of Professor Waldman's introductory lecture on chemistry—the
opening "recapitulation of the history of chemistry and the various
improvements made by different men of learning," followed by "a
cursory view of the present state of the sciences," an explanation of
several key terms and a few preparatory experiments—which comes
not so much from Davy's *Discourse* as from Davy's later textbook,
Elements of Chemical Philosophy (London: 1812), which Percy Shelley
ordered from Thomas Hookham on July 29, 1812.[5] This may be the
book listed in Mary's *Journal* on October 29, 30, November 2 and 4,
1816, when Mary notes that she "read Davy's 'Chemistry' with

Shelley" and then alone. A glance at the table of contents of this book would have given Mary Shelley the outline she attributes to Waldman: a brief history, followed by a discussion of several specific elements and compounds, with descriptions of experiments performed. The contents probably also provided her with the description of the lectures on natural philosophy that Victor Frankenstein attended in Geneva while still living at home:

> Some accident prevented my attending these lectures until the course was nearly finished. The lecture being therefore one of the last was entirely incomprehensible to me. The professor discoursed with the greatest fluency of potassium and boron, of sulphates and oxyds, terms to which I could affix no idea. (36)

Davy's *Discourse*, written to attract and keep a large audience, provided Mary Shelley with both the content and the rhetoric of Waldman's final panegyric on modern chemistry, the panegyric that directly inspired Victor Frankenstein's subsequent research. Waldman concludes

> the ancient teachers of this science . . . promised impossibilities, and performed nothing. The modern masters promise very little; they know that metals cannot be transmuted, and that the elixir of life is a chimera. But these philosophers, whose hands seem only made to dabble in dirt, and their eyes to pour over the microscope or crucible, have indeed performed miracles. They penetrate into the recesses of nature, and shew how she works in her hiding places. They ascend into the heavens; they have discovered how the blood circulates, and the nature of the air we breathe. They have acquired new and almost unlimited powers; they can command the thunders of heaven, mimic the earthquake, and even mock the invisible world with its own shadows. (42)

Davy, in his celebration of the powers of chemistry, asserted that "the phenomena of combustion, of the solution of different substances in water, of the agencies of fire; the production of rain, hail, and snow, and the conversion of dead matter into living matter by vegetable organs, all belong to chemistry."[6] Arguing that chemistry is the basis of many other sciences, including mechanics, natural history, minerology, astronomy, medicine, physiology, pharmacy, botany, and zoology, Davy insists

> how dependent, in fact, upon chemical processes are the nourishment and growth of organized beings; their various alterations of form, their constant production of new substances; and, finally, their death and decomposition, in which nature seems to take unto herself those

> elements and constituent principles which, for a while, she had lent
> to a superior agent as the organs and instruments of the spirit of life!
> (8)

After detailing the necessity of chemical knowledge to all the
operations of common life, including agriculture, metal-working,
bleaching, dyeing, leather-tanning, and glass and porcelain-making,
Davy paints an idealistic portrait of the contemporary chemist, who is
informed by a science that

> has given to him an acquaintance with the different relations of the
> parts of the external world; and more than that, it has bestowed
> upon him powers which may be almost called creative; which have
> enabled him to modify and change the beings surrounding him, and
> by his experiments to interrogate nature with power, not simply as a
> scholar, passive and seeking only to understand her operations, but
> rather as a master, active with his own instruments. (16)

Here Davy introduces the very distinction Mary Shelley wishes to draw
between the scholar-scientist who seeks only to understand the
operations of nature and the master-scientist who actively interferes
with nature. But where Davy obviously prefers the master-scientist,
Mary Shelley sees his instrumental activities as profoundly dangerous.

Davy sketches a visionary picture of the master-scientist of the
future, who will discover the still unknown general laws of chemistry:

> For who would not be ambitious of becoming acquainted with the
> most profound secrets of nature; of ascertaining her hidden
> operations; and of exhibiting to men that system of knowledge which
> relates so intimately to their own physical and moral constitution?
> (17)

These are Waldman's chemists, who "penetrate into the recesses of
nature and show how she works in her hiding places." The result of
such activity, Davy confidently predicts, will be a more harmonious,
cooperative, and healthy society. True, he cautions, "We do not look
to distant ages, or amuse ourselves with brilliant, though delusive
dreams, concerning the infinite improveability of man, the annihilation
of labour, disease, and even death" (22). But even as Davy apparently
disavows the very dreams that would inspire Victor Frankenstein,
Davy claims for his own project something very similar: "we reason by
analogy from simple facts. We consider only a state of human
progression arising out of its present condition. We look for a time that
we may reasonably expect, for a bright day of which we already
behold the dawn" (22). Having boldly stated the social benefits to be

derived from the pursuit of chemistry, Davy concludes his *Discourse* by insisting on the personal gratifications to be gained: "it may destroy diseases of the imagination, owing to too deep a sensibility; and it may attach the affections to objects, permanent, important, and intimately related to the interests of the human species," even as it militates against the "influence of terms connected only with feeling" and encourages instead a rational contemplation of the universal order of things (26).

In fairness to Davy, he had a great deal of skepticism about the very field that Victor Frankenstein chooses to enter, the new field of chemical physiology. Commenting on just the kind of enterprise Frankenstein pursues, the search for the principle of life itself, Davy warns

> if the connexion of chemistry with physiology has given rise to some visionary and seductive theories; yet even this circumstance has been useful to the public mind in exciting it by doubt, and in leading it to new investigations. A reproach, to a certain degree just, has been thrown upon those doctrines known by the name of the chemical physiology; for in the applications of them speculative philosophers have been guided rather by the analogies of words than of facts. Instead of slowly endeavouring to lift up the veil concealing the wonderful phenomena of living nature; full of ardent imaginations, they have vainly and presumptuously attempted to tear it asunder. (9)

Mary Shelley clearly heeded Davy's words, for she presents Victor Frankenstein as the embodiment of hubris, of that Satanic or Faustian presumption which blasphemously attempts to tear asunder the sacred mysteries of nature.

But in contrast to Davy, Mary Shelley doubted whether chemistry itself—insofar as it involved a "mastery" of nature—produced only good. She substituted for Davy's complacent image of the happy scientist living in harmony with both his community and himself the frightening image of the alienated scientist working in feverish isolation, cut off both physically and emotionally from his family, friends, and society. Victor Frankenstein's scientific researches not only bring him no physical or emotional pleasure but they also leave him, as Laura Crouch has observed, disgusted with the entire scientific enterprise.[7] Detached from a respect for nature and from a strong sense of moral responsibility for the products of one's research, purely objective thought and scientific experimentation can and do produce monsters. Mary Shelley might have found trenchant support for her view in Humphry Davy's praise for one of chemistry's most notable achievements: "in leading to the discovery of gunpowder, [chemistry] has changed the institutions of society, and rendered war more independent of brutal strength, less personal, and less barbarous."[8]

In contrast to Davy, Erasmus Darwin provided Mary Shelley with a powerful example of what she considered to be "good" science, a careful observation and celebration of the operations of all-creating nature with no attempt radically to change either the way nature works or the institutions of society. Percy Shelley acknowledged the impact of Darwin's work on his wife's novel when he began the Preface to the 1818 edition of *Frankenstein* with the assertion that "the event on which this fiction is founded has been supposed, by Dr. Darwin, and some of the physiological writers of Germany, as not of impossible occurrence" (1). To what suppositions, theories and experiments, by Erasmus Darwin and others, did Percy Shelley allude? Mary Shelley, in her Preface to the 1831 edition, referred to an admittedly apocryphal account of one of Dr. Darwin's experiments. During one of Byron's and Shelley's many long conversations to which she was "a devout but nearly silent listener," Mary Shelley recalled

> various philosophical doctrines were discussed, and among others the nature of the principle of life, and whether there was any probability of its ever being discovered and communicated. They talked of the experiments of Dr. Darwin (I speak not of what the doctor really did or said that he did, but, as more to my purpose, of what was then spoken of as having been done by him), who preserved a piece of vermicelli in a glass case till by some extraordinary means it began to move with voluntary motion. (227)

Even though Mary Shelley acknowledges that the animated piece of vermicelli is probably a fiction, Erasmus Darwin's theories have significant bearing on her purpose in *Frankenstein*.

Erasmus Darwin was most famous for his work on evolution and the growth of plants, and it is this work that Mary Shelley affirmed. Victor Frankenstein is portrayed as a direct opponent of Darwin's teachings, as an anti-evolutionist and a parodic proponent of an erroneous "Creation Theory." The basic tenets of Erasmus Darwin's theories appear in his major works, *The Botanic Garden* (1789, 1791), *Zoonomia; or the Laws of Organic Life* (1793), *Phytologia* (1800), and *The Temple of Nature* (1803).[9]

Eighteenth-century scientists generally conceived of the universe as a perfect, static world created by divine fiat at a single moment in time. This universe, metaphorically represented as a Great Chain of Being, manifested myriad and minute gradations between species, but these relationships were regarded as fixed and permanent, incapable of change. As Linnaeus, the great eighteenth-century classifier of all known plant-life, insisted in his *Systema Naturae* (1735), "Nullae species novae"—no new species can come into existence in a divinely ordered, perfect world. But by the end of the eighteenth century, under pressure from Herschel's new discoveries in astronomy, Cuvier's paleontological researches, William Smith's studies of fossil stratification, Sprengel's work on botanical cross-breeding and fertilization, and observations made with an increasingly powerful microscope, together with a more diffuse Leibnizian "natural theology" that emphasized the study of nature's varied interactions with human populations, the orthodox Linnaean concept of an immutable physical universe had begun to weaken.[10]

Erasmus Darwin was inspired by the researches of Comte du Buffon, the "father of evolution,"[11] who in his huge *Histoire naturelle* (44 volumes, 1749–1804) had described myriads of flora and fauna and interspersed among them comments on the progressive "degeneration" of life forms from earlier and more uniform species, often caused by environmental or climatic changes. Although he adhered to the concept of the *scala naturae* and the immutability of species, Buffon was the first to discuss seriously such central evolutionary problems as the origin of the earth, the extinction of species, the theory of "common descent," and in particular the reproductive isolation between two incipient species.[12] Significantly, it was to. Buffon that Victor Frankenstein turned after his early disillusionment with the alchemists, and Buffon whom he "still read . . . with delight" (36).[13] But it was Erasmus Darwin who for English readers first synthesized and popularized the concept of the evolution of species through natural selection over millions of years.

By 1803, Darwin had accepted, on the basis of shell and fossil remains in the highest geological strata, that the earth must once have been covered by water and hence that all life began in the sea. As Darwin concisely summed up this theory of evolution in *The Temple of Nature*:

> Cold gills aquatic form respiring lungs,
> And sounds aerial flow from slimy tongues.
>
> (*The Temple of Nature*, I, 11. 333–34)

Meditating on the suggestion that mankind descended from "one family of monkeys on the banks of the Mediterranean" that learned to use and strengthen the thumb muscle and "by this improved use of the sense of touch . . . acquired clear ideas, and gradually became men," Darwin speculated perhaps all the productions of nature are in their progress to greater perfection! an idea countenanced by modern discoveries and deductions concerning the progressive formation of the solid parts of the terraqueous globe, and consonant to the dignity of the Creator of all things. (*The Temple of Nature*, 54)

Darwin further suggested that such evolutionary improvement is the direct result of sexual selection:

> A great want of one part of the animal world has consisted in the desire of the exclusive possession of the females; and these have acquired weapons to bombard each other for this purpose, as the very thick, shield-like, horny skin on the shoulder of the boar is a defense only against animals of his own species, who strike obliquely upwards, nor are his tushes for other purposes, except to defend himself, as he is not naturally a carnivorous animal. So the horns of the stag are not sharp to offend his adversary, but are branched for the purpose of parrying or receiving the thrusts of horns similar to his own, and have therefore been formed for the purpose of combating other stags for the exclusive possession of the females; who are observed, like the ladies in the times of chivalry, to attend the car of the victor.
>
> (*Zoonomia*, 1794, I:503)

Erasmus Darwin anticipated the modern discovery of mutations, noting in his discussion of monstrous births that monstrosities, or mutations, may be inherited: "Many of these enormities of shape are propagated, and continued as a variety at least, if not as a new species of animal. I have seen a breed of cats with an additional claw on every foot." (*Zoonomia*, 1794, I:501).

In relation to *Frankenstein*, Erasmus Darwin's most significant evolutionary concept was that of the hierarchy of reproduction. Again and again, in *Zoonomia*, in *The Botanic Garden*, in *Phytologia*, and in *The Temple of Nature*, Darwin insisted that sexual reproduction is at a higher evolutionary level than hermaphroditic or solitary paternal propagation. As Darwin commented in his Note on "Reproduction" for *The Temple of Nature*:

> The miscroscopic productions of spontaneous vitality, and the next most inferior kinds of vegetables and animals, propagate by solitary generation only; as the buds and bulbs raised immediately from seeds, the lycoperdon tuber, with probably many other fungi, and the polypus, volvox, and taenia. Those of the next order propagate both by solitary and sexual reproduction, as those buds and bulbs which produce flowers as well as other buds or bulbs; and the aphis and probably many other insects. Whence it appears, that many of those vegetables and animals, which are produced by solitary generation,

gradually become more perfect, and at length produce a sexual progeny.

A third order of organic nature consists of hermaphrodite vegetables and animals, as in those flowers which have anthers and stigmas in the same corol; and in many insects, as leeches, snails, and worms; and perhaps all those reptiles which have no bones . . .

And, lastly, the most perfect orders of animals are propagated by sexual intercourse only. (36–37)

This concept of the superiority of sexual reproduction over paternal propagation was so important to Darwin that it forced him to revise radically his concept of reproduction in his third, "corrected" edition of *Zoonomia* (1801). In 1794, Darwin had argued, following Aristotle, that male plants produce the seed or embryon, while female plants provide only nourishment to this seed, and by analogy, had contended "that the mother does not contribute to the formation of the living ens in normal generation, but is necessary only for supplying its nutriment and oxigenation" (*Zoonomia*, 1794, I:487). He then attributed all monstrous births to the female, saying that deformities result from either excessive or insufficient nourishment in the egg or uterus (497). But by 1801, Darwin's observations of both animal and vegetable hybrids had convinced him that both male and female seeds contribute to the innate characteristics of the species:

> We suppose that redundant fibrils with formative appetencies are produced by, or detached from, various parts of the male animal, and circulating in his blood, are secreted by adapted glands, and constitute the seminal fluid, and that redundant molecules with formative aptitudes or propensities are produced by, or detached from, various parts of the female, and circulating in her blood, are secreted by adapted glands, and form a reservoir in the ovary; and finally that when these formative fibrils, and formative molecules, become mixed together in the uterus, that they coalesce or embrace each other, and form different parts of the new embryon, as in the cicatricula of the impregnated egg. (*Zoonomia*, 1801, II:296–97)

Interestingly, while Darwin no longer attributed monstrous births to uterine deficiencies or excesses, he continued to hold the *male imagination* at the moment of conception responsible for determining both the sex of the child and its outstanding traits:

> I conclude, that the act of generation cannot exist without being accompanied with ideas, and that a man must have at this time either a general idea of his own male form, or of the forms of his male organs; or of an idea of the female form, or of her organs, and that this marks the sex, and the peculiar resemblances of the child to either parent. (*Zoonomia*, 1794, I:524; 1801, II:270)

The impact of the female imagination on the seed in utero is less intense, argued Darwin, because its impact lasts for a longer period of time and is therefore more diffuse. It follows that Darwin, in 1801, attributed the bulk of monstrous births to the *male* imagination, a point of obvious relevance to *Frankenstein*.

Erasmus Darwin's work on what he called "the economy of vegetation" has equally significant implications for *Frankenstein*. Darwin's comments in *Phytologia* on plant nutrition, photosynthesis, and the use of fertilizers and manures for the first time put gardening and agriculture on a sound scientific basis.[14] Again and again in this lengthy work, Darwin emphasized the necessity to recycle all organic matter. His discussion of manures runs to over twenty-five thousand words and is by far the largest section in this book on plant agriculture. The best manures, Darwin reports, are

> organic matters, which ... will by their slow solution in or near the surface of the earth supply the nutritive sap-juice to vegetables. Hence all kinds of animal and vegetable substances, which will undergo a digestive process, or spontaneous solution, as the flesh, fat, skin, and bones of animals; with their secretions of bile, saliva, mucus; and their excretions of urine and ordure; and also the fruit, meal, oil, leaves, wood of vegetables, when properly decomposed on or beneath the soil, supply the most nutritive food to plants. (*Phytologia*, 254)

He urges every gardener and farmer to save all organic matter for manure, "even the parings of his nails and the clippings of his hair" (*Phytologia*, 241), and further urges the heretical notion that the soil nourished by the decomposition of human bodies ought to be available for growing plants. Mourning the waste of rich soil in churchyards and cemeteries, he argues that

> proper burial grounds should be consecrated out of towns, and divided into two compartments, the earth from one of which, saturated with animal decomposition, should be taken away once in ten or twenty years, for the purposes of agriculture; and sand or clay, or less fertile soil, brought into its place. (*Phytologia*, 243)

Mary Shelley was introduced to Darwin's thought by her father and again by her husband, who had been heavily influenced by Darwin's evolutionary theories while writing *Queen Mab*. Percy Shelley first read *The Botanic Garden* in July 1811, as he reported to Thomas Hogg, and in December 1812 he ordered Darwin's *Zoonomia* and *The Temple of Nature* from the booksellers Hookham and Rickman.[15] The extensive impact of Darwin's theories of evolution and agriculture and his poetic language on Percy Shelley's Notes to *Queen Mab*, "The Cloud," "The Sensitive Plant," and *Prometheus Unbound* has been well-documented.[16] It is clear that Darwin's work remained vivid in Percy Shelley's mind throughout the period in which Mary Shelley was writing *Frankenstein*, as his prefatory comment to the novel testifies.

Reading *Frankenstein* in the context of Darwin's writings, we can see that Mary Shelley directly pitted Victor Frankenstein, that modern Prometheus, against those gradual evolutionary processes of nature so well described by Darwin. Rather than letting organic life-forms evolve slowly over thousands of years according to natural processes of sexual selection, Victor Frankenstein wants to originate a new life-form quickly, by chemical means. In his Faustian thirst for knowledge and power, he dreams:

> Life and death appeared to me ideal bounds, which I should first break through, and pour a torrent of light into our dark world. A new species would bless me as its creator and source; many happy and excellent natures would owe their being to me. (49)

Significantly, in his attempt to create a new species, Victor Frankenstein substitutes solitary paternal propagation for sexual reproduction. He thus reverses the evolutionary ladder described by Darwin. And he engages in a concept of science that Mary Shelley deplores, the notion that science should manipulate and control rather than describe, understand, and revere nature.

Moreover, his male imagination at the moment of conception is fevered and unhealthy; as he tells Walton:

> Every night I was oppressed by a slow fever, and I became nervous to a most painful degree; ... my voice became broken, my trembling hands almost refused to accomplish their task; I became as timid as a love-sick girl, and alternate tremor and passionate ardour took the place of wholesome sensation and regulated ambition. (51)

Under such mental circumstances, according to Darwin, the resultant creation could only be a monster. Frankenstein has further increased the monstrousness of his creation by making a form that is both larger and more simple than a normal human being. As he acknowledges to Walton:

> As the minuteness of the parts formed a great hindrance to my speed, I resolved, contrary to my first intention, to make the being of a gigantic stature; that is to say, about eight feet in height, and proportionably large. (49)

Darwin had observed that nature moves "from simpler things to more compound" (*Phytologia*, 118). In defying nature's law, Victor Frankenstein has created not a more perfect species but a degenerate one.

In his attempt to override evolutionary development and to create a new species sui generis, Victor Frankenstein becomes a parodic perpetrator of the orthodox creationist theory. On the one hand, he denies the unique power of God to create organic life. At the same time he confirms the capacity of a single creator to originate a new species. By playing God, Victor Frankenstein has simultaneously upheld the creationist theory and parodied it by creating only a monster. In both ways, Victor Frankenstein has blasphemed against the natural order of things. He has moved down rather than up the evolutionary ladder—he has constructed his creature not only out of dead human organs collected from charnel houses and dissecting rooms, but also out of animal organs and tissue removed from "the slaughter-house" (50). And he has denied the natural mode of human reproduction through sexual procreation.

Victor Frankenstein has perverted evolutionary progress in yet another way. Despite Darwin's insistence that all dead organic matter—including decomposing human flesh and bones found in cemeteries—ought to be saved for compost-heaps and manure, Victor Frankenstein has removed human flesh and bones from graveyards. And he has done so not in order to generate life organically through what Darwin described as "spontaneous animal vitality in microscopic cells"[17] but to create a new life-form through chemical engineering. Frankenstein has thus disrupted the natural life-cycle. His attempt to speed up the transformation of decomposing organic material into new life-forms by artificial means has violated the rhythms of nature.

Mary Shelley's novel implicitly invokes Darwin's theory of gradual evolutionary progress to suggest both the error and the evils of Victor Frankenstein's bad science. The genuine improvement of the species can result only from the conjunction of male and female sexuality. In trying to have a baby without a woman, Victor Frankenstein has failed to give his child the mothering and nurturance it requires, the very nourishment that Darwin explicitly equated with the female sex. Victor Frankenstein's failure to embrace his smiling creature with parental love, his horrified rejection of his own creation, spells out the narrative consequences of solitary paternal propagation. But even if Frankenstein had been able to provide his child with a mother's care, he could not have prevented his creature's ostracism and misery. At best he would have produced another Elephant Man, a benevolent but still much maligned freak.

It is therefore a triple failure of imagination that curses Victor Frankenstein. First, by not imaginatively identifying with his creation, Frankenstein fails to give his child the parental support he owes to it. He thereby condemns his creature to become what others behold, a monster. Secondly, by imagining that the male can produce a higher form of evolutionary species by lateral propagation than by sexual procreation, Frankenstein defines his own imagination as profoundly anti-evolutionary and thus anti-progressive. Third, in assuming that he can create a perfect species by chemical means, Frankenstein defies a central tenet of Romantic poetic ideology: that the creative imagination must work spontaneously, unconsciously, and above all organically, creating forms that are themselves organic heterocosms.

Moreover, in trying to create a human being as God created Adam, out of earth and water, all at once, Victor Frankenstein robs nature of something more than fertilizer. "On a dreary night in November, . . . with an anxiety that almost amounted to agony," Victor Frankenstein infused "a spark of being into the lifeless thing that lay" at his feet (52). At that moment Victor Frankenstein became the modern Prometheus, stealing fire from the gods to give to mankind and thus overthrowing the established, sacred order of both earth and heaven. At that moment he transgressed against nature.

To understand the full implications of Frankenstein's transgression, we must recognize that Victor Frankenstein's stolen "spark of life" is not merely fire; it is also that recently discovered caloric fluid called electricity. Victor's interest in legitimate science was first aroused by the sight of lightning destroying an old oak tree; it was then that he learned of the existence of electricity and replicated Benjamin Franklin's experiment with kite and key to draw down "that fluid from the clouds" (35). In the late eighteenth century, there was widespread interest in the implications of Franklin's and Father Beccaria's discoveries of the existence of atmospheric mechanical electricity generated through such machines as the Leyden jar. Many scientists explored the possibility, derived from Newton's concept of the ether as an elastic medium capable of transmitting the pulsations of light, heat, gravitation, magnetism, and electricity, that the atmosphere was filled with a thin fluid that was positively and negatively charged and that could be identified as a single animating principle appearing under multiple guises (as light, heat, magnetism, etc.). Erasmus Darwin speculated that the perpetual necessity of the human organism for breathing suggests that "the spirit of animation itself is thus acquired from the atmosphere, which if it be supposed to be finer or more subtle than the electric matter, could not long be retained in our bodies and must therefore require perpetual renovation" (*Botanic Garden*,

Canto I, Note to line 401). And Humphry Davy, founder of the field of electrochemistry, first gave authoritative voice to a theory of matter as electrically charged atoms. In his *Elements of Chemical Philosophy*, Davy argued:

> Whether matter consists of indivisible corpuscles, or physical points endowed with attraction and repulsion, still the same conclusions may be formed concerning the powers by which they act, and the quantities in which they combine; and the powers seem capable of being measured by their electrical relations, and the quantities on which they act of being expressed by numbers. (57)

He further concluded that

> it is evident that the particles of matter must have space between them; and ... it is a probable inference that [each body's] own particles are possessed of motion; but ... the motion, if it exists, must be a vibratory or undulatory motion, or a motion of the particles round their axes, or a motion of particles round each other. (95)

Reading Darwin and Davy encouraged Percy Shelley in scientific speculations that he had embarked upon much earlier, as a school-boy at Dr. Greenlaw's Syon House Academy in 1802. Inspired by the famous lectures of Dr. Adam Walker, which he heard again at Eton, Shelley began ten years of experiments with Leyden jars, microscopes, magnifying glasses, and chemical mixtures. His more memorable experiments left holes in his clothes and carpets, attempted to cure his sister Elizabeth's chilblains with a galvanic battery, and electrified a family tomcat. Shelley early learned to think of electricity and the processes of chemical attraction and repulsion as modes of a single polarized force. Adam Walker even identified electricity as the spark of life itself. At the conclusion of his discussion of electricity in his *A System of Familiar Philosophy*, Walker enthused

> Its power of exciting muscular motion in apparently dead animals, as well as of increasing the growth, invigorating the stamina, and reviving diseased vegetation, prove its relationship or affinity to the *living principle*. Though, Proteus-like, it eludes our grasp; plays with our curiosity; tempts enquiry by fallacious appearances and attacks our weakness under so many perplexing subtilties; yet it is impossible not to believe it the soul of the material world, and the paragon of elements![18]

Percy Shelley's basic scientific concepts had long been familiar to Mary Shelley, ever since the early days of their relationship when he ritually celebrated his birthday by launching fire balloons.[19] That Percy Shelley endorsed Adam Walker's identification of life with electricity is everywhere apparent in his poetry. The imagery of *Prometheus Unbound* explicitly associates electricity with love, light, and life itself, as in the final act of the poem where the Spirit of the Earth, earlier imaged as a Cupid-figure linked to his mother Asia/Venus, becomes a radiant orb—or "ten thousand orbs involving and involved"—of pure energy. And on the forehead of the spirit sleeping within this "sphere within sphere" is a "star" (or negative electrode) that shoots "swords of azure fire" (the blue flames of electrical discharges) or

> *Vast beams like spokes of some invisible wheel*
> *Which whirl as the orb whirls, swifter than thought,*
> *Filling the abyss with sun-like lightnings,*
> *And perpendicular now, and now transverse,*
> *Pierce the dark soil, and as they pierce and pass,*
> *Make bare the secrets of the earth's deep heart.*
> (*Prometheus Unbound*, IV, 241, 243, 270, 271, 274–79)

When Victor Frankenstein steals the spark of being, then, he is literally stealing Jupiter's lightning bolt, as Benjamin Franklin had proved. But in Percy Shelley's terms, he is stealing the very life of nature, the source of both love and electricity.

To appreciate fully the science that lies behind Victor Frankenstein's endeavors, however, we must remember that in the 1831 edition of *Frankenstein*, Mary Shelley explicitly associated electricity with galvanism. Victor Frankenstein is there disabused of his belief in the alchemists by a "man of great research in natural philosophy" who introduces him to "a theory which he had formed on the subject of electricity and galvanism" (238); and in her Preface, Mary Shelley linked the attempt to give life to dead matter with galvanism. After referring to Dr. Darwin's vermicelli experiment, she writes:

> Not thus, after all, would life be given. Perhaps a corpse would be reanimated; galvanism had given token of such things: perhaps the component parts of a creature might be manufactured, brought together, and endued with vital warmth. (227)

In 1791 the Bolognese physiologist Luigi Galvani published his *De Viribus Electricitatis in Motui Musculari* (or *Commentary on the Effects of Electricity on Muscular Motion*)[20] in which he came to the conclusion that animal tissue contained a heretofore neglected innate vital force, which he called "animal electricity" but which was subsequently widely known as "galvanism." This force activated both nerves and muscles when they were connected by an arc of metal wires connected to a pile of copper and zinc plates. Galvani believed that his new vital force was a form of electricity different from both the "natural" form of electricity produced by lightning or by the torpedo fish and electric eel and the "artificial" form produced by friction (ie. static electricity). Galvani argued that the brain is the most important source of the production of this "electric fluid" and that the nerves acted as conductors of this fluid to other nerves and muscles, the tissues of which act much like the outer and inner surfaces of the widely used Leyden jar. Thus the flow of animal electric fluid provided a stimulus which produced contractions or convulsions in the irritable muscle fibres.

Galvani's theories made the British headlines in December, 1802, when in the presence of their Royal Highnesses The Prince of Wales, the Duke of York, the Duke of Clarence, and the Duke of Cumberland, Galvani's nephew, disciple and ardent defender, Professor Luigi Aldini of Bologna University, applied a Voltaic pile connected by metallic wires to the ear and nostrils of a recently killed ox-head. At that moment, "the eyes were seen to open, the ears to shake, the tongue to be agitated, and the nostrils to swell, in the same manner as those of the living animal, when irritated and desirous of combating another of the same species."[21] But Professor Aldini's most notorious demonstration of galvanic electricity took place on January 17, 1803. On that day he applied galvanic electricity to the corpse of the murderer Thomas Forster. The body of the recently hanged criminal was collected from Newgate where it had lain in the prison yard at a temperature of 30 degrees Fahrenheit for one hour by the President of the College of Surgeons, Mr. Keate, and brought immediately to Mr. Wilson's Anatomical Theatre where the following experiments were performed. When wires attached to a pile composed of 120 plates of zinc and 120 plates of copper were connected to the ear and mouth of the dead criminal, Aldini later reported, "the jaw began to quiver, the adjoining muscles were horribly contorted, and the left eye actually opened."[22] When the wires were applied to the dissected thumb muscles they "induced a forcible effort to clench the hand"; when applied to the ear and rectum, they "excited in the muscles contractions much stronger . . . The action even of those muscles furthest distant from the points of contact with the arc was so much increased as almost to give an appearance of re-animation." And when volatile alkali was smeared on the nostrils and mouth before the Galvanic stimulus was applied, "the convulsions appeared to be much increased . . . and extended from the muscles of the head, face, and neck, as far as the deltoid. The effect in this case surpassed our most sanguine expectations," Aldini exulted, and remarkably concluded that "vitality might, perhaps, have been restored, if many circumstances had not rendered it impossible."[23] Here is the scientific prototype of Victor Frankenstein, restoring life to dead bodies.

In further experiments conducted by Aldini in 1804, the bodies of human corpses became violently agitated and one even raised itself as if about to walk; arms alternately rose and fell; and one forearm was made to hold a weight of several pounds, while the fists clenched and beat violently the table upon which the body lay. Natural respiration was also artificially reestablished and, through pressure exerted against the ribs, a lighted candle placed before the mouth was several times extinguished.[24]

Aldini's expriments on the severed heads of oxen, frogs legs, dogs' bodies, and human corpses were replicated widely throughout Europe in the early 1800s. His colleagues at Bologna, Drs. Vassali-Eandi, Rossi, and Giulio, reported to the Academy of Turin on August 15, 1802, that they had been able to excite contractions even in the involuntary organs of the heart and digestive system,[25] while applications of galvanic electricity to vegetables, animals, and humans were conducted in Germany by F. H. A. Humboldt, Edmund Schmück, C. J. C. Grapengiesser, and Johann Caspar Creve.[26] Their experiments were reported in 1806 by J. A. Heidmann in his *Theorie der Galvanischen Elektrizität*, while the theoretical implications of galvanism were expounded by Lorenz Oken in his influential *Lehrbuch der Naturphilosophie* (Leipzig, 1809–10). Oken argued that polarity is the first and only force in the world; that galvanism or electrical polarity is therefore the principle of life; and that organic life is galvanism in a state of homogeneous mass.[27]

Events so notorious and so widely reported in the popular press must have been discussed in both the Shelley and the Godwin households at the time and would have been recalled, however inaccurately, by Shelley and Byron in their conversations about the possibility of reanimating a corpse. Indeed, the popular interest in galvanic electricity reached such a pitch in Germany that a Prussian edict was passed in 1804 forbidding the use of decapitated criminals' heads for galvanic experiments. It is probably to these events, as well as to the experiments of Humboldt, Grapengiesser, and Creve and the expositions of Heidmann and Oken that Percy Shelley referred in his Preface to *Frankenstein* when he insisted that "the event on which this fiction is founded has been supposed, by Dr. Darwin and some of the physiological writers of Germany, as not of impossible occurrence" (6). Even though Erasmus Darwin never fully endorsed the revolutionary theory of Galvani and Volta that electricity is the cause of mucular motion, he was convinced that electricity stimulated plant growth.[28]

Mary Shelley's familiarity with these galvanic experiments came not only from Shelley and Byron, but also from Dr. William Polidori. As a medical student with a degree from the University of Edinburgh, Polidori had been exposed to the latest galvanic theories and experiments by the famous Edinburgh physician, Dr. Charles Henry Wilkinson, whose review of the literature, *Elements of Galvanism in Theory and Practice*, was published in 1804. Dr. Wilkinson continued research on galvanism and developed his own galvanic treatments for intermittent fevers, amaurosis, and quinsy, with which he reported several successes.[29]

Mary Shelley based Victor Frankenstein's attempt to create a new species from dead organic matter through the use of chemistry and electricity on the most advanced scientific research of the early nineteenth century. Her vision of the isolated scientist discovering the secret of life is no mere fantasy but a plausible prediction of what science might accomplish. As such, *Frankenstein* has rightly been hailed as the first legitimate example of that genre we call science fiction. Brian Aldiss has tentatively defined science fiction as "the search for a definition of man and his status in the universe which will stand in our advanced but confused state of knowledge (science), and is characteristically cast in the Gothic or post-Gothic mold." And Eric Rabkin and Robert Scoles have identified the conventional elements of science fiction as "speculation and social criticism, hardware and exotic adventure."[30] We might expand these criteria to say that science fiction is a genre that (1) is grounded on valid scientific research; (2) gives a persuasive prediction of what science might be able to accomplish in the foreseeable future; and (3) offers a humanistic critique of either specific technological inventions or the very nature of scientific thinking.

Frankenstein is notable both for its grasp of the nature of the seventeenth-century scientific revolution and for its perspicacious analysis of the dangers inherent in that enterprise. Mary Shelley provides us with the first portrait of what the popular media has since caricatured as the "mad scientist," a figure that finds its modern apotheosis in Stanley Kubrick's Dr. Strangelove (1964). But Mary Shelley's portrait of Victor Frankenstein is both more subtle and more persuasive than subsequent media versions.

Mary Shelley recognized that Frankenstein's passion for his scientific research is a displacement of normal emotions and healthy human relationships. Obsessed by his vision of the limitless power to be gained from his newly discovered capacity to bestow animation, Victor Frankenstein devotes all his time and "ardour" to his experimental research, the creating of a human being. He becomes oblivious to the world around him, to his family and friends, even to his own health.

As he admits, "my cheek had grown pale with study, and my person become emaciated with confinement" (49) as "a resistless, and almost frantic impulse, urged me forward; I seemed to have lost all soul or sensation but for this one pursuit" (50). In his compulsive desire to complete his experiment, he ignores the beauty of nature and stops corresponding with his father and Elizabeth. "I could not tear my thoughts from my employment, loathsome in itself; but which had taken hold of my imagination. I wished, as it were, to procrastinate my feelings of affection, until the great object of my affection was compleated" (manuscript version of 50:29–33). Frankenstein has clearly substituted his scientific research for normal emotional interactions. His only "object of affection" has become the experiment on the laboratory table before him.

In his ability to substitute work for love, a dream of personal omnipotence for a dream of familial interdependence, Victor Frankenstein possesses a personality that has recently been characterized by Evelyn Fox Keller as typical of the modern scientist. Keller argues from her psychological survey of physicists working at Harvard University that the professional scientific demand for "objectivity" often masks a prior psychological alienation from the mother, an alienation that can lead scientists to feel uncomfortable with their emotions and sexuality. The scientists she studied, when compared to the norm, typically felt more estranged from their mothers, were more emotionally repressed, had a relatively low sex-drive, and tended to feel more comfortable with objects than with people.[31] Their professional detachment often precluded a concern with ethics and politics in their research. They preferred to leave the problems resulting from the social application of their discoveries to others. Frankenstein's failure to take personal responsibility for the outcome of his experiment thus anticipates the practice of many modern scientists.

Mary Shelley developed the character of Victor Frankenstein as a calculated inversion of the eighteenth-century "man of feeling." Influenced by Shaftesbury's philosophical argument that sympathy is the basis of human morality and by the fictional treatments of this idea—Henry Mackenzie's The Man of Feeling, Godwin's Fleetwood, or The New Man of Feeling, Laurence Sterne's A Sentimental Journey and Rousseau's La Nouvelle Héloïse which she heard Percy Shelley read aloud that summer of 1816—Mary Shelley embodied in Victor Frankenstein the very opposite of the sentimental hero. Her isolated protagonist has given both "heart and soul" to his work, callously indifferent to the anxiety his silence might cause his father and his fiancée. As such he has truly "lost all soul" (50). He has cut himself off from all moral feeling, from the capacity either to perceive or to enact goodness, as Shaftesbury defined it.

That Mary Shelley endorsed the ideal of the man of feeling as a moral exemplar is revealed not only in her association of the alienated Victor Frankenstein with Faust and Satan but also in her cameo portrait of the Russian boat-master whom Walton employs. This character functions in the novel as a moral touchstone of disinterested sympathy from which to measure the fall of both Frankenstein and Walton. The master "is a person of an excellent disposition, and is remarkable in the ship for his gentleness, and the mildness of his discipline" (14). He is entirely altruistic. When the girl he had obtained permission to marry told him that she loved another man, he not only gave her up but bestowed his small fortune on his impoverished rival and then tried to persuade her father to consent to the love-match. When her father refused, thinking himself honor-bound to the sea-master, the master left Russia and refused to return until the girl had married her lover. But despite the master's noble character, Walton finds the master's sympathetic involvement in the communal life of the ship narrow and boring.

Walton is aware of his own emotional limitations. Throughout the novel, he desperately seeks a friend, some man who would "participate my joy, . . . sympathize with me, . . . approve or amend my plans . . . [and have] affection enough for me to endeavour to regulate my mind" (13–14). Walton's desire is modelled directly on Godwin's Fleetwood, who also desperately sought a friend:

> I saw that I was alone, and I desired to have a friend, . . . a friend . . . whose kindness shall produce a conviction in my mind, that I do not stand alone in the world . . . a friend, who is to me as another self, who joys in all my joys, and grieves in all my sorrows, not with a joy or grief that looks like compliment, not with a sympathy that changes into smiles when I am no longer present, though my head continues bent to the earth with anguish. . . . Friendship, in the sense in which I felt the want of it, has been truly said to be a sentiment that can grasp but one individual in its embrace.[32]

But Godwin's novel clearly demonstrates that Fleetwood's sentimental desire for a "brother of my heart" masks a selfish need to possess the beloved entirely. His jealousy leads to a paranoic suspiciousness that destroys the only genuine friendship Fleetwood ever finds, that with his wife Mary Macneil. In contrast, Mary Macneil articulates an ideal of true friendship, a concept that Godwin had learned from Mary Wollstonecraft:

I am not idle and thoughtless enough, to promise to sink my being and individuality in yours. I shall have distinct propensities and preferences ... In me you will have a wife, and not a passive machine. But, whenever a question occurs of reflection, of experience, of judgment, or of prudential consideration, I shall always listen to your wisdom with undissembled deference. In every thing indifferent, or that can be made so, I shall obey you with pleasure. And in return I am sure you will consider me as a being to be won with kindness, and not dictated to with the laconic phrase of authority.[33]

From the perspective provided by Godwin's *Fleetwood*, we can see that Walton's concept of friendship, which some have hailed as the positive moral value in the novel,[24] is badly flawed. Walton seeks an alter-ego, a mirror of his self who will reflect back his own joys and sorrows, adding only the wisdom that an older Walton would in time have discovered for himself. Rather than a relationship of genuine altruism and self-sacrifice, or a partnership of independent yet mutually supportive persons, Walton's concept of friendship is in fact another form of egoism. He is therefore given the friendship of his genuine alter-ego, Victor Frankenstein, a "friendship" that, being none, is found only to be lost. As Walton laments, "I have longed for a friend; I have sought one who would sympathize with and love me. Behold, on these desert seas I have found such a one; but, I fear, I have gained him only to know his value, and lose him." (209)

Both Walton and Frankenstein devote their emotional energy not to empathic feelings or domestic affections but to egoistic dreams of conquering the boundaries of nature or of death. Not only have they diverted their libidinal desires away from normal erotic objects, but in the process they have engaged in a particular mode of thinking which we might call "scientific." Frankenstein and Walton are both the products of the scientific revolution of the seventeenth century. They have been taught to see nature "objectively," as something separate from themselves, as passive and even dead matter—as the "object of my affection"—that can and should be penetrated, analyzed, and controlled. They thus accord nature no living soul or "personhood" requiring recognition or respect.

Wordsworth had articulated the danger inherent in thinking of nature as something distinct from human consciousness. A reader of Wordsworth, Mary Shelley understood nature in his terms, as a sacred all-creating mother, a living organism or ecological community with which human beings interact in mutual dependence. To defy this bond, as both Frankenstein and Walton do, is to break one's ties with the source of life and health. Hence Frankenstein literally becomes sick in the process of carrying out his experiment: "every night I was oppressed by a slow fever, and I became nervous to a most painful degree" (51); and at its completion, he collapses in "a nervous fever" that confines him to his sickbed for several months.

But Mary Shelley's critique of objective, rationalistic thought goes beyond Wordsworth's organicist notion that "we murder to dissect." Perhaps because she was a woman, she perceived that inherent in most scientific thought was a potent gender identification. Professor Waldman taught Frankenstein that scientists "penetrate into the recesses of nature, and shew how *she* works in *her* hiding places" (42, my emphasis). In Waldman's trope, nature is a passive female who can be penetrated in order to satisfy male desire. Waldman's metaphor is derived directly from the writings of the leading British scientists of the seventeenth and eighteenth centuries. Francis Bacon had heralded the seventeenth-century scientific revolution as a calculated attempt to enslave female nature. Bacon's metaphor of a passive, possessable female nature strikingly altered the traditional image of nature as Dame Kind, an "all-creating" and bounteous Mother Earth who singlehandedly bore and nourished her children. But it was Bacon's metaphor that structured most of the new scientific writing in England in the eighteenth century. Isaac Barrow, Newton's teacher, declared that the aim of the new philosophy was to "search Nature out of her Concealments, and unfold her dark Mysteries,"[35] while Robert Boyle noted contemptuously that "some men care only to know Nature, others desire to command her."[36] Henry Oldenburg, a future Secretary of the Royal Society, invoked Bacon to support his assertion that the "true sons of learning" are those men who do not remain satisfied with the well-known truths but rather "penetrate from Nature's ante-chamber to her inner closet."[37] As Brian Easlea concludes, many seventeenth-century natural philosophers and their successors viewed the scientific quest as a virile masculine penetration into a passive female nature, a penetration that would, in Bacon's words, not merely exert a "gentle guidance over nature's course" but rather "conquer and subdue her" and even "shake her to her foundations."[38] This vision of nature was visually encoded in Ernest Barrias' large, bare-breasted female statue that in 1902 was placed at the entrance of the grand staircase of the Faculté de Médecine of the Université de Paris, bearing the inscription: "LA NATURE SE DEVOILANT DEVANT LA SCIENCE."

Carolyn Merchant, Evelyn Fox Keller, and Brian Easlea have drawn our attention to the negative consequences of this identification of nature as the passive female.[39] Construing nature as the passive Other has led, as Merchant shows, to the increasing destruction of the environment and the disruption of the delicate ecological balance between humankind and nature. Moreover, as Keller has suggested in her studies of how the social construction of gender has affected the making of science, the professional scientific demand for "objectivity" and detachment often masks an aggressive desire to dominate the female sex object. The result can be a dangerous division between what C. P. Snow called the "two cultures," between the power-seeking practices of science and the concerns of humanists with moral responsibility, emotional communion, and spiritual values. The scientist who analyzes, manipulates, and attempts to control nature unconsciously engages in a form of oppressive sexual politics. Construing nature as the female Other, he attempts to make nature serve his own ends, to gratify his own desires for power, wealth, and reputation.

Frankenstein's scientific project is clearly an attempt to gain power. Inspired by Waldman's description of scientists who "acquired new and almost unlimited powers" (42), Frankenstein has sought both the power of a father over his children, and, more omnipotently, of God over his creation. More subtly, yet more pervasively, Frankenstein has sought power over the female. He has "pursued nature to her hiding places" (49) in an attempt not only to penetrate nature and show how her hidden womb works but actually to steal or appropriate that womb. To usurp the power of reproduction is to usurp the power of production as such. Marx identified childbirth as the primary example of pure, or unalienated, labor. Victor Frankenstein's enterprise can be viewed from a Marxist perspective as an attempt to exploit nature or labor in the service of a ruling class. Frankenstein wishes to harness the modes of reproduction in order to become the acknowledged, revered, and gratefully obeyed father of a new species. His project is thus identical with that of bourgeois capitalism: to exploit nature's resources for both commercial profit and political control.[40]

Among these resources are animal and human bodies. Collecting bones and flesh from charnel-houses, dissecting rooms, and slaughter-houses, Frankenstein sees these human and animal organs as nothing more than the tools of his trade, no different from his other scientific instruments. In this sense he is identical with the factory owner who gathers men, his disembodied "hands" as Dickens's Bounderby would say, to manipulate his machines. We can therefore see Frankenstein's creature, as Franco Moretti has suggested, as the proletariat, "a *collective* and *artificial* creature,"[41] dehumanized by the mechanized modes of technological production controlled by the industrial scientist and, in modern times, by the computer. Elizabeth Gaskell first identified Frankenstein's monster with the nineteenth-century British working-class in *Mary Barton* (1848):

> The actions of the educated seem to me typified in those of
> Frankenstein, that monster of many human qualities, ungifted with a
> soul, a knowledge of the difference between good and evil.
>   The people rise up to life; they irritate us, they terrify us, and we
> become their enemies. Then, in the sorrowful moment of our
> triumphant power, their eyes gaze on us with a mute reproach. Why
> have we made them what they are; a powerful monster, yet without
> the inner means for peace and happiness? (Chapter 15)

But this misshapen and alienated worker, Frankenstein's monster, has
the power to destroy his maker, to seize the technology of production
(the creature carries the secret of his own creation in his pocket) and
force it to serve his own ends.

In the second edition of the novel, Mary Shelley further identifies
Frankenstein's capitalist project with the project of colonial imperial-
ism. Clerval here announces his intention to join the East India
Company:

> He came to the university with the design of making himself
> complete master of the oriental languages, as thus he should open a
> field for the plan of life he had marked out for himself. Resolved to
> pursue no inglorious career, he turned his eyes towrd the East, as
> affording scope for his spirit of enterprise. (243-44)

Frankenstein's enthusiastic affirmation of Clerval's plan signals Mary
Shelley's recognition of the expanding and increasingly dangerous
degree of cultural and scientific control over the resources of nature,
whether dead matter or living races. Her awareness of the similarity
between Frankenstein's scientific enterprise and Clerval's imperialist
project may have been triggered by the Parliamentary Debates on the
slave trade in 1824. The foreign secretary and leader of the House of
Commons, George Canning, in a speech opposing the freeing of the
Negro slaves in the West Indies, explicitly identified the slaves with
Frankenstein's monster:

> To turn [the Negro] loose in the manhood of his physical strength, in
> the maturity of his physical passions, but in the infancy of his
> uninstructed reason, would be to raise up a creature resembling the
> splendid fiction of a recent romance; the hero of which constructs a
> human form, with all the corporeal capabilities of man, and with the
> thews and sinews of a giant; but being unable to impart to the work
> of his hands a perception of right and wrong, he finds too late that he
> has only created a more than mortal power of doing mischief, and
> himself recoils from the monster which he has made.[42]

Writing during the early years of Britain's industrial revolution and the age of Empire, Mary Shelley was aware of the damaging consequences of a scientific, objective, alienated view of both nature and human labor. Uninhibited scientific and technological development, without a sense of moral responsibility for either the processes or products of these new modes of production, could easily, as in Frankenstein's case, produce monsters. A creature denied both parental love and peers; a working class denied access to meaningful work but condemned instead, in Ruskin's words, to make the same glass bead over and over; a colonized and degraded race: all are potential monsters, dehumanized by their uncaring employers and unable to feel the bonds of citizenship with the capitalist society in which they live. Moreover, these workers can become more powerful than their makers. As Frankenstein's creature asserts, "You are my creator, but I am your master;—obey!" (165), a prophecy whose fulfillment might take the form of bloody revolutions in which the oppressed overthrow their masters.

Even more important is Mary Shelley's implicit warning against the possible dangers inherent in the technological developments of modern science. Although we have not yet discovered Frankenstein's procedure for reanimating corpses, recent research in biochemistry—the discovery of DNA, the technique of gene-splicing, and the development of extra-uterine fertilization—has brought us to the point where human beings are able to manipulate life-forms in ways previously reserved only to nature and chance. The replacement of natural childbirth by the mechanical eugenic control systems and baby-breeders envisioned in Aldous Huxley's *Brave New World* or Marge Piercy's *Woman on the Edge of Time* is now only a matter of time and social will. Worse by far, of course, is the contemporary proliferation of nuclear weapons systems resulting from the Los Alamos Project and the political decision to drop atomic bombs on Hiroshima and Nagasaki in 1945. As Jonathan Schell has so powerfully reminded us in *The Fate of the Earth*, as such docudramas as "The Day After" (1983) and "Threads" (1984) have starkly portrayed, a morally irresponsible scientific development has released a monster that can destroy human civilization itself. As Frankenstein's monster proclaims, "Remember that I have power; . . . I can make you so wretched that the light of day will be hateful to you" (165). Mary Shelley's tale of horror is no fantastical ghost story, but rather a profound insight into the probable consequences of "objective"—gendered—or morally insensitive scientific and technological research.

CHAPTER SIX

Usurping the Female

In constituting nature as female—"I pursued nature to her hiding places" (49)—Victor Frankenstein participates in a gendered construction of the universe whose negative ramifications are everywhere apparent in the novel. The uninhibited scientific penetration and technological exploitation of female nature is only one dimension of a patriarchal encoding of the female as passive and possessable, the willing receptacle of male desire. The destruction of the female implicit in Frankenstein's usurpation of the natural mode of human reproduction symbolically erupts in his nightmare following the animation of his creature, in which his bride-to-be is transformed in his arms into the corpse of his dead mother—"a shroud enveloped her form, and I saw the grave-worms crawling in the folds of the flannel" (53). By stealing the female's control over reproduction, Frankenstein has eliminated the female's primary biological function and source of cultural power. Indeed, for the simple purpose of human survival, Frankenstein has eliminated the necessity to have females at all. One of the deepest horrors of this novel is Frankenstein's implicit goal of creating a society for men only: his creature is male; he refuses to create a female; there is no reason that the race of immortal beings he hoped to propagate should not be exclusively male.[1]

Mary Shelley, doubtless inspired by her mother's *A Vindication of the Rights of Woman*, specifically portrays the consequences of a social construction of gender which values men over women. Victor Frankenstein's nineteenth-century Genevan society is founded on a rigid division of sex-roles: the man inhabits the public sphere, the woman is relegated to the private or domestic sphere.[2] The men in Frankenstein's world all work outside the home, as public servants

(Alphonse Frankenstein), as scientists (Victor), as merchants (Clerval and his father), or as explorers (Walton). The women are confined to the home. Elizabeth, for instance, is not permitted to travel with Victor and "regretted that she had not the same opportunities of enlarging her experience and cultivating her understanding" (151). Inside the home, women are either kept as a kind of pet (Victor "loved to tend" on Elizabeth "as I should on a favorite animal" [30]) or they work as house-wives, child-care providers, and nurses (Caroline Beaufort Frankenstein, Elizabeth Lavenza, Margaret Saville), or servants (Justine Moritz).

As a consequence of this sexual division of labor, masculine work is segregated from the domestic realm. Hence intellectual activity is divorced from emotional activity. Victor Frankenstein cannot do scientific research and think lovingly of Elizabeth and his family at the same time. His obsession with his experiment has caused him "to forget those friends who were so many miles absent, and whom I had not seen for so long a time" (50). It is this separation of masculine work from the domestic affections that causes Frankenstein's downfall. Because Frankenstein cannot work and love at the same time, he fails to feel empathy for the creature he is constructing, callously making him eight feet tall simply because "the minuteness of the parts formed a great hindrance to my speed" (49). He then fails to love or feel any parental responsibility for the freak he has created. And he remains so self-absorbed that he cannot imagine his monster might threaten someone other than himself when he swears to be with Victor "on his wedding-night."

This separation of the sphere of public (masculine) power from the sphere of private (feminine) affection also causes the destruction of many of the women in the novel, as Kate Ellis has observed.[3] Caroline Beaufort dies unnecessarily because she cannot restrain herself from attending her favorite Elizabeth before she has fully recovered from smallpox. She thus incarnates a patriarchal ideal of female devotion and self-sacrifice (this suggestion is strengthened in the 1831 revisions where she deliberately risks her life to save Elizabeth). She is a woman who is devoted to her father in wealth and in poverty, who nurses him until his death, and then marries her father's best friend to whom she is equally devoted.

The division of public man from private woman also means that women cannot function effectively in the public realm. Despite her innocence of the crime for which she is accused, Justine Moritz is executed for the murder of William Frankenstein (and is even half-persuaded by her male confessor that she is responsible for William's death). And Elizabeth, fully convinced of Justine's innocence, is unable to save her. The impassioned defense she gives of Justine arouses public approbation of Elizabeth's generosity but does nothing to help Justine, "on whom the public indignation was turned with renewed violence, charging her with the blackest ingratitude" (80). Nor can Elizabeth save herself on her wedding night. Both these deaths are of course directly attributable to Victor Frankenstein's egotistical concern for his own suffering (the creature will attack only him) and his own reputation (people would think him mad if he told them his own monster had killed his brother).

Mary Shelley underlines the mutual deprivation inherent in a family and social structure based on rigid and hierarchical gender-divisions by portraying an alternative social organization in the novel: the De Lacey family. The political situation of the De Lacey family, exiled from their native France by the manipulations of an ungrateful Turkish merchant and a draconian legal system, points up the injustice that prevails in a nation where masculine views of competition and chauvinism reign. Mary Shelley's political attack on a society founded on patriarchy and the unequal distribution of power and possessions is conveyed not only through the manifest injustice of Justine's execution and of France's treatment first of the alien Turkish merchant and then of the De Lacey family, but also through the readings in political history that she assigns to the creature. From Plutarch's *Parallel Lives of the Greeks and Romans* and from Volney's *Ruins, or A Survey of the Revolutions of Empires*, the creature learns both of masculine virtue and of masculine cruelty and injustice. "I heard of the division of property, of immense wealth and squalid poverty; . . . I learned that the possessions most esteemed . . . were, high and unsullied descent united with riches." He then asks incredulously, "Was man, indeed, at once so powerful, so virtuous, and magnificent, yet so vicious and base?" (115). Implicit in Mary Shelley's attack on the injustice of patriarchal political systems is the suggestion that the separation from the public realm of feminine affections and compassion has caused much of this social evil. Had Elizabeth Lavenza's plea for mercy for Justine, based on her intuitively correct knowledge of Justine's character, been heeded, Justine would not have been wrongly murdered by the courts. As Elizabeth exclaims:

> how I hate [the] shews and mockeries [of this world]! when one creature is murdered, another is immediately deprived of life in a slow torturing manner; then the executioners, their hands yet reeking with the blood of innocence, believe that they have done a great deed. They call this *retribution*. Hateful name! when that word is pronounced, I know greater and more horrid punishments are going to be inflicted than the gloomiest tyrant has ever invented to satiate his utmost revenge. (83)

In contrast to this pattern of gender inequality and political injustice, as I suggested earlier, the De Lacey family represents an alternative ideology: a vision of the polis-as-egalitarian-family, of a society based on justice, gender equality, and mutual affection. Felix willingly sacrifices his own welfare to ensure that justice is done to the Turkish merchant. In the impoverished De Lacey household, all work is shared equally in an atmosphere of rational companionship, mutual concern, and love. As their symbolic names suggest, Felix embodies happiness, Agatha goodness. They are then joined by Safie (*sophia* or wisdom). Safie, the daughter of the Turkish merchant, is appalled both by her father's betrayal of Felix and by the Islamic oppression of women he endorses. She has therefore fled from Turkey to Switzerland, seeking Felix. Having reached the De Lacey household, she promptly becomes Felix's beloved companion and is taught to read and write French. Safie, whose Christian mother instructed her "to aspire to higher powers of intellect, and an independence of spirit, forbidden to the female followers of Mahomet" (119), is the incarnation of Mary Wollstonecraft in the novel. Wollstonecraft too travelled alone through Europe and Scandinavia. More important, she advocated in *A Vindication of the Rights of Woman* that women be educated to be the "companions" of men and be permitted to participate in the public realm by voting, working outside the home, and holding political office.

But what is lost in the novel is this alternative female role-model of an independent, well-educated, loving companion, as well as this alternative bourgeois family structure based on sexual equality and mutual affection, perhaps because the De Lacey family lacks the mother who might have been able to welcome the pleading, pitiable creature. When Safie flees with the De Lacey family, we as readers are deprived of the novel's only alternative to a rigidly patriarchal construction of gender and the family; so too Mary Shelley herself was deprived of a feminist role-model and a supportive family when her mother died and was subsequently denounced in the popular British press as a harlot, atheist, and anarchist. Safie's disappearance from the novel reflects Mary Shelley's own predicament. Like Frankenstein's creature, she has no positive prototype she can imitate, no place in history. That unique phenomenon envisioned by Mary Wollstonecraft, the wife as the lifelong intellectual equal and companion of her husband, did not exist in the world of nineteenth-century Europe experienced by Mary Shelley.

The doctrine of the separate spheres which Victor Frankenstein endorses encodes a particular attitude to female sexuality which Mary Shelley subtly exposes in her novel. This attitude is manifested most vividly in Victor's response to the creature's request for a female companion, an Eve to comfort and embrace him. After hearing his creature's autobiographical account of his sufferings and aspirations, Frankenstein is moved by an awakened conscience to do justice towards his Adam, promising to create a female creature on condition that both leave forever the neighborhood of mankind. After numerous delays, Frankenstein finally gathers the necessary instruments and materials together into an isolated cottage on one of the Orkney Islands off Scotland. There he proceeds to create a female being. Once again Frankenstein becomes ill: "my heart often sickened at the work of my hands. . . . my spirits became unequal; I grew restless and nervous" (162).

Disgusted by his enterprise, Frankenstein finally determines to stop his work, rationalizing his decision to deprive his creature of a female companion in terms that repay careful examination. Here is Frankenstein's meditation:

> I was now about to form another being, of whose dispositions I was alike ignorant; she might became ten thousand times more malignant than her mate, and delight, for its own sake, in murder and wretchedness. He had sworn to quit the neighborhood of man, and hide himself in deserts; but she had not; and she, who in all probability was to become a thinking and reasoning animal, might refuse to comply with a compact made before her creation. They might even hate each other; the creature who already lived loathed his own deformity, and might he not conceive a greater abhorrence for it when it came before his eyes in the female form? She also might turn with disgust from him to the superior beauty of man; she might quit him, and he be again alone, exasperated by the fresh provocation of being deserted by one of his own species.
>
> Even if they were to leave Europe, and inhabit the deserts of the new world, yet one of the first results of those sympathies for which the daemon thirsted would be children, and a race of devils would be propagated upon the earth, who might make the very existence of the species of man a condition precarious and full of terror. Had I a right, for my own benefit, to inflict this curse upon everlasting generations? . . . I shuddered to think that future ages might curse me as their pest, whose selfishness had not hesitated to buy its own peace at the price perhaps of the existence of the whole human race. (163)

What does Victor Frankenstein truly fear, that causes him to end his creation of a female? First, he is afraid of an independent female will, afraid that his female creature will have desires and opinions that cannot be controlled by his male creature. Like Rousseau's natural man, she might refuse to comply with a social contract made before her birth by another person. She might assert her own integrity and the revolutionary right to determine her own existence. Moreover, those uninhibited female desires might be sadistic. Frankenstein imagines a female "ten thousand times" more evil than her mate, who would "delight" in murder for its own sake. Third, he fears that his female creature will be more ugly than his male creature, so much so that even the male will turn from her in disgust. Fourth, he fears that she will prefer to mate with ordinary males. Implicit here is Frankenstein's horror that, given the gigantic strength of this female, she would have the power to seize and even rape the male she might choose. And finally, he is afraid of her reproductive powers, her capacity to generate an entire race of similar creatures. What Victor Frankenstein truly fears is female sexuality as such. A woman who is sexually liberated, free to choose her own life, her own sexual partner (by force, if necessary), and to propagate at will can appear only monstrously ugly to Victor Frankenstein, for she defies that sexist aesthetic that insists that women be small, delicate, modest, passive, and sexually pleasing—but available only to their lawful husbands.

Horrified by this image of uninhibited female sexuality, Victor Frankenstein violently reasserts a male control over the female body, penetrating and mutilating the female creature at his feet in an image which suggests a violent rape: "trembling with passion, [I] tore to pieces the thing on which I was engaged" (164). The morning after, when he returns to the scene, "the remains of the half-finished creature, whom I had destroyed, lay scattered on the floor, and I almost felt as if I had mangled the living flesh of a human being" (167). However he has rationalized his decision to murder the female creature, Frankenstein's "passion" is here revealed as a fusion of fear, lust, and hostility, a desire to control and even destroy female sexuality.

Frankenstein's fear of female sexuality is endemic to a patriarchal construction of gender. Uninhibited female sexual experience threatens the foundation of patriarchal power: the establishment of patrilineal kinship networks together with the conveyancing of both property and prestige by inheritance entailed upon a male line. Percy Shelley's struggles with his father and the Chancery Court had made Mary acutely aware of the patriarchal system of entail. And Shelley's failure to gain legal guardianship of his children by Harriet Westbrook Shelley—even after her death in December 1816, the Court had refused to grant custody to Percy Shelley, awarding Ianthe and Charles Shelley to foster parents instead—further sharpened her awareness of the lengths to which a patriarchal legal system would go to prevent and punish illegitimate sexual liaisons. In her depiction of the patriarchal society of Geneva, Mary portrayed the consequences of such systematic social and legal suppression of sexual desire. All the women in her novel are sexually repressed, even sexless. Caroline Beaufort is a devoted daughter and chaste wife. Elizabeth Lavenza's relationship with her fiance Victor is that of a sister. And even Safie suffers from this social control of sexuality: she permits Felix to kiss her, but only on the hand.

In this context, the murder of Elizabeth Lavenza on her wedding night becomes doubly significant. As several critics have noted, the scene of her death is based on a painting Mary Shelley knew well, Henry Fuseli's famous "The Nightmare" (Plate VIII, bottom). The corpse of Elizabeth lies in the very attitude in which Fuseli placed his succubus-ridden woman: "She was there, lifeless and inanimate, thrown across the bed, her head hanging down, and her pale and distorted features half covered by her hair." (193) Fuseli's woman is an image of female erotic desire, both lusting for and frightened of the incubus (the night marra, or spirit) that rides upon her, brought to her bed-chamber by the stallion that leers at her from the foot of her bed. Both the presence of this incubus and the woman's posture of open sexual acceptance leave Fuseli's intentions in no doubt.[4] Invoking this image, Mary Shelley alerts us to what Victor fears most: his bride's sexuality. Significantly, Elizabeth would not have been killed had Victor not sent her into their wedding-bedroom *alone*. Returning to the body of the murdered Elizabeth, Victor "embraced her with ardour; but the deathly languor and coldness of the limbs told me, that what I now held in my arms had ceased to be the Elizabeth whom I had loved and cherished" (193). Victor most ardently desires his bride when he knows she is dead. The conflation with his earlier dream, when he thought to embrace the living Elizabeth but instead held in his arms the corpse of his mother, signals Victor's most profound erotic desire, a necrophiliac and incestuous desire to possess the dead female, the lost mother.

To put this point another way, we might observe that Victor Frankenstein's most passionate relationships are with men rather than with women. He sees Clerval as "the image of my former self" (155), and his "friend and dearest companion" (181), as his true soul-mate. His description of Clerval's haunting eyes—"languishing in death, the dark orbs nearly covered by the lids, and the long black lashes that fringed them" (179)—verges on the erotic. Similarly, Walton responds to Frankenstein with an ardor that seems homoerotic. Having desired "the company of a man who could sympathize with me; whose eyes would reply to mine" (13), Walton eagerly embraces Frankenstein as "a celestial spirit" (23) whose death leaves him inarticulate with grief. "What can I say," Walton writes to his sister, "that will enable you to understand the depth of my sorrow?" (216). Finally, Frankenstein dedicates himself to his scientific experiment with a passion that can be described only as sexual. As Mary Shelley originally described

Frankenstein's obsession, "I wished, as it were, to procrastinate my feelings of affection, until the great object of my affection was compleated." Frankenstein's homoerotic fixation upon his creature, whose features he had selected as "beautiful" (52) in a parody of Pygmalion and Galatea, was underlined by Mary Shelley in a revision she made in the Thomas copy of *Frankenstein* now in the J. Pierpont Morgan Library. Describing his anxious enslavement to his task, Frankenstein confesses: "my voice became broken, my trembling hands almost refused to accomplish their task; I became as timid as a love-sick girl, and alternate tremor and passionate ardour took the place of wholesome sensation and regulated ambition" (51:31–35). In place of a heterosexual attachment to Elizabeth, Victor Frankenstein has substituted a homosexual obsession with his creature.[6] In his case this fixation is energized by his profound desire to reunite with his dead mother, a desire that can be fulfilled only by Victor's becoming himself a mother.

At every level, Victor Frankenstein is engaged upon a rape of nature, a violent penetration and usurpation of the female's "hiding places," of the womb. Terrified of female sexuality and the power of human reproduction it enables, both he and the patriarchal society he represents use the technologies of science and the laws of the polis to manipulate, control, and repress women. Thinking back on Elizabeth Lavenza strangled on her bridal bier and on Fuseli's image of female erotic desire that she encodes, we can now see that at this level Victor's creature, his monster, realizes his own most potent lust. The monster, like Fuseli's incubus, leers over Elizabeth, imaging Victor's own repressed desire to rape, possess, and destroy the female. Victor's creature here becomes just that, his "creature," the instrument of his most potent desire: to usurp female reproductive power so that only men may rule.

However, in Mary Shelley's feminist novel, Victor Frankenstein's desire is portrayed as horrible, unattainable, and finally self-destructive. For nature is not the passive, inert, or "dead" matter that Frankenstein imagines.[7] Frankenstein assumes that he can violate nature and pursue her to her hiding places with impunity. But nature both resists and revenges herself upon his attempts. During his research, nature denies to Victor Frankenstein both mental and physical health: "my enthusiasm was checked by my anxiety, and I appeared rather like one doomed by slavery to toil in the mines, or any other unwholesome trade, than an artist occupied by his favourite employment. Every night I was oppressed by a slow fever, and I became nervous to a most painful degree" (51). When his experiment is completed, Victor has a fit that renders him "lifeless" for "a long, long time" and that marks the onset of a "nervous fever" that confines him for many months (57). Victor continues to be tormented by anxiety attacks, bouts of delirium, periods of distraction, and madness. As soon as he determines to blaspheme against nature a second time, by creating a female human being, nature again punishes him: "the eternal twinkling of the stars weighed upon me, and . . . I listened to every blast of wind, as if it were a dull ugly siroc on its way to consume me" (145). His mental illness returns: "Every thought that was devoted to it was an extreme anguish, and every word that I spoke in allusion to it caused my lips to quiver and my heart to palpitate" (156); "my spirits became unequal; I grew restless and nervous" (162). Frankenstein's obsession with destroying his creature finally exposes him to such mental and physical fatigue that he dies at the age of twenty-five.

Moreover, nature pursues Victor Frankenstein with the very electricity he has stolen. Lightning, thunder, and rain rage around him. The November night on which he steals the "spark of being" from nature is dreary, dismal, and wet: "the rain . . . poured from a black and comfortless sky" (54). He next glimpses his creature during a flash of lightning as a violent storm plays over his head at Plainpalais (71). Significantly, the almighty Alps, and in particular Mont Blanc, are represented in this novel as female, as an image of omnipotent fertility.[8] On his wedding day, Victor admires "the beautiful Mont Blanc, and the assemblage of snowy mountains that in vain endeavour to emulate *her*" (190; my italics). Before Frankenstein's first encounter with his creature among the Alps, "the rain poured down in torrents, and thick mists hid the summits of the mountains" (91). Setting sail from the Orkney island where he has destroyed his female creature in order to throw her mangled remains into the sea, Frankenstein wakes to find his skiff threatened by a fierce wind and high waves which portend his own death: "I might be driven into the wide Atlantic, and feel all the tortures of starvation, or be swallowed up in the immeasurable waters that roared and buffeted around me. I . . . felt the torment of a burning thirst; . . . I looked upon the sea, it was to be my grave" (169). Frankenstein ends his life and his pursuit of the monster he has made in the arctic regions, surrounded by the aurora borealis, the electromagnetic field of the North Pole. The atmospheric effects of the novel, which most readers have dismissed as little more than the traditional trappings of Gothic fiction, in fact manifest the power of nature to punish those who transgress her boundaries. The elemental forces that Victor has released pursue him to his hiding places, raging round him like avenging Furies.

Finally, naure prevents Frankenstein from constructing a normal human being. His unnatural method of reproduction produces an unnatural being. His bride is killed on his wedding night, cutting off his chance to engender his own children. Nature's revenge is absolute: he who violates her sacred hiding places is destroyed.

Mary Shelley's novel thus portrays the penalties of raping nature. But it also celebrates an all-creating nature loved and revered by human beings. Those characters capable of deeply feeling the beauties of nature are rewarded with physical and mental health. Even Frankenstein in his moments of tranquillity or youthful innocence can respond powerfully to the glory of nature. As Walton notes, "the starry sky, the sea, and every sight afforded by these wonderful regions, seems still to have the power of elevating his soul from earth" (23). In Clerval's company Victor becomes again "the same happy creature who, a few years ago, loving and beloved by all, had no sorrow or care. When happy, inanimate nature had the power of bestowing on me the most delightful sensations. A serene sky and verdant fields filled me with ecstacy." (65) Clerval's relationship to nature represents one dimension of the moral and political ideology espoused in the novel. Since he "loved with ardour . . . the scenery of external nature" (154), nature endows him with a generous sympathy, a vivid imagination, a sensitive intelligence, and an unbounded capacity for devoted friendship. His death annihilates the possibility that Victor Frankenstein might regain a positive relationship with nature.

Mary Shelley envisions nature as a sacred life-force in which human beings ought to participate in conscious harmony. Elizabeth Lavenza gives voice to this ideal in her choice of profession for Ernest Frankenstein:

> I . . . proposed that he should be a farmer. . . . A farmer's is a very healthy happy life; and the least hurtful, or rather the most beneficial profession of any. My uncle [wanted him] educated as an advocate . . . but . . . it is certainly more creditable to cultivate the earth for the sustenance of man, than to be the confidant, and sometimes the accomplice, of his vices. (59)

Nature nurtures those who cultivate her and who work toward the welfare and sustenance of others. Perhaps this is why, of all the members of Frankenstein's family, only Ernest survives. Had Victor Frankenstein's eyes *not* become "insensible to the charms of nature" (50) and the affections of family and friends, he would not have violated Mary Shelley's moral credo:

> A human being in perfection ought always to preserve a calm and peaceful mind, and never to allow passion or a transitory desire to disturb his tranquillity. I do not think that the pursuit of knowledge is an exception to this rule. If the study to which you apply yourself has a tendency to weaken your affections, and to destroy your taste

for those simple pleasures in which no alloy can possibly mix [e.g. "the beautiful season"], then that study is certainly unlawful, that is to say, not befitting the human mind. (51)

As an ecological system of interdependent organisms, nature requires the submission of the individual ego to the welfare of the family and the larger community. Like George Eliot after her, Mary Shelley is profoundly committed to an ethic of cooperation, mutual dependence, and self-sacrifice. The Russian sea-master willingly sacrifices his own desires that his beloved and her lover may marry; Clerval immediately gives up his desire to attend university in order to nurse his dear friend Victor back to health; Elizabeth offers to release her beloved Victor from his engagement should he now love another. Mary Shelley's ethical vision thus falls into that category of moral thinking which Carol Gilligan has recently identified as more typically female than male. According to Gilligan's analysis, where men have tended to identify moral laws as abstract principles which clearly differentiate right from wrong, women have tended to see moral choice as imbedded in an ongoing shared life. As Gilligan contrasts them, a male "ethic of justice proceeds from the premise of equality—that everyone should be treated the same" while a female "ethic of care rests on the premise of nonviolence—that no one should be hurt."[9] Nancy Chodorow and Dorothy Dinnerstein have attributed this traditional female morality to the daughter's greater identification with the mother.[10] Whereas the son has learned to assert his separateness from the mother (and the process of mothering), the daughter has learned to represent that gendered role and thus has felt more tightly (and ambivalently) bound to the mother. Less certain of her ego boundaries, the daughter has been more likely to engage in moral thinking which gives priority to the good of the family and the community rather than to the rights of the individual.

Insofar as the family is the basic social unit, it has historically encapsulated the system of morality practiced by the culture at large. The Frankenstein family embodies a masculine ethic of justice, one in which the rights and freedoms of the individual are privileged. Frankenstein pursues his own interests in alchemy and chemistry, cheerfully ignoring his family obligations as he engages "heart and soul" in his research, and is moreover encouraged to leave his family and fiancée for two years ("for a more indulgent and less dictatorial parent did not exist upon earth" [130]). In contrast, the De Lacey family embodies a female ethic of care in which the bonding of the family unit is primary. Felix blames himself most because his self-sacrificing action on behalf of the Turkish merchant involved his family in his suffering. Agatha and Felix perform towards their father "every little office of affection and duty with gentleness; and he rewarded them by his benevolent smiles" (106). They willingly starve themselves that their father may eat. Safie's arrival particularly delighted Felix but also "diffused gladness through the cottage, dispelling their sorrow as the sun dissipates the morning mists" (112). In portraying the De Laceys as an archetype of the egalitarian, benevolent, and mutually loving bourgeois family, Mary Shelley clearly displayed her own moral purpose, which Percy Shelley rightly if somewhat vaguely described in his Preface as "the exhibition of the amiableness of domestic affection, and the excellence of universal virtue" (7).

Mary Shelley's grounding of moral virtue in the preservation of familial bonds (against which Frankenstein, in his failure to parent his own child, entirely transgresses) entails an aesthetic credo as well. While such romantic descendants as Walter Pater and Oscar Wilde would later argue that aesthetics and morality, art and life, are distinct, Mary Shelley endorsed a neoclassical mimetic aesthetic that exhorted literature to imitate ideal nature and defined the role of the writer as a moral educator. Her novel purposefully identifies moral virtue, based on moderation, self-sacrifice, and domestic affection, with aesthetic beauty. Even in poverty, the blind old man listening to the sweetly singing Agatha is "a lovely sight, even to me, poor wretch! who had never beheld aught beautiful before" (103). In contrast, Frankenstein's and Walton's dream of breaking boundaries is explicitly identified as both evil and ugly. As Walton acknowledges, "my day dreams are . . . extended and magnificent; but they want (as the painters call it) *keeping*" (14). "Keeping," in painting, is defined by the OED as "the maintenance of the proper relation between the representation of nearer and more distant objects in a picture; hence in a more general sense, 'the proper subserviency of tone and colour in every part of a picture, so that the general effect is harmonious to the eye'." Walton introduces Mary Shelley's ethical norm as an aesthetic norm. Both in life and in art, her ideal is a balance, a golden mean between conflicting demands, specifically here between large and small objects. In ethical terms, this means that Walton must balance his dreams of geographical discovery and fame against the reality of an already existing set of obligations (to his family, his crew, and the sacredness of nature). Similarly Frankenstein should have better balanced the obligations of great and small, of parent and child, of creator and creature. Frankenstein's failure to maintain proportion or *keeping* is thus at one with his failure to preserve "a calm and peaceful mind" (51). His mistake is thus in Mary Shelley's eyes both a moral and an aesthetic failure, one that appropriately results in the creation of a monster both hideous and evil.

CHAPTER SEVEN

Problems of Perception

My discussion of the moral and aesthetic dimensions of Mary Shelley's conceptions of nature and the family leads us back to an even more basic philosophical question. How does Mary Shelley conceive of nature as such? In other words, what *is* nature, both the external world and human nature? *Frankenstein* insistently raises this question. It is the question that Victor is trying to answer, namely, "whence . . . did the principle of life proceed?" (46). And it is the question that haunts his creature, who repeatedly asks "Who was I? What was I? Whence did I come? What was my destination?" (124).

As the characters wrestle with this ontological problem, the novel presents diametrically opposed answers. The creature insists that his innate nature is innocent, benevolent, loving. He is Rousseau's noble savage, born free but everywhere in chains, a Blakean man of innocent energy. Confronting Frankenstein for the first time, he asserts "I was benevolent and good; misery made me a fiend" (95). At the end of his autobiographical narration, the creature repeats that "My vices are the children of a forced solitude that I abhor; and my virtues will necessarily arise when I live in communion with an equal" (143). Frankenstein, in opposition, claims that his creature is innately evil, a vile insect, a devil: "Abhorred monster! fiend that thou art! the tortures of hell are too mild a vengeance for thy crimes. Wretched devil!" (94). If the creature represents innate human nature, as Mary Shelley's persistent authorial denomination of him as "creature" and Percy Shelley's editorial revision of "creature" to "being" suggest, then is a human being innately good or innately evil, a romantic child of innocence or an Augustinian child of original sin?

The question is vividly focused in the symbolic scene when the creature first sees himself. "How was I terrified, when I viewed myself in a transparent pool! At first I started back, unable to believe that it was indeed I who was reflected in the mirror; and when I became fully convinced that I was in reality the monster that I am, I was filled with the bitterest sensations of despondence and mortification" (109). This important passage suggests that in this novel identity is a process not so much of knowing (re-cognition) as of *seeing*. Even though the creature is unable to recognize himself, "unable to believe it was indeed I," his eyes convince him that "I was in reality the monster that I am."

As a unique being, an original, the creature functions in the novel as the sign of the unfamiliar, the unknown. He is a sign detached from a visual or verbal grammar, without diachronic or synchronic context, without precursor or progeny.[1] As such, he poses the fundamental epistemological problem: how is he to be perceived? In the novel, all the characters impose a semiotic construction upon the creature. They read his features or interpret his appearance as having a determinate meaning. In effect, they endorse the contemporary theories of Johann Caspar Lavater and Franz Gall. Lavater's treatise on physiognomy argued that the innate soul or character of the individual manifested itself in the person's physical appearance. The properly trained physiognomist could therefore determine a person's moral nature by correctly reading the meaning of his or her physical characteristics. Dr. Gall and his English-based disciple Johann Christoph Spurzheim reversed Lavater's theory and argued instead that the actual physical formation of the newborn infant determined its later moral nature. One could therefore identify a person's character by correctly reading the shape of his or her skull and body. This new "science" of phrenology was familiar to Mary Shelley. She had herself been physiognomically diagnosed as a three-week-old infant and had learned the basic tenets of Dr. Gall's system in 1814 from her friend Henry Voisey.[2]

The creature's unfamiliar physiognomy is consistently interpreted by the characters in the novel as monstrous, threatening, or evil. Victor Frankenstein, already prejudiced by his youthful "invincible repugnance to new countenances" (40), immediately construes his animated creature as a "wretch": "I beheld the wretch—the miserable monster whom I had created" (53). As his creature, grinning, leans forward to embrace his father, Frankenstein sees the gesture as an attempt "seemingly to detain me" (53) and quickly "escapes" from "the demoniacal corpse to which I had so miserably given life," exclaiming that "no mortal could support the horror of that countenance" (53).

That Frankenstein's response is an *arbitrary* semantic construction is made clear when he next encounters his creature. Seeing his gigantic form approach across the Mer de Glace, Frankenstein observes that "his countenance bespoke bitter anguish, combined with disdain and malignity" (94). But the creature resists this consistently negative reading of his appearance. When Frankenstein again violently rejects his offspring—"Begone! relieve me from the sight of your detested form"—his creature responds: " 'Thus I relieve thee, my creator,' he said, and placed his hated hands before my eyes" (96). The creature thus draws our attention to the possibility that Frankenstein is *misreading* his countenance, judging a mere appearance rather than the hidden reality.

Not only Frankenstein but all the other people the creature encounters immediately see his physiognomy as evil. The old man in his hut, "perceiving me, shrieked loudly, and, quitting the hut, ran across the fields with a speed of which his debilitated form hardly appeared capable" (100). The inhabitants of the nearby village "shrieked ... fainted ... attacked me, until, grievously bruised by stones and many other kinds of missile weapons, I escaped to the open country" (101). When Felix, Agatha and Safie finally see him:

> Who can describe their horror and consternation on beholding me? Agatha fainted; and Safie, unable to attend to her friend, rushed out of the cottage. Felix darted forward, and with supernatural force tore me from his father, to whose knees I clung: in a transport of fury, he dashed me to the ground, and struck me violently with a stick. (131)

The rustic whose drowning girlfriend he saves both tears her from the creature's arms and then shoots the creature. And even the young eyes of William Frankenstein, as the creature embraces him, instantly see the creature as evil: "As soon as he beheld my form, he placed his hands before his eyes, and uttered a shrill scream. . . 'Let me go,' he cried; 'monster! ugly wretch! you wish to eat me, and tear me to pieces—You are an ogre'—" (139).

Only two characters in the novel do not immediately interpret the creature as evil. The first of course is blind. Father De Lacey, unable to see the creature kneeling at his feet, listens instead to his eloquent speech and *hears* truth in the creature's assertion that "I have good dispositions; my life has been hitherto harmless, and, in some degree, beneficial; but a fatal prejudice clouds their eyes, and where they ought to see a feeling and kind friend, they behold only a detestable monster" (130). Father De Lacey replies, "I am blind, and cannot judge of your countenance, but there is something in your words which persuades me that you are sincere" (130). Here Father De Lacey articulates the reader's own response. The reader (as opposed to the filmgoer) has not *seen* the Monster, but only *heard* descriptions of his appearance. At this point in the novel, the reader's sympathies have shifted away from the horrified Frankenstein and toward the speaking creature, whose language is at least as powerful as the words earlier spoken about him. Mary Shelley gives the reader—through Father De Lacey—the opportunity to choose between two competing sets of information: that provided by those characters who see the monster but don't listen to him and that provided by Father De Lacey who listens to the creature but can't see him. But whether the blind De Lacey reads the creature's character correctly, we as readers can never know, for he is ripped out of the novel by his prejudging son.

Walton, because he has listened to the creature's autobiography, does not immediately reject him on the basis of a first impression, a single reading of his face. Confronting the creature for the first time at Frankenstein's deathbed, Walton is both repulsed—"Never did I behold a vision so horrible as his face, of such loathsome, yet appalling hideousness. I shut my eyes involuntarily . . ."—and, because he has thus eliminated his visual image of the creature, attracted to him: "I called on him to stay" (216). Hearing the creature's remorse, Walton's "first impulses, which had suggested to me the duty of obeying the dying request of my friend, in destroying his enemy, were now suspended by a mixture of curiosity and compassion" (217). Walton's responses to the creature continue to veer between sympathy—"I was at first touched by the expressions of his misery"—and hostility—"when I again cast my eyes on the lifeless form of my friend, indignation was re-kindled within me" (218). But Walton's final judgment on the creature is mute. After the creature's impassioned apologia pro vita sua, Walton says nothing. In the last sentence of the manuscript, he significantly loses "sight" of the creature "in the darkness and distance."

This last sentence thus underlines the basic problem of perception in the novel: how are we to *see* the innate being of the creature? Walton, who of all the characters knows him best, has "lost sight" of him. The creature's self-analysis acknowledges that he is both good and evil, but perhaps like King Lear more sinned against than sinning:

> Once I falsely hoped to meet with beings, who, pardoning my outward form, would love me for the excellent qualities which I was capable of bringing forth. I was nourished with high thoughts of honour and devotion. But now vice has degraded me beneath the meanest animal. No crime, no mischief, no malignity, no misery, can be found comparable to mine . . . the fallen angel becomes a malignant devil. . . . Am I to be thought the only criminal, when all human kind sinned against me? (219)

But neither Walton nor the author confirms the creature's self-analysis. At the end he remains lost "in darkness and distance."

The creature thus represents the confrontation of the human mind with an unknowable nature, with the experience that eighteenth-century philosophers called the sublime. The creature, in fact, inhabits those landscapes that Edmund Burke explicitly identified as the sources of the sublime. In his *A Philosophical Inquiry into the Origin of Our Ideas of the Sublime and the Beautiful* (1757), Burke characterised the sublime as "whatever is fitted in any sort to excite the ideas of pain and danger; that is to say, whatever is in any sort terrible, or is conversant about terrible objects, or operates in a manner analogous to terror, is a source of the *sublime*; that is, it is productive of the strongest emotions which the mind is capable of feeling."[3] A sublime landscape is one which seems to threaten the viewer's life. Burke defined the typical qualities of a sublime landscape as greatness of dimension (especially as contrasted with the finite limits of the human body) which gives rise to an idea of infinity; obscurity (which blurs the definition of boundaries); profound darkness or intense light; and sudden, sharp angles. Confronted with such overwhelming objects as towering mountains, huge dark caves, gloomy architectural ruins, or sudden blinding light, the human mind first experiences terror or fear and then, as the instinct of self-preservation is gradually relaxed, astonishment ("that state of the soul in which all its motions are suspended with some degree of horror"[4]), admiration, reverence, and respect. For one thus receives, according to Burke, a sensible impression of the Deity by whose power these overwhelming scenes are created.

The appearances of the creature in the novel are simultaneous with the revelation of the sublime. Approaching Secheron as night encloses the Alps, Frankenstein encounters a violent storm: "thunder burst with a terrific crash over my head. It was echoed from Salêve, the Juras, and the Alps of Savoy; vivid flashes of lightning dazzled my eyes, illuminating the lake, making it appear like a vast sheet of fire; then for an instant every thing seemed of a pitchy darkness" (71). As lightning flashes, Frankenstein's terrified eyes recognize in this landscape of Satan's Pandemonium the creature he had abandoned, "hanging among the rocks," the creature who is again lost in obscurity as the scene is "enveloped in an impenetrable darkness" (72). Frankenstein first speaks to his creature on the Mer de Glace above Chamounix, a landscape defined by eighteenth-century travellers as the locus of the sublime. The creature then follows him to an equally threatening, desolate landscape, the remotest of the Orkneys, "a rock, whose high sides were continually beaten upon by the waves" (161). The sublime nature of this northern Scottish coast was captured by Turner in his drawings of mountain torrents, stormy seas, Ben Arthur, and Ailsa Rock for his "Scottish Pencils" series done in 1801. The creature finally ends his existence among "the mountainous ices of the ocean" at the North Pole, in that frozen wasteland imaged in Caspar David Friedrich's *The Wreck of the "Hope"* (1821) as the ultimate apocalyptic sublime, where he is "lost in darkness and distance" (221).

The creature himself embodies the human sublime. His gigantic stature, his physical strength (as great as "the winds" or "a mountain stream," acknowledges Frankenstein [74]), his predilection for desert mountains and dreary glaciers (where he alone finds "refuge" [95]), and above all his origin in the transgression of the boundary between life and death, all render him both "obscure" and "vast," the touchstones of the sublime. Moreover, the creature's very existence seems to constitute a threat to human life. His appearance throughout the novel rouses "the strongest emotion which the mind is capable of feeling," a Gothic *frisson* of pure terror.

But Mary Shelley's calculated association of the creature with Burke's sublime is intended to do more than rouse a powerful aesthetic response in the reader. Thomas Weiskel has drawn our attention to the semiotic significance of sublime landscapes.[5] Encountering such a landscape, the human mind attempts to determine the meaning of the image before it. Burke and Kant suggested that the meaning of such an immense landscape is the infinite and incomprehensible power of God or nature (the thing-in-itself). In this reading, what is signified (divine omnipotence or the *Ding-an-sich*) is greater than the signifier (the landscape and our linguistic descriptions of it). Weiskel has called this the "negative" sublime, since the human mind is finally overwhelmed or negated by a greater, even transcendent power. In contrast, Wordsworth in the Mount Snowdon episode of *The Prelude* or Coleridge in "This Lime-tree Bower My Prison" suggested that the meaning of a sublime landscape may lie in its capacity to inspire the poetic imagination to a conception of its own power as a "mighty mind" or "almighty spirit."[6] In this reading, what is signified (the landscape) is less than the signifier (the poetic language produced by the creative imagination). Weiskel has called this the "positive" sublime, since the human mind finally confronts its own linguistic power.

With this distinction in mind, we can see that in semiotic terms, Frankenstein's creature brilliantly represents both the negative and the positive modes of the sublime. On the one hand, he is a vast power beyond human linguistic control. Like the wrath of God on judgment day, his revenge is boundless, imageless. His physical appearance is only a metaphor for the havoc he can wreak on the entire human race. As he warns Frankenstein:

Slave, I before reasoned with you, but you have proved yourself
unworthy of my condescension. Remember that I have power; you
believe yourself miserable, but I can make you so wretched that the
light of day will be hateful to you. You are my creator, but I am your
master;—obey! (165)

In this reading of the creature as the negative sublime, he signifies the
power of universal human destruction, the unthinkable, unimaginable,
unspeakable, experience of a deluge or a holocaust. He is the thing-in-
itself, the elemental "chaos" of external nature, those "dark, shapeless
substances" which precede and annihilate the forms of life.[7] As Mary
Shelley reminded her readers in her Preface to the 1831 edition of
Frankenstein: "Invention . . . does not consist in creating out of void,
but out of chaos; the materials must, in the first place, be afforded: it
can give form to dark, shapeless substances, but cannot bring into
being the substance itself." (226) As the *Ding-an-sich*, the dark
shapeless substance itself, the creature is forever displaced by the
mind's own "inventions," its categorizing or structuring perceptual
processes. In this sense, the creature represents the positive sublime, an
arbitrary semantic system, that invented meaning which the human
mind imposes on the chaos of nature. The creature is that which is
"always already" linguistically structured in visual or verbal signs, his
countenance both "bespoke" and "expressed". Mary Shelley here relies
on a Kantian anthropology even as she anticipates its most sophisticated modern revisions. Like Sapir, Whorf, Lévi-Strauss, and Derrida,
she suggests that the basic Kantian categories which structure the
mind's phenomenological perceptions of nature are not space, time,
unity, and causality, but rather the conventions of visual and verbal
languages. Victor Frankenstein construes the unknown in linguistic
terms: his creature's countenance "bespoke bitter anguish, combined
with disdain and malignity"; it "expressed the utmost extent of malice
and treachery" (94, 164). In this novel, such linguistic readings become
social realities. The interpretations of nature that human minds supply
become ideologies, phenomenological constructions of their material
existence.

The semiotic significance of *Frankenstein* was recognized in the first
dramatic production of the novel. H. M. Milner's play bill for
*Frankenstein: or, The Man and the Monster. A Romantic Melo-
Drama, in Two Acts*, first performed at the Royal Cobourg Theatre in
London on July 3, 1826, listed the monster in the dramatis personae
thus: "*************** [played by] Mr. O. Smith." Milner thus drew
attention to the unknowability, the purely fictive semantic significance,
of the creature. Mary Shelley commented approvingly when she saw

Thomas Cooke in the role on August 29 that "this nameless mode of naming the unnameable is rather good."[8] But Milner imposed his own reading upon the creature in his description of scene 2 as "Friendly Intentions of the Monster misinterpreted from his tremendous appearance, and met with Violence." Like most readings of Mary Shelley's text, this one radically simplifies the semiotic significance of the creature.

But Mary Shelley's purposes are primarily ethical rather than epistemological or aesthetic. She wishes us to see that human beings typically interpret the unfamiliar, the abnormal, and the unique as evil. In other words, humans use language, their visual and verbal constructions of reality, to name or image the human and the nonhuman and thus to fix the boundaries between us and them. In so doing, as Foucault has pointed out in *Madness and Civilization* and *Discipline and Punish*, we use language as an instrument of power, to define the borderline between reason and madness, between the socially acceptable and the criminal, and thus to control the terrors of the unknown.[9]

As Mary Shelley's novel illustrates, this linguistic process of naming or imaging becomes a discourse of power that results in the domination of the ideology of a ruling class and leads directly to the creation of evil. By consistently seeing the creature's countenance as evil, the characters in the novel force him to *become* evil. Whatever his innate nature might be, the creature becomes a monster because he, like Polyphemus before him,[10] has been denied access to a human community, denied parental care, companionship, love. His violent rage and malignant murders—of William, Justine, Clerval, Elizabeth, and finally, in consequence, of Alphonse and Victor Frankenstein—are the result of a humanly engendered semiotic construction of the creature as terrifying and horrible. Mary Shelley strikingly shows us that when we see nature as evil, we make it evil. What is now proved was once only imagined, said Blake. The moment Victor Frankenstein sees his creature again, he conceives him to be the murderer of his brother: "No sooner did that idea cross my imagination, than I became convinced of its truth" (71). Having conceived his creature as a "devil" and his "enemy," Frankenstein has made him so.

Moreover, because we can consciously know only the linguistic universes we have ourselves constructed, if we read or image the creature as evil, we write ourselves as the authors of evil. In Blake's pithy phrase, "we become what we behold." Victor Frankenstein becomes the monster he semiotically construes. As Victor confesses, "I considered the being whom I had cast among mankind . . . nearly in the light of my own vampire, my own spirit let loose from the grave, and forced to destroy all that was dear to me" (72). Frankenstein becomes the monster he names, just as in the popular imagination informed by the cinematic versions of Mary Shelley's novel, his name "Frankenstein" becomes the monster.

Victor's identification with his creature is underlined by the novel's persistent association of both men with the fallen Adam and with Satan. Reading Elizabeth's letter, Victor "dared to whisper paradisiacal dreams of love and joy; but the apple was already eaten, and the angel's arm bared to drive me from all hope" (186); "like the archangel who aspired to omnipotence," he confesses to Walton, "I am chained in an eternal hell" (208). The creature too is both Adam and Satan, as he explicitly reminds Victor: "I ought to be thy Adam; but I am rather the fallen angel, whom thou drivest from joy for no misdeed" (95). Increasingly, Victor resembles his creature: "When I thought of him, I gnashed my teeth, my eyes became inflamed" (87). Finally, the boundary between Victor and his creature is annihilated. In his nightmare, the creature literally enters his body. "I felt the fiend's grasp *in* my neck, and could not free myself from it; groans and cries rung *in* my ears" (181; italics mine). Metaphorically, the creature becomes Frankenstein's "own vampire" (72), cannibalistically devouring his creator.

During their final chase across the frozen Arctic wastes, Frankenstein and his creature are indistinguishable. Hunter and hunted blur into one consciousness, one spirit of revenge, one despair, one victim. Victor swears on the grave of William, Elizabeth, and his father to live in order "to execute this dear revenge": "Let the cursed and hellish monster drink deep of agony; let him feel the despair that torments me." He is immediately echoed by the loud and fiendish laugh of his creature: "I am satisfied: miserable wretch! you have determined to live, and I am satisfied" (200). Victor both pursues and is pursued by his creature. Not only does the monster leave marks to guide Frankenstein, but he enters Frankenstein's very soul. As Victor says, "I was cursed by some devil, and carried about with me my eternal hell" (201). Even those "good spirits" who leave food for Frankenstein and whom he had "invoked to aid" him are in fact his own monster, equally bent on revenge. Finally, both Frankenstein and his creature are lost in darkness among the frozen Arctic wastes. By the end of the novel, we cannot separate the wretched, solitary Frankenstein from the wretched, solitary monster. Even Frankenstein's passionate suffering, which has led at least one critic to hail him as a romantic hero,[11] has been more than shared by his creature. As the monster addresses the corpse of Victor, in the original manuscript, "Blasted as you wert, my agony is superior to yours; for remorse is the bitter sting that rankles in my wounds and tortures me to madness" (220:34–221:2). The creature has become his creator, the creator has become his creature.

Many readers have noticed that the monster becomes an alter-ego or double for Victor Frankenstein, a pattern of psychological mirroring that Mary Shelley borrowed from her father's doubles, Caleb Williams and Falkland. But to date these readings have focused on the monster as a manifestation of Frankenstein's repressed desires, whether Oedipal, egotistical, narcissistic, or masochistic.[12] It is true that the monster acts out Frankenstein's subliminal hostility to women by killing his bride on his wedding night. But such psychological interpretations do not account for the larger philosophical questions centrally at issue in the novel. What, finally, is being? Whence did the principle of life proceed? By reading his creation as evil, Frankenstein constructs a monster. The novel itself however leaves open the question of what the creature essentially *is*. Clearly, this being has the capacity to do good; equally clearly, it has the capacity to do evil. But whether it was born good and corrupted by society, or born evil and justly subjected to the condemnation of society, or neither, the novel does not tell us.

Instead *Frankenstein* shows us that in the world that human beings phenomenologically construct, the unknown is imaged, read, and written as "malignant." We thereby create the injustice and evil that we imagine. This is Mary Shelley's final critique of the Romantic ideology. By empowering the imagination as the final arbiter of truth and the poet as the (unacknowledged) legislator of the world, this ideology frees the imagination to construct whatever reality it desires. But the human imagination, left to its own devices, as the rationalist Theseus warned in *A Midsummer Night's Dream*, sees "more devils than vast hell can hold" or in the night, "imagining some fear," supposes every bush a bear. As *Frankenstein* illustrates, the abnormal is more likely to be seen as monstrous than with Titania's eyes of love which "can transpose to form and dignity . . . things base and vile, holding no quantity."

Mary Shelley's answer to the ontological and epistemological issues raised in *Frankenstein*, then, is a radical skepticism, a skepticism that she derived from David Hume and Immanuel Kant, whose ideas she had discussed with Percy Shelley. Since the human mind can never know the thing-in-itself, it can know only the constructs of its own imagination. As the creature says, "the human senses are insurmountable barriers to our union" (141). Because the mind is more likely to respond to the unknown with fear and hostility than with love and acceptance, an unfettered imagination is more likely to construct evil than good. Thus we can finally identify the monster with the poetic imagination itself, as Irving Massey has suggested: "the monster is the imagination, which reveals itself as a hideous construct of the dead parts of things that were once alive when it tries to realize itself, enter the world on the world's terms."[13] The liberation of the imagination advocated by the Romantic poets was regarded by Mary Shelley as both promiscuous and potentially evil. For imaginative creation is not necessarily identical with moral responsibility, as Walter Pater and Oscar Wilde later demonstrated, or closer to home, as Byron and Percy Shelley illustrated. Mary Shelley firmly believed that the romantic imagination must be consciously controlled by love, specifically a mothering love that embraces even freaks. As Victor Frankenstein admits: "If the study to which you apply yourself has a tendency to weaken your affections, and to destroy your taste for those simple pleasures in which no alloy can possibly mix, then that study is certainly unlawful, that is to say, not befitting the human mind." (51)

In advocating this ideal of self-control, of moderation and domestic decorum, Mary Shelley is endorsing an ideology grounded on the trope of the loving and harmonious bourgeois family. She is taking a considered ethical, political, and aesthetic position, a position that is essentially conservative. Human nature may not *be* evil, but human beings are more likely to *construe* it as evil than as good. Since the imagination is motivated by fears, frustrated desires, and fantasies of power, it must be curbed by a strenuous commitment to the preservation of a moral society. In Mary Shelley's view, that moral order traditionally based itself on a reading of nature as sacred. So long as human beings see nature as a loving mother, the source of life itself, they will preserve organic modes of production and reproduction within the nuclear family and will respect the inherent rights of every life-form. They will, moreover, protect and nurture all the products of nature—the old, the sick, the handicapped, the freaks—with love and compassion.

At the aesthetic level, this ideology entails the privileging of the beautiful over the sublime and a reversal of the eighteenth-century ordering of the arts. For as Burke wrote, the sublime appeals to the instinct of self-preservation and rouses feelings of terror that result in a lust for power, domination, and continuing control. But the beautiful appeals to the instinct of self-procreation and rouses sensations of both erotic and affectional love. Significantly, in Mary Shelley's novel, the idealized figure of Clerval consistently prefers the gently undulating and brightly colored landscapes of the beautiful, as painted by Claude Lorraine and Richard Wilson, and the variegated picturesque landscapes celebrated by Uvedale Price and William Gilpin. In a moment of innocence regained, Frankenstein and Clerval find ecstasy in "a serene sky and verdant fields" and "the flowers of spring" (65). Clerval explicitly rejects the landscapes of the sublime (as painted by Salvator Rosa or John Martin):

> I have seen this lake agitated by a tempest, when the wind tore up whirlwinds of water, and gave you an idea of what the water-spout must be on the great ocean, and the waves dash with fury the base of the mountain, where the priest and his mistress were overwhelmed by an avalanche, and where their dying voices are still said to be heard amid the pauses of the nightly wind; I have seen the mountains of La Valais, and the Pays de Vaud: but this country, Victor, pleases me more than all these wonders. The mountains of Switzerland are more majestic and strange; but there is a charm in the banks of this divine river, that I never before saw equalled. Look at that castle which overhangs yon precipice; and that also on the island, almost concealed amongst the foliage of those lovely trees; and now that group of labourers coming from among their vines; and that village half-hid in the recess of the mountain. Oh, surely, the spirit that inhabits and guards this place has a soul more in harmony with man, than those who pile the glacier, or retire to the inaccessible peaks of the mountains of our own country. (153)

By valuing the picturesque and the beautiful above the sublime, Clerval affirms an aesthetic grounded on the family and the community rather than on the individual. Images of cooperation (between human beings—the village; between man and nature—the laborers among the vines) are of a higher aesthetic order than images of isolation and destruction (the dying priest and his forbidden mistress; the inaccessible mountain peaks).

Clerval thus prefers an aesthetic grounded on the female rather than on the male. Isaac Kramnick has shown us that a gender division is imbedded in Burke's descriptions of the sublime and the beautiful. The sublime is masculine, the beautiful is feminine. The sublime has the qualities Burke associated with his powerful, demanding, violent, unloving father. It is vast, dark, and gloomy; "great, rugged and negligent;" "solid and ever massive;" awesome in its infinite power; capable of arousing only fear, terror, and abject admiration. In contrast, the beautiful is associated with Burke's gentle, shy, devoted mother. It is "small," "smooth and polished," "light and delicate," gently undulating, regular. It produces in the beholder only feelings of affection and tenderness, a nurturant sense of well-being.[14] Clerval's aesthetic of the beautiful is thus grounded in a conscious sympathy between the human mind and a benevolent female nature.

When Mary Shelley first saw the Alps, an experience she recorded in her *History of a Six Weeks Tour* (1817), she responded to their grandeur, not with terror or a conviction of human finitude, but with a wholeness of vision that discovered the vital and life-giving among the frozen wastes, the beautiful within the sublime, the female within the male:

> The scenery of this days journey was divine, exhibiting piny mountains barren rocks, and spots of verdure surpassing imagination. After descending for nearly a league between lofty rocks, covered with pines, and interspersed with green glades, where the grass is short, and soft, and beautifully verdant, we arrived at the village of St. Sulpice. (41)

And at the "desolate" summit of Montanvert, her eyes passed over the barren ice-fields to seek out the life which struggled to survive in their midst:

> We went on the ice; it is traversed by irregular crevices, whose sides of ice appear blue, while the surface is of a dirty white. We dine on the mountain. The air is very cold, yet many flowers grow here, and, among others, the rhododendron, or *Rose des Alpes*, in great profusion.[15]

Even among the most conventionally sublime landscapes, Mary Shelley typically sought out the elements of the beautiful, systematically construing nature not as a punishing or death-dealing force but as a maternal, nurturing, life-giving power, just as, in *Frankenstein*, she construed Mont Blanc and the attendant Alps as mighty images of female fertility. Clerval's reading of mother nature is here, in 1818, her own.

Frankenstein promotes the belief that the moment we foreswear an ecological reading of mother earth, the moment we construe nature as Frankenstein does, as the dead mother or as inert matter, at that moment we set in motion an ideology grounded on patriarchal values of individualism, competition, aggression, egoism, sexism, and racism. We set in motion the imperialist ideology that, as Mary Shelley reminds us, enslaved Greece and destroyed Mexico and Peru (51). We legislate a society capable both of developing and of exploding an atomic bomb, of annihilating itself in a nuclear holocaust. "You are my creator, but I am your master!"

Significantly, at the end of Mary Shelley's novel, the monster is still alive. Victor Frankenstein has vowed to return his creature to the cemetery whence he came, but that vow is fulfilled by neither Frankenstein nor his double, Walton. We have only the monster's word that he will destroy himself on a fiery pile at the North Pole. To believe him may be to engage in a fantasy as deceptive as Walton's vision of a coming together of fire and ice, a tropical paradise, at the North Pole. Mary Shelley left the ending of her novel open. The creature is "lost sight of . . . in the darkness and distance," lost in the unnameable, yet still present as the power of the unknown. But she has taught us that if we do not consciously embrace the unknown with nurturing affection, we may unconsciously construe it as the Other—alien, threatening, sublime. The absence of a mothering love, as *Frankenstein* everywhere shows, can and does make monsters, both psychological and technological. Mary Shelley's mythic vision of a manmade monster reverberates even more frighteningly today than it did in 1818.

yet why were these gentle beings un 16
happy — they possessed a delightful house
for such it was in my eyes and every
lux ury. they had a fire to warm
them when chill and delicious viands
when hungry — they were dressed
in excel
lent clothes and still more they enjoy
ed one anothers company and
interchanged each day looks of affection & kindness
What did their tears mean? Did they
really express pain? I was at first
unable to solve these questions but
perpetual attention and time
explained to me many of the appear
ances which at first seemed
enigmatic & you pretty Pecksie!

If a desire for ~~my unhappiness~~ revenge remained
to you in death it would be better satisfied in
my life than in my destruction — ~~But~~ But it was
not so. You wished for my extinction that I
might not cause greater ~~wretchedness~~ to others —
now you will not deprive my life for my
own misery. ~~In destroying too~~ ~~Miserable~~ Blasted
as you were my ~~wretchedness~~ agony is superior to
yours for remorse ~~is~~ the bitter sting that
rankles in my wounds & tortures me to
madness.

But soon, he cried clasping his hand
I shall die and what I now feel will no
longer be felt — soon these thoughts the
burning miseries will be extinct. I
shall ascend my pile triumphantly &
flame that consumes my body will g
enjoyment ~~it I shall exchange~~ to my mind.

He sprung from the cabin win—
as he said this ~~on the~~ upon an ice raft tha
lay close to the vessel ~~&~~ & pushing hi
self off he was carried away by the
waves and I soon lost sight of him
in the darkness & distance

14. ENGRAVING ENTITLED "LE PEUPLE MANGEUR DE ROIS"

CHAPTER EIGHT

Love, Guilt and Reparation:
The Last Man

Mary Shelley's idealization of the bourgeois family was both intensified and threatened by her personal experiences as a wife and mother in the years following the publication of *Frankenstein* in March, 1818. She soon lost a second child. The daughter whom she had carried while writing her novel, Clara Everina, died on September 24, 1818. Less than a year later, on June 7, 1819, her only surviving and favorite child, William, died of malaria in Rome. In part justly, Mary Shelley blamed her husband for the deaths of both these children.

In August 1818, Percy Shelley, in an attempt to help Claire negotiate a visit with Allegra, her daughter by Byron who was then under Byron's protection in a convent near Venice, accompanied Claire from Lucca to Venice to intercede with the estranged Byron. Percy, having lied to Byron that Mary and his children were with him, insisted that Mary travel across northern Italy to Este in the August heat in less than five days.[1] Despite the fact that the one-year-old Clara was ill when Percy met them in Este, he consistently failed to get reliable medical advice on her behalf from the doctor in Padua. After the baby's illness dragged on for three weeks, aggravated by her teething, Percy arranged an appointment with the doctor in Padua for 8 a.m. When Clara arrived at the end of the five-hour journey from Este with diarrhea, dehydrated and suffering mild convulsions, Percy—who was eager to continue his stimulating conversations with Byron—refused to leave her in the care of the Paduan doctor, insisting they proceed directly to Venice where they could consult Byron's physician. By the time Clara Everina arrived in Venice, her convulsions were severe. She died within an hour. As Percy Shelley's biographer, Richard Holmes, comments, "the death of little Clara, to which Shelley's carelessness and unconcern had distinctly contributed, brought to a state of crisis the already strained relations between husband and wife."[2]

Characteristically, Mary repressed her anger and nursed her grief in isolation. But after the death of her remaining child, the three-year-old William, in Rome the following summer, Mary withdrew from her husband into a prison of grief and despair which he could not penetrate, in part because its walls were formed of her unspoken anger at him. As she wrote to her good friend Marianne Hunt three weeks after William's death, on June 29, 1819, "We came to Italy thinking to do Shelley's health good—but the Climate is not any means warm enough to be of benefit to him & yet it is that that has destroyed my two children."[3]

During the summer of 1819, Percy Shelley further alienated Mary. Not only did he fail to share her profound grief at the deaths of her children, retiring instead into his tower at the Villa Valsovano every day to write, but when he emerged, he preferred to go on long walks with Claire or to take Spanish lessons from Maria Gisborne rather than to commiserate with the inconsolable Mary. As he explained in verse:

> My dearest Mary, wherefore hast thou gone,
> And left me in this dreary world alone?
> Thy form is here indeed—a lovely one—
> But thou art fled, gone down the dreary road,
> That leads to Sorrow's most obscure abode;
> Thou sittest on the hearth of pale despair,
> Where
> For thy own sake I cannot follow thee
> Do thou return for mine.[4]

While Percy Shelley's biographers justify his behavior as necessary to protect his own psychic and poetic health in the face of Mary's "severe nervous breakdown,"[5] they fail to see that, from Mary's point of view, Percy's behavior constituted a betrayal of their relationship, of the familial bond that cemented their sexual liaison, of the very ideology of the family to which her entire life was committed. Even taking into account the extreme severity of Mary's depression and misery, it seems that her husband could have offered her more comfort. Characteristically, Percy Shelley emotionally abandoned those women who could not give him the affection and support he craved and sought out those who could, in this case Claire and Maria Gisborne. Or he hid in a world of poetry and books. As Richard Holmes revealingly comments, Shelley's rooftop study "became his fortress of physical and intellectual light. He ascended into it, closing behind him the darkness and human misery below."[6]

Obsessed by grief, unable to emerge from her "bad spirits," Mary found relief only in the writing of *Mathilda*,[7] which she began, bitterly, on Percy's birthday, August 4, 1819. Into this novella she projected much of the hostility she felt toward her husband—and her father, who had also abandoned her during these months of misery. *Mathilda* is a father-daughter incest fantasy in which the incestuous father commits suicide and the chaste daughter's putative friend and soul-mate, a young poet named Woodville, finally abandons her. Focusing first on the character of Woodville, we can see the extent to which this novella articulates Mary Shelley's basic grievances against her husband, grievances which had already erupted in *Frankenstein*.

After Mathilda's father, in his guilt at his illicit passion, has destroyed himself, Mathilda stages her own suicide and retires to a lonely hermitage in northern Scotland, where for two years she lives like a nun, devoted to the love she still feels for her father and mourning his fateful passion and untimely death. Into her "deathlike solitude" of deep despair comes the poet Woodville, who is also consumed with grief for the death of his adored fiancée Elinor. Woodville befriends Mathilda and repeatedly urges her to confess the cause of her sorrow that he may relieve her agony.

The character of Woodville, originally named Lovel (love/evil[8]), manifests the ambivalence that Mary Shelley felt toward her husband. On the surface, Woodville is an idealized portrait of Percy Shelley. He is handsome, charming, outwardly sympathetic, and full of admirable idealism and sensitivity. A world-famous poet at twenty-three, Woodville is described as "glorious," universally loved, innocent, generous, free from all mortal vice. An "angel with winged feet," he believes in the divinity of genius and "like Adam and Prometheus must pay the penalty of rising above his nature by being the martyr to his own excellence" (55).

Mathilda finally consents to share her suffering with Woodville. He comes to the appointed hour and, in despair, Mathilda offers him a cup of poison that she has prepared for them both to drink. Here Mary Shelley's most murderous impulses toward her husband burst through the surface of her fiction. But Woodville refuses the poison, claiming that so long as his poems can give pleasure to others, so long as he has the capacity to bring hope or happiness even for an hour to another human being, he has an obligation to live to lighten their suffering—and besides, his poor old mother needs him. Woodville then abruptly leaves Mathilda. When asked to share fully another's suffering and depression, he quickly retreats into an insistence on his own altruism that sounds like a rationalization of self-promoting careerism. His character thus embodies the contradictory personality that Mary Shelley perceived in her husband and which she had earlier projected, in *Frankenstein*, as the separate but complementary characters of Clerval and Victor Frankenstein.

Writing *Mathilda* gave Mary Shelley some relief from her misery, and the birth of Percy Florence on November 6, 1819 alleviated her most acute depression and partially reconciled her to her husband. However, she was much distressed by his continuing financial entanglement with their nursemaid Elise and her unscrupulous husband Paolo Foggi (who was blackmailing the Shelleys, probably with the threat to publish a claim that the baby girl born in Naples on December 27, 1818, and registered on February 27, 1819, by Percy Shelley as Elena Adelaide Shelley, the daughter of himself and "Mary Godwin," was in fact the child of Shelley and Elise, a claim which may have been true).[9] But Percy Shelley's sudden death by drowning on July 8, 1822 was a devastating blow to Mary Shelley. She was still mourning the deaths of William and Clara. And she herself had been further weakened by a miscarriage on June 16, from which she was saved from bleeding to death only by Percy's prompt action in placing her in a tub of ice. It was six months before she could write fiction again, and a year and a half before she could undertake a novel.

When she picked up her pen in February, 1824, to begin what many critics consider her second-finest work, *The Last Man*, she projected into her novel all the guilt and resentment she felt towards her husband and the political ideology he espoused. *The Last Man* thus functions both as an attempted exorcism and as social analysis and criticism. In psychological terms, the novel enabled Mary Shelley to gain distance from and some control over her profound anger and loss. But the price she paid for this control was high, no less than an enduring definition of herself as the devoted widow of an irreplaceable genius. In social terms, the novel pits her ideology of the egalitarian bourgeois family against those human and natural forces which undermine it: male egoism, female masochism, and death. In political and philosophical terms, *The Last Man* first undercuts the dominant systems of government of the early nineteenth century and then shows that all cultural ideologies are but meaningless fictions.

The repressed hostility which Mary Shelley felt toward both her husband and her father that had erupted in *Mathilda* had also caused her, during the period between William's death in June 1819 and Percy Shelley's departure on his fatal trip to Leghorn in July 1822, to withdraw both emotionally and sexually from her husband. Hurt by his lack of sympathy for her intense grief, she had been unable to respond to his demands and enthusiasms with her former energy and commitment, although she still loved and depended upon him. Increasingly, Percy had complained of her reserve and had sought solace elsewhere. In "Epipsychidion" (1821), his celebration of erotic love dedicated to Emilia Viviani, the Italian damsel in distress whom he hoped to rescue from her convent in Pisa during the winter of 1820–21, Percy described Mary as "the cold chaste Moon" who put him, like Endymion, to sleep:

> And all my being became bright or dim
> As the Moon's image in a summer sea,
> According as she smiled or frowned on me;
> And there I lay, within a chaste cold bed:
> Alas, I then was nor alive nor dead.—(11. 296–300)

In the spring of 1822, he complained to Claire that Mary continued "to suffer terribly from languor and hysterical affections."[10] A month later he asked Trelawney to procure a small quantity of prussic acid for him because, even though he had "no intention of suicide at present ... it would be a comfort to me to hold in my possession that golden key to the chamber of perpetual rest."[11] And on June 22 he dreamt that "he saw the figure of himself strangling" his wife.[12] Only two days after Mary's miscarriage, he lamented to their mutual friends, the Gisbornes:

> I only feel the want of those who can feel, and understand me. Whether from proximity and the continuity of domestic intercourse, Mary does not. The necessity of concealing from her thoughts that would pain her, necessitates this, perhaps. It is the curse of Tantalus, that a person possessing such excellent powers and so pure a mind as hers, should not excite the sympathy indispensable to their application to domestic life.

Turning immediately to his current source of emotional consolation, he continued:

> The Williams's are now on a visit to us, and they are people who are very pleasing to me. But words are not the instruments of our intercourse. I like Jane more and more, and I find Williams the most amiable of companions. She has a taste for music, and an elegance of form and motions that compensate in some degree for the lack of literary refinement.[13]

Both his letters and fervent poems to Jane Williams, as well as her later comments to Leigh Hunt and Thomas Jefferson Hogg, testify to the degree to which Percy Shelley, feeling estranged from Mary, had come to depend on the fun-loving, cheerful Jane for sympathy and psychological support.[14]

Mary Shelley was of course fully aware of her husband's dissatisfactions and of his flirtations with Emilia Viviani and Jane Williams, but she was too weakened physically by her pregnancies and miscarriage and emotionally by her grief and ambivalence to confront him openly. Perhaps she feared the consequences of her own liberated anger. Certainly that unacknowledged anger was deep and enduring. Nonclinical depression is usually caused by repressed anger,[15] and Mary's neurotic depression or what she called her "bad spirits" had dominated her emotional life since the summer of 1819.

She trusted to time to heal the breach between herself and her husband. But time and nature (and possibly Percy Shelley's own suicidal impulses) had betrayed her, and his unexpected death left her with much unfinished emotional business to transact with him. Two poetic elegies, written shortly after Percy Shelley's death, reveal the dynamics of her psychological turmoil. In "The Choice," a poem transcribed at the end of her "Journal of Sorrow—/Begun 1822/But for my Child it could not/End too soon" (as she wrote inside the front cover), Mary Shelley confessed to Percy:

> *How fierce remorse and unreplying death*
> *Waken a chord within my heart, whose breath,*
> *Thrilling and keen, in accents audible,*
> *A tale of unrequited love doth tell.*
> *It was not anger—while thy earthly dress*
> *Encompassed still thy soul's rare loveliness,*
> *All anger was atoned by many a kind*
> *Caress or tear that spoke the softened mind:—*
> *It speaks of cold neglect, averted eyes*
> *That blindly crushed thy heart's fond sacrifice.*
> *My heart was all thy own—but yet a shell*
> *Closed in its core, which seemed impenetrable,*
> *Till sharp-toothed misery tore the husk in twain*
> *Which gaping lies nor may unite again—*
> *Forgive me! let thy love descend in dew*
> *Of soft repentance and regret most true;* (11. 25–40).[16]

Clearly Mary Shelley was overwhelmed by guilt, a guilt that aroused "fierce remorse" and that required both forgiveness and "repentance." We can comprehend the intensity of this guilt only if we recognize that it was energized by her awareness that at certain times in her life, Mary Shelley had almost wished her husband were dead. This repressed desire had erupted in *Mathilda* at the moment when Mathilda offers Woodville a cup of poison to drink with her. Now that her most sinful wish had come true, she felt it was a just retribution for which she must pay the full price, the price of her life.

Even worse, Percy Shelley's last years had not been happy, for which she blamed herself. Her guilt was exacerbated over the years by Percy's loyal friends, Leigh Hunt and Jane Williams, who held her responsible for his misery. The usually friendly Hunt claimed that he had as great a right to Percy's unburnt heart as Mary and treated her, in the months after Percy's death, with unwonted coldness, while Jane Williams—even as she professed friendship—told both Hunt and Hogg that Mary had caused Percy much pain.[17] In an attempt at reparation, Mary committed herself to the preservation of Percy Shelley's memory:

> *My trembling hands shall never write thee—dead.*
> *Thou liv'st in Nature—love—my memory,*
> *With deathless faith for aye adoring thee—*
> *The wife of time no more—I wed Eternity—*
> ("The Choice," Abinger Dep.d.311/4, 11. 118–21)

She would placate Percy Shelley's spirit by publishing his poems, writing his biography, and thus giving him a posthumous "life"—even a literary immortality. And the poet she would present to the public would be perfect, an angel come to earth. As she told her friend Maria Gisborne:

> I was fortunate in having [been] fearlessly placed by destiny in the hands of one, who a superior being among men, a bright planetary spirit enshrined in an earthly temple, raised me to the height of happiness—so far am I now happy that I would not change my situation as His widow with that of the most prosperous woman in the world—and surely the time will at length come when I shall be at peace & my brain & heart be no longer alive with unutterable anguish. I can conceive but of one circumstance that could afford me the semblance of content—that is the being permitted to live where I am now in the same house, in the same state, occupied alone with my child, in collecting His manuscripts—writing his life, and thus to go easily to my grave.[18]

The capital H of "His" in this passage clearly prefigures her conscious deification of her dead husband.

Mary Shelley's devotion to and idealization of Percy Shelley manifest her genuine love for him. At the same time, they exist in inverse proportion to the anger she wished to mask or deny. Unable to admit, in her intense guilt at having caused him to suffer, that he had faults—"it was not anger," she protests too much—she overcompensated by recreating Percy Shelley in the image of a living god. And in so doing, she both denigrated herself and rendered it impossible to establish normal, healthy relationships with other men.[19] Always the shadow of Percy Shelley came between them, as she herself predicted in a poem addressed to her husband after his death:

> *There is an anguish in my Breast*
> *A sorrow all undreamed, unguessed—*
> *A war that I must ever feel—*
> *A secret I must still conceal—*
> *I stand upon the Earth alone*
> *To none my secret spirit known*
> *With none to sooth the speechless stings*
> *Of my wild heart's imaginings*
> *With none to glory in my fame*
> *Or halo with sweet joy my name—*
> *The Star of Love for me hath set . . .*
> . . . .
> *From none the smile thou canst not give*
> *My buried Love will I receive—*
> *Genius and taste, if such there be,*
> *Too late, I consecrate to thee.*
> *O what have I to do with pride*
> *It withered when mine Angel died*
> *And but one thought remains to me*
> *My heart's lone deep dull agony—*[20]

Her desire to publish a hagiography of Percy Shelley was blocked by his father, who was embarrassed by any public mention of his renegade, revolutionary, and atheistic son. Mary Shelley therefore satisfied her need to consecrate herself to Percy by appending long biographical notes to her 1824 and 1839 editions of his poetry—notes which both deified the poet and rewrote their past history together, as when she asserted that his last two months on earth "were the happiest which he had ever known" (1824)—and by painting idealized portraits of him in her novels, most immediately in *The Last Man*. But even here, her genuine ambivalence—that secret war within her breast—reveals itself.

Readers have long recognized that *The Last Man* is a *roman à clef*. In the figures of Adrian, Earl of Windsor, and Lord Raymond, Mary Shelley projected and tried to come to terms with both Percy Shelley and Lord Byron.[21] But at a more philosophical level, the novel tests Mary Shelley's ideology of the family against the realities of human egotism and temporal mutability—of an implacable nature which annihilates individual achievements and family relationships through chance, accident, and death. In this grimly pessimistic novel—the first English example of what we might call apocalyptic or "end-of-the-world" fiction—Mary Shelley finally demonstrates that no ideology, including her own theory of the egalitarian bourgeois family, can survive the onslaught of death.

Adrian, the "hero" of the novel, is the son of the British King who abdicated his throne in 2073 that a republic might be instituted. Adrian shares the democratic principles of his nation and rejects his mother's demand that he reclaim the throne. Instead, he devotes himself to study and is "imbued beyond his years with learning and talent" (13).[22] His face and form are Percy Shelley's: he is "a tall, slim, fair boy, with a physiognomy expressive of the excess of sensibility and refinement" who appears before the narrator like an angel—"the morning sunbeams tinged with gold his silken hair, and spread light and glory over his beaming countenance" (17). His benevolence, his sincerity, and his "thrilling voice, like sweetest melody" arouse universal affection, even among his enemies. His adolescence is dedicated to love and poetry, but is blighted when his beloved Evadne rejects him. Like the poet of "Alastor," he is driven mad by despair, a madness from which he recovers only after a severe fever has permanently impaired his health.

Despite his physical weakness, he ardently supports the cause of freedom and even fights for a year with the Greeks against their Turkish oppressors. At home, he urges his countrymen to effect a greater equalization of wealth and privilege and "to introduce a perfect system of republican government into England" (30). But he refuses to use his position as Earl of Windsor to gain personal political power. Not until England is ravaged by the deadly plague that has annihilated Constantinople and devasted Europe does Adrian determine to "sacrifice himself for the public good" (182) and to accept the position of Lord Protector of England. With courage and unflagging energy, he then comforts the sick, takes what preventive measures he can against the unstoppable epidemic, and leads his ever-diminishing band of countrymen south toward the Alps and a warmer climate. When factions develop among his followers, he heroically hurls himself between their armed forces, eloquently reminding them that the plague is their common enemy and that each human life is sacred. Like "an angel of peace" (277), he reunites and governs his countrymen.

But even as Mary Shelley paints Adrian as a paragon of benevolence, idealism, courage, and self-sacrifice, her resentment cracks this perfect facade. Adrian never marries, never accepts responsibility for a family: "the sensitive and excellent Adrian, loving all, and beloved by all, yet seemed destined not to find the half of himself, which was to complete his happiness" (65). Thus Mary Shelley points to the narcissistic egoism of her husband, his never-satisfiable demand for that perfect soul-mate who could only be his own self.

Adrian, moreover, is incapable of working pragmatically to achieve his political ideals. Only *after* the plague has brutally eliminated all distinctions of wealth and class can he assume leadership over a levelled, egalitarian society. As Hugh Luke first observed, he is subtly associated in this regard with Merrivale, the old astronomer who, "learned as La Place, guileless and unforeseeing as a child," is "too long-sighted in his view of humanity to heed the casualties of the day" (209) and who remains oblivious to the sufferings of his wife and children until poverty, hunger, and the plague have killed them all.[23]

This oblique criticism of Percy Shelley's insensitivity to the needs of his wife and children is finally articulated through the character of Adrian himself. War, disease, and the plague destroy all but three of the human race, sparing only Adrian, the narrator Lionel Verney, and his niece Clara. At this point, Adrian urges the reluctant Verney to accede to Clara's request that they all sail from Italy to Greece to visit the tomb of her parents. Verney warns against the dangers of the ocean and the impassable distances to be crossed, but Adrian insists that they can easily make the journey. In the ensuing storm at sea, Adrian and Clara are both drowned, leaving only Verney alive on earth. Here Mary Shelley vividly focuses her persistent anger at her husband's irresponsibility and insensitivity to his family's welfare. Like Percy Shelley, Adrian seems oddly oblivious to his responsibility for the living, for the human race itself (for only he and Clara could have propagated without incest another generation of human beings), and carelessly sacrifices both his own life and that of the young girl who significantly bears the name of Mary Shelley's dead daughters. Despite her overt celebration of her dead husband's genius and "angelic" character, Mary Shelley had not forgiven him for contributing to Clara Everina Shelley's death, or to his own.

Her personal grievance was strengthened by her larger ideological commitment to what Temma Kaplan has recently called a "female consciousness," a concept Kaplan explains this way: "Female consciousness centers upon the rights of gender, on social concerns, on survival. Those with female consciousness accept the gender system of their society; indeed, such consciousness emerges from the division of labor by sex, which assigns women the responsibility of preserving life." The doctrine of the separate spheres that permeates the bourgeois society represented in *The Last Man* contains a definition of the woman's role as the creator and preserver of human life. Adrian's failure to protect either his own or Clara's life points up the political critique Mary Shelley wishes to make of the division of labor on the basis of sex in her contemporary society. The domination of masculine values in the public realm can lead to the extinction of human life, even—as she had suggested earlier in *Frankenstein*—of the human species itself. Only if men as well as women define their primary personal and political responsibility as the nurturance and preservation of human life, only if they too embrace a "female consciousness," will humanity survive. Mary Shelley thus anticipates Temma Kaplan's recognition that the drive to secure the universal right to life "has revolutionary consequences insofar as it politicizes the networks of everyday life."[24]

Her critique of male egoism also informs her characterization of Lord Raymond, where Mary Shelley comes to terms with her fascination with Lord Byron. After Percy's death, Mary had half-expected Byron to become her protector. She welcomed his offers of help (Byron wrote to Sir Timothy Shelley on her behalf, asking for an allowance for her and her child) and looked to him for both financial and emotional guidance. But Byron disappointed her. Caught up in his own plans to fight for Greek independence, he could not long be bothered with the distraught widow and abruptly withdrew his support.[25] Mary Shelley had counted on Byron to lend her the funds for her trip back to England. But when she finally sailed, it was only Trelawney who would give her the £20 she needed for the journey. Still her emotions toward Byron remained charged. The mere sound of his voice invoked the absent Percy Shelley and filled her with an "unspeakable melancholy." When she learned of his death at Missolonghi, she felt she had lost a close friend. As she cried out to her Journal on May 15, 1824:

> Can I forget his attentions and consolations to me during my deepest misery? Never.
> Beauty sat on his countenance and power beamed from his eye. His faults being, for the most part, weaknesses, induced one readily to pardon them.
> Albe—the dear, capricious, fascinating Albe—has left this desert world![26]

Lord Raymond is presented as the antithesis of Adrian: a proud man of personal ambition, practical worldly knowledge, and intense sexual passions. After fighting heroically in the Greek wars of independence, Raymond returns to England and schemes with the Countess of Windsor to marry her daughter Idris and restore the monarchy. But on the eve of success, Raymond throws over his worldly ambitions to marry the impoverished Perdita Verney, with whom he is passionately in love. Here Mary Shelley, who has given many of her own personality traits to Perdita, reveals one of her own half-conscious fantasies: that Byron would give up Theresa Guiccioli and his dreams of military glory in order to marry her (Raymond and Perdita retire to the very cottage at Bishopsgate where Mary and Percy Shelley had enjoyed an idyllic three months).[27] Raymond, however, cannot long be content with the loving family offered by Perdita and the intellectually stimulating companionship of Adrian, Lionel Verney, and his wife (the Idris whom Raymond never loved and who chose to marry Verney instead). After five years, Raymond's ambition draws him back into politics. He becomes Lord Protector, and in his first year successfully institutes a series of practical reforms and building projects designed to prevent the plague, distribute food abundantly to all, and improve the cultural life of the nation. Perdita joins him in all his benevolent schemes and for three years they are blissfully happy.

But eventually Raymond discovers Evadne, who had always loved him, living in direst poverty. In trying to help her, he falls half in love with her. When his secret visits to Evadne are discovered by Perdita, he cannot acknowledge his own duplicities and proudly refuses to discuss his feelings with his wife. Their perfect communion is thus destroyed, the foundation of their marriage is wrecked, and Perdita finally leaves Raymond. Still in love with Perdita but unable to apologize, Raymond turns to dreams of military glory instead. He heroically conquers Constantinople, only to triumph over a city emptied by the plague, which crashes around him in a fatal explosion when he alone has the courage to enter its silenced streets. In her portrait of Raymond, Mary Shelley reiterated the judgment on political ambition she had earlier given against Castruccio in her novel *Valperga* (1823): military and civic glory is too often won at the expense of family relationships and the suffering of the innocent. At the same time she exorcised her fascination with Byron: his pride and lack of control over his personal passions tainted even his most noble achievements.

Writing *The Last Man* enabled Mary Shelley to distance herself from her emotional response to the loss of both Percy Shelley and Byron. But she purchased this double distance at a cost. By acknowledging the failures of her real and desired lovers to sustain the family bonds she craved, she called into question the viability of the bourgeois family and forced herself to recognize the precariousness of the ideology to which she had committed her life. Confronted with male ambition, vanity, irresponsibility, and hypocrisy, the family may not survive. It can be shattered as easily as the marriage of Perdita and Raymond. And if the family is destroyed, what social roles are left for women to play? We need to look more closely at the female characters in *The Last Man*, for they embody the range of female experience as Mary

Shelley comprehended it. And that experience is both restricted and finally self-destructive.

The figures of Perdita and Idris, both self-images of Mary Shelley, define the roles of women within the domestic sphere even as they alert us to the potentially negative consequences of an ideological construction of the woman as primarily a member of a family unit, as a daughter, wife, and mother. Perdita, the outcast and "orphaned" child from Shakespeare's *Winter's Tale*, shares Mary Shelley's form and temperament. She is pale, fair, with dark, deep eyes, "full of noble feeling" but with cold, distrusting manners and an overactive imagination. Mary Shelley often reproached herself for her inability to communicate her most powerful emotions.[28] Perdita, too, "could love and dwell with tenderness on the look and voice of her friends, while her demeanour expressed the coldest reserve" (11). When, against all her expectations, her beloved Raymond chooses her, thus realizing her most cherished fantasy, she blossoms into an enchanting woman, open-hearted and more self-confident. Supporting him with enthusiasm in his Protectorship, she becomes the perfect wife and hostess, both dignified and benevolent.

Perdita conceives of herself only as a part of her husband: "her whole existence was one sacrifice to him" (84). For five years they are inseparable, their passionate love as intense as at its birth. But when Perdita discovers Raymond's visits to Evadne, she knows that he is no longer hers. Here Mary Shelley explicitly denies her husband's self-serving declaration in "Epipsychidion" that "Love in this is not like gold or clay / To divide is not to take away." She believes that the unique love between a devoted husband and wife cannot be shared without destroying the very intimacy and trust on which it is grounded:

> The affection and amity of a Raymond might be inestimable; but, beyond that affection, embosomed deeper than friendship, was the indivisible treasure of love. Take the sum in its completeness, and no arithmetic can calculate its price; take from it the smallest portion, give it but the name of parts, separate it into degrees and sections, and like the magician's coin, the valueless gold of the mine, is tuned to vilest substance. There is a meaning in the eye of love; a cadence in its voice, an irradiation in its smile, the talisman of whose enchantments one only can possess; its spirit is elemental, its essence single, its divinity an unit. (93)[29]

Perdita cannot tolerate living the sham of a lost love and finally determines to leave Raymond. But when she hears that he has been wounded in battle, her never-wavering passion for him carries her to Greece, where she both nurses him back to health and, when he is accidentally killed by a falling temple during his final attack on Constantinople, determines to die and be buried in his tomb rather than live without him in England.

Perdita thus embodies Mary Shelley's own passion for her husband, which she here projects as both constant and finally self-destructive. For without Raymond, Perdita cannot survive. Not even her daughter Clara can bind her to life. Through Perdita's suicide by drowning, Mary Shelley imaginatively realizes her own guilt-ridden need for atonement. Perdita's death is a displacement of Mary's desire to rejoin the dead Percy, a desire obsessively reiterated in her letters and Journal.[30] But Perdita's death also embodies Mary Shelley's recognition that the gender-determined role of devoted wife within the bourgeois family is inherently suicidal: the wife submerges her identity into that of her husband, sacrificing her self to his welfare.

Mary Shelley's second self-projection in the novel, Idris, is portrayed above all as a mother. She is a shadowy figure, so idealized in her high-born beauty, sensitivity, and loyalty as to be almost an abstraction of female perfection. The blessed love between Idris and Lionel Verney is frequently asserted but rarely described, perhaps because Lionel Verney is another projection of Mary Shelley and she found it difficult to give substance to a love-affair with herself. Idris becomes a rounded character only in her relationships with her children. Here she embodies Shelley's experience as a mother: "Idris, the most affectionate wife, sister and friend, was a tender and loving mother. The feeling was not with her as with many, a pastime; it was a passion." (163) When her second child dies of fever, her "triumphant and rapturous emotions of maternity" are dashed "with grief and fear" (163). Ever after, Idris is filled with a pervasive and unremitting anxiety for the welfare of her remaining two sons. As the plague advances, she is slowly destroyed by this anxiety: "she compared this gnawing of sleepless expectation of evil to the vulture that fed on the heart of Prometheus" (219). When her oldest son Alfred dies of the plague, Idris—debilitated by long nervous fear and a hysterical search in a cold winter storm for Verney and a doctor—soon succumbs to pneumonia. In Idris Mary Shelley projects both her own obsessive grief for her dead Clara Everina and William (the death of Verney's last son, Evelyn, is a detailed description of William Shelley's death from malaria [316–17]) and her enduring and excessive anxiety for the health of her only surviving child, Percy Florence, for whose sake alone she claimed to continue living.[31] By implying that such maternal suffering is as intense and unending as that of Prometheus, Mary

Shelley underlines the heroic but self-destructive dimensions of motherhood. Because Idris identifies so closely with her children, she has no life of her own—her sons' deaths annihilate her as well.

In this novel, women can find fulfillment neither within the family nor outside it. In contrast to Perdita and Idris who define themselves entirely as wives and mothers, the Countess of Windsor has strong political ambitions—she wishes to restore the monarchy and rule over England. But she is defeated by her gender. The English would never accept her, a foreign woman, as monarch. Hence she must channel her ambitions through her son, or her daughter's husband. Blocked by her husband's decision to abdicate, by her son's republicanism, by her daughter's rejection of a suitably highborn match, by Raymond's own desire to marry Perdita, she can never achieve her desires. After her daughter's death, she acknowledges that her ambition has been both futile and counterproductive, cutting her off from the love and nurturance of her children. While Mary Shelley makes it clear that the Countess of Windsor would have been a tyrannical ruler, no different from Castruccio, she also suggests that a woman cannot even gain access to the corridors of political power. The Countess is significantly absent from the Parliamentary debates concerning the Protectorship.

Mary Shelley's portraits of the Countess of Windsor, Perdita, and Idris all convey her belief that, in the future world (the novel is set in 2073–2100) as well as the present, a rigid division of sex-roles denies to women a fully satisfying life. In the public realm, her female characters depend on and serve men, either to realize their own political ambitions, as does the Countess of Windsor, or to function socially as hostess and wife, as does Perdita. As Perdita cries:

> He . . . can be great and happy without me. Would that I also had a career! Would that I could freight some untried bark with all my hopes, energies, and desires, and launch it forth into the ocean of life—bound for some attainable point, with ambition or pleasure at the helm! But adverse winds detain me on shore. (117)

Again in the private domestic realm, her women depend on others to satisfy their emotional needs, whether their husbands or their children. As Perdita explains the nature of woman's love to her brother:

> Lionel, you cannot understand what women's love is. . . . [Raymond] gave me an illustrious name and noble station; the world's respect reflected from his own glory: all this joined to his own undying love, inspired me with sensations towards him, akin to those with which we regard the Giver of life. I gave him love only. I devoted myself to him: imperfect creature that I was, I took myself to task, that I might

become worthy of him. I watched over my hasty temper, subdued my burning impatience of character, schooled my self-engrossing thoughts, educating myself to the best perfection I might attain, that the fruit of my exertions might be his happiness. I took no merit to myself for this. He deserved it all— ... I was ready to quit you all, my beloved and gifted companions, and to live only with him for him. I could not do otherwise, even if I had wished; for if we are said to have two souls, he was my better soul, to which the other was perpetual slave. (103–4)[32]

In both the public and the private spheres depicted in *The Last Man*, women have only a *relational* identity, as wife or mother. They are never self-centered or self-sufficient. And while this relational identity can contribute to the welfare and survival of the family, it is also extremely precarious. It is easily destroyed by human infidelity (the betrayal of Raymond) or the greater power that rules over all human experience, that of Chance, Accident, and Death. Mary Shelley here undermines her ideology of the family by acknowledging that it confines and eventually even destroys the women who enact it.

This pessimistic assessment of the future of the family is summed up in the fate of Clara, the ideal daughter and projected self that Mary desired.[33] An orphan, matured beyond her years by suffering, Clara is sensitive, loving, intelligent, and inspired with a passionate interest in philosophy and literature. She is devoted to her uncle and his family and functions as a second mother to her younger cousins. Lionel cherishes her as a daughter and when only she and his infant son Evelyn are left to him, he vows to devote his life to their happiness. But at the age of puberty, the amiable Clara—whose inner life has hitherto been hidden from us—suddenly changes:

> She lost her gaiety, she laid aside her sports, and assumed an almost vestal plainness of attire. She shunned us, retiring with Evelyn to some distant chamber or silent nook; nor did she enter into his pastimes with the same zest as she was wont, but would sit and watch with sadly tender smiles, and eyes bright with tears, yet without a word of complaint. She approached us timidly, avoided our caresses, nor shook off her embarrassment till some serious discussion or lofty theme called her for awhile out of herself. (315)

Clara's transformation is never explained, but we can speculate as to its source. With her dawning sexuality, Clara may have realized that her future—and the future of the human race—demanded from her a sexual liaison and motherhood. Her choice of mates is restricted to an incestuous union with her uncle/father Lionel or her infant cousin (until Evelyn also dies of typhus fever), or a more legitimate union with

Adrian. Her inability to contemplate the latter with pleasure is final testimony to Mary Shelley's ambivalence toward Percy. She cannot imagine a perfect harmony between Adrian and a woman, not even her ideal future self. Significantly, our last glimpse of Clara is of the half-drowned virgin clasped to Adrian's breast: "The lightning showed me the poor girl half buried in the water at the bottom of the boat; as she was sinking in it Adrian caught her up, and sustained her in his arms." (323) But Adrian cannot keep her. When Lionel last sees Adrian, he is alone, clinging to an oar, overwhelmed by the surging water. Adrian can sustain neither Clara nor himself. Perhaps it was Clara's unconscious recognition of Adrian's inability to love her with sufficient commitment that urged her to a union not with the living but the dead. Despite the idyllic weeks she shared with Lionel and Adrian in Italy, on the Brenta and in Venice, Clara yearns to visit her parents' graves. It is the very urgency of her desire that drives them on their fatal voyage. Clara finally feels more bonded to the dead than to the living. Her death is Mary Shelley's final comment on the future possibility of female fulfillment and even survival within a family to which men do not make an equal commitment.

The only alternative that Mary Shelley presents in *The Last Man* to this female experience of dependency and self-destruction within the family is a stoical solipsism rendered endurable only by an escapist imagination. We need to look closely at Mary Shelley's depiction of the value and limitations of the poetic imagination here, for this novel presents an even more devastating critique of the Romantic ideology than does *Frankenstein*. Having lost his family, Lionel Verney becomes a writer, the narrator of the tale we read.

We have always known that the last man, Lionel Verney, is actually the last woman, Mary Shelley—she so identified herself in her Journal on May 14, 1824:

> The last man! Yes, I may well describe that solitary being's feelings, feeling myself as the last relic of a beloved race, my companions extinct before me.[34]

Throughout the novel, Mary Shelley draws parallels between Lionel Verney's situation and her own. Both were "outcasts" in childhood; both possessed a scholarly temperament, a literary imagination, and a preference for domestic pleasures and affections; both were in love with Adrian/Shelley and credited him with their salvation from intellectual ignorance and emotional misery. Both find themselves at last enduring an almost unimaginable experience of isolation and loneliness. As Mary Shelley recorded in her Journal:

> At the age of seven-and-twenty, in the busy metropolis of native England, I find myself alone, deserted by the few I knew, disdained, insulted ... (December 3, 1824)
>
> Here I am again—here—alone—truly—most truly alone—for it is not only that I rise to solitude and, spending a lonely day, commune only with my melancholy self—but to my corroding cares—to the many evils of my situation & my sad disappointments, I have no solace or support of any kind. I am sick of myself.... My head aches. My heart—my hapless heart—is deluged in bitterness.... I strive to study, I strive to write, but I cannot live without loving and being loved, without sympathy; if this is denied to me, I must die. Would that the hour were come! (September 5, 1826)[35]

When Lionel Verney is finally deprived of all human companionship, he turns—like Mary Shelley herself—to creative composition for comfort. As she began *The Last Man* she recorded her rare pleasure: "I feel my powers again, and this is, of itself, happiness; the eclipse of winter is passing from my mind. I shall again feel the enthusiastic glow of composition; again, as I pour forth my soul upon paper, feel the winged ideas arise, and enjoy the delight of expressing them."[36] Inspired by the monuments of Rome and a desire to celebrate the "matchless specimens of humanity" that created such grandeur, Lionel Verney determines to write an account of the plague and the annihilation of mankind.

Significantly, he consciously works within a female literary tradition, invoking both Ann Radcliffe's *The Italian* and Madame de Staël's *Corinne* in his imaginative appropriation of Rome (336). But Lionel Verney also encodes the literary archetypes of male isolation: Charles Brockden Brown's egocentric Arthur Mervyn, the dying Macbeth, the stranded Robinson Crusoe, the guilt-ridden and blasted Ancient Mariner (187, 203, 326, 340). In contrast to such prototypes, Lionel Verney cannot even hope for human communication. He can dedicate his tale only to "the illustrious dead" (339).

Explicit in Mary Shelley's account of the last man is the assertion that her tale has no living readership, no audience. That this unread tale is written by a woman rather than a man is documented in the "Author's Introduction," where Mary Shelley tells us that she has functioned as the editor of the fragmentary leaves of a prophecy found in the cave of the Cumaean Sibyl. Mary Shelley thus invokes the ultimate female literary authority, the oracle of the Sibyl, to authenticate her prophetic vision. But even as she constructs a female literary tradition, from the Sibyl through her own editorship, she terminates that tradition. Her novel posits the end of writing as such: it is a manuscript left on the tombs of Rome for no one to read by a writer who has abandoned authorship in order to voyage aimlessly, an ancient mariner encountering no wedding-guest but only life-in-death. Finally, Mary Shelley implies, the female writer—like Lionel Verney—will not be read, her voice will not be heard, her discourse will be silenced forever.

Moreover, Shelley suggests that the products of the creative imagination so glorified by the Romantic poets may be worthless. At best their consolation is temporary, if delusive, as Verney finds when he enters Constantinople, seeking the already dead Raymond: "For a moment I could yield to the creative power of the imagination, and for a moment was soothed by the sublime fictions it presented to me. The beatings of my human heart drew me back to blank reality" (145). Insubstantial dreams in themselves, at worst they become "tales of sound and fury, signifying nothing" when they can reach no living ear or mind. Here the skeptical version of the idealist epistemology that underpins both *The Last Man* and *Frankenstein* becomes visible. If to be is to be perceived, if the human mind can never know the thing in itself but only its linguistic constructions of it, then reality exists only in the collective minds of all perceivers. As Percy Shelley had put it in "Mont Blanc," "The everlasting universe of things / Flows through the mind." But unlike Bishop Berkeley or her husband, Mary Shelley posits no overarching mind of God, no eternal Power, no transcendental subject, to guarantee the truth or endurance of mental things. Once all human perceivers are dead, history ends. The death of the last man is the death of consciousness. It is moreover the death of the universe, since the Cumaean Sibyl prophesies a point in the future, "2100 Last Year of the World," when time and space—as experienced duration and extension—terminate. Since reality is a set of language systems, the death of Lionel Verney is the death of narration, the final period. This is Mary Shelley's sweeping critique of the Romantic poetic ideology: the constructions of the imagination cannot transcend the human mind, which is inherently finite, mutable, and mortal.

Engendered by Mary Shelley's personal despair and "constitutional pessimism,"[37] *The Last Man* generates from this radical skeptical standpoint a social and political critique of farreaching significance. We have already seen how the novel pits Mary Shelley's ideology of the family against those forces which here triumph over it: the forces of male egotism, female masochism, and plague-induced death. In undermining the family as the preserver of cultural value and social stability, Shelley does more than undercut her own ideology. She also reveals the failures of the dominant political ideologies of her day—both radical (republican or democratic) and conservative (monarchical). Finally she denies the authority of all ideologies, all systems of belief.

As Lee Sterrenburg has observed, *The Last Man* functions as an anatomy of political revolution and gradual reform after the defeat of Napoleon in 1815.[38] By 1825, the possibility that a violent political revolution could produce either immediate or long-term political reform seemed increasingly unlikely. The republican ideals of the French Revolution, as well as the Rousseauistic faith that political revolutions were a necessary and natural bloodletting capable of restoring a diseased body-politic to health, had been undermined by the brutalities of both the Terror and Napoleon's imperial campaigns. And the romantic notion that the beauty of nature could offer an adequate compensation for political disappointments had been rejected as socially irresponsible by even its most ardent English proponents, Wordsworth and Coleridge. The conservative belief in a divinely ordained monarchy and a hierarchically ordered and gradually evolving social system modelled on the feudal family and troped as a great chain of being had been permanently weakened by the rise of capitalism, the growing strength of the bourgeoisie, and the intellectual appeal of a meritocracy. In the decades following the defeat of Napoleon, a widespread postrevolutionary despair was articulated in many artistic depictions of the apocalyptic ending of human history.[39] It is within this cultural context that Mary Shelley's *The Last Man* puts forth a particularly devastating critique of the range of political options still available.

Godwin's and Percy Shelley's conviction that mankind might be perfected through the improvement of reason and love under a democratic government is tested in *The Last Man* through the actions both of Ryland, the leader of the people's party, and of Adrian, the ardent espouser of republican principles. Ryland, whose appearance and character are based on those of the radical British journalist and politician William Cobbett,[40] eloquently defends the rights of the common man against Lord Raymond's attempts to restore the monarchy:

> Ryland began by praising the present state of the British empire [under the republican government initiated in 2073]. He recalled past years to their memory; the miserable contentions which in the time of our fathers arose almost to civil war, the abdication of the late king, and the foundation of the republic. He described this republic; shewed how it gave privilege to each individual in the state, to rise to consequence, and even to temporary sovereignty. He compared the royal and republican spirit; shewed how the one tended to enslave the minds of men; while all the institutions of the other served to

raise even the meanest among us to something great and good. He shewed how England had become powerful, and its inhabitants valiant and wise, by means of the freedom they enjoyed. As he spoke, every heart swelled with pride, and every cheek glowed with delight to remember, that each one there was English, and that each supported and contributed to the happy state of things now commemorated. (41–42)

But equal freedoms mean equal responsibilities, sacrifices, and limitations. In the period of economic expansion celebrated by Ryland, an egalitarian society can provide adequately for all its members. But in a time of scarcity, of restricted resources, all must be equally deprived. Mary Shelley subtly reveals the inability of Ryland's democratic ideology to confront the necessity to distribute equally the burden of disaster. When the limited resource is life itself, freedom from the plague, who is to be saved? At first the wealthier members of English society willingly share their land and goods with the refugees fleeing from the plague in Europe:

The high-born ladies . . . would have deemed themselves disgraced if they had now enjoyed, what they before called a necessary, the ease of a carriage. . . . . It was more common, for all who possessed landed property to secede to their estates, attended by whole troops of the indigent, to cut down their woods to erect temporary dwellings, and to portion out their parks, parterres and flower-gardens, to necessitous families. Many of these, of high rank in their own countries, now, with hoe in hand, turned up the soil. (172)

While the plague thus completes the process of social levelling advocated by a democratic ideology, it also demands that all must die equally. When confronted with the brute reality that in a classless society, all must suffer as well as benefit equally, Ryland immediately abdicates the Lord Protectorship. In order to protect himself from the contagion of his countrymen, he barricades himself within his northern estate in a futile attempt to preserve his own life. Ryland's frantic abdication of political responsibility is Mary Shelley's skeptical view of the excessive optimism inherent in a democratic ideology: a socialist government perhaps succeeds only if there is enough for every individual. In a scarcity economy, the equal distribution of resources may not be the best way to protect and preserve the human race.

Inherent in Godwin's and Percy Shelley's political ideology were more extreme utopian concepts that Mary Shelley's novel specifically calls into question. Adrian repeats the visionary ideas that Godwin had propounded in *Political Justice* (1793) and that Percy Shelley had endorsed in *Prometheus Unbound*: the conviction that the improved powers of the rational mind could conquer disease and even death. As Godwin argued, "We are sick and we die ... because we consent to suffer these accidents." When the rational mind has reached its full powers, Godwin claimed, "there will be no disease, no anguish, no melancholy and no resentment." At that point, he speculated, man "will perhaps be immortal."[41] Or as Percy Shelley put it in *Prometheus Unbound*:

> Gentleness, Virtue, Wisdom, and Endurance,
> These are the seals of that most firm assurance
>   Which bars the pit over Destruction's strength;
> And if, with infirm hand, Eternity,
> Mother of many acts and hours, should free
>   The serpent that would clasp her with his length;
> These are the spells by which to reassume
> An empire o'er the disentangled doom.
> . . . .
> ... This, like thy glory, Titan, is to be
> Good, great and joyous, beautiful and free;
> This is alone Life, Joy, Empire, and Victory.
>   (IV:562–69, 577–79)

Adrian endorses these utopian beliefs when he cries out to Verney:

> Look into the mind of man, where wisdom reigns enthroned; ... [and] Love, and her child, Hope, which can bestow wealth on poverty, strength on the weak, and happiness on the sorrowing. ...
>   Oh, that death and sickness were banished from our earthly home! that hatred, tyranny, and fear could no longer make their lair in the human heart! ... The choice is with us; let us will it, and our habitation becomes a paradise. For the will of man is omnipotent, blunting the arrows of death, soothing the bed of disease, and wiping away the tears of agony. (53–54)

But Mary Shelley shows that the powers of the human mind are feeble in comparison to those of all-controlling nature. In her novel, no one can determine the cause, the mode of transmission, or the cure of the fatal plague that sweeps across the earth. As Sterrenburg concludes, "utopian hopes prove futile in *The Last Man* because nature is impervious to human will and human rationality."[42]

But even as Mary Shelley criticizes the utopian idealism of her father and husband, she also undercuts the conservative political ideology articulated by Edmund Burke. Initially she invokes Burke's arguments for a constitutional monarchy and a traditional class-system with approval, assigning them both to the successful politician Lord Raymond and to her own authorial spokesman, Lionel Verney.

Raymond gains the Protectorship by his persuasive condemnation of the "commercial spirit of republicanism, . . . [of] a bartering, timorous commonwealth" (43). He then institutes a benevolent reign in which he markedly improves the social and cultural condition of England. And Lionel Verney, gazing on the playing fields of Eton, hails "the future governors of England":

> the men, who, when our ardour was cold, and our projects completed or destroyed for ever, when, our drama acted, we doffed the garb of the hour, and assumed the uniform of age, or of more equalizing death; here were the beings who were to carry on the vast machine of society. . . . thus man remains, while we the individuals pass away.

Verney here explicitly endorses Burke's view in *Reflections on the French Revolution* that "the human race, the whole, at one time, is never old, or middle-aged, or young, but, in a condition of unchangeable constancy, moves on through the varied tenour of perpetual decay, fall, renovation, and progression." (165) Mary Shelley clearly has more sympathy for Edmund Burke's vision of an organic society developing naturally toward an ever-higher form of being, guided by enlightened and benevolent rulers who institute gradual reforms in pragmatically effective ways, than she has for the impractical, visionary utopianism of Godwin and Percy Shelley.

Nonetheless, she recognizes that Burke's conservative ideology also rests on a heuristic fiction, a trope: the image of the body politic as a natural organism. If society is an organism, then it is subject to disease. Burke had himself defined this disease as the "plague" of revolution currently festering in France, a plague which "the precautions of the most severe quarantine ought to be established against" lest it infect that "course of succession [which] is the healthy habit of the British constitution."[43] Mary Shelley takes Burke's metaphor literally. Even the healthy British constitution cannot long resist the ravages of a deadly plague that can be neither confined nor cured. Finally, all organisms, both individual and social, are subject to the overriding power of Nature, Chance, and Accident. The body politic can die as well as grow.

In taking Burke's metaphor of the plague literally, Mary Shelley participates in a figurative practice which Margaret Homans has perceptively identified as characteristic of the female Gothic tradition. In a patriarchal culture where women are identified with nature, with the object or thing in itself, women writers are apt to blur the distinction between the literal and the figurative. They can thereby assert their own identities as subjects by both literalizing the metaphoric and troping the literal. As Homans comments:

> It could be that women write the Gothic, where all sorts of
> literalizations occur, not because Nietzsche was in some way right
> that they are incapable of any liberating transcendence, but because
> they have been excluded from it and must continually confront and
> defend against accepting that exclusion.[44]

Mary Shelley assumes that consciousness functions entirely within a
linguistic universe in which the figural and the literal are but differing
signs or linguistic markers. The plague is thus both literal and
metaphorical. Her radical epistemological skepticism forces her to
insist upon the fictiveness and temporality of all imaginative constructs.
It also forces her to fuse the literal and the figurative in one continuous
language system. Since in her view, conscious experience occurs only
within the prison-house of language, the destruction of language—or
all language-speakers and recorded texts—is the destruction of human
life. Her plague is the narrative sign for all the forces that work against
the survival of human life, both the physical (literal) and the mental
(figurative).

In the place of the metaphor put forth by both Godwin and Burke of
history as progress toward perfection, Mary Shelley offers the
metaphor of human history as motion that can suddenly stop. By the
end of her novel, only one human being remains alive on earth. She
thus introduces a powerful trope that in recent years has increasingly
dominated our cultural consciousness: the trope of history as a
narrative that reaches an abrupt and final conclusion, whether by
biological epidemic (AIDS, cancer), chemical warfare, invasion from
outer space, or nuclear holocaust. Since this metaphor denies ultimate
significance to all human events, Shelley's novel is on the deepest level
anti-political and anti-ideological. She suggests that all conceptions of
human history, all ideologies, are grounded on metaphors or tropes
which have no referent or authority outside of language.

When Mary Shelley establishes nature as the final arbiter of human
destiny in *The Last Man*, she directly challenges two fundamental
romantic assumptions that had supported her own ideology in
Frankenstein: the beliefs that nature can be the source of moral
authority and that the human mind can create meanings of permanent
value. Wordsworth, at a climactic moment of high rhetorical
confidence, had argued that the mighty minds of nature and of man
worked in harmony, and that the "higher minds" of the most
imaginative poets derived from this "communion with the invisible
world" a full comprehension of the meaning of human experience, for

hence came "religion, faith, / And endless occupation for the soul / . . . sovereignty within and peace at will, / . . . cheerfulness in every act of life / . . . truth in moral judgments and delight / That fails not in the external universe" (*Prelude*, 1805, XIII:111–19). Wordsworth's precarious vision rested on a teleological paradigm of the development of human consciousness from a primal unity with nature through a phase of alienation and isolated self-consciousness to a higher consciousness of the workings of the philosophic mind as a dimension of the workings of nature.

Mary Shelley explicitly denies this paradigm of natural supernaturalism by portraying the "child of nature," her orphaned narrator Lionel Verney, as an aggressive, embittered outcast, somewhat like her earlier rejected monster in *Frankenstein*. Deliberately alluding to Wordsworth's celebrations of the life of the shepherd, Mary Shelley's Cumberland sheep boy is hardly more than a savage whose only law "was that of the strongest" and whose only concept of virtue "was never to submit" (9). As Verney concludes:

> I cannot say much in praise of such a life; and its pains far exceeded its pleasures. There was freedom in it, a companionship with nature, and a reckless loneliness; but these, romantic as they were, did not accord with the love of action and desire of human sympathy, characteristic of youth. (8)

Verney eagerly abandons his brutal shepherd life to participate in the social pleasures offered by Adrian—friendship, learning, gamesmanship, military struggle, and politics. But in Verney's case, all such social interactions finally terminate in the destructions of the plague. He ends in the solitude in which he began, but worse, since he has learned to appreciate the value of those social relationships which he can never know again.

Mary Shelley not only reverses the Wordsworthian model of the growth of the mind, as Hugh Luke has observed.[45] She also undercuts the romantic concept that nature can be a source of cultural meaning. For insofar as nature is the *Ding-an-sich* or thing in itself, by definition it exists outside of language or the phenomenological consciousness of human beings. Thus it can never enter into language, can never authorize systems of cultural meaning. As Homans has rightly observed:

> That we might have access to some original and final ground of meaning is a necessary illusion that empowers acts of figuration; at the same time, literal meaning would hypothetically be fatal to any

text it actually entered, collapsing it by making superfluous those very figures, and even all language acts.[46]

But we must go one step further than Homans does and recognize that the "literal" itself, insofar as it is a linguistic construction or sign, is necessarily figurative.

The nature troped in *The Last Man* is closer to Tennyson's image of "Nature . . . red in tooth and claw" than to Mary Shelley's earlier figuring of nature in *Frankenstein* as a sacred life-force and nurturing mother. In a passage that explicitly refutes Percy Shelley's invocation of the west wind as both destroyer *and* preserver, Lionel Verney addresses the power of nature:

> Then mighty art thou, O wind, to be throned above all other viceregents of nature's power; whether thou comest destroying from the east, or pregnant with elementary life from the west; thee the clouds obey; the sun is subservient to thee; the shoreless ocean is thy slave!
>
> . . . Why dost thou howl thus, O wind? . . . alas, what will become of us? . . .
>
> What are we, the inhabitants of this globe, least among the many that people infinite space? Our minds embrace infinity; the visible mechanism of our being is subject to merest accident. Day by day we are forced to believe this. He whom a scratch has disorganized, he who disappears from apparent life under the influence of the hostile agency at work around us, had the same powers as I—I also am subject to the same laws. In the face of all this we call ourselves lords of the creation, wielders of the elements, masters of life and death, and we allege in excuse of this arrogance, that though the individual is destroyed, man continues for ever.
>
> Thus, losing our identity, that of which we are chiefly conscious, we glory in the continuity of our species, and learn to regard death without terror. But when any whole nation becomes the victim of the destructive powers of exterior agents, then indeed man shrinks into insignificance, he feels his tenure of life insecure, his inheritance on earth cut off. (166–67)

In this central passage, Mary Shelley undercuts the political ideologies of both Godwin and Burke. More important, she moves beyond the poetic theories of Wordsworth and Percy Shelley which assume that language constructs and communicates meaning. If the human race can be eliminated, as it is in her novel, then the very concept of meaning is, finally, meaningless. Where human discourse cannot occur, linguistically constituted meaning cannot exist and human consciousness is annihilated.

Significantly, Mary Shelley sets the final scene of the plague's devastation on the very banks of the Arve where Percy Shelley wrote

"Mont Blanc" and raised the epistemological question whether the universe could have a meaning not constituted by human thought:

> And what were thou, and earth, and stars, and sea,
> If to the human mind's imaginings
> Silence and solitude were vacancy?
>
> ("Mont Blanc," 142–45)

As Adrian and his few remaining followers cross into Switzerland, they are suddenly confronted with one of nature's most sublime landscapes:

> Below ... lay the placid and azure expanse of lake Leman; ... But beyond, and high above all, as if the spirits of the air had suddenly unveiled their bright abodes, placed in scaleless altitude in the stainless sky, heaven-kissing, companions of the unattainable ether, were the glorious Alps, clothed in dazzling robes of light by the setting sun. And, as if the world's wonders were never to be exhausted, their vast immensities, their jagged crags, and roseate painting, appeared again in the lake below, dipping their proud heights beneath the unruffled waves—palaces for the Naiads of the placid waters. (305)

Adrian's followers, overcome by the sheer grandeur of nature's beauty, are moved beyond tears. One cried out: "God reveals his heaven to us; we may die blessed." But Mary Shelley's invocations of both pagan Naiads and Christian heavens serve only to highlight the fact that no deity presides over this plague, only an indifferent nature. Human attempts to interpret their experiences in terms of an ontological moral force or a providential design are here rendered nugatory.

This perception is sharpened by a sudden surge of music among the Alps—"the language of the immortals, disclosed to us as testimony of their existence" (306). Seeking its source, Verney discovers a young woman playing Haydn's "New Created World" on a cathedral organ while her blind old father listens beside her. In the world of *The Last Man*, a new-created world exists only in Haydn's imagination. The only comfort humanity can find must be in fictions that human beings themselves create.

Mary Shelley's conception of the last man is thus in deliberate contrast to the other early nineteenth-century treatments of the last man theme, all of which used the trope of the end of civilization to point either an ethical or a religious moral.[47] Byron's "Darkness" (itself derived from Pope's vision of chaotic night in "The Dunciad") and Thomas Hood's "The Last Man" (1826) had satirized mankind's innate greed, aggression, and cowardice, which would compel even the last two men on earth to turn against each other. In a more religious vein, the visual depictions of the Deluge and the Last Man by Philippe de Loutherbourg and John Martin, Cousin de Grainville's novel *The Last Man: or, Omegarius and Syderia, A Romance in Futurity* (trans. 1806), and Thomas Campbell's poem "The Last Man" (first published in 1823 and probably the immediate inspiration for Mary Shelley's May 14, 1824 Journal entry and title) all invoke a Christian framework and the possibility of a finer life elsewhere, whether on earth or in heaven. Campbell's last man triumphantly defies both darkness and death because he knows "This spirit shall return to Him / That gave its heavenly spark" and "robb'd the grave of Victory,— / And took the sting from Death!" (61–62, 69–70). But Mary Shelley explicitly denies a religious interpretation of her plague. The illiterate who insists that the plague is God's punishment for human sin and that he and his followers constitute an "Elect" that will be saved is explicitly condemned as an "Imposter" whose deceived followers perish along with everyone else.

And her intentions go far beyond satire. By quoting her portraits of Father De Lacey and Agatha in the blind old man and his music-playing daughter, Mary Shelley deliberately undercuts the ideology of the egalitarian bourgeois family that sustained *Frankenstein*. Implicit in *Frankenstein* was a belief in the primacy of the domestic affections and in the restorative power of a maternal, "beautiful" nature. But in *The Last Man*, all pastoral idylls—whether set among the woods of Windsor or on the shores of Lake Como—are abruptly shattered by the advent of the plague. Even though nature continues to provide scenes of both sublime grandeur and beautiful delight that pleasure the human senses, she remains indifferent to the preservation of human life.

Therefore all human values must, like Haydn's music, be engendered out of the human imagination. But such values, including the value of the domestic affections that Lionel Verney celebrates throughout *The Last Man*, finally depend entirely on individual commitment. And since individuals are mutable, often unable to control their passions (as in the case of Lord Raymond) and always unable to control their final destiny, such values are necessarily temporal and mutable. As Verney says at the very beginning of his tale, "My fortunes have been . . . an exemplification of the power that mutability may posssess over the varied tenor of man's life" (5). Mary Shelley's novel recognizes only one controlling Power—not Percy Shelley's Necessity, but Mutability.

Mary Shelley's skepticism thus cuts through the fabric, not only of her own ideology of the egalitarian family and a sacred mother nature, but of *all* ideologies. The domestic affections can be sustained only by individual human beings, but those human beings are inherently mutable and mortal. Nature offers scenes of beauty, but such scenes only mock the human conviction that nature never did betray the heart that loved her. A romantic ideology that grounds cultural meaning in the creations of the imagination or a dialectically developing phenomenological consciousness is destroyed by the disappearance of the human mind itself.

The Last Man thus opens the way to twentieth-century existentialism and nihilism.[48] Like Camus's *The Plague*, it asserts that all meaning resides, not in an indifferent universe, but in human relationships and language-systems which are inherently temporal and doomed to end. Further, *The Last Man* initiates the modern tradition of literary deconstruction. It is the first work to demonstrate that all cultural ideologies rest on nonreferential tropes, tropes written as literal but nonetheless inherently figural, tropes as arbitrarily motivated and mutable as the mortal mind. But as the author of the first fictional example of nihilism, Mary Shelley expresses the emotional desolation that such philosophical conviction brings as has no writer since.

That this experience of emotional and intellectual despair was first voiced by a woman is, I think, no accident. For Mary Shelley had been taught to conceive of her self only in relational terms, as a daughter/wife/mother. As she told Robert Dale Owen in 1827, referring to the powerful feminist Frances Wright:

> Do not imagine that she is capable always of taking care of herself:—she is certainly more than any woman, but we have all in us—& she is too sensitive & feminine not largely to partake in this inherent part of us—a desire to find a manly spirit where on [to] lean—a manly arm to protect & shelter us.[49]

Lacking a firm conviction in her own ego, grounding her identity entirely on her relationships with others, Mary Shelley was acutely aware of the fragility and temporality of those very relationships and acts of engagement through which ideological meaning can alone be represented and sustained.

CHAPTER NINE

Revising *Frankenstein*

By the time Mary Shelley revised *Frankenstein* for republication in Colburn and Bentley's Standard Novels Series in 1831, her philosophical views had changed radically.[1] The 1831 *Frankenstein* is as different from the 1818 *Frankenstein* as Wordsworth's 1850 *Prelude* is different from his 1805 version, and in somewhat the same ways. By 1831, the deaths of her second daughter, her son William, and her husband, followed by Bryon's death and Jane Williams's betrayal of her friendship—together with her financially straightened circumstances and her guilt-ridden and unshakeable despair—all convinced Mary Shelley that human events are decided not by personal choice or free will but by material forces beyond our control. As she confessed to Jane Williams Hogg in August, 1827:

> The power of Destiny I feel every day pressing more & more on me, & I yield myself a slave to it, in all except my moods of mind, which I endeavour to make independant of her, & thus to wreathe a chaplet, where all is not cypress, in spite of the Eumenides.[2]

The biographical origin of her new vision of nature's relationship to humanity is registered in the novel itself. Elizabeth Lavenza Frankenstein now dies, not at Coligny, but on the shores of Lake Como, the place where Mary and Percy Shelley had first sought a home when they returned to Italy in the spring of 1818. After 1822, Italy figures conflictingly in Mary Shelley's imagination as both the locus of radiant light and warmth and peace, a heavenly haven to which she nostalgically yearned to return, and as the site of youthful disillusion, the place where natural beauty is forever shadowed by relentless death.

Thus she described it in 1840 when she again visited the shores of Lake Como with her son Percy Florence:

> There I left the mortal remains of those beloved—my husband and my children, whose loss changed my whole existence, substituting, for happy peace and the interchange of deep-rooted affections, years of desolate solitude, and a hard struggle with the world; ...[3]

As Wordsworth put it in his "Elegiac Stanzas," "I have submitted to a new control / ... a deep distress hath humanised my Soul." In the midst of that desolate solitude, in 1831, Mary Shelley reshaped her horror story to reflect her pessimistic conviction that the universe is determined by a destiny blind to human needs or efforts. As in *The Last Man*, nature is no longer a supportive mother, but rather an indifferent power entirely capable of betraying the heart that loves her.

In 1818 Victor Frankenstein possessed free will or the capacity for meaningful moral choice—he could have abandoned his quest for the "principle of life," he could have cared for his creature, he could have protected Elizabeth. In 1831 such choice is denied to him. He is the pawn of forces beyond his knowledge or control.[4] Again and again, Mary Shelley reassigns human actions to chance or fate. By happenstance, lightning struck when a scientist was standing nearby to explain the nature of electricity and galvanism. By "one of those caprices of the mind" to which youth is peculiarly susceptible, Victor then gave up his interest in alchemy and instead turned to the study of mathematics. As he now comments:

> Thus strangely are our souls constructed, and by such slight ligaments are we bound to prosperity or ruin. When I look back, it seems to me as if this almost miraculous change of inclination and will was the immediate suggestion of the guardian angel of my life—the last effort made by the spirit of preservation to avert the storm that was even then hanging in the stars, and ready to envelope me. Her victory was announced by an unusual tranquillity and gladness of soul ...
>
> It was a strong effort of the spirit of good; but it was ineffectual. Destiny was too potent, and her immutable laws had decreed my utter and terrible destruction. (239)

His decision to return to the study of chemistry is now attributed to "Chance—or rather the evil influence, the Angel of Destruction" (24). The deaths of both William Frankenstein and Justine are portrayed by Victor as a curse ("the work of my thrice-accursed hands") imposed by "inexorable fate" (246).

Some readers might wish to argue that this rhetoric of fatalism was introduced to emphasize Victor Frankenstein's capacity for self-deception, rationalization, and self-serving attempts to win his audience's sympathy, rather than to express the author's own views. But the fact that the female characters also propound this new concept of destiny suggests otherwise. Elizabeth now claims that the routines of her peaceful life are governed by exterior forces: "The blue lake, and snow-clad mountains, they never change;—and I think our placid home, and our contented hearts are regulated by the same immutable laws" (243). And Justine envisions Heaven as a divine "will" to which we must "learn . . . to submit in patience" (246)

Mary Shelley thus replaces her earlier organic conception of nature with a mechanistic one. She now portrays nature as a mighty machine, a juggernaut, impelled by pure force. She turns directly to Percy Shelley's "Mont Blanc," borrowing for the first time his concept of Power or energy as the creator, preserver, and destroyer of all visible phenomena. Victor Frankenstein, alone like the poet of "Mont Blanc," visits the ravine of the Arve, and sees the very image of creation and destruction Percy Shelley had described:

> The immense mountains and precipices that overhung me on every side—the sound of the river raging among the rocks, and the dashing of the waterfalls around, spoke of a power mighty as Omnipotence—and I ceased to fear, or to bend before any being less almighty than that which had created and ruled the elements, here displayed in their most terrific guide. (248)

> I stood beside the sources of the Arveiron, which take their rise in a glacier, that with slow pace is advancing down from the summit of the hills, to barricade the valley. The abrupt sides of vast mountains were before me; the icy wall of the glacier overhung me; a few shattered pines were scattered around; and the solemn silence of the glorious presence-chamber of imperial Nature was broken only by the brawling waves, or the fall of some vast fragment, the thunder sound of the avalanche, or the cracking, reverberated along the mountains of the accumulated ice, which, through the silent working of immutable laws, was ever and anon rent and torn, as if it had been but a plaything in their hands. (249)

But where Percy Shelley, confronted with such Power—"the secret Strength of things / Which governs thought, and to the infinite dome / Of Heaven is as a law"—saw silence and solitude as a vacancy that might be peopled by the human mind's imaginings, Mary Shelley presents "the silent workings of immutable laws" as inexorable, beyond human control. She foreswears the positive sublime for the negative sublime. The landscape can manifest only the omnipotent, death-dealing power of "imperial" nature.

Human beings thus become "playthings," far weaker than mountains of ice, mere puppets in the hands of destiny. Mary Shelley adopts a behavioristic model of human nature. Human beings are, like nature itself, only machines manipulated by external forces. As Frankenstein describes his response to Professor Waldman's lecture, "one by one the various keys were touched which formed the mechanism of my being: chord after chord was sounded, and soon my mind was filled with one thought, one conception, one purpose (241)." Frankenstein is entirely passive: "My internal being was in a state of insurrection and turmoil; I felt that order would thence arise, but I had no power to produce it" (241). Even morally good human beings are but "creatures of an angelic nature and celestial mechanism" (255).

Since fate controls human destiny, Victor Frankenstein's downfall is caused not so much by his own "presumption and rash ignorance" (245) as by bad influences. Frankenstein's curiosity about the workings of nature is presented as innocent and healthy. It is accidentally perverted by his reading of Cornelius Agrippa. His father, who "was not scientific" (238), was unable to explain Agrippa's errors—Mary Shelley removed the suggestion that Alphonse Frankenstein willfully "neglected" to educate his son on this occasion (32.25–28). And Professor Waldman, who now functions as a kind of Mephistopheles, tempts his student's innocent thirst for knowledge with "words of fate, enounced to destroy me. As he went on, I felt as if my soul were grappling with a palpable enemy" (241). Frankenstein can therefore not be held entirely responsible for his actions; an arrow shot by a devil has poisoned him. As he insists, he is "encompassed by a cloud which no beneficial influence could penetrate. The wounded deer dragging its fainting limbs to some untrodden brake, there to gaze upon the arrow which had pierced it, and to die—was but a type of me" (247)

Frankenstein's sin is no longer identified at least in part with his failure to love and take responsibility for his creature. Rather, it is his initial decision to construct a human being that is his only error. Even before the creature is born, while doing the experiments now described as an "unearthly occupation" (252), Frankenstein "shunned my fellow-creatures as if I had been guilty of a crime" (242). His scientific experiments as such, involving "harrowing sensations" and the total loss of "self-command" (252), become "unhallowed arts" (247). Frankenstein even suggests that the creature's evil acts may be the result of a predestined moral nature—"the monstrous Image, which I had endued with the mockery of a soul still more monstrous" (255)

Not only is Victor Frankenstein held less responsible for his actions, but his actions are presented more positively. Although he still abandons his creature in callous horror, he is moved to create a female creature both by his aroused sense of obligation to his Adam and by a new and passionate desire to "save" his family, whom he "loved . . . to adoration" (252). His failure to confess the existence of his monster is attributed not only to a self-serving pride ("My tale was not one to announce publicly; its astounding horror would be looked upon as madness by the vulgar" [245]), but also to a genuine wish to spare his father greater suffering: "I could not bring myself to disclose a secret which would fill my hearer with consternation, and make fear and unnatural horror the inmates of his breast" (256). To some degree the author has muted her criticisms of her protagonist in the 1831 text. Perhaps in deference to her dead husband and his reading of her novel, Mary Shelley now presents Victor Frankenstein more as a victim of circumstances than as the active author of evil.

Walton and Clerval, Frankenstein's alter-egos, are now portrayed in ways that reflect more positively on Frankenstein himself. Walton's similarity to Frankenstein is emphasized. "You are pursuing the same course, exposing yourself to the same dangers which have rendered me what I am," says Victor (232–33). Walton commits Frankenstein's hubristic error when he admits his Satanic willingness to sacrifice his crew to his own ambition. Both Walton and Frankenstein share the condition of Coleridge's Ancient Mariner. Despite Walton's claim that he will "kill no albatross . . . in the land of mist and snow" (15), both Walton and Frankenstein come to feel that they are living under a "ban" that deprives them of human "companionship" (252). But the allusion to the "Ancient Mariner" also suggests that Frankenstein's and Walton's crimes are unintentional, accidental.[5] Moreover, Walton's sin is balanced against a new remorse. Walton confesses that "it is terrible to reflect that the lives of all these men are endangered through me. If we were lost, my mad schemes are the cause" (258). Even the concept of friendship shared by these two men has developed from a desire merely to extend one's ego to a desire to improve one's self. As Victor responds to Walton, "I agree with you; . . . we are unfashioned creatures, but half made up, if one wiser, better, dearer than ourselves—such a friend ought to be—do not lend his aid to perfectionate our weak and faulty natures" (232).

Significantly, Clerval no longer appears in the novel as Frankenstein's better half, a moral touchstone against which we can clearly measure Frankenstein's failures. Frankenstein's desire for scientific knowledge is now presented as the counterpart of Clerval's desire for knowledge concerning "the moral relations of things" (237). Clerval is now equally ambitious for fame—"his hope and his dream was to become one among those whose names are recorded in story, as the gallant and adventurous benefactors of our species" (237). Above all, Clerval has become another Promethean figure. He defies his father's injunction against attending university: Clerval "said little; but when he spoke, I read in his kindling eye and in his animated glance a restrained but firm resolve, not to be chained to the miserable details of commerce" (240). He gains his father's consent, not through gentle persuasion, but through a harsher and more rebellious sarcasm; as he sneers, "all necessary knowledge [is] not comprised in the noble art of book-keeping" (242). Clerval now intends to become, not his father's partner, but a colonial imperialist, using his "mastery" of Oriental languages as Frankenstein uses his scientific instruments and Walton his crew, to dominate and exploit the resources of nature. Clerval "turned his eyes toward the East, as affording scope for his spirit of enterprise" (243–44), convinced that "he had in his knowledge of its various languages, and in the views he had taken of its society, the means of materially assisting the progress of European colonisation and trade" (253).

More important, Mary Shelley undercuts her earlier ideology of the loving, egalitarian family. Maternal love is strikingly associated with self-destruction when Caroline Beaufort intentionally sacrifices her life to nurse the infectious Elizabeth. The lengthened description of the Frankenstein marriage sets up an ideal of the domestic affections only to undercut it by identifying Caroline Beaufort as a "fair exotic" who requires to be "sheltered . . . from every rougher wind" (233–34), a time-consuming responsibility that leads Alphonse Frankenstein entirely to withdraw from public life. Their attentive nurturing of their oldest son still provides a striking contrast to Frankenstein's failuire to care for his creature:

> With the deep consciousness of what they owed towards the being to which they had given life, added to the active spirit of tenderness that animated both, it may be imagined that while during every hour of my infant life I received a lesson of patience, of charity, and of self-control, I was so guided by a silken cord, that all seemed but one train of enjoyment to me. (234)

But however negatively this passage reflects upon Victor, it also suggests that even the most devoted parental care cannot prevent pedagogical mistakes—in Victor's case, those caused by his father's ignorance.

Elizabeth Lavenza's place in the Frankenstein household is both more legitimate and more oppressed. No longer a blood-cousin, she is an orphan adopted by Caroline Frankenstein; no incestuous overtones accrue to her marriage to Victor. But she is now presented to Victor as a "present," a "gift" that is entirely his to cherish and possess (235). As such, he comes to regard her as his "more than sister" (235). By 1831, Elizabeth Lavenza has become the prototype of the Victorian "angel in the house." Victor describes her as "a being heaven-sent," "bearing a celestial stamp in all her features," "fairer than pictured cherub" (235). Significantly, the two moments in the 1818 edition at which Elizabeth expressed her own views in opposition to the patriarchy are cut from the 1831 edition. No longer does Elizabeth protest against her uncle's plans for Ernest (59) or denounce the tyrannical, vengeful *retribution* of the law-courts (83). Bound by the "immutable laws of nature" and her dependence on the Frankenstein family, Elizabeth Lavenza has become a cypher, the woman as the silenced Other.

By 1831, Mary Shelley had lost faith in the possibility that a generous, loving, and nurturant response to both human and physical nature might create a world without monsters. The Russian sea-master is now "wholly uneducated," "as silent as a Turk," and guilty of an "ignorant carelessness" (230). Elizabeth's chosen profession for Ernest is no longer that of the constructive farmer but rather that of the destructive military soldier, controlling "foreign" lands. Above all, nature is imaged as an "imperial" tyrant, a mighty power whose constant changes spell only death to the living.

By coming to construe nature in the way that Waldman and Frankenstein did in the 1818 edition, as a mighty and amoral machine, Mary Shelley significantly decreased the critical distance between herself and her protagonist. In her added Introduction to the novel, Mary Shelley represents herself much as she now represents Frankenstein, as a victim of destiny. She was compelled to write by her parents' example, by Byron's challenge, by Percy Shelley's expectations; her "imagination, unbidden, possessed and guided" her (227); she is still "averse to bringing myself forward in print" (222). She ends with a defensive lie: "I have changed no portion of the story, nor introduced any new ideas or circumstances" (229). Thus Mary Shelley both disclaimed responsibility for her hideous progeny and insisted that she had remained passive before it, "leaving the core and substance of it untouched" (229). For invention "can give form to dark, shapeless substances, but cannot bring into being the substance itself" (226). Imperial nature, the substance itself, is thus triumphant. Before it, Mary Shelley's human invention, her imagination, "unbidden," could only mould shapeless darkness into a hideous monster. Like Victor Frankenstein, she has become the unwilling "author of unalterable evils."

CHAPTER TEN

Fathers and Daughters, or "A Sexual Education"

After her return to London in 1823, Mary Shelley found herself impoverished, both financially and emotionally. She immediately sought support: economically, by writing novels, stories, encyclopedia articles, and reviews, and psychologically, by turning to Jane Williams, her father, and any acquaintance who would give her an entry into that "society" whose affection and approval she so craved. Despite the pessimistic conclusions of *The Last Man* and the revised *Frankenstein*, she clung to her vision of the family as the only possible source of psychological satisfaction and cultural meaning for women. Forsaking the genres of Gothic and futurist fiction to utilize instead the more popular and commercially viable forms of the historical and the sentimental novel, Mary Shelley explored her ideology of the domestic affections within more realistic settings, variously the Guelf-Ghibelline conflicts of fourteenth-century Italy (in *Valperga*, which she had completed in 1821), the Yorkish uprisings of fifteenth-century England (in *Perkin Warbeck*), and the fashionable world of early nineteenth-century English society (in *Mathilda*, *Lodore*, and *Falkner*).

Not all of Mary Shelley's novels deserve detailed critical attention in the context of the issues pursued in this book. *Perkin Warbeck* (1830), for instance, is a thoroughly researched and well-told adventure story which vividly recounts Perkin Warbeck's attempts to reclaim the English throne (Mary Shelley was convinced that Warbeck was indeed the Duke of York, escaped from the Tower after Richard III murdered his older brother). The novel compellingly illustrates the ways in which historical and political forces control individual destinies and in particular, the ways in which personal loyalties and domestic affections

177

are systematically sacrificed to the ambitions of power-seeking men. It thus sets Mary Shelley's ideology of the family against the forces of historical determinism, suggesting that the masculine betrayal of family bonds is a practice inherited from the past. But it does not engage these conflicts in a compellingly personal way.[1] Nor does *Valperga; or, the Life and Adventures of Castruccio, Prince of Lucca* (1823) satisfactorily synthesize its mass of historical detail, "raked," said Percy Shelley, "out of fifty old books,"[2] into a coherent narrative. Nonetheless, three of its characters—Castruccio, Euthanasia and Beatrice—throw additional light on Mary Shelley's primary concern with love, family relationships, and the disastrous political and personal consequences of masculine ambition and egotism.

It is in her novels of sentiment, her portrayals of contemporary English society, that Mary Shelley's continuing commitment to the bourgeois family energizes some of her more powerful writing. *Mathilda* (1819; published, 1959), *Lodore* (1835), and *Falkner* (1837) all celebrate the domestic affections: all depict idyllic relationships between fathers (or father-substitutes) and daughters. They strongly affirm her ideology of the egalitarian family, insisting that men as well as women must sacrifice their personal ambitions and desires to the welfare of the family.

But these three novels also reveal the contradiction at the core of this ideology. For the nineteenth-century middle-class family was not in fact egalitarian, as British family historians have documented.[3] These novels show what can happen when bourgeois fathers do love and care for their children, and especially their daughters. The fathers in these novels produce, not monsters, perhaps, yet still mutilated lives, women whose selves are less than whole. However loving, these fathers seduce their daughters into a relationship in which they remain forever dependent upon and subsidiary to a male. Significantly, in each of these novels, the narrative's overt affirmation of the bourgeois family and the loving and cooperative daughter or wife stumbles over an event or a character that powerfully reveals the damage done to women who define themselves primarily in terms of their roles within the familial hierarchy. What makes these neglected novels worth reading is just the tension they reveal between Mary Shelley's psychic need to idealize the bourgeois family and her painful recognition of how much participation in such a family can hurt a woman.

Mary Shelley strongly believed that a woman's greatest fulfillment came from a loving relationship with another person. Her lifelong, never fully gratified desire for a stable, supportive family led her to conceive of her own identity exclusively in relational terms. As she matured from the eighteen-year-old girl who wrote *Frankenstein* into a wife, mother, and early widow, Mary Shelley characteristically described her self in relation to someone else: as the daughter of Godwin and Wollstonecraft; as the mistress, wife, and devoted widow of the poet Shelley; as the mother of Percy Florence Shelley. As a girl, she had never been able to imagine herself as the heroine of her own daydreams and heroic fantasies. As an adult, she could not imagine herself as a leader, or even as an independent person; she relied on others for guidance and direction. In 1838 she explained her inability to take a stand on behalf of women's rights and other radical political causes as the consequence of her particular temperament:

> I recoil from the vulgar abuse of the inimical press. . . . I am silent therefore from prudence. I will not put myself so far forward—for then I cannot pause, but shall be dragged further. Proud & sensitive, I act on the defensive—an inglorious position.
>
> To hang back, as I do, brings a penalty. I was nursed and fed with a love of glory. To be something great and good was the precept given me by my Father. Shelley reiterated it. Alone and poor, I could only be something by joining a party; and there was much in me – the woman's love of looking up, and being guided, and being willing to do anything if any one supported and brought me forward—which would have made me a good partisan. But Shelley died, and I was alone. My Father, from age and domestic circumstances & other things, could not "*me faire valoir*," none else noticed me— . . . My total friendlessness & want of connection, . . . my being poor, my horror of pushing, and inability to put myself forward unless led, cherished and supported,—all this has sunk me in a state of loneliness no other human being ever before, I believe, endured— except Robinson Crusoe. How many tears and spasms of anguish this solitude has cost me, lies buried in my memory.
>
> . . . If I write the above, it is that those who love me may hereafter know that I am not all to blame, nor merit the heavy accusations cast on me for not putting myself forward. I *cannot* do that; it is against my nature. As well cast me from a precipice and rail at me for not flying.[4]

Mary Shelley conceived of herself as a follower, a worshipper at the altar of another. As a child, her father "was my God—& I remember many childish instances of the excess of attachment I bore for him," she confessed to Jane Williams.[5] She then transferred that devotion to her husband.

After Percy Shelley's death, having lost confidence in male companionship, Mary turned to women for emotional support. She demanded of them the intensity and commitment of a lover or a mother and was constantly disappointed. She assumed on her return to England in 1823 that she and Jane Williams would live together forever. Yearning to return to Italy, she informed Leigh Hunt in June, 1825:

> the hope & consolation of my life is the society of Mrs W[illiams].
> To her, for better or worse I am wedded—while she will have me & I
> continue in the love-lorn state that I have since I returned to this
> native country of yours—I go or stay as she or rather our joint
> circumstances decide—which now with ponderous chain and heavy
> log enroot us in Kentish Town.[6]

But her adored Jane betrayed her trust. Behind Mary's back Jane went
to both Leigh Hunt and Hogg, maliciously condemning her for the way
she had treated Percy in their last year together. Moreover, Jane
preferred the company of men; in 1827 she went to live with Thomas
Jefferson Hogg. Mary's later female friends consistently deserted her,
for other women, for their husbands, or for circumstantial necessity.
Isabella Robinson emigrated to Paris with her lesbian "husband" Mary
Diana Dods (*alias* Walter Sholto Douglas, *nom de plume* David
Lyndsay) in 1828; Anne Frances Hare went to Italy with her husband
in 1830; Georgiana Beauclerk left London in disgrace in 1832; Lady
Paul died in April 1833; and Louisa Robinson married and sailed to
India in 1834. As Mary Shelley lamented in her Journal on December 2,
1834: "destiny [is] ever at hand to turn everything against me—have I
friend, she dies or goes abroad."[7] She later confessed to Trelawney in
1835:

> I do not wonder at your not being able to deny yourself the pleasure
> of Mrs Nortons society—I never saw a woman I thought so
> fascinating—Had I been a man I should certainly have fallen in love
> with her—As a woman—ten years ago—I should have been spell
> bound & had she taken the trouble she might have wound me round
> her finger—Ten years ago I was so ready to give myself away—&
> being afraid of men, I was apt to get *tousy-mousy* [an allusion to
> Byron's sardonic description of excessive romantic "enthusiasm" as
> "entusymusy"] for women—experience & suffering have altered all
> that— ... I am now proof as Hamlet says both against man and
> woman.[8]

Disappointed in her male and female friendships, Mary emotionally
turned back to her first love, her father. On her return to London in
1823, Godwin welcomed her with all the affection of which he was
capable. He set his "heart & soul" on her staying with him in England,
making her "returning to Italy an affair of life and death with him," so
much so that Mary acquiesced, telling Leigh Hunt that "in this world it
always seems one's duty to sacrifice one's own desires, & that claim
ever appears the strongest which claims such a sacrifice."[9] Daughter
and father lived within blocks of each other and saw each other almost
daily. In his Diary Godwin frequently made the revealing slip of
identifying Mary Shelley, no longer as MWS, but as MWG, the

daughter who in person as well as name has become a substitute for her beloved mother Mary Wollstonecraft Godwin. Mrs. Godwin faded into the background as Godwin and Mary consulted each other frequently on the writing projects she pursued to pay his debts as well as her own. Despite her loyalty to her father, Mary soon found that his financial troubles (Godwin declared bankruptcy in 1825) prevented him from giving her the emotional support and economic protection she needed. As she acknowledged in her Journal on January 18, 1824, "My Father's situation, his cares and debts, prevent my enjoying his society."[10]

Nonetheless she refused all offers of marriage, in spite of the attentions of several male admirers, most persistently John Howard Payne and Prosper Mérimée. To Edward John Trelawney, who had loyally befriended her during and after the terrible days of Shelley's disappearance and death in 1822 and who finally suggested nine years later that fate might have, "without our choice, united us," she wrote

> you tell me not to marry—but I will—any one who will take me out of my present desolate & uncomfortable position—Any one—& with all this do you think that I shall marry?—Never—neither you, nor any body else—Mary Shelley shall be written on my tomb—and why? I cannot tell—except that it is so pretty a name that tho' I were to preach to myself for years, I never should have the heart to get rid of it—[11]

When a man did arouse her interest, as in the cases of Bryan Waller Procter, Washington Irving, or Aubrey Beauclerk, she found no responsive sympathy and condemned her foolish vanity. "[Procter's] visits . . . have ceased—it is four months since I have seen him—so much for my powers of attraction," she wrote with bitter irony in her Journal on September 3, 1824.

She became a devoted mother as well as a devoted daughter. As she confided to her Journal on February 24, 1823, "our Child demands all my care now that you have left us. I must be all to him: the Father, Death has deprived him of; the relations, the bad world permits him not to have." Often she felt that she was living only for her son. "Oh, my child! what is your fate to be? You alone keep me; you are the only chain that links me to time—but for you," she cried out in her despair on October 5, 1822, "I should be free."[13] She determined to give Percy Florence the education of a gentleman and to reconcile him with his grandfather, Sir Timothy Shelley, in the hope that he might someday claim the baronetcy entailed upon his father's male heirs. When Sir Timothy's grudging allowance of £200 per annum together with her journalism and novel-writing efforts failed to produce the income necessary to board Percy Florence at Harrow, Mary Shelley gave up her London life of theatre-going and social visits, incarcerating herself in a flat in Harrow for three years so that Percy could be a day-scholar.

Perhaps the greatest emotional satisfaction of her adult life came from the knowledge that Percy was devoted to her. He even invited her to accompany him and two Cambridge University friends on their summer holidays in Italy in 1840 and again in 1842. Mary Shelley recorded her intense delight at this invitation in her Journal on the eve of her departure, on June 1, 1840:

> Yet, though I no longer dream all things attainable, I enjoy what is, and while I feel that whatever I have lost of youth and hope, I have acquired the enduring affection of a noble heart, and Percy shows such excellent dispositions that I feel I am much the gainer in life.[14]

She described the pleasures of the trips themselves in her *Rambles in Germany and Italy in 1840, 1842 and 1843* (1844). In 1848, when Percy Florence was 28, four years after the long-awaited death of Sir Timothy and Percy's accession to the baronetcy, Mary Shelley found him the ideal wife, Jane St. John, a sweet, thoughtful, unambitious young widow with literary tastes who loved the rather stolid, easy-going Percy, admired her mother-in-law (who remained a welcome member of the household), and idolized the poet Shelley, to whom a room at Boscombe Manor was kept as a shrine for as long as Lady Jane Shelley lived. Assured that her son was now financially secure and emotionally happy, Mary Shelley lost the will to live. Having long suffered from psychosomatic illnesses—headaches, nervous irritability, depression—she finally succumbed to a mysterious paralysis and died on February 1, 1851, at the age of 53.

Mary Shelley's career demonstrates that it was possible for an intelligent woman in the early nineteenth century to support herself financially through writing (in her case, a combination of novels, short stories, articles for Lardner's Cabinet Cyclopedia, and magazine reviews) and, with the help of a reluctantly given allowance from her father-in-law, to raise a well-educated, well-adjusted son. But Mary Shelley herself gained relatively little satisfaction from her adult life. She never found the unconditional love she had craved since childhood. Her father, even at his most devoted, remained ungenerous, self-absorbed, and demanding. The female friends to whom she turned with intense affection, seeking the response of a mother or a lover, all disappointed her. Her limited financial circumstances prevented her from gaining the secure place in "society" that might have satisfied her need for a supportive family. As she cried out to her Journal on March 8, 1831:

God grant that after these few months are elapsed I may be able to take refuge in Nature & solitude from the feverish misery of my present existence. Here gaunt poverty & cruel privation dog my pleasures close—cares beset me—& fair expectations die. Could I concenter my affections round a home I should ask no more—the luxuries of wealth are nothing to me—I ask only a home with one or two who would find the solace of their life in my care & affection—but this is denied me—& I am miserable beyond words.[15]

Her frequent brushes with death—the losses of four children, of her husband, of such friends as Byron, John and Maria Gisborne, and Lady Paul—left her fatalistic and chronically depressed, excessively anxious for Percy Florence's health and welfare, and prone to an intense loneliness which she felt unable to alleviate. Her Journal entries record her recurrent melancholy:

March 30, 1823—I cannot write. Day after day I suffer the most tremendous agitation. I cannot write, or read, or think—there is a whirlwind within me that shakes every nerve. I take exercise & do every thing that may prevent my body from influencing evilly my mind; but it will not do—whether it be the anxiety for letters that shakes a frame not so strong as hitherto—whether it be my annoyances here—whether it be my regrets, my sorrows, and despair, or all these—I know not, but I am a wreck.

January 18, 1824—I have now been nearly four months in England and if I am to judge of the future by the past and the present, I have small delight in looking forward. . . . I am imprisoned in a dreary town—I see neither fields, nor hills, nor trees, nor sky—the exhilaration of enrapt contemplation is no more felt by me . . . Writing has become a task, my studies irksome, my life dreary. . . . My imagination is dead, my genius lost, my energies sleep.

September 5, 1826—My head aches. My heart—my hapless heart—is deluged in bitterness. Great God! if there be any pity for human suffering, tell me what I am to do. I strive to study, I strive to write, but I cannot live without loving and being loved, without sympathy. If this is to be denied to me, I must die. Would that the hour were come!

September 26, 1827—How dark—how very dark the future seems—I shrink in fear from the mere imagination of coming time. Is any evil about to approach me? Have I not suffered enough?

December 18, 1830—I have felt my solitude more entirely but never more painfully than now. I seem deserted—alone in the world—cast off—the victim of poverty & neglect—Thus it is—to be poor & so cut off from society—to pass my days in seclusion—how well could I bear it had I one hope to cheer me—one joy to shed its brightness over my darkling lot—How many years I cherished the expectation of seeing one whom I might love—who could protect & guard me—Fate has written that this is never to be—

> December 2, 1834—occupation is the medicine of my mind—I write the 'Lives' in the morning & I read novels and memoires of an evening—such is the variety of my days . . .
>
> My heart and soul is bound up in Percy. My race is run. I hope absolutely nothing except that when he shall be older and I a little richer to leave a solitude, very unnatural to anyone and peculiarly disagreeable to me.
>
> June 1, 1840—Long oppressed by care, disappointment, and ill health, which all combined to depress and irritate me, I felt almost to have lost the spring of happy reveries. On such a night it returns—[16]

Although Mary Shelley's spirits usually rose in the company of others, at the core of her being, the grim, despairing mood of *The Last Man* never left her. She was a person who lived in the past. Her novels turned again and again for their material either to the historical past or to her own adolescence and early womanhood, where she relived in fantasy her idealized relationships with both her father and her husband.

Mathilda (1819), *Lodore* (1835), and *Falkner* (1837) ask to be considered as a group, simply because all three works use and reuse material which was for Mary Shelley obsessive. All three portray at length an idyllic relationship between a loving father and a devoted adolescent daughter, a relationship uninhibited by the presence of other family members. All three heroines—indistinguishable from one another—receive from their fathers or guardians what Mary Shelley defined in *Lodore* as "a sexual education." Lord Lodore "fashioned his offspring to be the wife of a frail human being, and instructed her to be yielding, and to make it her duty to devote herself to his happiness, and to obey his will."[17] Lodore's program is based on Rousseau's theory of female education in *Emile*. Rousseau had insisted that "the first and most important qualification in a woman is good-nature or sweetness of temper: formed to obey a being so imperfect as man, often full of vices, and always full of faults, she ought to learn betimes even to suffer injustice and to bear the insults of a husband without complaint."[18] Taking Milton's Eve as their model, whom Lord Lodore considered "the embodied ideal of all that is adorable and estimable in her sex" (I:38), all three father-guardians mold women who embody the nineteenth-century bourgeois ideal of the pure and modest Proper Lady.[19]

Ethel Lodore, raised by her father in the wilds of America as his constant companion, is brave but pliant: "Nothing was dreaded, indeed, by her, except his disapprobation; and a word or look from him made her, with all her childish vivacity and thoughtlessness, turn as with a silken string, and bend at once to his will" (I:30). She becomes a veritable angel in the house: "She had no fears, no deceit, no untold thought within her. Her matchless sweetness of temper prevented any cloud from ever dimming her pure loveliness: her voice cheered the heart, and her laugh rang so true and joyous on the ear, that it gave token in itself of the sympathizing and buoyant spirit which was her great charm" (I:33). As a result of her father's educational theories—"to cultivate her tastes and enlarge her mind, yet so to controul her acquirements, as to render her ever pliant to his will" (I:37)—Ethel Lodore "seldom thought, and never acted, for herself" (I:41). All her thoughts were for her father's happiness, and he in turn was inspired "with more than a father's fondness. He lived but for her and in her" (I:42).

When Lord Lodore is suddenly killed in a duel, Ethel, at eighteen, cannot imagine living without him: "She was in love with death, which alone could reunite her to the being, apart from whom she believed it impossible to exist" (I:288). But Ethel, brought to London by her aunts to save her health, encounters again the handsome young man who had been her father's second in the fatal duel. Seeing in Edward Villiers her father's friend, Ethel promptly falls in love with him and, despite Villiers's shaky financial circumstances, marries him. After an idyllic honeymoon in Italy, they return to London to find bailiffs waiting. Mary Shelley here recounts her and Percy's experience of hiding from his creditors in the fall and winter of 1814–15, suffusing the lovers' grim lodgings (the Villiers finally end up together in debtors' prison) with the radiance of mutual passion and undying loyalty. Ethel continues to feel, yet never for herself, only for her beloved Edward. In effect, she redirects her love for her father into an identical self-sacrificing love for her husband. As Mary Shelley described her to a possible publisher, Charles Ollier, "In the daughter I have tried to pourtray [sic] in its simplicity, & all the beauty I could muster, the *devotion* of a young wife for the husband of her choice."[20]

Ethel's example of pure devotion finally inspires her long-estranged mother, Lady Lodore, to an act of similar self-sacrifice. She secretly uses her small fortune to pay off Villiers's debts and, having thereby lost her home and place in society, retires to a small cottage in Wales. Lady Lodore is amply rewarded for her maternal devotion. She gains a new empathy for the beauties of nature:

> "Yes," she thought, "nature is the refuge and home for women: they have no public career—no aim nor end beyond their domestic circle; but they can extend that, and make all the creations of nature their own, to foster and do good to ... But throw aside all vanity, no longer seek to surpass your own sex, nor to inspire the other with

feelings which are pregnant with disquiet or misery, and which seldom end in mutual benevolence, turn your steps to the habitation which God has given as befitting his creatures, contemplate the lovely ornaments with which he has blessed the earth;—here is no heart-burning nor calumny; it is better to love, to be of use to one of these flowers, than to be the admired of the many—the mere puppet of one's own vanity." (III:297–98)

Here Mary Shelley reinvokes the conception of nature as a nurturant and benevolent mother which she had endorsed in the first edition of *Frankenstein*. However, her intervening representations of nature in both *The Last Man* and the second edition of *Frankenstein* (1831) as an implacable and indifferent mutability should alert us to the sentimentalization or fictiveness of this rhetoric.

This passage again asserts Mary Shelley's conviction that a woman finds her greatest fulfillment within the family. Lady Lodore is soon reunited with her long-lost daughter in a powerful scene of mutually passionate affection. As Mary Shelley said to Charles Ollier, Lady Lodore is "The Mother who after sacrificing *all* to the world at first—afterwards makes sacrifices not less entire, for her child—finding all to be Vanity, except the genuine affections of the heart."[11] Moreover, Lady Lodore gains a husband, Horatio Saville, Viscount of Maristow, who embodies Mary Shelley's image of the ideal man. A scholar who had long loved Lady Lodore, Horatio Saville

was outwardly mild, placid, and forbearing, and thus obtained the reputation of being cold—though those who study human nature ought to make it their first maxim, that those who are tolerant of the follies of their fellows—who sympathize with, and assist their wishes, and who apparently forget their own desires, as they devote themselves to the accomplishment of those of their friends, must have the quickest feelings to make them enter into and understand those of others, and the warmest affections to be able to conquer their wayward humours, so that they can divest themselves of selfishness, and incorporate in their own being the pleasures and pains of those around them. (II:24–25)

This self-revelatory passage is Mary Shelley's own apologia pro vita sua, a defense against the charges of "coldness" and "unfeelingness" brought against her by Leigh Hunt, Jane Williams, and Percy Shelley. But it is also a potent ideological assertion that men as well as women should suppress their egotistic desires and sacrifice their personal welfare to the betterment of their family and friends.[22] And the primary sacrifice should be that of parents for their children, as the modest Saville, a man of Keatsian negative capability and a "proper gentleman," recognizes. When Lady Lodore agrees to marry him, the author insists that

> she respects, admires, in some sense it may be said, that she adores her husband; but even while consenting to be his, and thus securing her own happiness, she told him that her first duties were towards Ethel—and that he took a divided heart, over the better part of which reigned maternal love. Saville, the least egoistic of human beings, smiled to hear her name that a defect, which was in his eyes her crowning virtue. (III:306)

The same authorial commitment to the family informs *Falkner*, where the orphaned Elizabeth Raby is raised almost singlehandedly by her Byronic protector, John Falkner, into another figure of Eve. Elizabeth is passionately devoted to her guardian, while Falkner in turn comes to feel not only concern and affection for his ward but even an emotional dependency upon her. Together they share an idyllic parent-child relationshp, isolated (by their constant travelling) from other society. "What is so often a slothful, unapparent sense of parental and filial duty was with them a living, active spirit, for ever manifesting itself in some new form."[23] When Falkner is wounded fighting for the cause of Greek independence, Elizabeth bravely rescues him and nurses him back to health. En route to England she is aided by a stranger, Gerard Neville, who possesses "gentleness, and almost feminine delicacy of attention, joined to all a man's activity and readiness to do the thing that was necessary to be done" (I:217). Gerard, admiring the passionate filial devotion which Elizabeth shows to Falkner, falls in love with her. Entering London society for the first time, Elizabeth feels alienated:

> She loved friends, but hated acquaintance. Nor was this strange. Her mind was quite empty of conventional frivolities. . . . To unbend with her was to converse with a friend—to play with children—or to enjoy the scenes of nature with one who felt their beauties with her. (I:254)

Although she takes pleasure only in the company of Gerard Neville, who teaches her to love poetry, and whose affection she increasingly reciprocates, when Elizabeth is forced to choose between Neville and Falkner (who twenty years earlier forcibly abducted Neville's mother and inadvertently caused her death and dishonor), she finds she cannot abandon the only parent she has ever known. As Mary Shelley told Maria Gisborne, "I took upon fidelity as the first of human virtues—& am going to write a novel to display my opinion."[24] Elizabeth visits Falkner, who has confessed to the crime he committed twenty years before and is now in jail, bringing forgiveness, sympathy, and hope for a future together. Falkner, thinking of Elizabeth, articulates his passionate love for her:

> He loved her with a feeling, which, though not paternal, was as warm as ever filled a father's breast. His passions were ardent, and all that could be spared from remorse, were centred in his adopted child. He had looked on her, as the prophet might on the angel, who ministered to his wants in the desert: in the abandonment of all mankind, in the desolation to which his crime had led him, she had brought love and cheer. She had been his sweet household companion, his familiar friend, his patient nurse—his soul had grown to her image, and when the place was vacant that she had filled, he was excited by eager longings for her presence, that even made his man's heart soft as a woman's with very desire. (III:127–28)

Elizabeth's and Falkner's mutual fidelity is finally rewarded when Neville (inspired by love for Elizabeth and by a sense of the justice owed to Falkner) and Elizabeth together locate Osborne, the man who drove Falkner's coach on the night of Alithea Neville's abduction and can testify that her death was in fact accidental. Falkner is thereby cleared of the charge of murder and released. Elizabeth and Gerard agree to marry, and Gerard even manages to overcome his lifelong hatred of "his mother's destroyer" and invites Falkner to live with them, in what is then described as a paradise of equality, mutual respect, and ever-increasing domestic affection.

A similarly idyllic father-daughter relationship is portrayed in *Mathilda* (1819) where Mathilda, who is raised by her aunt after her mother's death in childbirth, is reunited with her father when she is sixteen. Having yearned throughout her youth to be her father's "consoler" and "companion," Mathilda is ecstatic when her father returns; he greets her with intense affection and eagerly accompanies her on long walks through the glorious countryside of western Scotland during which he enthusiastically describes all his travels, feelings, and future plans. She is the devoted, affectionate daughter. He is the cherishing father. For six months, their happiness together is unalloyed:

> My improvement was his delight; he was with me during all my studies and assisted or joined with me in every lesson. We saw a great deal of society, and no day passed that my father did not endeavour to embellish by some new enjoyment. The tender attachment that he bore me, and the love and veneration with which I returned it cast a charm over every moment. The hours were slow for each minute was employed; we lived more in one week than many do in the course of several months and the variety and novelty of our pleasures gave zest to each. (17)

Up to this point, *Mathilda* purveys the ideology that underpins the first edition of *Frankenstein* and overtly informs the later *Lodore* and *Falkner*: the belief that a loving, caring parent will produce a loving, caring child, that a sympathy with natural beauty is morally redemptive, and that human beings find their greatest fulfillment in the mutually self-sacrificing relationships of the egalitarian family. But blatantly in *Mathilda* and more subtly in *Lodore* and *Falkner*, flaws appear in this ideology of the family, cracks which I now wish to peer into from a modern feminist orientation. While each of these three works articulates Mary Shelley's passionate desire for an intensely loving relationship with both her father and her husband, while each imaginatively satisfies her obsessive need for a tightly bonded nuclear family, each narrative also contains elements which acknowledge the very fictiveness, the impossibility, of such wish-fulfillments. In other words, Mary Shelley's ideological commitments come into conflict with her historical experience of the bourgeois family and that contradiction is registered in these fictions.

We should first observe that in all of Mary Shelley's fictional celebrations of the family, the mother is absent. In *Frankenstein*, Caroline Beaufort Frankenstein dies during her son's childhood and the De Lacey family is without a mother. Mathilda's mother Diana dies in childbirth; and the aunt who dutifully raises her "had the coldest [heart] that ever filled a human breast: it was totally incapable of any affection" (8). Elizabeth Raby's mother dies when her daughter is hardly five years old, leaving her an orphan. Lady Lodore, caught up in her social whirl, shamefully neglects her daughter and is completely estranged from her husband, who takes his daughter away to America when Ethel is twelve. And the death of Alithea Neville leaves Gerard without a mother. The striking absence of loving mothers in these fictions reflects Mary Shelley's own motherless childhood. But more important, it undercuts her idealization of the egalitarian family because it makes it impossible for her to ground that ideology on a detailed examination of a sustained mother-child or husband-wife relationship.

Since by the time she wrote *Falkner* in 1837, Mary Shelley had raised a seventeen-year-old son, it is revealing that she could present a passionately loving mother-child relationship (that between Alithea and Gerard Neville) only as a violent rupture. Perhaps her self-definition as devoted mother could not bear the critical analysis that extended fictional representation might require. Perhaps her obsessive fixation on her own father caused her to fear as much as desire the presence of a mother in her idealized nuclear family, since the mother could threaten and even displace the daughter's relationship with the father (as Mrs. Godwin had displaced Mary Godwin). Perhaps Mary Shelley omitted the mother from her idealized family because she found it impossible even to imagine a fully realized egalitarian marriage, given her own subservient relationship with Percy Shelley.

Whatever the reason, the husband-wife and mother-child relationships that one would have expected to be central to Mary Shelley's celebration of the family are absent from her fiction. Lady Lodore's belated concern for Ethel, after twenty years of separation, rings hollowly. And in the only short story in which she developed a mother-son relationship at length, Mary Shelley stopped work on her manuscript at the very point at which the foster-mother's love, encouragement, and excellent educational stimulation seem to have produced a clever but arrogant and egotistical young man. Unable to portray a son who disappointed his mother, Mary Shelley left her tale, tentatively entitled "Cecil," unfinished.[25]

The only mother-child relationship that Mary Shelley depicts at length, that between Cornelia Lodore and her mother Mrs. Santerre, is portrayed entirely negatively. It was Mrs. Santerre who first alienated Lord Lodore from his wife by insisting that her daughter devote her primary energies to becoming a social success rather than a loyal wife, and by claiming a greater share of Cornelia's affections than Lodore received. In other words, Mrs. Santerre is presented as the sexist stereotype of the domineering and insensitive mother-in-law, the woman who destroys domestic harmony by demanding from the wife more attention than the husband gets. Cornelia Lodore is redeemed from her mother's evil influences only when she willingly sacrifices the self she has become—her role in society, her friendships, and her fortune—and instead immerses herself in nature and the new domestic circle constituted by her daughter and her second husband. Since Mary Shelley's fiction avoids detailed representations of lasting and mutually beneficial mother-child and husband-wife relationships, her ideology of the egalitarian family is effectively divorced from a realistic praxis, a demonstration of how it actually works. As a result, her beliefs are presented in an idealized, abstract, and sentimental rhetoric, a rhetoric that is finally unpersuasive.

More important, these three fictions show that her ideology has potentially dangerous consequences for women. Inherent in Lord Lodore's definition of the female as the innocent Eve or Proper Lady who self-sacrificingly fulfills the roles of devoted daughter, wife, and mother, is a sexual and psychological exploitation of women of which modern feminist theory has made us very much aware.[26] These three works portray women who find their self-definition and their self-fulfillment through familial love, love for their fathers and for their husbands. But they also reveal the destructiveness of such love when it sustains the dependent relationship of a younger woman upon a dominant, older man. Ethel Lodore and Elizabeth Raby, having idolized their loving fathers throughout childhood, seek out marriages which replicate the same pattern of worshipful dependence. Edward Villiers, literally her father's "second," immediately assumes the role of Ethel's protector, and is rewarded with her willingness to sacrifice every material and social advantage for his sake. Gerard Neville falls in love with Elizabeth Raby because he admires her daughterly devotion to Falkner and, in effect, demands the same total commitment to himself and his cause, a commitment Elizabeth eagerly makes. And when her devotion to her lover conflicts with her devotion to her guardian, Elizabeth miraculously manages to reconcile both these father-figures into one loving nuclear family. The implausibility of the novel's sentimental ending is acknowledged in the author's "this was not a cause for words or reason" (III:314). By the end of *Falkner*, Neville and Falkner—lifelong enemies—have in effect been fused into the same person, the idol of the angelic Elizabeth's worship.

While *Lodore* and *Falkner* present these "father-daughter" marriages without overt irony, and even identify them with Mary's own marriage to Percy Shelley, *Mathilda* demonstrates that Mary Shelley was aware of their psychological danger. For in *Mathilda*, the loving father is not replaced by a younger, socially acceptable father-substitute. Instead the father himself becomes his daughter's lover. *Mathilda* thus explicitly identifies the relationship of a powerful, loving man with a submissive, adoring younger woman as father-daughter incest. Since *Mathilda* constitutes Mary Shelley's most radical critique of her ideological commitment to the bourgeois family—a critique that she was never able to publish in her own lifetime[27]—it deserves detailed attention.

Mary Shelley wrote this eighty-page novella between August 4 and September 12, 1819, during the severe depression which followed the death of William on June 7. The plot can be briefly summarized. Mathilda is the daughter of a beautiful, intelligent woman named Diana and her passionately devoted husband, a wealthy and self-indulgent young man of rank who marries her after having overcome his family's objections to their early union. This young couple enjoys fifteen months of romantic bliss. Then Mathilda is born, but a few days later, her mother dies of complications resulting from childbirth. Mathilda's father, distraught with grief, gives the newborn child to his older half-sister to raise and immediately leaves the country. Mathilda is reared in isolation by her cold, austere aunt in rural Scotland. All through her youth she dreams of her father's return and of the passionate affection with which she will greet him. When Mathilda is sixteen, her father comes back. He and Mathilda immediately become intensely close and spend several halcyon months together. In the autumn, her aunt dies and Mathilda and her father move to London, where a suitor begins to court the beautiful girl, now grown to look exactly like her mother. Her father abruptly dismisses the suitor, claiming that his daughter is too young for such attentions. Soon after, Mathilda notices with alarm and pain that her father has begun to avoid her company. She seeks him out. He both responds to and rejects her affectionate embraces, and then departs abruptly for the family mansion in Yorkshire where he had lived with his beloved wife and which he has not seen since her death. To her joy, Mathilda is summoned a few days later to join him there.

On arrival, however, she finds her father as moody and withdrawn as he was in London. Convinced that he is suffering some great grief that she might relieve by sharing with him, Mathilda pursues her father on his lonely walk to the summit of a cliff and pitifully begs him to confess his troubles. Angrily, he refuses to speak his heart. Mathilda, in a paroxysm of pain, insists that he must hate her. At this, her father answers violently, "Yes, yes, I hate you! You are my bane, my poison, my disgust! Oh! No!" And then his manner changes, and fixing his eyes on Mathilda with an expression that convulses every nerve in her body, he cries out, "you are none of all these; you are my light, my only one, my life.—My daughter, I love you!" (30). As Mathilda stands in "speechless agony," her father in a frenzy of desire and despair, sinks fainting to the earth.

Appalled by this incestuous love, Mathilda abandons her father, convinced that she can never speak to him again, and flees to her room where she composes a farewell letter to him. That night, after she has refused to come down for dinner, her father approaches her room. She hides in a corner, but he does not enter. Mathilda goes to sleep and immediately dreams that she has risen to seek out her father and inform him of her decision to leave him. At length she spies him in the woods, dressed in a flowing white robe and appearing "unearthly," even "deadily pale" (35). She follows him to the brow of a steep cliff. Just as she arrives he plunges off the precipice into the sea. When she wakes, her servant brings her a letter from her father, begging her understanding and forgiveness, describing "the hell of passion which has been implanted in me to burn until all be cold, and stiff, and dead," and promising that he will depart and she will never hear from him again (40). Mathilda immediately intuits that her father, despite his protestations that he does not intend to die, has left on a suicidal journey. Again she pursues him, in a blinding storm, through town and field, toward the sea. One day later she reaches the beach only to see through the opened door of a cottage a bed on which lies "something stiff and straight . . . , covered by a sheet" (45). She sinks "lifeless" beside this, the corpse of her father.

Mathilda then stages her own suicide and retires to a lonely hermitage on the heaths of northern Scotland, where for two years she lives like a nun, devoted to the love she still feels for her father and mourning his fateful passion and untimely death. She is here found by Woodville, the Shelleyean poet who both proffers and finally refuses sympathy. After Woodville departs, urging Mathilda to hope for new affection and a happier life, she strolls through the woods, thinking of Dante's Matilda gathering flowers beside a lovely river that flows "dark, dark, yet clear, moved under the obscure / Eternal shades, whose interwoven looms / The rays of moon or sunlight ne'er endure."[28] Losing her way, Mathilda spends the night on the cold autumnal heath, wakened by a rainstorm that brings on a high fever and leaves her dying from a rapid consumption. As she awaits her imminent death, she pens a final letter to Woodville, the confession of her father's incestuous passion that is the novella we read.

In this story Mary Shelley projects and displaces her deepest and most ambivalent feelings toward her father during the painful summer of 1819.[29] Godwin had been horrified by Mary's elopement with Percy Shelley, and for two-and-a-half years, he had rigidly refused to see or correspond with her. But Godwin abruptly forgave Mary and Percy after their marriage on December 30, 1816, and even boasted of the excellent match his daughter had made. As he hypocritically wrote to his brother, Hull Godwin, on February 21, 1817:

> The piece of news I have to tell, however, is that I went to church with this tall girl some little time ago to be married. Her husband is the eldest son of Sir Timothy Shelley, of Field Place, in the county of Sussex, Baronet. So that, according to the vulgar ideas of the world, she is well married, and I have great hopes the young man will make her a good husband. You will wonder, I daresay, how a girl without a penny of fortune should meet with so good a match. But such are the ups and downs of this world. For my part I care but little, comparatively, about wealth, so that it should be her destiny in life to be respectable, virtuous, and contented.[30]

As Godwin's judicious biographer, Don Locke, comments, "It was a fittingly dishonest epitaph to Godwin's most dishonourable years."[31] Godwin's behavior tormented Mary, who continued to love him despite his manifest cruelty, duplicity, and selfishness. For Godwin continued to threaten to withhold his affection from Mary unless she persuaded Percy to lend him the ever larger sums of money to which his (self-serving) theory of the just distribution of wealth convinced him he was entitled.[32]

The worst instance of Godwin's emotional manipulation of Mary occurred just after William's death, in the summer of 1819. Informed of his grandson's death from malaria and Mary's deep depression, Godwin wrote twice. Only the second letter survives, perhaps because Mary or Percy destroyed the first. We do know Percy's reaction to this first letter: he was outraged by Godwin's callousness. On August 15, 1819, he denounced it to Leigh Hunt:

> We cannot yet come home. Poor Mary's spirits continue dreadfully depressed. And I cannot expose her to Godwin in this state. I wrote to this hard-hearted person, (the first letter I had written for a year), on account of the terrible state of her mind, and to entreat him to try to soothe her in his next letter. The *very* next letter, received yesterday, and addressed to her, called her husband (me) "a disgraceful and flagrant person" tried to persuade her that I was under great engagements to give him *more* money (after having given him £4,700), and urged her if she ever wished a connection to continue between him and her to force me to get money for him.—He cannot persuade her that I am what I am not, nor place a shade of enmity between her and me—but he heaps on her misery, still misery.—I have not yet shewn her the letter—but I must.[33]

In his next letter, written on September 9, 1819, Godwin harshly denounced his daughter: "I cannot but consider it as lowering your character in a memorable degree, and putting you among the commonality and mob of your sex, when I had thought you to be ranked among those noble spirits that do honour to our nature. Oh! what a falling off is here! ... you have lost a child; and all the rest of the world, all that is beautiful, and all that has a claim upon your kindness, is nothing, because a child of three years old is dead!"[34] Throughout this history of emotional rejection and financial exploitation, Mary remained passionately attached to Godwin. In October, 1817, she was reluctant to go to Italy without Godwin's approval, confessing to Percy that "I know not whether it is early habit or affection but the idea of his silent quiet disapprobation makes me weep as it did in the days of my childhood."[35] And throughout her marriage, she begged Percy to pay Godwin's debts.

In *Mathilda*, Mary Shelley both articulates her passionate devotion to her father and takes revenge for his cruelty toward her.[36] At a psychobiographical level, the novella is pure wish-fulfillment. Mary Shelley first portrays a paradise of idyllic father-daughter affection, a mutually fulfilling, intense communion between two companions who take endless pleasure in each other's minds and emotions. Wandering over the heaths of Scotland where Mary Shelley had been so happy with her adolescent friends Christy and Isabel Baxter, Mathilda and her father experience the ideal platonic passion that Mary had long yearned to share with Godwin, who as her only parent embodied her earliest and most powerful love-object.

But in her fantasy, Mary reverses the power dynamic of her relationship with Godwin. Now it is the father, not the daughter, who loves with an overwhelming and self-destructive passion. And it is the daughter, not the father, who rejects the proffered passion. Mary Shelley's anger at Godwin's brutal disregard for her feelings surfaces in the destruction of Mathilda's father. In a passion fraught with psychological complexity, Mathilda—after dreaming, or wishing, her father's death—finds and sinks beside his corpse, as it lies, covered with a sheet, "stiff and straight." The phallic reference is inescapable. Mathilda here embodies Mary Shelley's most powerful, and most powerfully repressed, fantasy: the desire both to sexually possess and to punish her father.

Mathilda experiences an ecstasy of incestuous necrophiliac desire that leaves her exhausted, consummated, "lifeless," yet yearning for a repetition of this experience. From the moment of his death, Mathilda wishes only to reunite with her father, to embrace him passionately in the grave. As she tells Woodville, "death the skeleton" is to her as "beautiful as Love" (64) and she finds her progressive decay "sweet." Ending her narrative, she writes, "I shall not see the red leaves of autumn; before that time I shall be with my father. . . . In truth I am in love with death; no maiden ever took more pleasure in the contemplation of her bridal attire than I in fancying my limbs already enwrapt in their shroud: is it not my marriage dress? Alone it will unite me to my father when in an eternal mental union we shall never part" (77–78). In this Freudian dream-work, Mary Shelley both consummates and purges her incestuous fantasies.

But this obsession with incest is ideological as well as psychological. Mary Shelley's novella calls into question the bourgeois sexual practices of her day, practices which defined the young, submissive, dutiful, daughter-like woman as the appropriate love-object for an older, wiser, economically secure, and "fatherly" man. By calling her heroine Mathilda, Mary Shelley registered her conviction that a daughter-like woman is not a legitimate love-object for men. In all the literary sources upon which Mary Shelley consciously drew, Mathilda is the forbidden sexual partner.

In Dante's *Purgatorio*, which Mathilda's mother had been reading just before she died and which Mary Shelley herself was reading with

Percy in February and again in August 1819,[37] Matilda is the Pilgrim's last temptation before his ultimate encounter with Beatrice in "the car all light." Mary Shelley explicitly identifies her heroine with Dante's Matilda: "I pictured to myself a lovely river such as that on whose banks Dante describes Matilda gathering flowers .... and thought it would be sweet when I wandered on those lovely banks to see the car of light descend with my long lost parent to be restored to me" (74). In the *Purgatorio*, Matilda is the Lady of Innocence, Eve before the fall, who gathers flowers in the Garden of Eden. But the Pilgrim's response to her shows that he is not yet free from all mortal desire, from the sins of the flesh. Looking at Matilda, Dante's pilgrim is immediately reminded of Venus, gazing with the radiant desire of newborn love, and he hates the rivulet that parts him from Matilda with the hatred that Leander felt for the Hellespont that separated him from his passionately beloved Hero.[38] Dante clearly includes these pagan allusions to mark the distance the pilgrim must yet travel before he can transcend all earthly desire and receive the pure and blessed vision brought by Beatrice. Insofar as Dante's pilgrim is distracted from his ultimate spiritual goal by the lovely Matilda, he is led astray, seduced by the desires of the flesh. Mathilda thus figures that very female innocence that must be neither lustfully desired nor sexually possessed by a man.

Again, in the tradition of Gothic fiction which stands behind both *Mathilda* and *Frankenstein*, Mathilda is consistently the name of the forbidden woman. In Matthew Lewis's *The Monk* (1796), which Mary Shelley read on September 22, 1814,[39] and of which she was reminded in August 1816 when "Monk" Lewis's forthcoming visit to Byron was announced,[40] Mathilda is the devil's handmaiden. It is she who actively seduces the monk Ambrosio into a life of debauchery, hypocrisy, and finally the murder of his mother and the incestuous rape of his sister. In Horace Walpole's *The Castle of Otranto* (1764), Matilda is the daughter of the Gothic villain Manfred, the Count of Otranto, who proposes to divorce his own wife and to marry his dead son's fiancée, Isabella, in a union that the Friar Jerome denounces as "an incestuous design on thy contracted daughter."[41] To further his evil design, Manfred promises to tender his own daughter Matilda to Isabella's father. In this double marriage, the two daughters function as equivalent coins in the marriage exchange to be traded and sexually possessed by two fathers in an act intended to be seen by the reader as a monstrous perversion, as incest.

Closer to home, Percy Shelley had sustained this Gothic association of evil erotic passion with the name of Matilda. Heavily influenced in his youth by the sentimental Gothic tales of Charlotte Dacre Byrne, whose nom de plume was "Rosa Matilda," Percy Shelley adopted the name of Matilda for the impassioned female protagonist of his own early Gothic tale, *Zastrozzi, A Romance* (1810). In Percy Shelley's tale, Matilda, the Contessa di Laurentini, joins with the villain Zastrozzi in an attempt to murder Julia, the beloved fiancée of the man she adores and wants for herself, Verezzi. By the end of this rather preposterous story, Matilda has seduced Verezzi into marriage by claiming that Julia has died, seen Verezzi kill himself when he discovers that Julia is alive, and in despair murdered Julia. In Percy Shelley's fiction, too, Matilda is the illegitimate love-object.

Mary Shelley's theoretical concern with incest was inspired not only by her "excessive & romantic attachment" to her father,[42] but also by her conversations with Percy Shelley and Byron, both of whom had shown an intense interest in the varieties and symbolic implications of incest. During the summer in which Mary was writing *Mathilda*, Shelley completed his verse tragedy of father-daughter incestuous rape, *The Cenci*, having discussed in detail with Mary the arrangement of its scenes.[43] During the preceding year, he had repeatedly urged Mary to translate *Mirra* (1785), Alfieri's tragedy about daughter-father incest.[44] He had, moreover, celebrated brother-sister incest in his earlier poem, "Laon and Cythna" (1817-18). And during the summer of 1816, Mary had copied Byron's *Manfred*, another verse drama implicitly concerned with sibling incest.

In *The Cenci*, Percy Shelley developed Horace Walpole's trope of parent-child incest as a representation of the father's excessive political power and tyranny over his sons. As Peter Thorslev has noted, in both *The Cenci* and *The Castle of Otranto* we find

> the sense of the past as being parasitic upon the future; of fathers, authorities, institutions, and traditions having outlived their usefulness, but being unwilling to grow old gracefully and wither away and even attempting grotesquely to renew their youth by devouring their young or by reproducing upon them.[45]

In contrast, Percy Shelley and Byron affirmed sibling incest as the appropriate love for the romantic hero, since only the sister can fully sympathize with the alienated poet in his rejection of social conventions, established political authorities, and moral laws.

But Mary Shelley's analysis of parent-child incest is very different from that found either in *The Cenci* or in the Gothic tradition. The Gothic novel written by men presents the father's incestuous rape of his daughter as the perverse desire of the older generation to usurp the sexual rights of the younger generation, while the Gothic novel written by women represents incest as a cultural taboo which functions to repress the sexual desires of women. In the female Gothic novel, as Cynthia Griffin Wolff has observed, the archetypal Gothic building with its walled exterior and too easily penetrated interior chambers, crypts, and secret passages represents the "woman's body . . . when she is undergoing the seige of conflict over sexual stimulation or arousal."[46] This metaphor makes possible a narrative strategy in which the heroine's involvement with (and final escape from) her villain-lover, who is often related to her in a way that makes his desire incestuous, enables her to experience sexual desire (the penetration of her "house") in a "safe" way.

While *Mathilda* alludes to both the male and female Gothic representations of incest, it implies a more radical analysis of the symbolic function and significance of father-daughter incest in Western culture. Influenced by her mother's *A Vindication of the Rights of Woman* to take a critical view of the role and education of women in her society, Mary Shelley in *Mathilda* attacks the underlying psychosexual structure of the bourgeois family. In a society where the father or male is the dominant authority and wielder of power and the female is taught to love and obey, the father-daughter relationship becomes a paradigm for all male-female relationships. Women are urged to remain daughters (or children) and to marry "father figures," men who are older, wiser, stronger, and more economically powerful than they. This ideology pervades the fiction of Jane Austen, where the older and wiser Mr. Knightly, her father's close friend, is depicted as the appropriate husband for Emma Woodhouse and the wealthier and more powerful Mr. Darcy as the ideal mate for Elizabeth Bennet. Walpole's Count of Otranto only expresses a widely held cultural belief when he urges his putative daughter-in-law to marry him instead of his son on the grounds that "Instead of a sickly boy, you shall have a husband in the prime of his age, who will know how to value your beauties, and who may expect a numerous offspring."[47]

Mary Shelley's *Mathilda* shows that in a society where such "father-daughter" relationships are the norm, both inside and out of the marriage bed, natural heterosexuality becomes a kind of incest. The desire of Mathilda's father for her is identical with his desire for his wife Diana. As he writes to Mathilda, "in my madness I dared say to myself—Diana died to give her birth; her mother's spirit was transferred into her frame, and she ought to be as Diana to me" (40). When wives are child-brides, there can be no meaningful distinction between wives and daughters, between women and children. As Mary Wollstonecraft had sardonically noted in *A Vindication*, the women of her time were viewed "as if they were in a state of perpetual childhood, unable to stand alone."[48] Marriage between a man and a girl young enough to be his daughter and whom he treats as his daughter is, Mary Shelley's tale suggests, incest—if not in the physical, then in the psychological sense.

Mary Shelley saw clearly that the generational hierarchy of the bourgeois family produces father-daughter incest. When a social structure that gives parents the right to govern their children is combined with the inevitable channelling of sexual desire into familial relationships (what Freudians have called the family romance), it creates the situation portrayed in *Mathilda*, a situation in which the father has sexual as well as psychological and economic mastery over his daughter. Father-daughter incest thus becomes the most obvious flaw in Mary Shelley's vision of the egalitarian bourgeois family, the point at which the inherent inequality of the family is starkly revealed. Even where husbands and wives are equal, father and mothers continue to dominate their sons and daughters. *Mathilda* draws our attention not simply to the increasingly well documented prevalence of father-daughter incest in Western societies, but more fundamentally to the injustice and potential psychological damage wrought by any family, both bourgeois and working-class, in which parents exercise power over children.[49]

Mary Shelley's primary focus is on Mathilda herself, the incest victim. Having been sexually desired by her father, Mathilda has been denied the possibility of natural growth, of the development of an autonomous, integrated selfhood or sexual identity.[50] The object and the cause of her father's desire, Mathilda feels intensely identified with that desire. As she remarks, "infamy and guilt were mingled with my portion; unlawful and detestable passion had poured its poison into my ears and changed all my blood, so that it was no longer the kindly stream that supports life but a cold fountain of bitterness corrupted in its very source" (61). Imprisoned in the role of daughter-bride, Mathilda can conceive of no future for herself: she can be, must be, the bride of death.

Mathilda's inability to imagine an adult life in society for herself is partly caused by the absence of her mother. Diana's death in childbirth, together with the withdrawn, emotionally repressed character of Mathilda's aunt, gave this young girl no positive role-model of the adult woman. The absence from this novella of a successful, happy, nurturant woman may in part project Mary Shelley's own childhood anger at her mother's death. Mary Wollstonecraft's death was experienced by her daughter as a painful absence that not only deprived her of a mother's love and protection but left her prey to an "excessive and romantic attachment" to her father. In this sense, both Mary Shelley and Mathilda reenact the psychological drama of the mother-daughter relationship in a typical father-daughter incest family, one in which the daughter experiences her mother as absent. Often the mother is consciously or subliminally aware of the incestuous relationship between her daughter and husband but does nothing to prevent or stop it, either because she is too frightened of the husband, too fearful of the legal or social consequences of publicizing an incestuous liaison, too physically or emotionally incapacitated, or, in a few cases, too psychologically dependent on her daughter to play the role of "the little mother" in the household.[51] The daughter characteristically feels more hostility to this passive, "absent" mother (who has failed to protect her or even openly betrayed her) than toward her father whose actions can be said to be motivated by a kind of love. The deaths both of Diana and of Mathilda's aunt, however much they reflect Mary Shelley's biographical circumstances, may also express the childish anger toward the absent mother felt by the abandoned daughter.

Mary Shelley's *Mathilda* shows us that a culture in which women can play no role but that of daughter, even in their marriages, denies its females the capacity for meaningful growth, since a woman's future self—even her daughter—can only replicate her present self. Procreation thus gives life, not to the future, but only to the past. When the child-bride's daughter is also her sister and peer, significant generational and psychological development becomes impossible. Mathilda's necrophilia and subconscious suicide (or "self"-consumption) are the inevitable consequences of a patriarchal, father-daughter relationship. Written at the moment in her own life when Mary Shelley had been violently deprived of the only other family role available to her, that of a mother, *Mathilda* can be read as her most critical examination of her own ideology of the bourgeois family, an ideology that offers women no social role outside the father's house and psychosexual domination.

Even without the benefit of having read *Mathilda*, we might hear the incestuous overtones of Lord Lodore's relationship with his daughter. Having taken Ethel away from her mother just as Ethel reaches puberty, Lodore teaches her to be "ever pliant to his will" and loves her "with more than a father's fondness. He lived but for her and *in* her" (I:42, my italics). A similar pattern of what we can now recognize as incestuous love recurs in Falkner's relationship with his adopted daughter, Elizabeth Raby. In prison, Falkner can think only of Elizabeth, whose presence he desires with a passion that is clearly erotic:

His passions were ardent, and all that could be spared from remorse, were centred in his adopted child . . . . when the place was vacant

that she had filled, he was excited by eager longings for her presence,
that even made his man's heart soft as a woman's with very desire.
(III:127–28)

Incest is not the only flaw in the ideology of the bourgeois family in these three novels. The daughter who dedicates herself to pleasing and obeying her father and husband often feels an anger she is unable to express at the man who satisfies his own emotional and sexual needs at the expense of hers. In *Mathilda* this female anger surfaces in Mathilda's dream following her father's declaration of erotic love, a dream in which she pursues her father to his death. Her repressed desire to punish her father is then gratified in the exhausting consummation she experiences beside his corpse.

The same female hostility to the dominating father surfaces in *Lodore* and *Falkner*, albeit in more indirect ways. When Lord Lodore is killed in a duel undertaken to preserve his honor but without thought for the impact his death might have on the daughter for whom he had assumed total responsibility, Ethel's guilty anger—her resentment of her father's decision to value her needs as less than his honor, together with her passionate grief for him—renders her suicidal: "She was in love with death, which alone could reunite her to the being, apart from whom she believed it impossible to exist" (*Lodore*, I:288). Unable to voice her anger, Ethel—like Mathilda—turns her resentment of her total dependence on her father against herself. She blames herself for not reconciling him to his past humiliations in his relationship with her mother and his natural son so as to prevent the duel of honor that caused his death. She is further mortified when she learns that her father suffered even in her company. As Mary Shelley comments, remembering her own guilt-ridden remorse after Percy Shelley's death:

> When we love one to whom we have devoted our lives with undivided affection, the idea that the beloved object suffered any grief while with us, jars with our sacred sorrow. We delight to make the difference between the possession of their society, and our subsequent bereavement, entire in its contrasted happiness and misery; we wish to have engrossed their whole souls, as they do ours, at the period of regret, and it is the most cruel theft, to know that we have been deprived of any of the power we believed that we possessed, to influence their entire being. (I:281)

The conflation of the author's grief for her dead husband with her heroine's grief for her dead father further supports the implicit identification of fathers with husbands in these novels. In both cases, the female's discovery that the male has a life larger than her own, feelings and experiences which she does not share, arouses hostility and guilt. Psychologically, she turns her angry jealousy of his greater opportunities and power against herself. As Karen Horney first pointed out, female masochism is a frequent outcome of the repressed female hostility generated from the daughter's subordinate role within the hierarchical bourgeois family.[52] Both Mary Shelley and her heroines exhibit the classic symptoms of such masochistic behavior.

But *Lodore* shows us that at the level of narrative control, female anger can be directed at the men who aroused it. Mathilda's father kills himself and Lord Lodore is unexpectedly trapped and punished by his past. His reckless action in depriving his daughter of her mother is repaid by his own early death. As the author comments:

> A strange distortion of vision blinded this unfortunate man to the truth, which experience so perpetually teaches us, that the consequences of our actions *never die*: that repentance and time may paint them to us in different shapes; but though we shut our eyes, they are still beside us, helping the inexorable destinies to spin the fatal thread, and sharpening the implement which is to cut it asunder. (I:250)

Mary Shelley here represents her narrative control as fate, a fate that inevitably punishes the man who thought he could evade responsibility for his own failures as a father and a husband. In effect, Lord Lodore is doubly punished: he loses both his life and his daughter, whose affections are finally fully engaged by her new husband and by the very mother from whom Lodore had hoped to separate her.

This narrative pattern of punishing the father is even more overt in *Falkner*, where, as Mary Poovey has observed, the loving adopted daughter Elizabeth Raby literally forces her father-figure into a confrontation with his past crime, a confrontation which leads both to his confession and his public humiliation.[53] From the moment that Elizabeth, who has hitherto been totally absorbed by her passionate devotion to her rescuer and guardian, encounters Gerard Neville, she is roused by his obvious suffering into a passionate desire to comfort him and to redress his wrongs. Her warm sympathy for Neville is of course a constant thorn in Falkner's side, for Falkner knows that he alone has caused all of Neville's agony, first by depriving him in his infancy of his adored mother Alithea and secondly by giving birth to the scandal that Alithea voluntarily deserted her husband and children. Since Neville never doubted his mother's love and loyalty, this scandal has kept him on the rack throughout his childhood and further alienated his embitterd father from him. Elizabeth Raby, however unconsciously, thus plays the same role in relation to Falkner that Godwin's Caleb

Williams played in relation to his employer and father-figure Falkland: innocent persecutor and revenging fury. In drawing this parallel with her father's novel, Shelley alerted us to Elizabeth's narrative function as unintentional but justified avenger.

More important, she constructed a narrative strategy through which she could represent Elizabeth's repressed anger at the man who, even as he idolized and tenderly cared for her, completely controlled her existence. For the author leaves us in no doubt that Falkner's decision to raise Elizabeth Raby as his daughter and to take her with him on his constant travels from England to Russia and finally Greece is a decision that is unfair to Elizabeth. However indebted Falkner feels to Elizabeth for preventing his suicide, however responsible he feels for the child who would otherwise have been raised by the very woman he inadvertently destroyed, Falkner has no right to deprive Elizabeth Raby of all contact with her natural family, with her homeland and native culture, with the companionship of peers, and with an education appropriate to a girl of her breeding. The latter defect is partially remedied by the employment of an English governess during Elizabeth's twelfth year, a cold and discreet woman who teaches Elizabeth self-discipline and needlework ("and thus Elizabeth escaped for ever the danger she had hitherto run of wanting those feminine qualities without which every woman must be unhappy—and, to a certain degree, unsexed" [I:116]). Yet Elizabeth continues to feel the want of female society and friendship. She compensates by devoting herself entirely to Falkner, sharing his every physical and intellectual activity, even as he prepares to enter the war for Greek independence in which he expects to atone his early crime by his death. Suspecting Falkner's suicidal intentions, Elizabeth is forced to "early learn the woman's first and hardest lesson, to bear in silence the advance of an evil, which might be avoided, but for the unconquerable will of another" (I:178).

Elizabeth's unacknowledged resentment of Falkner's callous uncon-cern for her needs and sufferings, of his complete domination of her existence, is displaced into the narrative structure. Even as she courageously rescues Falkner from the Greek battlefield and devotedly nurses him back to health, Elizabeth innocently forces Falkner to associate more and more with Gerard Neville, the very man whose existence is a constant reminder of his greatest sin. It is Elizabeth's fervent espousal of Neville's cause—"I think that, in all he is doing [to vindicate his lost mother], he is obeying the most sacred law of our nature, exculpating the innocent, and rendering duty to her who has a right, living or dead, to demand all his love" (II:93)—that finally forces Falkner to send Neville his confession: he had abducted Alithea

Neville, whom he had long loved and planned to marry, entirely against her will; in her frenzied efforts to escape Falkner's clutches and return to her child, she had drowned in a flash flood. In making this confession, Falkner assumes that he is signing his death warrant. He expects to be challenged by Neville to a duel in which Falkner will not even discharge his pistol. Elizabeth's loyalty to justice and her insistence on the primacy of the mother-son bond have thus constituted a fatal attack on Falkner's life.

The overt narrative conclusion—Falkner is not killed but rather arrested and forced to confess publically his role in Alithea Neville's accidental death—sentimentally redeems Falkner to live happily ever after in the household of Elizabeth Raby and Gerard Neville. But inherent in this conclusion is a transformation of Falkner's character that effectively kills off the Byronic hero whose history of passionate love, crime, remorse, and misguided self-redemption we have been reading. In this sense, Falkner has been entirely destroyed by Elizabeth. The humbled old man whom Neville can embrace is not the man who abducted both Alithea Neville and Elizabeth Raby. That double abduction of two women from their legitimate families, however justified by love, has been fully punished. Female anger at the arrogant domination of the patriarchal male has produced the narrative displacements of Mary Shelley's fiction and illuminated another of the faultlines that crack apart the ideology of the bourgeois family and the primacy of the domestic affections overtly propounded in *Falkner*.

But even as we trace these fissures in the ideological structure of *Falkner*, we must acknowledge that the strongest energies in the rhetorical figurings of the novel are directed at an affirmation of parent-child relationships. Elizabeth Raby experiences a paradise of intellectual stimulation and emotional gratification during the years she spends with Falkner in Europe and Greece. Her genuine devotion to him renders her unable to accept Neville's proposal until Falkner's name has been cleared and his blessing has been bestowed on their union. Even more potently, the novel idealizes the mother-son relationship. The greatest agony portrayed here is not Falkner's but Alithea Neville's. Suddenly deprived of her small son, she goes almost berserk with despair and risks (and loses) her life to return to him. The public redemption of an injustly slandered mother is the highest moral obligation the novel endorses, and Gerard Neville's unwavering devotion to his mother's honor is an unquestioned ideal throughout the novel. Echoing as it does Mary Shelley's own attempts to honor her mother's memory and to redress the damage done her reputation by Godwin's loving but imprudent publications, Neville's actions constitute a sentimental and unquestioned moral virtue which is rewarded by the love of the angelic Elizabeth Raby, whose very name invokes the pure Aurora Raby who sat by Eden's door and held out the possibility of experiencing heaven on earth to Byron's disillusioned Don Juan.

From a modern Anglo-American feminist perspective, the most glaring problem with the ideology of the family celebrated in Mary Shelley's novels is the fact that her female characters develop no sense of self, no independent integrity. Shelley's heroines conceive of themselves solely in relational terms, as a daughter or a wife or a mother. Since older women are generally absent from her novels, these self-definitions are all based on a relationship with a man, a father or a husband. An alternative female culture, distinguishable from a male culture, does not exist here. The female protagonists have neither sisters nor friends with whom they might develop a constructive and extra-familial concept of female identity. The ideal female, in Mary Shelley's view, is one whose life is shaped by service to her family.

Mary Shelley sets this ideal of the self-sacrificing female against what she regards as the greatest human evil, the selfish egotism displayed by many of her male protagonists, from Victor Frankenstein through Castruccio and Mathilda's father to Lodore and Falkner. All these men willingly sacrifice the good of others to forward their own ambitions, to satisfy their own desires, to protect their own reputation and honor. They are indifferent to the feelings and needs of even those whom they most love. Frankenstein is responsible for Elizabeth's death, Castruccio for Euthanasia's, Mathilda's father for Mathilda's. Lodore, in his decision to duel and die for his honor, irresponsibly abandons his daughter, while Falkner selfishly deprives his beloved ward of a normal family life. In contrast to this male egotism, a female ethic of care, service, and self-sacrifice appears noble.

But there is a price to be paid for an identity constructed entirely in relational terms, and Mary Shelley's fictions register this cost even as they overtly celebrate this virtue. Her heroines discover that, having created themselves only in relation to men, they cannot live without those men. When Mathilda's father dies, she defines herself as the "bride of death" and consciously prepares her own death, first faking her own suicide and then willing her fatal consumption. Ethel Lodore, who "seldom thought, and never acted, for herself," reacts to her father's death by falling "in love with death, which alone could reunite her to the being, apart from whom she believed it impossible to exist" (I:41, 228). Cornelia Lodore is redeemed from her mother's evil influences only when she voluntarily sacrifices the self she has become—her role in society, her friendships, her fortune—to submerge herself in nature and her second family. And Elizabeth Raby can conceive of her life only in relation to Falkner, whom she nurses both on the battlefield and in jail, and whom she refuses to abandon even when she marries. These women fail to develop an autonomous self that can survive independently of the men whom they serve and love.

In one novel, however, Mary Shelley suggests that there might be an alternative identity and social role for women beyond those contained within the bourgeois family. Although a minor character, Fanny Derham leaps off the pages of *Lodore* simply because she doesn't fit into the ideology of the family overtly endorsed in the novel. Fanny, the daughter of Lodore's old school-friend, is explicitly contrasted to Ethel. Where Lodore gives his daughter a "sexual education" that she may become the perfect wife, Derham tries to educate "an immortal soul":

> The one fashioned his offspring to be the wife of a frail human being, and instructed her to be yielding, and to make it her duty to devote herself to his happiness, and to obey his will. The other sought to guard his from all weakness, to make her complete in herself, and to render her independent and self-sufficing. (III:21)

Fanny Derham, inspired by her father's teachings and educated by his excellent private library, becomes a scholar, a person who understands and reads with pleasure the writings of the classical and Judaeo-Christian poets and philosophers. She is a woman of courage and affection, and becomes a sincere friend to Ethel Lodore, whom she supports during her days with Edward in debtors' prison.

But Fanny buys her intellectual attainments and personal independence at a high price. She has no place in the domestic circles of bourgeois English society. As Mary Shelley comments:

> Such a woman as Fanny was more made to be loved by her own sex than by the opposite one. Superiority of intellect, joined to acquisitions beyond those usual even to men; and both announced with frankness, though without pretension, forms a kind of anomaly little in accord with masculine taste. Fanny could not be the rival of women, and, therefore, all her merits were appreciated by them. (III:10)

Since the prevailing norms of her culture will frustrate Fanny's desire to marry, and since the career of professional scholar or university educator is not open to women, Fanny's future appears bleak. But Mary Shelley feels too much sympathy for Fanny to permit her to suffer greatly. She gives Fanny, unexpectedly, an inheritance from her grandfather sufficient to enable her to continue her scholarly pursuits. As she ironically comments:

> Fanny was too young, and too wedded to her platonic notions of the supremacy of mind, to be fully aware of the invaluable advantages of pecuniary independence for a woman. She fancied that she could enter on the career—the only career permitted her sex—of servitude, and yet possess her soul in freedom and power. (III:222)

The modern feminist reader yearns to know more of Fanny's life and personal feelings, since her very existence calls into question the novel's overt celebration of the egalitarian bourgeois family with its canonization of the cooperative, self-sacrificing wife and husband. Fanny represents the possibility of an entirely independent, intellectual, self-reliant woman who develops deep and enriching friendships with other women as well as with men such as her father who can appreciate her mental gifts. But Mary Shelley refuses to tell us Fanny's story, and does so deliberately. *Lodore* ends, not with the final affirmation we might have expected of the egalitarian bourgeois family that Ethel and Edward Villiers and Lady Lodore and Horatio Saville have together created, but rather with Fanny Derham, whose story cannot be told.

Since these final pages articulate Mary Shelley's most conscious recognition of the limits and failures of her own ideology, they deserve to be quoted in full:

> One only remains to be mentioned: but it is not in a few tame lines that we can revert to the varied fate of Fanny Derham. She continued for some time among her beloved friends, innocent and calm as she was beautiful and wise; circumstances at last led her away from them, and she has entered upon life. One who feels so deeply for others, and yet is so stern a censor over herself—at once so sensitive and so rigidly conscientious—so single-minded and upright, and yet open as day to charity and affection, cannot hope to pass from youth to age unharmed. Deceit, and selfishness, and the whole web of human passion must envelope her, and occasion her many sorrows; and the unworthiness of her fellow-creatures inflict infinite pain on her noble heart: still she cannot be contaminated. She will turn neither to the right nor left, but pursue her way unflinching; and in her lofty idea of the dignity of her nature, in her love of truth and in her integrity, she will find support and reward in her various fortunes. What the events are, that have already diversified her existence, cannot now be recounted; and it would require the gift of prophecy to foretell the conclusion. In after times these may be told, and the life of Fanny Derham be presented as a useful lesson, at once to teach what goodness and genius can achieve in palliating the woes of life, and to encourage those, who would in any way imitate her, by an example of calumny refuted by patience, errors rectified by charity, and the passions of our nature purified and ennobled by an undeviating observance of those moral laws on which all human excellence is founded—a love of truth in ourselves, and a sincere sympathy with our fellow-creatures. (III:310–11)

Mary Shelley cannot tell us Fanny's story because in her experience, that story has not yet been lived. Fanny Derham embodies a female potentiality that Mary Wollstonecraft had described, and her presence in the novel is Mary Shelley's homage to her mother's radical feminist convictions.

But for Mary Shelley herself, the autonomous selfhood and unswerving integrity represented by Fanny Derham was not possible. On the one hand, she identified with Fanny Derham's genuine love of learning. The self-image Mary Shelley projected in her Journal and letters is that of a woman pursuing a rigorous program of intellectual development through a life of scholarship. As she confessed in her Journal:

> Literary labours, the improvement of my mind, and the enlargement of my ideas, are the only occupations that elevate me from my lethargy. (October 2, 1822)

> I lead an innocent life, and it may become a useful one. I have talent, I will improve that talent; . . . and if, while meditating on the wisdom of ages, and storing my mind with all that has been recorded of it, any new light bursts upon me, or any discovery occurs that may be useful to my fellows, then the balm of utility may be added to innocence. (February 24, 1823)

> Study has become to me more necessary than the air I breathe. In the questioning and searching turn it gives to my thoughts, I find some relief to wild reverie; in the self-satisfaction I feel in commanding myself, I find present solace; in the hope that thence arises, that I may become more worthy of my lost one, I find a consolation that even makes me less wretched than in my most wretched moments. (March 19, 1823)[54]

But Mary Shelley never achieved the intellectual self-fulfillment and psychological independence that she attributes to Fanny Derham. The last Journal entry reminds us that her sense of self-esteem depended on the recognition and approval of others, even of the dead husband to whom she continued to address Journal entries and verbal comments for the rest of her life. As Lady Jane Shelley recalled, Mary constantly invoked Percy Shelley's presence: "It was always: 'Shelley would think this; Shelley would say that; how amused Shelley would have been by this thing.' He was ever present with her. 'He always lives with me,' she would say."[55] Her decision not to tell Fanny's story is in effect a personal confession: the intellectually accomplished, economically self-sufficient, and emotionally self-reliant woman who can play a constructive social role outside the family does not exist in her experience.

Over a decade earlier, Mary Shelley's fiction had acknowledged the possibility that women might be able to live entirely and productively outside the family, in the public realm. But she raised that possibility only to deny it. In Safie, she had quickly sketched a woman with the courage and economic independence to travel alone across Europe, but had then assigned to that woman a strictly domestic motivation and role, as the future wife of Felix De Lacey. In *Valperga: or, The Life and Adventures of Castruccio, Prince of Lucca* (1823), she drew a full-scale portrait of a highly educated woman with the capacity for both passionate love and political leadership. Euthanasia dei Admirari, who inherits the Castle of Valperga, is raised by her scholarly father both to appreciate the history and literature of her country and to strive for a politically unified Italy:

> Her young thoughts darted into futurity, to the hope of freedom for Italy, of revived learning and the reign of peace for all the world: wild dreams, that still awake the minds of men to high song and glorious action. (I:30)

She falls in love with Castruccio, the Lord of Lucca, whom she sees as the man who can rescue Italy from the internecine struggles of the Guelfs and Ghibellines and restore the Roman republic for which she yearns. While Castruccio admires and loves her, he does not share Euthanasia's dream of a pax Romana but desires instead a Ghibelline oligarchy. Having "made a god of him she loved, believing every virtue and every talent to live in his soul" (I:189), Euthanasia is gradually disillusioned as Castruccio becomes increasingly devious and cruel in his military campaigns. She refuses to join him, preserving Valperga's neutrality, until finally Valperga is captured and she becomes a prisoner of the tyrant she both loves and condemns:

> Sometimes she thanked Providence that she had not become the wife of this man: but it was a bitter thankfulness. She had not been wedded to him by the church's rites; but her soul, her thoughts, her fate, had been married to his; she tried to loosen the chain that bound them eternally together, and felt that the effort was fruitless: If he were evil, she must weep; if his light-hearted selfishness allowed no room for remorse in his own breast, humiliation and sorrow was doubly her portion, and this was her destiny for ever. (III:15)

She repeatedly tries to persuade Castruccio to abandon his vengeful, bloodthirsty policies against the Guelfs and establish peace, but he refuses. Finally, thinking that only in this way can she save his life, Euthanasia joins a conspiracy against Castruccio. The conspiracy is betrayed and Castruccio sends Euthanasia to prison in Sicily. En route she is drowned: "She slept in the oozy cavern of the ocean; the sea-weed was tangled with her shining hair; and the spirits of the deep wondered that the earth had trusted so lovely a creature to the barren bosom of the sea, which, as an evil step-mother, deceives and betrays all committed to her care (III:261)." Euthanasia's fate, as her name suggests, registers Mary Shelley's conviction that a highly educated and loving woman dedicated to public political action in the revolutionary cause of universal peace cannot survive, either in wartorn fourteenth-century Italy or, by implication, in the imperialist England of her day. Euthanasia's death is therefore merciful, for in Shelley's view, her life could only be that of the imprisoned, disillusioned, and perpetually suffering idealist.

Significantly, in *Valperga* the self-sacrificing woman fares no better. Beatrice, the sainted virgin who falls in love with Castruccio and construes their sexual liaison as a religious revelation, follows him pathetically until she is imprisoned for heresy. But Castruccio feels no responsibility for Beatrice's sufferings and she finally dies, comforted only by Euthanasia. In the world of Machiavellian realpolitik that Castruccio constructs around him,[56] only the selfish and cruel can survive. *Valperga* is primarily an attack on male ambition and egotism, which corrupts the youthful, loyal, and idealistic Castruccio into a tyrant "daring, artful, bounteous and cruel; evil predominated in his character; and, if he were loved by a few, he was hated by most, and feared by all" (III:171). But it also emphasizes the inability of women, whether as adoring worshippers (like Beatrice) or active leaders (like Euthanasia), to influence political events or to translate an ethic of care—whether embodied in the domestic affections or in a political program of universal justice and peace—into historical reality.

Euthanasia and Fanny Derham together demonstrate that Mary Shelley never completely renounced her mother's vision of a well educated and entirely self-reliant woman. But the material circumstances of her life forced Mary Shelley to acknowledge that such a woman could not find a place in the middle-class English society of her day. The widespread denunciation of Mary Wollstonecraft as a revolutionary, atheist, and whore after the publication of Godwin's ill-judged *Memoirs* made it socially impossible for a respectable, educated woman of the early nineteenth century to advocate Wollstonecraft's lifestyle or to celebrate her as a leader of the women's movement. More personally, it eroded Mary Shelley's belief that her mother's life and career provided a viable alternative social role for women. The absence from her novels of independent, self-fulfilled, nurturant women records Mary Shelley's oblique recognition that such a woman does not survive in the world she knew.

In 1838, Mary Shelley justified her refusal actively to support her parents' revolutionary politics in the following terms:

> In the first place, with regard to "the good cause"—the cause of the advancement of freedom and knowledge, of the rights of women, &tc.—I am not a person of opinions. . . . That my parents and Shelley were of the former class, makes me respect it. . . . For myself, I earnestly desire the good and enlightenment of my fellow-creatures, and see all, in the present course, tending to the same, and rejoice; but I am not for violent extremes, which only bring on an injurious reaction. . . . Besides, I feel the counter-arguments too strongly. . . ; besides that, on some topics (especially with regard to my own sex), I am far from making up my mind. I believe we are sent here to educate ourselves, and that self-denial, and disappointment, and self-control, are a part of our education; that it is not by taking away all restraining law that our improvement is to be achieved; and, though many things need great amendment, I can by no means go so far as my friends would have me. When I feel that I can say what will benefit my fellow-creatures, I will speak; not before.[57]

In part Mary Shelley's desire to avoid extremes, to function within the laws and mores of established English society, was an economic necessity. In order to provide for her son, she had to write books that would be commercially successful. More important, she had to placate that arch-conservative Sir Timothy Shelley so as to sustain her son's allowance and preserve his inheritance intact.

But we should not regard her as compromising her ideals for material advantage. Mary Shelley was by temperament a conservative who endorsed a cultural and social tradition based on a model of monarchical democracy, class stability, and organic evolutionary growth. When advised to send her son to a school where they would teach him to think for himself, she is reported to have answered. "Teach him to think for himself? Oh, my God, teach him rather to think like other people!"[58] Her commitment to the bourgeois family derives in part from her conviction that only within the confines of that family have women found roles—as mothers, child-care providers, educators, and moral guardians—at once psychologically fulfilling, culturally valued, and historically viable. We must remember that Mary Shelley would extend the roles of mother, educator, and moral leader to men as well as women. Were men to mother their children with the same responsibility and sensitivity as women—and here Mary Shelley anticipates the modern psychoanalytic theories of Nancy Chodorow and Jean Baker Miller—they might well develop the same "female consciousness" or primary commitment to the preservation of human life historically possessed by women. The result would be a revolutionary redefinition of the way nations are governed and the way social institutions are structured; new practices of mediation and the peaceful resolution of conflict would replace traditional practices of competition and military warfare.

Of all Mary Shelley's later novels, *Lodore* most deserves to be read today for its honest recognition of the contradictions inherent within her ideology of the bourgeois family. Her affirmation of the domestic affections requires a sacrifice from both men and women of their independence and individual gratification. On the one hand, such a sacrifice prevents the evils engendered by a self-centred egotism and is rewarded by a satisfying sense of emotional union with another person. On the other hand, such a sacrifice can annihilate individual identity, arrest one's mental and emotional development, and leave one prone—if the marriage partner does not reciprocate one's commitment—to suicidal despair.

CHAPTER ELEVEN

Idealizing the Bourgeois Family:
Final Reflections

The death of Mary Wollstonecraft Godwin in childbirth not only deprived Mary Shelley of her mother, but left her with a perhaps never-satisfiable desire for the unconditional love of another person. Further frustrated by the apparent withdrawal of her father's affection, her unhappy interactions with her stepmother, the deaths of four of her five children and her troubled relationship with her husband (who died when she was only twenty-five), Mary Shelley displaced her desire for an all-consoling mother on to the world around her. She turned first to her father, then to "mother nature" (during her two-year stay in Scotland with the Baxter family), then to her husband, her female friends, and finally to an aristocratic "society" for the attention, approval, and financial support she craved.

These personal experiences produced a set of values, or ideology, which inform all her literary work. They led her to celebrate an idealized image of the middle-class, bourgeois family as a set of loving and egalitarian relationships, an image in part derived from her mother's concept in *A Vindication of the Rights of Woman* of the rational, educated woman as the "companion" of her husband. Her fictional celebrations of the bourgeois family generate such devoted parents as Father De Lacey, Alithea Neville, Cordelia Lodore (after her conversion), and Idris and Lionel Verney, together with such dutiful daughters and sons as Ethel Lodore, Elizabeth Raby, Gerard Neville, and Felix and Agatha De Lacey.

In the context of what we now know about the structure of the family in England in the early nineteenth century, Mary Shelley's vision, in which husbands and wives are regarded as equal providers of emotional and even financial support, was at odds with the prevailing practice. During the eighteenth century, as both Lawrence Stone and Randolph Trumbach have argued, some significant changes occurred in the middle- and upper-class English family. Stone documents a development away from the rigidly patriarchal family of the late Renaissance toward a more affectionate nuclear family in which individuals were granted more privacy and respect, a development energized in part by the Protestant Reformation, while Trumbach shows that there were increasingly contractual and hence egalitarian relationships between masters and servants and fathers and children in aristocratic families.[1] Alan MacFarlane's study of English love and marriage between 1300 and 1840 argues that the Malthusian marriage-system prevailed in England from the sixteenth century onward and Linda Pollock's research on parent-child relationships documents that affectionate bonds united English families as early as 1500.[2] Yet it seems clear that by 1800 a more intense cult of domesticity generated from the increasing number of non-arranged love-marriages in the seventeenth and eighteenth centuries idealized the nuclear family as the primary source of psychological and spiritual comfort.

The cult of domesticity was further strengthened among the upper and middle classes during the nineteenth century by the doctrine of the separate spheres (public man versus private woman) that was intensified by the industrial revolution and the increasing division of waged from unwaged labor. But this growing cultural affirmation of domesticity, registered in the increasing popularity of family portraits or "conversation pieces" in British art in the eighteenth century,[3] did not radically change the hierarchical relationship between husbands and wives or fathers and children that had prevailed since the feudal period. Trumbach admits that the increasing equality between masters and servants was not easily transferred to husband-wife or father-daughter relationships among the aristocracy where the surviving system of patrilineage demanded a double standard in the treatment of women.[4]

Mary Shelley's visionary family was rooted in her mother's lower-class, proto-industrial culture. The daughter of an impoverished Lancashire weaver who emigrated to London, Mary Wollstonecraft had been born into a world of cottage industries which expected husbands and wives to contribute equally to the family welfare. In this plebeian society, as David Levine and John Gillis have shown, the wife's domestic employment and earnings increased her social status.[5] By suggesting that bourgeois women, such as Lady Lodore or Agatha and Safie in *Frankenstein*, should act independently and contribute significantly to the family resources, Mary Shelley extended this lower-class expectation to the middle and upper classes. She thus put forth a revolutionary concept of the ideal structure of the English middle-class family as one in which both marriage partners participated in the emotional care and education of their children and were mutually respected as equals within the home.

In this context, I have interpreted *Frankenstein* as an extended analysis of what happens, both psychologically and socially, when such a family, and especially a loving parent, is absent. Mary Shelley's own anxieties about her capacity to be an adequate mother determined both the origin and the production of the novel (the ghost story contest and her subsequent dream, the structure of the novel, the revisions of her manuscript). Victor Frankenstein's failure to mother his child produces a monster at many levels of cultural meaning. Mary Shelley's celebration of the egalitarian bourgeois family has political, aesthetic, scientific, and philosophical implications. Politically, it endorses the conservative position espoused by Edmund Burke, a position that upholds the traditional, organically evolving, affectionate nuclear family and condemns the revolutionary irresponsibility of Promethean politics. Aesthetically, it entails an affirmation of the beautiful over the sublime, for the beautiful (as Burke had shown) is identified with the female procreation of the family while the sublime is associated with a solitary egoistic male triumph over death. In her view, "good" science recognizes and respects a sacred procreative life-force troped as "Mother Nature," whereas "bad" science construes nature as dead matter or a machine to be manipulated, controlled, and changed. At the philosophical level, Shelley's belief in the family implies that only a maternally loving, nurturant perception or linguistic construction of reality can prevent the semiotic construction of monsters.

Mary Shelley believed the egalitarian family to be the only social context in which both men and women could achieve emotional satisfaction, through powerful husband-wife and parent-child bonding. The loving family embodies an ethic of disinterested care that is the necessary foundation of a healthy body politic. Like Jane Austen and George Eliot, she believed that the progressive reform of civilization can happen only when individuals willingly give up their egotistical desires and ambitions in order to serve the greater good of the community.

Her ideology of the egalitarian bourgeois family thus subsumes but goes significantly beyond the ideology of the proper lady described by Mary Poovey. Shelley's concept of the family includes the proper lady as wife and daughter: the ideal woman functions as a modest, devoted, self-sacrificing servant of the needs of the family. Since Shelley's own writings celebrated the continued reproduction of the family, she experienced no conflict between her role as wife and mother and her desire to write. But it is critical to see that Mary Shelley, most explicitly in *Frankenstein* and *Lodore*, insisted that the role of the proper lady and mother *must also be filled by men* if the family is to survive. Her proper man is Horatio Saville: the exemplar of modest, selfless, devoted service to his wife and family, an ideal type first embodied in Clerval and later reborn in Gerard Neville. Had Adrian been able to fulfill this commitment to the preservation of human life in a loving union with Clara, civilization would not have ended with the last man, Lionel Verney.

In this sense, Mary Shelley's writings support a feminist position which argues that female culture is morally superior to male culture, that men should become more like women, more "feminine" in their behavior. Commenting on gender-difference in her Journal on December 3, 1825, she observed that "most women I believe wish that this [sic, for they] had been men—so do not I—change my sex & I do not think that my talents would be greater—& I should be like one of these—selfish, unkind—either persueing [sic] for their own ends or deserting—because those ends cannot be satisfied."[6] All her novels show the ways in which an uninhibited male egoism contributes to human suffering and may even cause the annihilation of human civilization. Mary Shelley would have us see that only a culture that mothers all its members, a behavior traditionally embodied in but not necessarily limited to the work of women, can prevent the making of monsters capable of destroying us all.

However, even as Mary Shelley's novels implicitly or overtly celebrate the egalitarian bourgeois family and the ethic of care it encodes, they also reveal the limits of that ideology. They consistently show what happens to a woman who defines her self solely in terms of the family. Drawing on her own experiences of childhood abandonment, frustrated desire, and lack of self-esteem, Mary Shelley acknowledges that in her contemporary culture, a devoted child can be abandoned by its father (as are Frankenstein's creature and Ethel Lodore), causing both resentful anger and monstrous revenge. Or a loving daughter can be exploited by a father to satisfy his emotional needs at the expense of hers, as is Mathilda, the object of her father's incestuous fantasies. Or a female may grow up with no sense of self-esteem or independent autonomy, leaving her helpless, even suicidal, at the disappearance of the man to whom she devoted herself, as are Ethel Lodore and Mathilda. A woman who defines herself exclusively in terms of her family relationships may also find herself without social security, both in the sense of economic solvency (as was Mary Shelley after her husband's death and her father's bankruptcy) and in the larger sense envisioned in *The Last Man*, where all human relationships are subject to disease (the plague), disruption, and death. But the alternative for women to marriage and life within the family, the educated, self-sufficient, and financially independent woman portrayed in the character of Fanny Derham in *Lodore*, does not find a place in the world depicted in Shelley's fiction.

This means, finally, that while celebrating the egalitarian bourgeois family, Mary Shelley acknowledges that it has never existed. There are no detailed examinations of such a family in her fiction: we leave the Villiers/Savilles just at the moment of their reunion; the family units in *The Last Man* are inexorably destroyed by disease (the diseases of ambition, suspicion, and anxiety as well as the literal plague); and the De Laceys are ripped out of *Frankenstein*, perhaps because that family again lacked the mother who alone might have been able to embrace the ugly but loving monster.

In terms of modern political theory, Mary Shelley was a feminist in the sense that her mother was, in that she advocated an egalitarian marriage and the education of women. But insofar as she endorsed the continued reproduction of the bourgeois family, her feminism is qualified by the ways in which her affirmation of the bourgeois family entails an acceptance of its intrinsic hierarchy, a hierarchy historically manifested in the doctrine of the separate spheres, in the domination of the male gender, and in the unequal distribution of power between parents and children. Nonetheless, since Shelley's personal experiences inspired her to document the ways in which the traditional middle-class family can mutilate the lives of women, modern feminists can find many useful insights in her work.

The "monsters" of my title thus refers not only to the creature produced by Victor Frankenstein's hubristic usurpation of natural reproduction, but also to the cultural ideologies that generate men who devalue women and women who are psychologically crippled because they can find no social opportunity to develop their innate capacities for autonomous selfhood, creative expression, or meaningful public work. From this perspective, Mary Shelley's novels can serve as a powerful warning to the modern age, showing us the damage wrought by a still dominant capitalist ideology that enables the masculine gender to control, exploit, and suppress the feminine and that endorses the reproduction of hierarchical power-systems both within the nuclear family and in society at large.

At the same time, her novels record one woman's fascination with a masculine domination. Mary Shelley's obsessive preference for egotistical male protagonists—Frankenstein, Castruccio, Mathilda's father,

Adrian Windsor, Raymond, Falkner, Lodore—registers her deep-seated ambivalence toward Percy Shelley, Byron, and Godwin. Even as she documents the damage caused by their arrogant selfishness, she acknowledges the power these male figures possess over her psychic life. She thus points to that troubling possibility discussed so perceptively by Tania Modleski in *Loving with a Vengeance*, that women raised within a hierarchical nuclear family experience sexual desire only in the terms permitted by the family romance. In other words, a woman's sexual fantasies can only reproduce the dynamics of the father-daughter relationship, whether the daughter's wily seduction of the more powerful father or the father's aggressive, virile conquest of the daughter. Mathilda's lifelong obsession with her father, Euthanasia's with Castruccio, Perdita's with Raymond, and Elizabeth's with Falkner all suggest that Mary Shelley's own sexuality and erotic desires were aroused only by masterful, self-confident, egotistical males, men like Godwin, Byron, and Percy Shelley, embodiments of the patriarchal power of their bourgeois culture. At the psychological as well as the ideological level, then, Mary Shelley's fictions are ruptured, broken apart by her contradictory desires: to find self-esteem and emotional satisfaction as wife and mother within an egalitarian family on the one hand, and on the other, to consummate her relentless desire for total absorption by the all-powerful parent, whether the father or the (in her case forever lost) mother.

In the ongoing feminist debate as to whether the Freudian family romance produces or only reproduces the patriarchal structure of bourgeois capitalism,[7] Mary Shelley's novels uncomfortably suggest that the female raised within the bourgeois family may never be able to escape the father's seduction. Insofar as her female protagonists choose husbands who replicate their fathers' powers of fascinating control, insofar as her heroines find no satisfying social existence outside the nuclear family, Mary Shelley vividly poses the question at the center of much current feminist theorizing. Can the culturally inherited roles of mother and wife be reconciled with the development of female autonomy and independence? Can the hierarchy of the bourgeois family structure—even where husbands do not govern wives, parents do govern children—be reconciled with gender equality? Mary Shelley's novels advocate the practices of mothering in all arenas of public and private life. At the same time they painfully uncover the ways in which even nurturant families can generate incestuous and sadomasochistic desires and reproduce exploitative sexual behaviors. In this sense, the nightmarish pessimism of *Frankenstein* and *The Last Man* pervades even Shelley's later, only apparently optimistic and comfortingly sentimental fictions.

Percy Shelley's Revisions of the Manuscript of *Frankenstein*

Percy Shelley genuinely improved the manuscript of *Frankenstein* in many small ways. He corrected three minor factual errors: he accurately dated Frankenstein's reference to Charles I and the Civil Wars to a period not "two" but "one and a half" centuries earlier (157:6); he redated Frankenstein's own creation of the monster to a period not "two" but "three" years before his arrival in Scotland (163:5); and he rightly permitted the newborn creature to mutter not "words" but only "inarticulate sounds" as he peers through Victor Frankenstein's bed-curtains (53:21). He eliminated some obvious grammatical mistakes. He removed his wife's dangling prepositions and a few awkward constructions, as when he revised her "as if an omen of my future misery if I should prosecute my journey" to "an omen, as it were, of my future misery" (37:16–17).

On several occasions, Percy clarified the text. Mary's rather vague comment on Frankenstein's disappointment with the goals of modern scientists—"and the expulsion of chimaera overthrew at the same time all greatness in the science"—became Percy's more eloquent and precise "The ambition of the inquirer seemed to limit itself to the annihilation of those visions on which my interest in science was chiefly founded. I was required to exchange chimeras of boundless grandeur for realities of little worth" (41:23–26). Waldman's lecture on chemistry now begins, not with Mary's sloppy "a kind of history," but with Percy's more specific "a recapitulation of the history" (42:6). And Frankenstein's insight into the cause of generation and life was clarified by Percy from the obscure comment that this information was "rather one that would direct my endeavours than show the prospect with any precise certainty" to the more logical "was of a nature rather to direct my endeavours so soon as I should point them towards the object of my search, than to exhibit that object already accomplished" (48:4–5). Mary's awkward account of the thunderstorm over Lake Geneva—"The most violent storm was exactly north of the town and at that part where the lake turns the promontory of Belrive and changing its course from south to north which it before pursued proceeds from west to east"— was simplified by Percy to the more concrete "The most violent storm hung exactly north of the town, over that part of the lake which lies between the promontory of Belrive and the village of Copêt" (71:11–14). Percy explicated the role of Goethe's *Werther* in the creature's education by defining the feelings the novel depicted as altruistic, "which had for their object something out of self" (123:28–29), and adding that they accorded well with "the wants which were forever alive in my own bosom" (124:1–2). He amplified the ontological dimension of the creature's agonized search for identity by adding to Mary's questions, "Who was I? What was I?" the more teleologically oriented "Whence did I come? What was my destination?" (124:17–18). And he specified Frankenstein's neglected obligations to his creature by adding to Mary's description of the relationship between God and Adam that Adam was "guarded by the especial care of his Creator; he was allowed to converse with, and acquire knowledge from beings of a superior nature" (125:20–22).

Percy frequently substituted more precise technical terms for Mary's cruder ones. His greater scientific learning enabled him to change Frankenstein's "workshop" into a "laboratory" (162:6), his chemical "machines" into "instruments" (46:10), and his area of specialization, "natural philosophy," into "natural philosophy in its general relations" (41:11). Similarly he added Waldman's observation that modern science is founded on the researches of the alchemists (42:33–43:1) and the comment that Frankenstein analyzed "all the minutiae of causation, as exemplified in the change from life to death, and death to life" (47:14–15). As the more sophisticated philosopher and linguist, Percy specified that the creature's first experience of fear was not conscious knowledge but "as it were instinctively" (98:12); that "sensations" (99:10) preceded conscious ideas; and that the development of the ability to distinguish one sensation from another is "gradual" (98:31). He revised Mary's account of the creature's response to Father De Lacey's smile of kindness and affection from "I felt my own hard nerves move and I was obliged to withdraw" to a more informed account of the development of the emotions: "I felt sensations of a peculiar and overpowering nature: they were a mixture of pain and pleasure, such as I have never before experienced, either from hunger or cold, warmth or food; and I withdrew from the window, unable to bear these emotions" (103:32–104:3). Percy's fascination with the nature of language and language acquisition led him to make several technical changes in Mary's account of the creature's linguistic development. Percy specified that the De Lacey's possessed a "method" of communicating not merely "ideas" but more generally their "experience and feelings" (107:16–17); that the mystery of language lies not so much in its "sounds" as in its "reference" (107:26); and that names are given to objects "of discourse" and must be "applied" to things (107:29–30). Finally, Percy's greater familiarity with legal procedures enabled him to revise Frankenstein's "tale" told to the magistrate Mr. Kirwin into a "deposition" (196:33), while his superior knowledge of sailing led him to correct Frankenstein's account, during his solo boat trip from Scotland to Ireland, of "leaving the rudder" to "fixing the rudder in a direct position" (168:35) and of his unsuccessful attempt to "turn the boat" to an attempt to "change my course" (169:8).

Some of Percy's revisions markedly improved the coherence and narrative continuity of the text. He occasionally sharpened the logic of his wife's ideas. When Frankenstein is nostalgically recalling his delight in his native landscape, Percy adds the comment that no one "but a native" could comprehend his pleasure (70:11). When the creature promises Frankenstein that he will leave him and his family in peace if Frankenstein will give him what he asks, Percy moved that condition to the front of the sentence, emphasizing its force (94:27–28). And again, he recast Justine's testimony that "I am at a stand. I have no enemy on earth that I know" to the stronger "I am checked. I believe that I have no enemy on earth" (79:8–9). He increased the credibility of Frankenstein's narrative by changing his assertion that he had passed three months on the ice pursuing the monster to a more plausible three weeks (204:31). Sometimes he introducd information necessary to our comprehension of events. For instance, he added to Frankenstein's account of his pursuit of the monster the fact that although Frankenstein saw the creature boarding a vessel bound for the Black Sea and "followed him," "he escaped me, I know not how" (220:31). And he made sense of Mary's comment that "again the frost came" after Frankenstein heard the threatening sea beneath the ice by adding "and made the paths of the sea secure" (204:28–29).

Percy occasionally improved Mary's paragraph transitions. After the creature has been rejected by the De Laceys and has spent a miserable night in the forest, Percy initiated the next paragraph with "The pleasant sunshine, and the pure air of day, restored me to some degree of tranquillity" (133:9–10), thus setting the scene for the creature's final disappointment. And he intensified the foreshadowing of the concluding line of Chapter III by changing Frankenstein's reference to his reviving cares and fears "which I had forgotten while on the water" to the more foreboding "which soon were to clasp me, and cling to me for ever" (191:18).

Percy several times enriched the thematic resonance of the text. He anticipated the disastrous results of Frankenstein's project by adding to his admission that he might have thrown Agrippa aside had his father bothered to explain Agrippa's flaws, the prophetic statement, "it is even possible, that the train of my ideas would never have received the fatal impulse that led to my ruin" (33:9–11). In a fine bit of prefigurative dramatic irony, he added to Frankenstein's reflections on his mother's death the comment that we must "learn to think ourselves fortunate, whilst one remains whom the spoiler has not seized" (38:28–29). By changing Frankenstein's eulogy of those alchemists or masters of science who sought "immortality and wealth" to "immortality and power," Percy perceptively focused our attention on Frankenstein's ultimate desire for omnipotence. He improved Mary's banal expression of Frankenstein's self-pity the morning after his creation—"Surely so wretched a creature had never before existed"—to the more perceptive "Mingled with this horror, I felt the bitterness of disappointment" (54:4–5). By describing Frankenstein's reaction to his discovery in terms of landscape—"I became dizzy with the immensity of the prospect which it illustrated" (47:17–18), he prepared for Mary's identification of the creature with the sublime. His added description of the Mer de Glace (93:23–26) gives substance to Mary's evocation of the sublime, justifies Frankenstein's pleasure in the scene, and further creates an additional dramatic irony, since Frankenstein's delight is immediately destroyed by the second appearance of the monster.

Percy further developed the complexity of the monster's character in several revisions. He stressed the generosity of the creature's bringing love-gifts of firewood to the De Lacey family by including Felix's reaction—"to his perpetual astonishment, he found his store always replenished by an invisible hand" (108:33–34). He anticipated the character of the monster's future crimes by adding to Frankenstein's forebodings the statement that "There was always scope for fear, so long as any thing I loved remained behind" (87:21–22) and increased our sense of Frankenstein's (and our own) danger by augmenting the creature's threatened evil with the warning "which it only remains for you to make so great, that not only you and your family, but thousands of others, shall be swallowed up in the whirlwinds of its rage" (96:4–6). By adding "after their sufferings in the lake of fire" to the creature's allusion to the daemons of hell in their retreat to Pandemonium (101:6), Percy Shelley both recalled the creature's double-edged experience of fire as warming and painful and also strengthened the identification of the creature with Satan. He further sharpened this identification by introducing a reference to the creature's discovery of his "accursed origin" (126:7) and by changing Mary's "for everywhere I see bliss while I alone am irrecoverably wretched" to the more telling "whom thou drivest from joy for no misdeed. Everywhere I see bliss, from which I alone am irrevocably excluded" (95:16–18). He kept before the reader's eye the ambiguity of the creature's appearance by referring to him not as "he" but as "the shape" (94:5). This phrase anticipates Percy's own imaging of power as Demogorgon, that "mighty darkness ... shapeless" (in *Prometheus Unbound*). On the other hand, he emphasized the creature's community with human beings by changing the monster's reference to "your fellow-creatures" to "any other being that wore the human form" (136:14–15).

Similarly, Percy stressed Victor Frankenstein's unique responsibility for his creature by interpolating the phrase "ought to be" in Mary's "I am thy Adam" and by his adding to the creature's account of his abuse at the hands of other human beings the phrase "who owe me nothing" (95:29). He further emphasized Frankenstein's responsibility by changing Frankenstein's reference to the condemned Justine from the bland "her" to "my unhappy victim" (80:25) and by adding that the curse upon Frankenstein's head was "as mortal as that of crime" (160:12).

In contrast to these positive changes is Percy Shelley's inclination for an inflated rhetoric, which I have explored earlier and of which I should perhaps give a few more examples. When Elizabeth, speaking of Justine, says "My aunt was very fond of her which caused her to give her an education," Percy Shelley eliminated the possibly confusing pronoun reference by the following: "My aunt conceived a great attachment for her, by which she was induced to give her an education superior to that which she had at first intended" (60:29–31). When Frankenstein considers, in Mary Shelley's words, "whether my marriage would hasten my fate. It might indeed a few months but if he suspected that I delayed on his account, he would certainly revenge himself some other way," Percy Shelley heightened it to

> my destruction might indeed arrive a few months earlier; but if my torturer should suspect that I postponed it, influenced by his menaces, he would surely find other, and perhaps more dreadful means of revenge. (186:21–24)

At least one howler came into the text at Percy's instigation. When Frankenstein heard Elizabeth's dying shriek, he "could feel the blood trickling in my veins," wrote Mary, to which Percy appended, "and tingling in my feet," a revision only slightly improved in the published "and tingling in the extremities of my limbs" (193:9).

The full extent of Percy Shelley's editorial policies will only become clear to the general reader when we have a complete transcript of the surviving fragments of the manuscript of *Frankenstein* in print, an editorial task which I hope will soon be undertaken.

CHAPTER ONE In Search of a Family

1. *The Monthly Review* (London: September-December, 1798), pp. 321–22.

2. Thomas Mathias, *The Shade of Alexander Pope* (London, 1799), p. 48. For a fuller discussion of the impact of Godwin's *Memoirs* on the reputation of Mary Wollstonecraft, see Donald Locke, *A Fantasy of Reason—The Life and Thought of William Godwin* (London: Routledge & Kegan Paul, 1980), pp. 133–39; Eleanor Flexner, *Mary Wollstonecraft* (New York: Coward, McCann & Geoghegan, 1972), pp. 264–65; and especially Claire Tomalin, *The Life and Death of Mary Wollstonecraft* (New York and London: Harcourt, Brace, Jovanovich, 1974), pp. 234–53.

3. William Godwin, *Memoirs of the Author of A Vindication of the Rights of Woman* (London, 1798), Second edition corrected, p. 195.

4. William Godwin, ed., *Posthumous Works of the Author of a Vindication of the Rights of Woman* (London: J. Johnson, 1798), III:5–6.

5. *Letters of Anna Seward* (Edinburgh and London, 1811), III:117.

6. *The Love Letters of Mary Hays (1779–1780)*, ed. A. F. Wedd (London: Methuen, 1925), p. 5.

7. *Portrait of a Whig Peer*, ed. Brian Connell (London: André Deutsch, 1957), p. 259. For a thorough discussion of the public response to *A Vindication of the Rights of Woman*, see Claire Tomalin, *Mary Wollstonecraft*, pp. 110–16.

8. Louisa Jones's letters to Godwin are on deposit at the Bodleian Library, in the Abinger Shelley Collection (Dep. c. 508).

9. C. Kegan Paul, *William Godwin, His Friends and Contemporaries* (London, Henry S. King & Co., 1876), I:313.

10. Louisa Jones to William Godwin, undated (Abinger Dep. c. 508).

11. C. Kegan Paul, *William Godwin*, I:364–65, 367, 370, 374.

12. Charles Lamb, *The Letters of Charles Lamb to which are added those of his sister Mary Lamb*, ed. E. V. Lucas (London: J. M. Dent & Sons, 1935), I:273, 304; Marshall's comment is quoted by Don Locke, *A Fantasy of Reason*, p. 206.

13. William Godwin to Mary Jane Clairmont, October 10, 1801; October 28, 1803. Godwin's correspondence with Mary Jane Clairmont Godwin is in the Abinger Collection in the Bodleian Library (Abinger Dep. c. 523).

14. William Godwin to Mary Jane Clairmont Godwin, April 2, 1805; April 5, 1805 (Abinger Dep. c. 523).

15. William Godwin to Mary Jane Clairmont Godwin, August 13, 1809 (Abinger Dep. c. 523).

16. *The Letters of Mary Wollstonecraft Shelley*, ed. Betty T. Bennett (Baltimore: Johns Hopkins University Press, 1980, 1983), II:215; dated October 30, 1834.

17. *Letters of Mary Shelley*, ed. Betty T. Bennett, I:363, dated August 7, 1823.

18. C. Kegan Paul, *William Godwin*, II:214.

19. C. Kegan Paul, *William Godwin*, II:213–14.

20. C. Kegan Paul, *William Godwin*, II:118–20.

21. Iona and Peter Opie discovered that Mary Godwin was the author of "Mounseer Nongtongpaw; or, The Discoveries of John Bull in a Trip to Paris" printed in 1808 "for the Proprietors of the Juvenile Library, 41, Skinner Street"; see their note on the poem in *A Nursery Companion*, ed. Iona and Peter Opie (Oxford: Oxford University Press, 1980), pp. 127–28. For the sake of comparison, I give the beginning and final verses of Charles Dibdin's original song "Mounseer Nongtongpaw":

> *John Bull for pastime took a prance,*
> *Some time ago, to peep at France;*
> *To talk of sciences and arts,*
> *And knowledge gain'd in foréign parts.*
> *Monsieur, obsequious, heard him speak,*
> *And answer'd John in heathen Greek:*
> *To all he ask'd, 'bout all he saw,*
> *'Twas, 'Monsieur, je vous n'entends pas.'*
>
> . . . .
>
> *John, to the Palais Royal come,*
> *Its splendour almost struck him dumb,*
> *'I say, whose house is that there here?'*
> *'Hosse! Je vous n'entends pas, Monsieur.'*
> *'What, Nongtongpaw again?' cries John,*
> *'This fellow is some mighty Don:*
> *No doubt has plenty for the maw,*
> *I'll breakfast with this Nongtongpaw. . .'*
>
> . . . .
>
> *But hold,—whose fun'ral's that? cries John:*
> *Je vous n'entends pas: What! is he gone?*
> *Wealth, fame, and beauty could not save*
> *Poor Nongtongpaw, then, from the grave:*
> *His race is run, his game is up;*
> *I'd with him breakfast, dine, and sup:*
> *But since he chooses to withdraw,*
> *Good night t'ye, Mounseer Nongtongpaw.*
>
> (Charles Dibdin, *The Songs of Charles Dibdin* [London: 1848], II:143.)

22. Aaron Burr recorded attending one such lecture, which the eight-year-old William Godwin read "from a little pulpit . . . with great gravity and decorum," after which the family had tea, "and the girls sang and danced an hour" (Aaron Burr, *The Private Journal of Aaron Burr* [New York: Harper & Brothers, 1858], II:307; dated February 15, 1812).

23. Mary Wollstonecraft Shelley, Introduction to *Frankenstein, or The Modern Prometheus* (London: Colburn and Bentley; Standard Novels Edition, 1831), p. v.

24. Peter Marshall claims that "Godwin taught the girls Roman, Greek and

English history, and they learned French and Italian from tutors. Fanny and Mary drew very well, but as Jane could never draw she learned music and singing instead" (*William Godwin* [New Haven: Yale University Press, 1984], p. 293). But Marshall's claim rests entirely on an extremely unreliable source, Claire Clairmont's heavily revised copy of her mother's letter to Lady Mountcashel, printed with a strong caveat by R. Glynn Grylls in *Claire Clairmont, Mother of Byron's Allegra* (London: John Murray, 1939), p. 277. Claire's accounts of her childhood, prepared in her old age in the 1870s for Trelawney, are highly suspect, designed as they are to present herself in the most favorable light possible. Peter Marshall's entire account of Godwin's family life—in Chapter 17—is seriously marred by his idealization of Godwin, his excessive hostility to Mary Jane Clairmont Godwin, his failure to consult the best available editions of the Shelley and Clairmont letters and journals, and most of all, by his acceptance as fact of Claire Clairmont's unreliable memoirs and revised copies of her mother's letters.

25. In fact, William Godwin, Jr., attended three schools (Charterhouse, 1811–14; Dr. Burney's School, 1814–17; and a "celebrated school for preparing youth for the pursuits of commerce at Woodford," 1818). In addition he was given a year's private tutoring in mathematics (1819) with Peter Nicholson in London Street, Fitzroy Square, before being apprenticed, first to the engineer Mr. Maudsley in 1820, and then to the architect Mr. Nash in 1821. William Godwin details this schooling in his Memoir of his son prefacing William Godwin, Jr.'s novel *Transfusion* (London: John Macrone, 1835), pp. v–vii.

26. William Godwin to Mary Jane Clairmont Godwin, May 20, 1811 (Abinger Dep. c. 523).

27. Mary Jane Clairmont Godwin to William Godwin, June 10, 1811 (Abinger Dep. c. 523).

28. *Letters of Mary Shelley*, ed. Betty T. Bennett, I:34, 161, 3, 322.

29. *The Journals of Claire Clairmont 1814–1827*, ed. Marion Kingston Stocking (Cambridge: Harvard Univesity Press, 1968), pp. 18–19.

30. Maud Brooke Rolleston, *Talks with Lady Shelley* (London: George G. Harrap & Co., 1925), pp. 33–34.

31. Elizabeth Hitchener met Godwin on July 14, 1812. Harriet Shelley shared her unfavorable impression of Godwin and reported to her friend Catherine Nugent: "He thinks himself such a very great *man*. He would not let one of his children come to *us* just because he had not seen our faces. . . . Such excuses sit not well upon so great a literary character as he is. I might have expected such an excuse from a woman of selfish and narrow mind, but not from Godwin." (Letter dated August 4, 1812; *The Complete Works of Percy Bysshe Shelley*, The Julian Edition, ed. Roger Ingpen and Walter E. Peck [London: Ernest Benn Limited; New York: Scribner's, 1926–30], X:15–16.)

32. Don Locke, *A Fantasy of Reason*, p. 217.

33. C. Kegan Paul, *William Godwin*, II:214.

34. William Godwin to Mary Jane Clairmont Godwin, May 18, 1811 (Abinger Dep. c. 523).

35. William Godwin, *St. Leon: A Tale of the Sixteenth Century* (London: G. G. & J. Robinson, 1799), p. 118–19. Don Locke identifies St. Leon's oldest daughter Julia with Fanny Godwin and argues for Godwin's preference for her, *A Fantasy of Reason*, pp. 217–18.

36. William Godwin to Mary Jane Clairmont Godwin, May 30, 1811 (Abinger Dep. c. 523).

37. Christy Baxter, Mary Shelley's childhood friend, was interviewed and her

account of the Godwin household published by Florence A. Marshall in *The Life and Letters of Mary Wollstonecraft Shelley* (London: Bentley, 1889), I:33–34.

38. William Godwin to William Thomas Baxter, June 8, 1812; reprinted in *Shelley and His Circle 1773–1822*, ed. Kenneth Neill Cameron and Donald H. Reiman (Cambridge: Harvard University Press, 1961–73), III:100–02.

39. On the Baxter family, see Enid Gauldie's forthcoming study of the William Baxter Family of Dundee. Enid Gauldie is the local historian and archivist of the Dundee Library, Dundee, Scotland.

40. Mary Wollstonecraft Shelley, *Mathilda*, ed. Elizabeth Nitchie (Chapel Hill: University of North Carolina Press, 1959), p. 16.

41. Mary Wollstonecraft Shelley, Introduction to *Frankenstein* (1831), p. vi.

42. Percy Bysshe Shelley to William Godwin, January 3, 1812, *The Letters of Percy Bysshe Shelley*, ed. Frederick L. Jones (Oxford: The Clarendon Press, 1964), I:219–21.

43. Percy Bysshe Shelley to William Godwin, January 10, 1812, *Letters of Percy Shelley*, ed. Frederick L. Jones, I:227–28.

44. C. Kegan Paul, *William Godwin*, II:207.

45. Richard Holmes gives a particularly full and convincing account of the Tan-yr-allt affair in his *Shelley—The Pursuit* (New York: E.P. Dutton, 1975), pp. 163–98.

46. On Harriet Shelley, see Newman Ivey White, *Shelley* (London: Secker and Warburg, 1941; revised edition, 1947)), I:323.

47. Percy Bysshe Shelley to Elizabeth Hitchener, October 16, 1811, *Letters of Percy Shelley*, ed. Frederick L. Jones, I:150.

48. For Shelley's financial dealings with Godwin, and Godwin's exorbitant demands upon Shelley, see Roger Ingpen, *Shelley in England* (London: Kegan Paul, 1917), pp. 412–13, 448–51, passim.

49. Thomas Jefferson Hogg, *The Life of Percy Bysshe Shelley* (London: Edward Moxon, 1858), II:537–38.

50. R. Glynn Grylls, *Claire Clairmont, Mother of Byron's Allegra*, pp. 14–15.

51. Further evidence of Shelley's persistent desire to surround himself with loving women appears in the scheme he hatched shortly after his return to London with Mary and Claire, the scheme to persuade his favorite sisters Elizabeth and Hellen to leave Mrs. Hugford's School in Hackney and live with him and the Godwin girls. Mary described this attempt in more political terms as a plan for "converting and liberating two heiresses" (*Mary Shelley's Journal*, ed. Frederick L. Jones [Norman, Oklahoma: University of Oklahoma Press, 1947], September 30, 1814, p. 17; cf. *Journals of Claire Clairmont*, ed. Marion Kingston Stocking, pp. 46–47).

52. *Maria Gisborne and Edward E. Williams, Shelley's Friends: Their Journals and Letters*, ed. Frederick L. Jones (Norman, Oklahoma: University of Oklahoma Press, 1951), pp. 39–41.

53. *The Elopement of Percy Bysshe Shelley and Mary Wollstonecraft Godwin, as narrated by William Godwin*, with Commentary by H. Buxton Forman (London: The Bibliophile Society, 1911), p. 16.

54. Mary Wollstonecraft Shelley, Review: "The English in Italy," *Westminster Review*, October 1826; printed as Appendix A in *Journals of Claire Clairmont*, ed. Marion Kingston Stocking, p. 442.

55. *Mary Shelley's Journal*, ed. Frederick L. Jones, August 7, 1814, p. 6.

56. *Mary Shelley's Journal*, ed. Frederick L. Jones, August 2, 1814, p. 5.

57. *Letters of Mary Shelley*, ed. Betty T. Bennett, I:3.

58. William Godwin, *Memoirs of the Author of A Vindication of the Rights of Woman* (1798), p. 129. Godwin met Mary Wollstonecraft for the first time in five years on January 8, 1796 at the home of Mary Hays; they dined together with a large party at Newton's on January 14, 1796; Godwin began reading her *Letters written . . . in Sweden* on January 25, and completed the book on February 3; and on February 13 he called on Mary Wollstonecraft but she was not at home. During February Mary Wollstonecraft attempted a final reconciliation with Gilbert Imlay, and when that failed, went to visit friends in Berkshire. When she came back to London, she returned Godwin's call on April 14, a meeting that initiated the love affair which was sexually consummated on July 16 (see Godwin's Diary, Abinger Shelley Collection, Bodleian Library, Dep. e. 202).

59. *Mary Shelley's Journal*, ed. Frederick L. Jones, p. 13.

60. Mary Wollstonecraft Shelley, *History of A Six Weeks Tour through a part of France, Switzerland, Germany, and Holland, with Letters descriptive of a Sail round the Lake of Geneva, and of the Glaciers of Chamouni* (London: T. Hookham, Jr., and C. and J. Ollier, 1817), pp. 35, 23–24. It is possible that the voiturier was annoyed because his customers had chosen the shortest and more picturesque but most difficult route, as André Koszul suggested in "Notes and Corrections to Shelley's 'History of a Six Weeks' Tour' (1817)," *MLR* 2 (October 1906): 61–62.

61. Mary Wollstonecraft Shelley, *History of a Six Weeks Tour*, pp. 50, 56, 68.

62. *Mary Shelley's Journal*, ed. Frederick L. Jones, p. 12.

63. Mary Wollstonecraft Shelley, *Six Weeks Tour*, p. 70.

64. *Mary Shelley's Journal*, ed. Frederick L. Jones, p. 9.

65. *Journals of Claire Clairmont*, ed. Marion Kingston Stocking, p. 31.

66. Jane details this reading, *Journals of Claire Clairmont*, ed. Marion Kingston Stocking, pp. 29, 33, 35, 39.

67. *Mary Shelley's Journal*, ed. Frederick L. Jones, p. 12; *Journals of Claire Clairmont*, ed. Marion Kingston Stocking, p. 31.

68. *Mary Shelley's Journal*, ed. Frederick L. Jones, p. 14.

69. *Journals of Claire Clairmont*, ed. Marion Kingston Stocking, p. 40, n.38.

70. *Mary Shelley's Journal*, ed. Frederick L. Jones, p. 24.

71. *Mary Shelley's Journal*, ed. Frederick L. Jones, entry for October 7, 1814, by Shelley, p. 18. For Claire's descriptions of these horrors, see *Journals of Claire Clairmont*, ed. Marion Kingston Stocking, p. 48.

72. *Journals of Claire Clairmont*, ed. Marion Kingston Stocking, p. 31; dated August 27, 1814.

73. John Harrington Smith first argued that Claire and Percy had become lovers at this time, although he rather quaintly asserted that "they fell only once," in "Shelley and Claire Clairmont," *PMLA* LIV (September 1939): 785–814. Smith based his claim on Claire's letters to Byron in which she compared her history to that of Adam Weishaupt who, Smith claims, seduced his sister-in-law, and to that of Maria Eleanora Schöning who was raped in Coleridge's account in *The Friend*, Part IV, Essay 1 (London: J. Brown, 1809–1810; repr. New York: Free Press, 1971), pp. 225–35. Claire further described Shelley as "the man whom I have loved, and for whom I have suffered much." In the context of this particular letter to Byron, "love" has a sexual rather than a platonic connotation. Claire Clairmont's

correspondence with Byron is reprinted in *The Works of Lord Byron*, ed. Rowland Prothero (London: John Murray, 1904), Vol. X, Appendix 7, see especially pp. 431, 437. John Harrington Smith further points to the secret correspondence between Claire and Shelley in the autumn of 1814 as substantiating his claim. On this basis he identifies Claire as the Comet in "Epipsychidion," as Constantia in the "Constantia" poems, and as the cruel lady in "Julian and Maddalo"—identificatons which suggest that Claire and Shelley had been but were no longer lovers. See also his "Shelley and Claire Again," *Studies in Philology* XLI (1944): 94–105 for further discussion.

74. Richard Holmes, *Shelley—The Pursuit*, p. 89–93.

75. For Hogg's letters to Elizabeth Shelley between January and June, 1811, and Percy Shelley's responses, see *Shelley and His Circle*, ed. Kenneth Neill Cameron and Donald H. Reiman, II: 668–94, 700–14, 797–809; for Hogg's attempted seduction of Harriet Shelley and Percy Shelley's response, see *Shelley and His Circle*, III: 24–62, 67–68.

76. *Mary Shelley's Journal*, ed. Frederick L. Jones, November 14, 1814, pp. 25–26.

77. *Letters of Mary Shelley*, ed. Betty T. Bennett, January 1, 1815, I:6.

78. Richard Holmes, *Shelley—The Pursuit*, p. 277.

79. Mary Shelley's Journal records Shelley's first conversation with Jane "concerning Jane's character" on August 21, 1814; on October 14, Shelley recorded "Jane's insensibility and incapacity for the slightest degree of friendship. . . . Beware of weakly giving way to trivial sympathies. . . . Converse with Jane; her mind unsettled; her character unformed; occasion of hope from some instances of softness and feeling; she is not entirely insensible to concessions; new proofs that the . . . truest virtue consists in an habitual contempt of self; a subduing of all angry feelings; a sacrifice of pride and selfishness;" and on November 14, he complained, "I wish this girl had a resolute mind. Without firmness, understanding is impotent, and the truest principles unintelligible" (*Mary Shelley's Journal*, ed. Frederick L. Jones, pp. 11, 20, 25).

80. On Shelley's financial situation in 1815–16, see Richard Holmes's especially clear account, *Shelley—The Pursuit*, pp. 283–85, 312–15; and Don Locke, *A Fantasy of Reason*, pp. 262–66.

81. *Mary Shelley's Journal*, ed. Frederick L. Jones, p. 39.

82. *Mary Shelley's Journal*, ed. Frederick L. Jones, entries for March, 9, 13, 19, 20, 1815; pp. 40–41.

83. *Mary Shelley's Journal*, ed. Frederick L. Jones, Dec. 6, 1814, p. 28.

84. *Mary Shelley's Journal*, ed. Frederick L. Jones, p. 40.

85. *Mary Shelley's Journal*, ed. Frederick L. Jones, p. 40.

86. *Mary Shelley's Journal*, ed. Frederick L. Jones, p. 46.

87. *Mary Shelley's Journal*, ed. Frederick L. Jones, pp. 46–7.

88. Claire Clairmont to Fanny Godwin, 28 May 1815, Abinger Dep. c. 478.

89. Claire Clairmont to Fanny Godwin, 28 May 1815, Abinger Dep. c. 478.

90. Claire Clairmont to Lord Byron, May 6, 1816, Abinger MS. Shelley Adds. c. 8; printed in *Shelley and Mary*, ed. Lady Jane Shelley (London: privately published, 1882), I:91.

91. *Letters of Mary Shelley*, ed. Betty T. Bennett, December 5, 1816, I:22.

92. *Letters of Mary Shelley*, ed. Betty T. Bennett, October 18, 1817, I:57.

93. *Journals of Claire Clairmont*, ed. Marion Kingston Stocking, p. 153.

94. *Letters of Mary Shelley*, ed. Betty T. Bennett, II:271.

95. Maud Brooke Rolleston, *Talks with Lady Shelley* (London: George G. Harrap & Co., 1925), p. 41.

96. Clara Mary Jane Clairmont's two notebooks of "Reminiscences, Anecdotes, Etc." are in the Ashley Manuscript Collection in the British Museum (Ashley 2820); the bulk of these passages were printed in Appendix B of R. Glynn Grylls's *Claire Clairmont*, pp. 254–55.

97. Clara Clairmont, "Reminiscences," Ashley 2820.

98. *Letters of Mary Shelley*, ed. Betty T. Bennett, dated July 27, 1815, I:15.

99. Mary Godwin to Percy Shelley, October 28, 1814; *Letters of Mary Shelley*, ed. Betty T. Bennett, I:3.

100. Mary Wollstonecraft Shelley, Introduction to *Frankenstein* (1831), p. vi.

CHAPTER TWO   Making a Monster

1. On the origin and nature of the *golem*, see Gershom G. Scholem, *On the Kabbalah and Its Symbolism*, trans. Ralph Manheim (London: Routledge & Kegan Paul, 1965), Chapt. 5; and Scholem's witty updating of the idea in his "The Golem of Prague and the Golem of Rehovot," in *The Messianic Idea of Judaism* (New York: Schocken Books, 1971), pp. 335–40.

2. This date is derived from Dr. Polidori's claim, on June 17, 1816, that "The ghost-stories are begun by all but me," in *The Diary of Dr. John William Polidori*, ed. William Michael Rossetti (London: Elkin Mathews, 1911), p. 125.

3. The major feminist readings of *Frankenstein* to date are those by Ellen Moers, in *Literary Women* (Garden City, New Jersey: Doubleday, 1976), pp. 91–99; Marc A. Rubenstein, " 'My Accursed Origin': The Search for the Mother in *Frankenstein*," *Studies in Romanticism* 15 (Spring 1976): 165–94; Sandra Gilbert and Susan Gubar, in *The Madwoman in the Attic* (New Haven: Yale University Press, 1979), 213–47; Barbara Johnson, "My Monster/My Self," *Diacritics* 12 (1982): 2–10; Devon Hodges, "*Frankenstein* and the Feminine Subversion of the Novel," *Tulsa Studies in Women's Literature* 2 (Autumn 1983): 155–64; Mary Poovey, *The Proper Lady and the Woman Writer—Ideology as Style in the Works of Mary Wollstonecraft, Mary Shelley and Jane Austen* (Chicago and London: University of Chicago Press, 1984), Chaps. 4–5; Mary Jacobus, "Is There a Woman in This Text?" *New Literary History* 14 (1982): 117–41; Burton Hatlin, "Milton, Mary Shelley and Patriarchy," in *Rhetoric, Literature, and Intepretation*, ed. Harry R. Garvin (Lewisburg, Pa.: Bucknell University Press, 1983), pp. 19–47; Margaret Homans, *Bearing the Word—Language and Female Experience in Nineteenth-Century Women's Writing* (Chicago: University of Chicago Press, 1986), Chap. 5; and the essays by George Levine, U. C. Knoepflmacher, Judith Wilt, and Kate Ellis included in *The Endurance of Frankenstein*, ed. George Levine and U. C. Knoepflmacher (Berkeley and Los Angeles, and London: University of California Press, 1979). For a complete bibliography of research on *Frankenstein* before 1983, see Frederick S. Frank, "Mary Shelley's *Frankenstein*: A Register of Research," *Bulletin of Bibliography* 40 (1983): 163–88.

4. Ellen Moers, "Female Gothic," in *Literary Women*, p. 93. This essay first appeared in *The New York Review of Books* on March 21, 1974.

5. Mary Wollstonecraft Shelley, Introduction to *Frankenstein, or The Modern Prometheus* (London: Colburn and Bentley; Standard Novels Edition, 1831), p. xi.

6. Mary Wollstonecraft Shelley, *Frankenstein, or The Modern Prometheus* (London: Lackington, Hughes, Harding, Mavor and Jones, 1818); all further references to *Frankenstein*, unless otherwise noted, will be to the only modern reprint of the first edition, edited by James Rieger (New York: Bobbs-Merrill, 1974; reprinted, Chicago: University of Chicago Press, 1982), and will be cited by page number only in the text. These phrases occur on pages 51 and 52 of the Rieger text.

7. Lawrence Stone, in *The Family, Sex and Marriage in England 1500–1800* (London: Weidenfeld and Nicolson, 1977), distinguishes three types of family structures: the Open Lineage Family, which he asserts was prevalent for the millenium prior to 1600 and characterized by its "permeability by outside influences" and "members' sense of loyalty to ancestors and to living kin" (p. 4); the Restricted Patriarchal Nuclear Family, which he argues came into dominance between 1530–1700 among the upper and middle classes, and in which the father assumed greater power and determined the nuclear family's particular loyalties to political and religious factions; and the Closed Domesticated Nuclear Family, which he says began to develop after 1640 and was "well established by 1750 in the key middle and upper sectors of English society." (8–9). It manifested four key features: "intensified affective bonding of the nuclear core at the expense of neighbors and kin; a strong sense of individual autonomy and the right to personal freedom in the pursuit of happiness; a weakening of the association of sexual pleasure with sin and guilt; and a growing desire for physical privacy" (p. 8). Alan MacFarlane (*Love and Marriage in England, Modes of Reproduction 1300–1840* [Oxford: Basil Blackwell, 1986]), Linda A. Pollock (*Forgotten Children—Parent-Child Relations From 1500–1900* [Cambridge: Cambridge University Press, 1983]), and Randolph Trumbach (*The Rise of the Egalitarian Family— Aristocratic Kinship and Domestic Relations in Eighteenth-Century England* [New York, San Francisco, London: Academic Press, 1978]) have criticized Stone's models on the grounds that the Malthusian marriage-system and the affectional nuclear family existed well before the sixteenth century, but their arguments do not sufficiently take into account the documented changes that occurred within the British family during the modern period. Within the context of Stone's classifications, Victor Frankenstein's attempt to create a family or race entirely dependent upon him is an example of the Restricted Patriarchal Nuclear Family, in which the father is, as Stone comments, virtually "a legalized petty tyrant within the home" (p. 7). The Patriarchal Family was becoming more rather than less prevalent in nineteenth-century England under the impact of the industrial revolution and the rigid separation of the public (wage-earning) from the domestic (unwaged) spheres (see Heidi Hartmann, "Capitalism, Patriarchy, and Job Segregation by Sex," in *Capitalist Patriarchy and the Case for Socialist Feminism*, ed. Zillah Eisenstein [New York and London: Monthly Review Press, 1979], 206–47).

8. Mary Shelley's extensive reading program is documented in her *Journal* (ed. Frederick L. Jones [Norman, Oklahoma: University of Oklahoma Press, 1947]); these books are listed on pp. 47–49, with the exception of Volney's *Ruins*. For knowledge of Volney, she probably relied on Percy Shelley, who read the book in 1814 (Newman Ivey White, *Shelley* [London: Secker and Warburg, 1941; revised edition, 1947], pp. I:277, 292, 419). For the impact of Volney on Percy Shelley's "The Revolt of Islam," which he was working on during the composition of *Frankenstein*, see Kenneth Neill Cameron, *Shelley—The Golden Years* (Cambridge: Harvard University Press, 1974), p. 315.

9. Gilbert and Gubar have emphasized this point, in *The Madwoman in the Attic* (New Haven: Yale University Press, 1979), pp. 238, 247. See also Marcia Tillotson, " 'A Forced Solitude': Mary Shelley and the Creation of Frankenstein's Monster," in *The Female*

Gothic, ed. Juliann E. Fleenor (Montreal and London: Eden Press, 1983): 167–75.

10. *Mary Shelley's Journal*, ed. Frederick L. Jones, p. 72. Claire Clairmont probably first introduced Mary Shelley to *Emile*, which she read during their trip back to England in September, 1814, (*The Journals of Claire Clairmont 1814–1827*, ed. Marion Kingston Stocking [Cambridge: Harvard University Press, 1968], pp. 39–40).

11. Jean Jacques Rousseau, *Emile*, trans. Barbara Foxley (New York: Dutton—Everyman's Library, 1911; repr. 1963), p. 5. All future references to this Everyman edition are cited in the text.

12. U. C. Knoepflmacher, "Thoughts on the Aggression of Daughters," *The Endurance of Frankenstein*, ed. George Levine and U. C. Knoepflmacher, pp. 88–119. William Veeder endorses this view in his *Mary Shelley & Frankenstein—The Fate of Androgyny* (Chicago: University of Chicago Press, 1986), pp. 161–71.

13. For an illuminating discussion of Rousseau's writings in relation to *Frankenstein*, see Paul A. Cantor, *Creature and Creator: Myth-making and English Romanticism* (New York: Cambridge University Press, 1984), pp. 4–25, 119–28.

14. For an excellent discussion of the parallels between David Hartley's model of psychological development and the Creature's formative experiences, see Sue Weaver Schopf, " 'Of what a strange nature is knowledge!': Hartleian Psychology and the Creature's Arrested Moral Sense in Mary Shelley's *Frankenstein*," *Romanticism Past and Present* 5 (1981): 33–52.

15. John Locke, *Some Thoughts Concerning Education*, ed. Peter Gay (New York: Bureau of Publications, Teachers College, Columbia University, 1964), p. 66.

16. John Locke, *Some Thoughts Concerning Education*, pp. 1–3.

CHAPTER THREE My Hideous Progeny

1. *Jean Rhys Letters 1931–1966*, ed. Francis Wyndham and Diana Melly (London: André Deutsch, 1984), dated March 9, 1966, p. 301.

2. Sandra Gilbert and Susan Gubar, *The Madwoman in the Attic* (New Haven: Yale University Press, 1979), p. 49.

3. *The Diary of Dr. John William Polidori*, ed. William Michael Rossetti (London: Elkin Mathews, 1911), pp. 122–25. James Rieger first noted this discrepancy in "Dr. Polidori and the Genesis of *Frankenstein*," *Studies in English Literature* 3 (1963): 461–72.

4. Barbara Johnson, "My Monster/My Self," *Diacritics* 12 (1982): 7. Margaret Homans has subtly explored the implications of Mary Shelley's identification of child-bearing with figurative writing (and the death of the mother), "with the bearing of men's words," in *Bearing the Word—Language and Female Experience in Nineteenth-Century Women's Writing* (Chicago: University of Chicago Press, 1986), pp. 100–19. See also Mary Jacobus, "Is There a Woman in This Text?" *New Literary History* 14 (1982): 117–14; repr. in *Reading Woman* (New York: Columbia University Press, 1986).

5. The text of *Frankenstein* incorporates certain anachronisms—quotations from poems not published until later, e.g. Wordsworth's "Tintern Abbey" (1798), Coleridge's revised "Rime of the Ancient Mariner" (1800), Byron's "Childe Harold's Pilgrimage," Canto III (1816)—which may undercut the chronology I have suggested here. But my dating has both psychological and political resonance in the novel.

6. Cynthia Griffin Wolff, "The Radcliffean Gothic Model: A Form for Feminine Sexuality," *Modern Language Studies* 9 (Fall, 1979): 101.

7. For an excellent analysis of the psychodynamic structures underpinning the formulae of such modern Gothic romances as the Harlequin and Mills and Boon series, see Tania Modleski, *Loving with a Vengeance: Mass-produced Fantasies for Women* (New York and London: Archon and Methuen, 1982).

8. Mary Poovey, *The Proper Lady and the Woman Writer—Ideology as Style in the Works of Mary Wollstonecraft, Mary Shelley and Jane Austen* (Chicago and London: University of Chicago Press, 1984), Chap. 4.

9. For a thematic reading of this narrative structure, see Richard J. Dunn, "Narrative Distance in *Frankenstein*," *Studies in the Novel* 6 (1974): 408–17.

10. E. B. Murray, "Shelley's Contribution to Mary's *Frankenstein*," *Keats-Shelley Memorial Bulletin* 29 (1978): 67.

11. George Levine, "The Ambiguous Heritage of *Frankenstein*," in *The Endurance of Frankenstein*, ed. George Levine and U. C. Knoepflmacher (Berkeley and Los Angeles, and London: University of California Press, 1979), p. 3.

12. Percy Shelley's unpublished review of *Frankenstein* is available in *The Complete Works of Percy Bysshe Shelley* (The Julian Edition), ed. Roger Ingpen and Walter E. Peck (London: Ernest Benn Limited; New York: Scribner's, 1926–30), VI:263—65. It is reprinted with an illuminating commentary in William Veeder, *Mary Shelley & Frankenstein* (Chicago: University of Chicago Press, 1986), Appendix C.

13. Mary Daly, *Beyond God the Father: Toward a Philosophy of Women's Liberation* (Boston: Beacon Press, 1973)·; cf. Judith Wilt, "*Frankenstein* as Mystery Play," in *The Endurance of Frankenstein*, ed. George Levine and U. C. Knopflmacher, pp. 31–48.

14. *The Letters of Percy Shelley*, ed. Frederick L. Jones (Oxford: The Clarendon Press, 1964), I:553.

15. *Letters of Percy Shelley*, ed. Frederick L. Jones, I:565.

16. *Letters of Percy Shelley*, ed. Frederick L. Jones, I:565.

17. *The Letters of Mary Wollstonecraft Shelley*, ed. Betty T. Bennett (Baltimore: Johns Hopkins University Press, 1980, 1983), I:42.

18. *Shelley's Prose*, ed. David Lee Clark (Albuquerque: University of New Mexico Press, 1954), p. 169.

19. *Letters of Percy Shelley*, ed. Frederick L. Jones, I:553.

20. *Letters of Mary Shelley*, ed. Betty T. Bennett, I:145–36; dated May 8, 1820.

21. Percy Shelley's review of Frankenstein is most easily accessible in William Veeder's *Mary Shelley and Frankenstein*, where it is printed as Appendix C. These quotations appear on pages 225–227.

CHAPTER FOUR   Promethean Politics

1. See Anne K. Mellor, *Blake's Human Form Divine* (Berkeley: University of California Press, 1974), for a discussion of the "divine analogy" and the "human form divine" in William Blake's poetry and art.

2. Ovid's *Metamorphoses*, Book I, lines 101–6, 111–12, translated by John Dryden, *The Works of John Dryden*, ed. A. B. Chambers and W. Frost (Berkeley: University

of California Press, 1974), IV:378–79. For Mary Shelley's reading of Ovid, see her *Journal*, ed. Frederick L. Jones (Norman, Oklahoma: University of Oklahoma Press, 1947), entries between April 8—May 13, 1815, pp. 43–47. Burton Pollin first identified Ovid as Mary Shelley's source for the Prometheus plasticator myth, "Philosophical and Literary Sources of *Frankenstein*," *Comparative Literature* 17 (1965): 102. For helpful discussions of the use of the Prometheus myth in *Frankenstein*, see David Ketterer, *Frankenstein's Creation: The Book, the Monster, and the Human Reality* (Victoria, British Columbia: Victoria University Press—English Literature Studies Number 16, 1979); and M. K. Joseph, Introduction to the 1831 edition of *Frankenstein, or The Modern Prometheus* (Oxford and New York: Oxford University Press, 1969, repr. 1984).

3. Byron had long admired Aeschylus' *Prometheus Bound*, which he asked Percy Shelley to translate from the Greek for him in July, 1816. In "Prometheus," Byron both identifies Prometheus as "a symbol and a sign/ To Mortals of their fate and force" (ll. 45–46) and projects his own distress at his divorce and the loss of his daughter into his description of Prometheus' "silent suffering": "All that the proud can feel of pain,/ The agony they do not show,/ The suffocating sense of woe,/ Which speaks but in its loneliness" (lines 8–11; Diodati, July 1816).

The link between Victor Frankenstein and Byron is further strengthened in the 1831 edition, where Mary Shelley borrows Byron's self-image of the poet as a greater Newton, no longer picking up pebbles on the seashore but venturing out onto the "ocean of eternity" (*Don Juan* 10:4), for Frankenstein himself:

> "I have described myself as always having been embued with a fervent longing to penetrate the secrets of nature. In spite of the intense labour and wonderful discoveries of modern philosophers, I always came from my studies discontented and unsatisfied. Sir Isaac Newton is said to have avowed that he felt like a child picking up shells beside the great and unexplored ocean of truth. Those of his successors in each branch of natural philosophy with whom I was acquainted, appeared even to my boy's apprehensions, as tyros engaged in the same pursuit" (238).

4. *Shelley and His Circle 1773–1822*, ed. Kenneth Neill Cameron and Donald H. Reiman (Cambridge: Harvard University Press, 1961–73), VI:841.

5. *Mary Shelley's Journal*, ed. Frederick L. Jones, p. 73. Mary Shelley's perception of a link between Aeschylus' *Prometheus Bound*, Percy Shelley's poetic persona, and her own novel may underlie her Journal entry for July 13, 1817: "Shelley translates 'Prometheus Desmotes' and I write it" (Bodleian Library: Abinger MS. Dep. d. 311/2). This entry is erroneously printed in *Mary Shelley's Journal*, p. 82.

6. Peter Dale Scott, "Vital Artifice: Mary, Percy, and the Psychopolitical Integrity of *Frankenstein*," *The Endurance of Frankenstein*, ed. George Levine and U. C. Knoepflmacher (Berkeley and Los Angeles, and London: University of California Press, 1979), pp. 175–83; William Veeder, *Mary Shelley & Frankenstein—The Fate of Androgyny* (Chicago: University of Chicago Press, 1986), pp. 92–95, 112–23, passim. See also Christopher Small, *Ariel Like a Harpy: Shelley, Mary and Frankenstein* (London: Gollancz, 1972); Richard Holmes, *Shelley—The Pursuit* (New York: E. P. Dutton, 1975), pp. 331–32; and Judith Weissman, "A Reading of *Frankenstein* as the Complaint of a Political Wife," *Colby Library Quarterly* XII (December 1976): 171–80.

7. For Percy Shelley's reading of Albertus Magnus, Paracelsus, Pliny, and Buffon, see Newman Ivey White, *Shelley* (London: Secker and Warburg, 1941; revised edition, 1947), I:41, 50–52, 158; on Shelley's obsession with alchemy and chemistry, see Thomas Jefferson

Hogg's account of his Oxford days, *The Life of Percy Bysshe Shelley* (London: Edward Moxon, 1858), I:33–34, 58–76.

8. On the association of the Illuminati and the University of Ingolstadt, see Ludwig Hammermayer, "Die letzte Epoche der Universität Ingolstadt: Reformer, Jesuiten, Illuminaten (1746–1800)," in *Ingolstadt: Die Herzogsstadt—Die Universitätsstadt—Die Festung* ed. Theodor Müller and Wilhelm Reissmüller (Ingolstadt: Verlag Donau Courier, 1974), pp. 299–357. The goals of the Illuminati are stated by L'Abbé Augustin Barruel in *Memoirs, Illustrating the History of Jacobinism*, trans. Robert Clifford (London, 1797–98), III:117, 228. For Percy Shelley's reading of Barruel, see *Mary Shelley's Journal*, ed. Federick L. Jones, entries for 23, 25 August and 9, 11 October, 1814. On Percy Shelley's use of Weishaupt's revolutionary doctrines, see Gerald McNiece, *Shelley and the Revolutionary Idea* (Cambridge: Harvard University Press, 1969), pp. 22–23, 97–101. For an account of Percy Shelley's revolutionary doctrines in "The Assassins," see Newman Ivey White, *Shelley*, I:682–83. On the impact of Barruel on *Frankenstein*, see Burton R. Pollin, "Sources of *Frankenstein*", p. 103 n23; and Horst Meller, "Prometheus im romantischen Heiligen-Kalendar," in *Antike Tradition und Neuere Philologien*, ed. Hans-Joachim Simmermann (Heidelberg: Carl Winter-Universitätsverlag, 1984), pp. 163–69.

9. On 22 October 1811, Percy Shelley wrote to his mother thus: "I suspect your motives for *so violently* so *persecutingly* desiring to unite my sister Elizabeth to the music master Graham, I suspect that it was intended to shield *yourself* from that suspicion which at length has fallen on you. If it is unjust, prove it" (*The Letters of Percy Bysshe Shelley*, ed. Frederick L. Jones [Oxford: The Clarendon Press, 1964], I:155). For a discussion of the injustice of this charge, see Newman Ivey White, *Shelley*, I:48, 166–67; on Percy Shelley's relationship with Edward Fergus Graham, see *Shelley and His Circle*, ed. Kenneth Neill Cameron and Donald H. Reiman, II:621–25, 646–48.

10. D. W. Harding identified Percy Shelley's "regressive yearnings" as a "longing for the return of an infantile kind of bliss in union with a mother–figure" (Introduction to *From Blake to Byron* ed. Boris Ford [London: Pelican Books, 1957], pp. 208–9). See also Edward Carpenter and George Barnefield, *The Psychology of the Poet Shelley* (London: Allen and Unwin, 1925); A. M. D. Hughes, *The Nascent Mind of Shelley* (Oxford: The Clarendon Press, 1947); and Eustace Chesser, *Shelley and Zastrozzi—Self-Revelation of a Neurotic* (London: Gregg/Archive, 1965). William Veeder reaches similar conclusions concerning Percy Shelley's psychological profile (*Mary Shelley & Frankenstein*, Chap. 2, passim).

11. Here Mary Shelley's resentment of her husband's unquestioning assumption of superior literary judgment may erupt in her choice of "mutilated," a word that focuses both her irritation and her guilt at making a monster.

The identification of Frankenstein as an author is strengthened by the images that link him both to the cursed, tale-telling Ancient Mariner and to Coleridge himself. Frankenstein explicitly identifies with the Mariner pursued by a "frightful fiend" (54); he also finds himself alone on a wide, wide sea and at the sight of land at last, "tears gushed from my eyes" (169). Moreover, Frankenstein uses Coleridge's image of the poet's mind as "the sole unquiet thing" in "Frost at Midnight" to define his own mental state: "I was often tempted, when all was at peace around me, and I the only unquiet thing that wandered restless in a scene so beautiful and heavenly . . . to plunge into the silent lake" (87).

12. The relationship between the Wordsworthian Narrator of "Alastor" and Percy Shelley is a vexed critical question. Earl R. Wasserman argued for an ironic distance between the Narrator and the author, in *Shelley—A Critical Reading* (Baltimore: Johns Hopkins University Press, 1971), pp. 11–46; Lisa Steinman saw a more complex irony in which both Narrator and visionary poet are modes of Percy Shelley's own skepticism concerning the limits and contradictions of consciousness, in "Shelley's Skepticism: Allegory

in 'Alastor'," *ELH* 45 (1978): 225–69; while Lloyd Abbey has reiterated an older critical tradition which assumed, as did Mary Shelley, that the Narrator spoke for the author, in his *Destroyer and Preserver—Shelley's Poetic Skepticism* (Lincoln, Nebraska and London: University of Nebraska Press, 1979), pp. 20–30.

13. For a brilliant discussion of how *Frankenstein* reads "Alastor" as the story of Percy Shelley's desire *not* to find the female object of his desire embodied in his wife, see Margaret Homans, *Bearing the Word—Language and Female Experience in Nineteenth-Century Women's Writing* (Chicago: University of Chicago Press, 1986), pp. 105–9.

14. For a detailed and insightful account of Walton's role in the novel, see Peter McInerney, "*Frankenstein* and the Godlike Science of Letters," *Genre* 13 (1980): 455–75.

15. Andrew Griffin has discussed the imagery of fire and ice in *Frankenstein* and *Jane Eyre* in "Fire and Ice in *Frankenstein*," in *The Endurance of Frankenstein*, ed. George Levine and U. C. Knoepflmacher, pp. 49—73; see also Irving Massey, *The Gaping Pig—Literature and Metamorphosis* (Berkeley and Los Angeles, and London: University of California Press, 1976), pp. 131–34.

16. Behind this necessarily simplistic description of the romantic ideology lie the more detailed and precise formulations contained in Mario Praz's *The Romantic Agony* (1933; trans. Angus Davidson, New York: Meridian Books, 1956); M. H. Abrams's *Natural Supernaturalism—Tradition and Revolution in Romantic Literature* (New York: Norton, 1971); my *English Romantic Irony* (Cambridge: Harvard University Press, 1980); and Jerome J. McGann's *The Romantic Ideology* (Chicago: University of Chicago Press, 1983).

17. Lee Sterrenburg, "Mary Shelley's Monster: Politics and Psyche in *Frankenstein*," in *The Endurance of Frankenstein*, ed. George Levine and U. C. Knoepflmacher, pp. 143–71. See also Ronald Paulson, "Gothic Fiction and the French Revolution," *ELH* 48 (1981); 532–54.

18. On the impact of Rousseau on *Frankenstein*, see Paul A. Cantor, *Creature and Creator: Myth-making and English Romanticism* (New York: Cambridge University Press, 1984), pp. 119–28; Jean de Palacio, *Mary Shelley dans son oeuvre* (Paris: Klincksieck, 1969), pp. 209—11; and Milton Millhauser, "The Noble Savage in Mary Shelley's *Frankenstein*," *Notes and Queries* CXC (1946): 248–50.

19. L'Abbé Augustin Barruel, *Memoirs, Illustrating the History of Jacobinism*, trans. Robert Clifford, III:414.

20. Edmund Burke, *Letters on the Proposals for Peace with the Regicide Directory of France, Letter I (1796)*, in *The Works and Correspondence of the Right Honourable Edmund Burke* (London, 1852), V:256.

21. Mary Wollstonecraft Shelley, "Life of William Godwin," p. 151 (Abinger Dep. c. 606/1); Mary Shelley never completed or published her biography of Godwin.

22. If Walton's first encounter with Frankenstein's creature takes place on Monday, July 31, 1797, as argued in the previous chapter, then on the basis of (not always consistent) internal evidence we might date the following events in Mary Shelley's narrative thus:

> Summer-Autumn, 1789—Frankenstein, now seventeen, decides to attend the University of Ingolstadt; mother dies (37–38)
>
> January, 1790—Frankenstein enters University of Ingolstadt (39)
>
> February, 1791—Frankenstein discovers the secret of life (45—47)
>
> November, 1792—Frankenstein animates his creature (52)
>
> Thursday, May 7, 1794—Death of William Frankenstein (67)

August, 1794—Frankenstein encounters creature in Alps (94)

March 27, 1795—Frankenstein goes to Oxford (156–157)

July-November, 1795–Frankenstein constructs female creature in Orkney Island (163)

January-March, 1796—Frankenstein in prison in Ireland (179)

June, 1796—Frankenstein marries Elizabeth Lavenza (188)

July, 1796-July, 1797—Frankenstein pursues creature north along Rhine, through Russia, to Arctic (200–4)

Monday, July 31, 1797–Walton's crew see creature passing ship (17)

August 1, 1797—Frankenstein taken aboard Walton's ship (206)

September 11, 1797—Death of Frankenstein (214).

The time frame of Mary Shelley's novel thus embraces the major events of the French Revolution, from its initiation by another Genevan, Necker (who persuaded Louis XVI to convene the Estates Général in August, 1788) and the storming of the Bastille on July 14, 1789; through the defeat of the Girondins by the Montagnards (May 31, 1793); the Terror; the execution of Robespierre (July 28, 1794); and the Coup of 18 Fructidor, Year V (September 4, 1797). In this context, we might see the creature's funeral pyre, "lost sight of . . . in the darkness and distance," as the final coup de grâce of the French Revolution, Bonaparte's coup of 18–19 Brumaire (November 9–10, 1799).

23. M. J. Guillaume, ed., *Procès-verbaux du Comité d'Instruction publique de la Convention Nationale* 2 (17 brumaire an II) (Paris, 1894): 779.

24. For a full discussion of the representation of the French Revolution as Hercules, see Lynn Hunt, *Politics, Culture, and Class in the French Revolution* (Berkeley: University of California Press, 1984), Chap. 3.

25. Joseph Fouché, "Declaration aux Citoyens de la Departmente de l'Aube," 29 June 1793, *Archives Parlementaires* (Troyes) 68:73; trans. Lynn Hunt.

26. Lynn Hunt, *Politics, Culture and Class in the French Revolution*, p. 101.

27. Mary Wollstonecraft Shelley, *History of A Six Weeks Tour through a part of France, Switzerland, Germany, and Holland, with Letters descriptive of a Sail round the Lake of Geneva, and of the Glaciers of Chamouni* (London: T. Hookham, Jr., and C. and J. Ollier, 1817), pp. 22–23.

28. Mary Wollstonecraft Shelley, *Six Weeks Tour*, p. 86.

29. Mary Wollstonecraft Shelley, "Notes" to the *First Collected Edition of The Poems of Percy Bysshe Shelley* (1839), reprinted in *The Complete Poetical Works of Percy Bysshe Shelley*, ed. Thomas Hutchinson (London: Oxford University Press, 1905; repr. 1960), p. 273 n1.

30. Mary Wollstonecraft Shelley, *Lives of the most Eminent Literary and Scientific Men of France*, for The Cabinet Cyclopedia, conducted by Rev. Dionysius Lardner (London: Longman et. al., 1838–39), II:179.

31. William Godwin, *Memoirs of the Author of A Vindication of the Rights of Woman* (London, 1798), pp. 127–28, Second edition corrected; *St. Leon: A Tale of the Sixteenth Century* (London: G. G. & J. Robinson, 1799), Preface, x–xii; *Thoughts Occasioned by a Perusal of Dr. Parr's Spital Sermon* (London, 1801), pp. 25–26. For a useful discussion of what Charles Lamb called "the famous fire cause," see Don Locke, *A Fantasy of*

Reason—The Life and Thought of William Godwin (London: Routledge & Kegan Paul, 1980), pp. 144–46, 167–79, 197–204.

32. For an insightful analysis of Mary Shelley's political position, see Jean de Palacio, *Mary Shelley dans son oeuvre*, pp. 185–236; Palacio concludes that "la position de Mary se situe entre ces extrêmes: c'est la position moyenne d'un esprit essentiellement libéral, mais non militant ni surtout révolutionnaire" (236). A far less convincing argument that Mary Shelley merely contradicted herself has been put forth by Sylvia Bowerbank in "The Social Order vs. The Wretch: Mary Shelley's Contradictory-Mindedness in *Frankenstein*," *ELH* 46 (1979) 418–31.

33. Mary Shelley, *Lives of the ... Men of France*, II:186.

34. Perhaps I should explain why I have defined the De Lacey family as bourgeois rather than as working class. Despite their recent impoverishment by the French government and their descent into the peasant or lower classes, the De Laceys retain the education and culture of the middle classes, as their literary and musical activities demonstrate. The novel presents their decline in social status as unjust, thus implying that they rightfully belong to a higher class. Moreover, as I have tried to show in this chapter, Mary Shelley's sympathies are consistently with the educated and cultured classes, not with the workers or peasants whom she found vulgar and disgusting. Here she distanced herself from her mother's more democratic principles, believing not that every individual was born equal but rather that females should receive the same education and cultural opportunities as the men of their class.

CHAPTER FIVE   A Feminist Critique of Science

1. Benjamin Farrington, trans., " 'Temporis Partus Masculus': An Untranslatea Writing of Francis Bacon," *Centaurus* I (1951): 197. For a full discussion of Bacon's use of gender metaphors, see Evelyn Fox Keller, *Reflections on Gender and Science* (New Haven and London: Yale University Press, 1985), Chap. 2.

2. A marginal note on the Thomas copy of the 1818 *Frankenstein* beside this passage, probably in Mary Shelley's own hand, comments "you said your family was not sientific [sic]" (reported by James Rieger, ed., *Frankenstein*, p. 35 n8).

3. On the importance of this introductory lecture to Humphry Davy's career, see Sir Harold Hartley, *Humphry Davy* (London: Nelson, 1966), p. 41. Roger Sharrock has traced Davy's debt to William Wordsworth's "Preface to *The Lyrical Ballads* of 1800" in "The Chemist and the Poet: Sir Humphry Davy and the Preface to the *Lyrical Ballads*," *Notes and Records of the Royal Society* 17 (1962): 57.

4. *Mary Shelley's Journal*, ed. Frederick L. Jones (Norman, Oklahoma: University of Oklahoma Press, 1947), p. 67; Laura Crouch has persuasively argued that the "Discourse" is the book listed by Mary Shelley in her Journal under Books Read in 1816 as "Introduction to Davy's Chemistry" ("Davy's *A Discourse, Introductory to a Course of Lectures on Chemistry*: A Possible Scientific Source of *Frankenstein*," *Keats-Shelley Journal*, 27 [1978]: 35–44). Mary Shelley would have known of Humphry Davy's work since childhood; she may even have been introduced to him when Davy dined with Godwin on February 16, 1801. See Samuel Holmes Vasbinder, "Scientific Attitudes in Mary Shelley's *Frankenstein*: Newtonian Monism as a Base for the Novel," *DAI* 37 (1976): 2842A (Kent State University).

5. *The Letters of Percy Shelley*, ed. Frederick L. Jones (Oxford: The Clarendon Press, 1964), I:319.

6. Sir Humphry Davy, *A Discourse, Introductory to a Course of Lectures on Chemistry* (London: John Johnson, 1802), pp. 5–6. All further references to this edition are cited in the text.

7. Laura Crouch, "Davy's *A Discourse*," p. 43.

8. Sir Humphry Davy, *Elements of Chemical Philosophy* (London, 1812), p. 58.

9. Erasmus Darwin, *The Botanic Garden* (London: John Johnson, Part I: "The Economy of Vegetation," 1791; Part II: "The Loves of the Plants," 1789); *Zoonomia: or The Laws of Organic Life* (London: John Johnson, 1794; third "Corrected" edition, 1801; *Phytologia: or the Philosophy of Agriculture and Gardening* (London: John Johnson, 1800); *The Temple of Nature* (London: John Johnson, 1803). All further references to these editions are cited in the text.

10. See Loren Eiseley, *Darwin's Century: Evolution and the Men Who Discovered It* (Garden City, New Jersey: Doubleday, 1958), Chaps. 1 and 2; and Ernst Mayr, *The Growth of Biological Thought: Diversity, Evolution, and Inheritance* (Cambridge: Belknap Press, 1982), pp. 301–41, for excellent summaries of pre-evolutionary and early evolutionary theories.

11. Mayr, *Growth of Biological Thought*, p. 335.

12. Mayr, *Growth of Biological Thought*, pp. 329–37.

13. Percy Shelley also read Buffon attentively. In his journal letter to Peacock of July 23, 1816, Shelley alludes to the first volume of Buffon's work, *La Théorie de la terre*, in the course of describing the glaciers of Mont Blanc: "I will not pursue Buffons sublime but gloomy theory, that this earth which we inhabit will at some future period be changed into a mass of frost" (*Letters of Percy Shelley*, ed. Frederick L. Jones, I:499).

14. Desmond King-Hele, *Erasmus Darwin* (London: Macmillan, 1963), p. 3.

15. *Letters of Percy Shelley*, ed. Frederick L. Jones, I:129, 342, 345.

16. For Erasmus Darwin's influence on Percy Shelley's thought and poetry, see Carl Grabo, *A Newton among Poets—Shelley's Use of Science in "Prometheus Unbound"* (Chapel Hill: University of North Carolina Press, 1930), pp. 22–74; Desmond King-Hele, *Erasmus Darwin*, pp. 144–51, and *Shelley—His Thought and Work* (London: Macmillan, 1960), pp. 162–64; Kenneth Neill Cameron, *The Young Shelley—Genesis of a Radical* (London: Victor Gollancz, 1951), pp. 121, 240; and Robert M. Maniquis, "The Puzzling *Mimosa*: Sensitivity and Plant Symbols in Romanticism," *Studies in Romanticism* VIII (1969): 129–55.

17. Erasmus Darwin discusses this process in *The Temple of Nature*, Additional Note 1: "Spontaneous Vitality of Miscroscopic Animals," pp. 1–11.

18. Adam Walker, *A System of Familiar Philosophy* (London, 1799), p. 391.

19. Richard Holmes, *Shelley—The Pursuit* (New York: E. P. Dutton, 1975), pp. 150, 344.

20. Luigi Galvani, *De Viribus Electricitatis in Motui Musculari. Commentarius* (Bologna, 1791); *Commentary on the Effects of Electricity on Muscular Motion*, trans. M. G. Foley, with notes and Introduction by I. Bernard Cohen (Norwalk, Conn.: Burndy Library, 1953).

21. John Aldini, *An Account of the Late Improvements in Galvanism, with a series of Curious and Interesting Experiments performed before the Commissioners of the French National Institute and repeated lately in the Anatomical Theatres of London; to which is added, An Appendix, containing the author's Experiments on the Body of a Malefactor executed at New Gate* (London: Cuthell and Martin, and J. Murray, 1803), p. 54. This book is an English translation of the original French text, *Essay Théorique et*

Expérimentale sur le Galvanisme published in Paris in 1802 and translated into German by F. H. Martens and published at Leipzig in 1804.

22. Aldini, *Galvanism*, p. 193.

23. Aldini, *Galvanism*, pp. 195, 194, 194.

24. These results are reported by Paul Fleury Mottelay, in his *Bibliographical History of Electricity and Magnestism* (London: C. Griffin & Co., Ltd., 1922), which gives a complete set of references to Aldini's experiments, pp. 305–7.

25. Reported by Dr. Giulio in Aldini, *Galvanism*, pp. 204–8.

26. See F. H. A. Humboldt, *Sur Galvanisme*, trans. J. F. N. Jadelot (Paris, 1799); Edmund Joseph Schmück, "On the action of galvanic electricity on the *mimosa pudica*," cited in Mottelay, *Bibliographical History of Electricity*, p. 332; C. J. C. Grapengieser, *Versuche den Galvanismus* (Berlin, 1801, 1802); and Johann Caspar Creve, *Beiträge zu Galvanis versuchen* (Frankfurt and Leipzig, 1793).

27. See Paul Mottelay, *Bibliographical History of Electricity*, pp. 402–4.

28. Erasmus Darwin, *The Botanic Garden*, Part I, p. 463.

29. Charles Henry Wilkinson, *Elements of Galvanism in Theory and Practice*, 2 Vols. (London, 1804), pp. 269–70. Wilkinson's treatise is heavily dependent upon the earlier dissertations on the subject of galvanism prepared by Johann C. L. Reinhold for his medical degree at Magdeburg in 1797 and 1798.

30. Brian W. Aldiss, *Billion Year Spree—The History of Science Fiction* (London: Weidenfeld and Nicholson, 1973), p. 8. Cf. Robert Scholes and Eric S. Rabkin, *Science Fiction: History, Science, Vision* (New York: Oxford University Press, 1977), p. 38. Aldiss, Scholes and Rabkin concur that *Frankenstein* is the first legitimate example of science fiction. For an analysis of the way *Frankenstein* has been misread by male science-fiction writers, see Judith A. Spector, "Science Fiction and the Sex War: A Womb of One's Own," *Literature and Psychology* 31 (1981): 21–32.

31. Evelyn Fox Keller, "Gender and Science," *Psychoanalysis and Contemporary Thought* I (1978): 409–33; see also her *Reflections on Gender and Science*, Chap. 4.

32. William Godwin, *Fleetwood or, the New Man of Feeling*, 3 Vols. (London, 1805; repr. New York and London: Garland, 1979) II:143–45.

33. William Godwin, *Fleetwood*, II: 278–79.

34. See, for example, Robert Kiely, *The Romantic Novel in England* (Cambridge: Harvard University Press, 1972), p. 166.

35. Isaac Barrow, *The Usefulness of Mathematical Learning Explained and Demonstrated* (London, 1734; repr. Frank Cass, 1970), pp. xxix–xxx.

36. Robert Boyle, *The Works of Robert Boyle*, ed. Thomas Birch, 6 Vols. (London, 1772), I:310.

37. Henry Oldenburg, *The Correspondence of Henry Oldenburg*, ed. A. R. Hall and M. B. Hall (Madison: University of Wisconsin Press, 1965), I:113.

38. Francis Bacon, *The Works of Francis Bacon*, ed. J. Spedding, R. L. Ellis, and D. N. Heath (new edn., 1879–90; Facsimile, Stuttgart-Bad Cannstatt, 1962, 7 Volumes), II:42, 373. For a discussion of the sexual metaphors utilized in much seventeenth- and eighteenth-century English scientific writing, see Brian Easlea, *Science and Sexual Oppression—Patriarchy's Confrontation with Woman and Nature* (London: Weidenfeld and Nicolson, 1981), p. 86; Chaps. 3, 4, 5.

39. Caroline Merchant, *The Death of Nature: Women, Ecology and the Scientific*

Revolution (San Francisco: Harper and Row, 1980); see also Evelyn Fox Keller, *Reflections on Gender and Science*, Chaps. 4–9; and Brian Easlea, *Science and Sexual Oppression*.

40. As Caroline Merchant concludes, "The removal of animistic, organic assumptions about the cosmos constituted the death of nature—the most far-reaching effect of the Scientific Revolution. Because nature was now viewed as a system of dead, inert particles moved by external, rather than inherent forces, the mechanical framework itself could legitimate the manipulation of nature. Moreover, as a conceptual framework, the mechanical order had associated with it a framework of values based on power, fully compatible with the directions taken by commercial capitalism" (*The Death of Nature*, p. 193).

For a useful study of the way *Frankenstein* condemns bourgeois patriarchy and the concept of male motherhood, see Burton Hatlen, "Milton, Mary Shelley and Patriarchy," in *Rhetoric, Literature and Interpretation*, ed. Harry R. Garvin (Lewisburg, Pa.: Bucknell University Press, 1983), pp. 19–47.

41. Franco Moretti, *Signs Taken for Wonders—Essays in the Sociology of Literary Form*, trans. S. Fischer, D. Forgacs, and D. Miller (London: Verso, 1983), p. 85.

42. George Canning, "Ameliorization of the Condition of the Slave Population in the West Indies (House of Lords)," [Hansard's] *Parliamentary Debates*, n.s. 10 (March 16, 1824), cols. 1046–1198 [1103].

CHAPTER SIX   Usurping the Female

1. Mary Shelley thus heralds a tradition of literary utopias and dystopias that depict single-sex societies, a tradition most recently appropriated by feminist writers to celebrate exclusively female societies. For an analysis of the strengths and weaknesses of such feminist utopian writing, in which female societies are reproduced by parthenogenesis, see my "On Feminist Utopias," *Women's Studies* (1982): 241–62. Leading examples of this genre include Charlotte Perkins Gilman's *Herland*, Sally Miller Gearhart's *The Wanderground*, Joanna Russ's *The Female Man*, James Tiptree, Jr.'s "Houston, Houston, Do You Read?" and Suzy McKee Charnas's trilogy *The Vampire Tapestry*.

2. On the gender division of nineteenth-century European culture, see Jean Elshtain, *Public Man, Private Woman: Women in Social and Political Thought* (Oxford: Robertson, 1981); and *Victorian Women—A Documentary Account of Women's Lives in Nineteenth-Century England, France, and the United States*, ed. E. Hellerstein, L. Hume, and K. Offen (Stanford: Stanford University Press, 1981). For a study of sex-roles in *Frankenstein*, see Kate Ellis, "Monsters in the Garden: Mary Shelley and the Bourgeois Family," in *The Endurance of Frankenstein*, ed. George Levine and U. C. Knoepflmacher (Berkeley and Los Angeles, and London: University of California Press, 1979), pp. 123–42; and Anca Vlasopolos, "*Frankenstein*'s Hidden Skeleton: The Psycho-Politics of Oppression," *Science-Fiction Studies* 10 (1983): 125–36.

William Veeder, in his insightful but occasionally reductive psychological study of Mary and Percy Shelley and *Frankenstein* (*Mary Shelley & Frankenstein—The Fate of Androgyny* [Chicago: University of Chicago Press, 1986]), wishes to define masculinity and femininity as the complementary halves of an ideally balanced androgynous or agapic personality which is destroyed or bifurcated by erotic self-love; his book traces the reasons why Mary Shelley's fictional characters realize or fail to achieve her androgynous ideal. While he is right to argue that Mary Shelley believed in balancing "masculine" and "feminine" characteristics, he consistently defines as innate psychological characteristics those patterns of learned behavior (masculinity, femininity) which I prefer to see as socially constructed gender roles. His readings thus unintentionally reinforce an oppressive biological determinism and sex stereotyping, even as they call attention to the dangers of extreme masculine and feminine behaviors.

3. Kate Ellis, "Monsters in the Garden," in George Levine and U. C. Knoepflmacher, *The Endurance of Frankenstein*, pp. 130–33. While Ellis rightly stresses Mary Shelley's condemnation of the inegalitarian sex roles in the nineteenth-century bourgeois family, she goes too far in arguing that Mary Shelley was opposed to the bourgeois family as such. As I argue in Chapter 4 and elsewhere, Mary Shelley continued to endorse a bourgeois family in which the sexes were equal but in which parents continued to govern children. In this sense, Mary Shelley was what we would now call a "liberal feminist," as opposed to her mother's more radical socialist feminism. But she shared her mother's conviction that women should receive the same education and cultural opportunities as the men of their class.

4. Henri Fuseli, *The Nightmare*, first version, 1781; courtesy of The Detroit Institute of Art. This famous painting was widely reproduced throughout the early nineteenth century and was of particular interest to Mary Shelley, who knew of her mother's early passionate love for Fuseli. H. W. Janson has suggested that Fuseli's representation of the nightmare is a projection of his unfulfilled passion for Anna Landolt, whose portrait is drawn on the reverse side (H. W. Janson, "Fuseli's *Nightmare*," *Arts and Sciences* 2 [1963]: 23–28). When Fuseli learned that Anna Landolt had married, he wrote to her uncle and his good friend Johann Lavater from London on June 16, 1779 that he had dreamed of lying in her bed and fusing "her body and soul" together with his own. Fuseli's painting is thus a deliberate allusion to traditional images of Cupid and Psyche meeting in her bedroom at night; here the welcomed god of love has been transformed into a demonic incubus of erotic lust (see also Peter Tomory, *The Life and Art of Henry Fuseli* [London: Thames and Hudson, 1972], 92ff; and the Catalogue Raisonnée by Gert Schiff, *Johann Heinrich Füssli* [Zurich: Verlag Berichthaus, 1973], 757–59).

Gerhard Joseph first noted the allusion to Fuseli's painting, "Frankenstein's Dream: The Child is Father of the Monster," *Hartford Studies in Literature* 7 (1975): 97–115, 109. William Veeder denies the association (*Mary Shelley & Frankenstein*, pp. 192–93) on the grounds that Elizabeth's hair half-covers her face; in this regard, it may be significant that Fuseli's woman's face is half-covered in shadow.

5. Paul A. Cantor has discussed Frankenstein's rejections both of normal sexuality and of the bourgeois life-style, in *Creature and Creator: Myth-making and English Romanticism* (New York: Cambridge University Press, 1984), pp. 109–15.

6. William Veeder has emphasized the homosexual bond between Frankenstein and his Monster (*Mary Shelley & Frankenstein*, pp. 89–92). Eve Kosofsky Sedgwick arrives at this conclusion from a different direction. In her *Between Men—English Literature and Male Homosocial Desire* (New York: Columbia University Press, 1985), she observes in passing that *Frankenstein*, like William Godwin's *Caleb Williams*, is "about one or more males who not only is persecuted by, but considers himself transparent to and often under the compulsion of, another male. If we follow Freud [in the case of Dr. Schreber] in hypothesizing that such a sense of persecution represents the fearful, phantasmic rejection by recasting of an original homosexual (or even merely homosocial) desire, then it would make sense to think of this group of novels as embodying strongly homophobic mechanisms" (pp. 91–92).

7. While I am in large agreement with Mary Poovey's intelligent and sensitive analysis of Frankenstein's egotistic desire (in *The Proper Lady and the Woman Writer: Ideology as Style in the Works of Mary Wollstonecraft, Mary Shelley and Jane Austen* [Chicago and London: University of Chicago Press, 1984], pp. 123–33), I do not share her

view that the nature we see in the novel is "fatal to human beings and human relationships." Poovey fails to distinguish between Frankenstein's view of nature and the author's and between the first and second editions of the novel in this regard.

8. On Mary Shelley's subversive representation of the traditionally masculinized Alps as female, see Fred V. Randel, *"Frankenstein*, Feminism, and the Intertextuality of Mountains," *Studies in Romanticism* 23 (Winter 1984): 515–32.

9. Carol Gilligan, *In A Different Voice—Psychological Theory and Women's Development* (Cambridge and London: Harvard University Press, 1982), p. 174.

10. See Nancy Chodorow, *The Reproduction of Mothering—Psychoanalysis and the Sociology of Gender* (Berkeley: University of California Press, 1978); Dorothy Dinnerstein, *The Mermaid and the Minotaur—Sexual Arrangements and Human Malaise* (New York: Harper & Row, 1976); cf. Nancy Friday, *My Mother/My Self—the Daughter's Search for Identity* (New York: Dell, 1977).

CHAPTER SEVEN Problems of Perception

1. On the epistemological issues raised by the monster, see L. J. Swingle, "Frankenstein's Monster and Its Romantic Relatives: Problems of Knowledge in English Romanticism," *Texas Studies in Literature and Language* 15 (1973): 51–65; and Joseph H. Gardner, "Mary Shelley's Divine Tragedy," *Essays in Literature* 4 (1977): 182–97. On the semiotic implications, see Peter Brooks, " 'Godlike Science/Unhallowed Arts': Language, Nature and Monstrosity," *Endurance of Frankenstein*, ed. George Levine and U. C. Knoepflmacher (Berkeley and Los Angeles, and London: University of Chicago Press, 1979), pp. 205–20; and Jerrold E. Hogle, "Otherness in *Frankenstein*: The Confinement/Autonomy of Fabrication," *Structuralist Review* 2 (1980): 20–48.

2. For Lavater's physiognomical theories, see Johann Caspar Lavater, *Essays on Physiognomy, Designed to Promote the Knowledge and Love of Mankind*, 4 Vols., trans. Henry Hunter (London, 1789–98). For the physiognomical analysis of the infant Mary Godwin, see R. Glynn Grylls, *Mary Shelley—A Biography* (London: Oxford University Press, 1938), pp. 10–11: the physiognomist Mr. Nicholson reported on September 18, 1797, that the three-week-old Mary Godwin's skull "possessed considerable memory and intelligence," while her forehead, eyes and eyebrows manifested a "quick sensibility, irritable, scarcely irascible" and her "too much employed" mouth showed "the outlines of intelligence. She was displeased, and it denoted much more of resigned vexation than either scorn or rage." Franz Joseph Gall's phrenological system was expounded by Johann Christoph Spurzheim in *The Physiognomical System of Drs. Gall and Spurzheim* (London, 1815). For Mary Shelley's familiarity with Dr. Gall's system, see her *Journal*, ed. Frederick L. Jones (Norman, Oklahoma: University of Oklahoma Press, 1947), p. 15; and *The Journals of Claire Clairmont 1814–1827*, ed. Marion Kingston Stocking (Cambridge: Harvard University Press, 1968), p. 44.

3. Edmund Burke, *A Philosophical Inquiry into the Origin of Our Ideas of the Sublime and the Beautiful* (London, 1757; repr. Philadelphia, 1806), p. 47.

4. Edmund Burke, *The Sublime and the Beautiful*, p. 77.

5. Thomas Weiskel, *The Romantic Sublime* (Baltimore: Johns Hopkins University Press, 1976).

6. For further discussion of this point, see my "Coleridge's 'This Lime-Tree Bower My Prison' and the Categories of English Landscape," *Studies in Romanticism* 18 (1979): 253–270.

7. We should recall here Mary Shelley's fascination with Poussin's *Deluge* (or *Winter*), the only painting she mentioned from her visit to the Louvre in 1814 (*Mary Shelley's Journal*, ed. Frederick L. Jones, p. 6). On the creature as an image of elemental Chaos, readers might wish to consult Frances Ferguson's "Legislating the Sublime," in *Studies in Eighteenth-Century British Art and Aesthetics*, ed. Ralph Cohen (Berkeley: University of California Press, 1985), pp. 128–47, which reaches rather different conclusions from mine.

8. *The Letters of Mary Wollstonecraft Shelley*, ed. Betty T. Bennett (Baltimore: Johns Hopkins University Press, 1980, 1983), I:378.

9. Michel Foucault, *Madness and Civilization*, trans. Richard Howard (New York: Vintage Books, 1961; *Discipline and Punish—The Birth of the Prison*, trans. Alan Sheridan (New York: Vintage Books, 1977, 1979).

10. Mary Shelley described *Frankenstein* as a defense of Polyphemus. Replying to Leigh Hunt's remark that "Polyphemus . . . always appears to me a pathetic rather than a monstrous person, though his disappointed sympathies at last made him cruel," Mary Shelley commented, "I have written a book in defence of Polypheme—have I not?" (*Letters of Mary Shelley*, ed. Betty T. Bennet, I:91, dated April 6, 1819). the allusion is to the one-eyed, uncouth, giant Cyclops Polyphemus, whose passionate love for the beautiful nymph Galatea is rejected; the story is recounted in Book 12 of Ovid's *Metamorphoses*. The scorned Polyphemus, in jealousy and despair, murders Galatea's lover Acis. I owe this observation to Aija Ozolins, "Dreams and Doctrine: Dual Stands in *Frankenstein*," *Science-Fiction Studies* 6 (1975): 106.

11. Robert Kiely, *The Romantic Novel in England* (Cambridge: Harvard University Press, 1972), p. 158. Kiely has been misled by the association of Victor Frankenstein with Percy Shelley into seeing the character of Frankenstein too positively, as a romantic "hero" whose "fault is more nature's than his." While Kiely acknowledges Frankenstein's egoism, he gives too much credit to Frankenstein's "superiority through suffering" and mistakenly identifies as a major theme in the novel the "idea that the genius, even in his failures, is unique, noble, and isolated from other men by divine right" (pp. 156, 158, 172).

12. On the relation of *Frankenstein* to *Caleb Williams*, see Katherine Richardson Powers, *The Influence of William Godwin on the Novels of Mary Shelley* (New York: Arno Press, 1980); Gay Clifford, "*Caleb Williams* and *Frankenstein*: First-Person Narration and Things as They Are," *Genre* 10 (1977): 601–17; and A. D. Harvey, "*Frankenstein* and *Caleb Williams*," *Keats-Shelley Journal* 29 (1980): 21–27.

On Frankenstein and his creature as psychological doubles or alter-egos, see among others, Masao Miyoshi, *The Divided Self* (New York: New York University Press, 1969), pp. 79–89; Martin Tropp, *Mary Shelley's Monster* (Boston: Houghton, 1976); J. M. Hill, "*Frankenstein* and the Physiognomy of Desire," *American Imago* 32 (1975): 335–58; Harold Bloom, "Afterword" to *Frankenstein* (New York: New American Library, 1965), pp. 212–23; Paul A. Cantor, *Creator and Creature: Myth-making and English Romanticism* (New York: Cambridge University Press, 1984), pp. 115–24; and William Veeder, *Mary Shelley and Frankenstein—The Fate of Androgyny* (Chicago: University of Chicago Press, 1986), pp. 89–92, passim. Paul Sherwin both develops and criticizes such Freudian interpretations in "*Frankenstein*: Creation as Catastrophe," *PMLA* 96 (1981): 883–903.

13. Irving Massey, *The Gaping Pig—Literature and Metamorphosis* (Berkeley and Los Angeles, and London: University of California Press, 1976), p. 129.

14. On the gender division in Burke's aesthetic theory, see Isaac Kramnick, *The Rage of Edmund Burke—Portrait of an Ambivalent Conservative* (New York: Basic Books, 1977), pp. 92–98.

15. *Mary Shelley's Journal*, ed. Frederick L. Jones, p. 53. I am indebted to Gary Harrison for bringing the importance of this passage to my attention.

CHAPTER EIGHT Love, Guilt and Reparation: *The Last Man*

1. On August 23, 1818, Shelley wrote to Mary demanding that she come "instantly" with William and Clara from the Bagni di Lucca to Este and issued the following traveling schedule—"You can pack up directly you get this letter & employ the next day in that. The day after get up at four oClock, & go post to Lucca where you will arrive at 6. Then take Vetturino for Florence to arrive the same evening. From Florence to Este is three days vetturino journey, & you could not I think do it quicker by the Post . . .—I don't think you can but *try* to get from *Florence* to *Bologna* in one day. Don't take the post for it is not much faster & very expensive. I have been obliged to decide all these things without you.—I have done for the best." (*The Letters of Percy Bysshe Shelley*, ed. Frederick L. Jones [Oxford: The Clarendon Press, 1964], I:36).

2. Richard Holmes, *Shelley—The Pursuit* (New York: E. P. Dutton, 1975), p. 447; cf. pp. 439–57.

3. *The Letters of Mary Wollstonecraft Shelley*, ed. Betty T. Bennett (Baltimore: Johns Hopkins University Press, 1980, 1983), I:101.

4. Percy Bysshe Shelley, *The Complete Poetical Works of Percy Bysshe Shelley*, ed. Thomas Hutchinson, with Notes by Mary Shelley (London: Oxford University Press, 1905; repr. 1960), p. 582. The final lines were first printed from Bodleian MS Shelley Adds. c. 12. p. 179 (rev.) by Judith Chernaik, *The Lyrics of Shelley* (Cleveland: Case Western Reserve University Press, 1972), p. 247.

5. Richard Holmes, *Shelley—The Pursuit*, p. 519.

6. Richard Holmes, *Shelley—The Pursuit*, p. 521.

7. Two entries from Mary Shelley's Journal, quoted by Elizabeth Nitchie, testify to the relief she gained from writing this novella during her depression (Mary Wollstonecraft Shelley, *Mathilda*, ed. Elizabeth Nitchie [Chapel Hill: University of North Carolina Press, 1959], p. 103; all further references to this, the only published edition of *Mathilda*, will appear in the text). The entry for October 27, 1822, records: "Before when I wrote Mathilda, miserable as I was, the inspiration was sufficient to quell my wretchedness temporarily." Another entry, for December 2, 1834, reminisces: "Little harm has my imagination done to me & how much good!—My poor heart pierced through & through has found balm from it—it has been the aegis to my sensibility—Sometimes there have been periods when misery has pushed it aside—& those indeed were periods I shudder to remember—but the fairy only stept aside, she watched her time—& at the first opportunity her . . . beaming face peeped in & the weight of deadly woe was lightened."

T. N. Potniceva's suggestion that *Mathilda* was a response to the despair that Mary Shelley felt over the political situation in England upon hearing of the Peterloo Massacre of August 16, 1819, in "Svoeobrazie romantičeskogo metoda v romane M. Šelli *Matil'da* (1819)," *Filologičeskie Nauki* 4:94 (1976): 33, is nullified by the fact that the Shelleys did not learn of the Peterloo Massacre until September 5 (*Letters of Percy Shelley*, ed. Frederick L. Jones, II:117).

8. Lovel also echoes "Love-Will," Mrs. Godwin's pet name for her son William, the half-brother who had displaced Mary in the Godwin household.

9. On Percy Shelley's possible affair with Elise, see Ursula Orange, "Elise, Nursemaid to the Shelleys," *Keats-Shelley Memorial Bulletin* 6 (1955): 24–34; and Richard

Holmes, *Shelley—The Pursuit*, pp. 463–74. The baby (whom Shelley referred to as his "Neopolitan charge") died on June 9, 1820. For a full review of the documents surrounding this episode, see Kenneth Neil Cameron, *Shelley—The Golden Years* (Cambridge: Harvard University Press, 1974), pp. 64–73. Although Cameron denies the possibility of Elise being the mother of Elena Adelaide on the grounds that the doctor who examined her in early December, 1818, feared only for a "miscarriage," it is possible that the baby was born quite prematurely; her health after birth was precarious. Paolo Foggi may have married Elise on the assumption that the child was his, only to discover afterwards that Elise had been pregnant before their sexual liaison began.

10. *Letters of Percy Shelley*, ed. Frederick L. Jones, II:427 (dated May 28, 1822).

11. *Letters of Percy Shelley*, ed. Frederick L. Jones, II:433 (dated June 18, 1822).

12. *Letters of Mary Shelley*, ed. Betty T. Bennett, I:245.

13. *Letters of Percy Shelley*, ed. Frederick L. Jones, II:435 (dated June 18, 1822).

14. On the relationship between Percy Shelley and Jane Williams during the period preceding his death, see the thoughtful account by Donald H. Reiman, "Shelley's 'The Triumph of Life': The Biographical Problem," *PMLA* 58 (1963): 536–50.

15. The classic statement of the causal relationship between repressed anger and nonclinical depression is Freud's *Mourning and Melancholia* (1917). See *The Complete Psychological Works of Sigmund Freud: The Standard Edition*, trans. James Strachey, in collaboration with Anna Freud, assisted by Alix Strachey and Alan Tyson (London: Hogarth Press and the Institute of Psychoanalysis, 1957), Vol. 14: 237–58.

16. Mary Wollstonecraft Shelley, "The Choice," Mary Shelley's Journal, Abinger Dep. d. 311/4; erroneously printed in *The Choice—A Poem on Shelley's Death*, ed. H. Buxton Forman (London: privately printed, 1876); a more accurate transcription of the poem is given by Diana Scott-Kilvert and Paula Feldman in their edition of Mary Shelley's Journal (Oxford: Clarendon Press, 1987), pp. 490–94. This poem was completed before November 27, 1823, when Mary Shelley asked Leigh Hunt to return it to her (*Letters of Mary Shelley*, ed. Betty T. Bennett, I:404).

17. Hunt was finally persuaded by Jane Williams to give Shelley's unconsumed heart to Mary Shelley. On the unseemly quarrel over Shelley's heart, see Hunt's letter to Mary Shelley after she had appealed to Byron to intercede (*The Letters of Mary W. Shelley*, ed. Frederick L. Jones [Norman: University of Oklahoma Press, 1944], I:187 n2) and John Gisborne's account (Maria Gisborne, *Maria Gisborne and Edward E. Williams, Shelley's Friends: Their Journals and Letters*, ed. Frederick L. Jones [Norman, Oklahoma: University of Oklahoma Press, 1951], pp. 88–89). On Hunt's dislike for and eventual reconciliation with Mary following Percy Shelley's death, see *Letters of Mary Shelley*, ed. Betty T. Bennett, I:300, 304, 354, 375.

Jane Williams had told Leigh Hunt on his arrival in Italy what she assumed that he already knew, that "the intercourse between Shelley & Mary was not as happy as it should have been." On her discussions with Leigh Hunt and Thomas Hogg concerning Percy Shelley's estrangement from Mary, see Jane Williams's letter to Hunt on April 28, 1824 (Maria Gisborne, *Journals and Letters*, pp. 165–67) and Hogg's letter to Jane Williams on August 17, 1823, in which he commented

> Oh, the cruel kindness of Trelawney! I fear indeed that nothing is left
> for Mary's friends, but to hope, that her return will be more
> auspicious than they can venture to augur. I tremble because of her
> want of tact (to borrow her favorite expression), & because of those
> wretches, the G[odwin]s, who wd sink a much better vessel with a

much better pilot—they have a talent for failing & for failing disgracefully. Her conversation will be painful, just as her letters are, because, to those, who saw behind the scenes, the subject of it is a mere fable; our loss is real; your's, dearest girl, I acknowledge, in spite of my hopes, irreparable, mine bad enough, but her's, however painful, is in fact imaginary for to suppose that matters cd have continued as they were, wd have been the vanity of vanities, & any other termination wd have been for her, except as to money-matters, infinitely worse. (Bodleian Library: Abinger Ms. Dep.c.535)

Mary did not discover that Jane had been impugning her behind her back until July 13, 1827 (see her Journal entries for July 13, 1827, February 12, 1828, November 23, 1833, and October 21, 1838 [Abinger Dep. d. 311/5]; and *Letters of Mary Shelley*, ed. Betty T. Bennett, I:568–69; II:25–26, 50).

18. *Letters of Mary Shelley*, ed. Betty T. Bennett, I:252; cf. Mary Shelley's Journal, entries for October 5, November 11, and December 19, 1822 (Abinger Dep. d. 311/4). William Walling has commented on how Mary Shelley's guilt led her to deify her dead husband and to denigrate her self as mere "cold moonshine" (*Mary Shelley* [New York: Twayne, 1972] pp. 76–77).

19. Mary Shelley's profound sense of unworthiness surfaces repeatedly in her Journal. On October 21, 1822, for instance, she wrote:

I am much given to self-examination . . . [which] even among the most perfect, causes diffidence, how much more therefore with one like me—who finds within herself so many defects.

And on June 3, 1823, she told her dead husband, "I was unworthy of you—I ever felt that—most bitterly & deeply now." Cf. her Journal entries for March 19, 1823; April 26, 1823; December 15, 1823 (Abinger Dep. d. 311/4). And she refused all subsequent offers of marriage.

20. This poem was discovered and published by R. Stanley Dicks, "Mary Shelley: An Unprinted Elegy on Her Husband?" *Keats-Shelley Memorial Bulletin* 28 (1977): 36–41. The poem was written on the end-papers of Mary Shelley's copy of *Dramas of the Ancient World* (1821–22) by "David Lyndsay" (the nom de plume of her friend Mary Diana Dods) and dated "Feby 1822." But as Dicks argues, this date is almost certainly an error. He posits a date one year later (February 1823), after Percy Shelley's death. I myself would suggest, on the basis of her reference to her "fame," a date two years later—February 1824—after Mary Shelley had returned to England in August, 1823, and found herself "famous" as the author of *Frankenstein*, then receiving a dramatic production at the English Opera House (cf. her letter to Leigh Hunt, September 11, 1823: *Letters of Mary Shelley*, ed. Betty T. Bennett, I:378).

21. Mary Shelley told Theresa Guiccioli that Adrian and Lord Raymond were "faint portraits" of Percy Shelley and Byron (*Letters of Mary Shelley*, ed. Betty T. Bennett, I:566). Her biographical allusions were noted, not always correctly, by Walter E. Peck, "The Biographical Element in the Novels of Mary Wollstonecraft Shelley," *PMLA* 38 (1923): 196–219. For more accurate identifications, see Elizabeth Nitchie, *Mary Shelley—Author of "Frankenstein"* (New Brunswick, New Jersey: Rutgers University Press, 1953), pp. 68–75, 94–95, 102–4.

22. All textual references to *The Last Man* are to the modern reprint, Mary Wollstonecraft Shelley, *The Last Man*, ed. Hugh J. Luke, Jr., (Lincoln: University of Nebraska Press, 1965).

23. Hugh J. Luke, Jr., Introduction to *The Last Man*, pp. xiv. P. D. Fleck has pointed out Mary Shelley's contemporaneous criticism of her husband's impractical idealism in her notes to his poems, in "Mary Shelley's Notes to Shelley's Poems and *Frankenstein*," *Studies in Romanticism* 6 (1966–67): 226–54.

24. Temma Kaplan, "Female Consciousness and Collective Action: The Case of Barcelona, 1910–1918," *Signs* VII (1982): 545–566, p. 545.

25. On March 17–19, 1823, Mary Shelley noted in her Journal that Byron

> "who has been called my protector & who at first seemed willing to become so, has resigned that office. That, to me, confiding & somewhat sanguine, has been a bitter blow.... For without my protector & my support, no circumstance that called me into active life, however fortunate it might be esteemed by others, but would bring with it almost unqualified pain—" (Abinger Dep. d. 311/4, f. 46)

Cf. *Letters of Mary Shelley*, ed. Betty T. Bennett, I:344. For Mary Shelley's relations with Byron after her husband's death, see Leslie Marchand, *Byron—A Biography* (London: John Murray, 1957), III:1017–18, 1037, 1079–86; on the portrait of Byron in *The Last Man*, see Ernest J. Lovell, Jr., "Byron and the Byronic Hero in the Novels of Mary Shelley," *Studies in English* 30 (1951): 158–83, and "Byron and Mary Shelley," *Keats-Shelley Journal* 2 (1953): 35–49.

26. Since Frederick L. Jones's transcriptions of Mary Shelley's Journal after Percy Shelley's death are appallingly incomplete and inaccurate, I have provided my own transcriptions; here of Abinger Dep. d. 311/4, f. 78. Readers should check all my transcriptions against the new edition of Mary Shelley's Journal, ed. Diana Scott-Kilvert and Paula Feldman (Oxford: Clarendon Press, 1987), which appeared after this book went to press.

Mary Shelley had earlier analyzed her intense emotional response to Byron in her Journal on October 19, 1822:

> I do not think that any person's voice has the same power of awakening melancholy in me as Albe's [Byron's]. I have been accustomed when hearing it to listen and to speak little; another voice, not mine, ever replied—a voice whose strings are broken.... when Albe speaks and Shelley does not answer, it is as thunder without rain—the form of the sun without heat or light ... and I listen with an unspeakable melancholy that yet is not all pain.
>
> The above explains that which would otherwise be an enigma— why Albe has the power by his mere presence & voice of exciting such deep and shifting emotions within me. For my feelings have no analogy either with my opinion of him, or the subject of his conversation. (Abinger Dep. d. 311/3)

And in 1830, she summed up her impression of Byron for John Murray:

> Our Lord Byron—the fascinating—faulty—childish—philosophical being—daring the world—docile to a private circle—impetuous and indolent—gloomy and yet more gay than any other—

Letters of Mary Shelley, ed. Betty T. Bennett, II:101; cf. I:421, 436; II:162–64.

27. G. Bebbington reported the discovery of the Shelleys' cottage in Bishopsgate and its similarity to Perdita's cottage in "*The Last Man*" in *Notes and Queries* 216 (May 1971): 163–65.

28. In her Journal on October 21, 1822, Mary Shelley revealed her own inability to communicate her deepest feelings to her friends, her shyness, her innate pride, and her resultant self-contempt:

> There is another thing which in my peculiar case renders my intercourse with others extremely disagreeable—no one seems to understand or to sympathize with me. They all seem to look on me as one without affections—without any sensibility—my sufferings are thought a cypher—& I feel my self degraded before them; knowing that in their hearts they degrade me from the rank which I deserve to possess—I feel dejected & cowed before them, feeling as if I might be the senseless person they appear to consider me. (Abinger Dep. d. 311/4)

The charge of coldness pursued Mary Shelley all her life, as Betty T. Bennett has observed (*Letters of Mary Shelley*, I:284n5).

29. William Walling has noted this rejoinder to "Epipsychidion," *Mary Shelley*, pp. 96–97.

30. Mary Shelley repeatedly voiced a desire to die and be reunited with her husband in her Journal:

> I cannot be destined to live long; a hatred of life must consume the vital principle—perfectly detached as I am from the world. . . . I feel that all is to me dead except the necessity of viewing a succession of daily suns illuminate the sepulchre of all I love. Well I shall commence my task, commemorate the virtues of the only creature on earth worth loving or living for, & then may be I may join him, Moonshine may-be united to her planet & wander no more, a sad reflection of all she loved, on earth. (October 5, 1822)

> No! No—I shall not live. I feel that my thread is short. . . . I go on from day to day & I know that I am unhappy—know that I desire death only as the sole relief to my misery—but suddenly I awake—it is a change from narrative to a drama—I feel the prison walls close about me—I feel in every trembling nerve that life has nought but bitterness for me—that young—I can hope no more—a palpable darkness surrounds me, & I on narrow pinacle of isolated rock, stand shuddering. (February 17, 1823)

> A long dreary winter is coming—and where shall I be next year. If a sybil said, in my grave, she were the foreteller of joy. I never, in all my woes, understood the feelings that led to suicide till now—When the blank grave appears a rest after this troubled dream, or any change preferable to this monotony of heaviness. (October 26, 1824)

Cf. entries for January 30, 1824, and December 31, 1833 (all Abinger Dep. d. 311/4–5); and *Letters of Mary Shelley*, ed. Betty T. Bennett, I:243, 252, 261, 283, 287, 291, 300, 305.

31. Mary Shelley repeatedly claimed that only her love and sense of responsibility for her child, Percy Florence, kept her alive; see her Journal entries for October 5, 1822, and February 24, 1823 (Abinger Dep. d. 311/4).

32. Mary Shelley endorsed Perdita's view of "woman's love" in her letter to Theresa Guiccioli on May 16, 1824:

> Every day one feels more within how little the world is worth when

the beloved object is gone. Didn't dear Byron himself say (he who knew so thoroughly the female heart) that the whole of a woman's existence depends on love, and therefore losing a love there is no other refuge than To love again and be again undone. But we, dear Guiccioli, are deprived of this refuge.

Letters of Mary Shelley, ed. Betty T. Bennett, I:421.

33. On the mother's tendency to identify with her daughter, see Nancy Chodorow, *The Reproduction of Mothering—Psychoanalysis and the Sociology of Gender* (Berkeley: University of California Press, 1978).

34. Mary Shelley's Journal, Abinger Dep. d. 311/4, f. 76. As Mary Shelley wrote to Thomas Hogg on February 28, 1823:

Miserable wreck as I am—left from the destruction of the noblest fabric of humanity, to tell of it—to mourn over it—& mark its ruin—who can visit me even in thought without a shudder—who can communicate with me without being shadowed by the misery which penetrates me.

Letters of Mary Shelley, ed. Betty T. Bennett, I:316. One of the first reviewers of *The Last Man* sarcastically wondered why the author did not choose "the last Woman? she would have known better how to paint her distress at having nobody left to talk to," *The Literary Gazette and Journal of Belle Lettres, Arts, Sciences, &c.* 473 (February 18, 1826): 102–3; in W. H. Lyles, *Mary Shelley: An Annotated Bibliography* (New York: Garland, 1975) pp. 174–75.

35. Mary Shelley's Journal, Abinger Dep. d. 311/54 f. 91; Dep. d. 311/5, ff. 3–4. Mary Shelley recorded her recurrent and painful loneliness in her Journal and letters:

"Tears fill my eyes; well may I weep, solitary girl! The dead know you not; the living heed you not. You sit in your lone room, and the howling wind, gloomy prognostic of winter, gives not forth so despairing a tone as the unheard sighs your ill-fated heart breathes." (October 26, 1824)

Cf. her Journal entries for October 5 and 21, 1822; Sepembter 5, 1826; December 5, 1827; December 28, 1830; and March 8, 1831—all Abinger Dep. d. 311/4–5—and *Letters of Mary Shelley*, ed. Betty T. Bennett, I:304, 311–12, 415, 452, 463; II:214, 281. "Loneliness has been the curse of my life," she observed in her Journal on December 2, 1834 (Abinger Dep. d. 311/5, f. 55).

For a Freudian analysis of the dynamic by which a powerful love-hate relationship with a parent or spouse can produce both guilt and an enduring sense of loneliness, see Melanie Klein, "On the Sense of Loneliness" (1963) in *Envy and Gratitude and Other Works*, ed. Masud R. Khan (London: Hogarth Press, 1980), pp. 300–13.

36. Mary Shelley's Journal, Abinger Dep. d. 311/4, f. 79. Mary Shelley celebrated the capacity of her imaginative activities to bring her solace in her Journal entries for October 27, 1822; November 10, 1822; and December 2, 1834 (Abinger Dep. d. 311/4–5). But she also recognized that creative activity alone did not guarantee her the audience and sympathy she craved:

I once dreamt that the thoughts labouring in this brain might shape themselves to such words as might weave a chain to bind the thoughts of my fellow-creatures to me in love & sympathy—but it is not so—the sands drink up the waters that flowed from the deepest fountains of my soul, & nor verdure nor stain shows where they fell. . . . (December 15, 1823; Abinger Dep. d. 311/4, f. 64).

37. Muriel Spark uses this phrase in *Child of Light—A Reassessment of Mary Wollstonecraft Shelley* (Hadleigh, Essex: Tower Bridge Publications, Ltd., 1951; repr. 1987), p. 120. William Godwin also noted a melancholic strain in his daughter which he attributed to her mother. "How differently are you and I organized!" he wrote to Mary Shelley on October 9, 1827:

> In my seventy-second year I am all cheerfulness, and never anticipate the evil day with distressing feelings till to do so is absolutely unavoidable. Would to God you were my daughter in all but my poverty! But I am afraid you are a Wollstonecraft. We are so curiously made that one atom put in the wrong place in our original structure will often make us unhappy for life.

See C. Kegan Paul, *William Godwin, His Friends and Contemporaries* (London: Henry S. King & Co., 1876; repr. New York: AMS Press, 1970), II:299.

38. Here I am much indebted to Lee Sterrenburg's fine essay "*The Last Man*: Anatomy of Failed Revolutions," *Nineteenth Century Fiction* 33 (1978): 324–47.

39. On the prevalence of apocalyptic themes in English art between 1755 and 1840, see Morton D. Paley, *The Apocalpytic Sublime* (New Haven and London: Yale University Press, 1986). For literary treatments of the theme, see Laurence Goldstein, *Ruins and Empire: The Evolution of a Theme in Augustan and Romantic Literature* (Pittsburgh: University of Pittsburgh Press, 1977), pp. 143–62; George Steiner, *In Bluebeard's Castle: Some Notes towards the Redefinition of Culture* (New Haven: Yale University Press, 1971), Chap. 1; and A. J. Sambrook, "A Romantic Theme: The Last Man," *Forum for Modern Language Studies* 2 (1966): 25–33.

40. As early as September, 1817, Mary Shelley had distrusted the motives behind William Cobbett's calls for democratic reform. As she wrote to Shelley:

> Have you seen Cobbett's 23 No. to the Borough mongers—Why he appears to be making out a list for a proscription—I actually shudd{er} to read it—a revolution in this country would {not?} be *bloodless* if that man has any power in it He is I fear somewhat of a Marius perhaps of a Marat—I like him not—I fear he is a bad man—He encourages in the multitude the worst possible human passion *revenge* or as he wouild probably give it that abominable *Christian* name retribution. (*Letters of Mary Shelley*, ed. Betty T. Bennett, I:49)

41. William Godwin, *An Enquiry Concernig Political Justice* (London: G. G. J. and J. Robinson, 1793), II:869, 872, 871.

42. Lee Sterrenburg, "*The Last Man*," p. 335.

43. Edmund Burke, *Reflections on the Revolution in France*, ed. William B. Todd (New York: Holt, Rinehart and Winston, 1959), pp. 107–8.

44. Margaret Homans, "Dreaming of Children: Literalization in *Jane Eyre* and *Wuthering Heights*," in *The Female Gothic*, ed. Juliann E. Fleenor (Montreal and London: Eden Press, 1983), pp. 257–79; p. 259.

However, I would argue against Homans's assumption, both here and in her recent *Bearing the Word* (1986), that language enables us to differentiate precisely the literal from the figurative (is a "tableleg" literal or figurative, for instance?). I believe that language, by which I mean all systems of visual, verbal, aural, and sensory signs that convey meaning, is itself a figurative construction of that material reality or *Ding-an-sich* which exists for the conscious mind only as it is linguistically structured. As Benjamin Lee Whorf and Edward Sapir would put it, all conscious experience presupposes a symbolic language. *The Last Man* endorses this concept of linguistic determinism, which Percy Shelley had articulated in *Prometheus Unbound*:

> *Language is a perpetual Orphic song,*
> *Which rules with Daedal harmony a throng*
> *Of thoughts and forms, which else senseless and shapeless were.*
>
> (Act IV, 415–17)

45. Hugh J. Luke Jr., Introduction to *The Last Man*, pp. xvii–xviii.

46. Margaret Homans, "Dreaming of Children," p. 257.

47. On Mary Shelley's sources for the theme of the last man, see Jean de Palacio, "Mary Shelley and The 'Last Man': A Minor Romantic Theme," *Revue de Littérature Comparée* 42 (1968): 37–49; and Henry R. Majewski, "Grainville's 'Le Dernier Homme',," *Symposium* 17 (1963): 114–22.

48. Robert Lane Snyder also reaches this conclusion in "Apocalypse and Indeterminacy in Mary Shelley's *The Last Man*," *Studies in Romanticism* 17 (1978): 435–52.

49. *Letters of Mary Shelley*, ed. Betty T. Bennett, II:17.

CHAPTER NINE   Revising *Frankenstein*

1. Mary Poovey has perceptively discussed the role of fatalism in the 1831 revisions of *Frankenstein*, albeit to different purposes (*The Proper Lady and the Woman Writer—Ideology as Style in the Works of Mary Wollstonecraft, Mary Shelley and Jane Austen* [Chicago and London: University of Chicago Press, 1984], pp. 133–42). Jean de Palacio has stressed only the stylistic dimensions of these changes which he defines as a process "d'allongement et de commoration" (*Mary Shelley dans son oeuvre* [Paris: Klincksieck, 1969], pp. 576–85; 584).

2. *The Letters of Mary Wollstonecraft Shelley*, ed. Betty T. Bennett (Baltimore: Johns Hopkins University Press, 1980, 1983), I:572.

3. Mary Wollstonecraft Shelley, *Rambles in Germany and Italy in 1840, 1842, and 1843* (London: Edward Moxon, 1844), pp. 1–2.

4. For a telling study of the role of fate in the 1831 edition of *Frankenstein*, see John R. Reed, "Will and Fate in *Frankenstein*," *Bulletin of Research in the Humanities* 83 (1980): 319–38.

5. For a discussion of Coleridge's "The Rime of the Ancient Mariner" as a discourse of open-ended indeterminacy rather than of moral didacticism, see my *English Romantic Irony* (Cambridge: Harvard University Press, 1980), Chap. 5.

CHAPTER TEN   Fathers and Daughters, or "A Sexual Education"

1. For a sympathetic study of the historical sources of *Perkin Warbeck* and its relationship to other historical novels, see Jean de Palacio, *Mary Shelley dans son oeuvre* (Paris: Klincksieck, 1969), pp. 146–80. For a study of the political implications of the novel, see Betty T. Bennett, "The Political Philosophy of Mary Shelley's Historical Novels: *Valperga* and *Perkin Warbeck*," in *The Evidence of the Imagination*, ed. Donald H. Reiman, Michael C. Jaye, and Betty T. Bennett (New York: New York University Press, 1978), pp. 354–71.

2. *Letters of Percy Shelley*, ed. Jones, II:245; this letter, to Thomas Love Peacock, is dated November 8, 1820.

3. For a discussion of the historical developments in the nineteenth-century English family, see Chapter 11: "Idealizing the Bourgeois Family."

4. Mary Shelley's Journal, entry for October 21, 1838, Abinger Dep. d. 311/4: ff 77–78, 80, 90.

5. *The Letters of Mary Wollstonecraft Shelley*, ed. Betty T. Bennett (Baltimore: Johns Hopkins University Press, 1980, 1983), I:296; dated December 5, 1822.

6. *Letters of Mary Shelley*, ed. Betty T. Bennett, I:491; dated June 27, 1825.

7. Mary Shelley's Journal, Abinger Dep. d. 311/5: f 53. Betty T. Bennett first identified Walter Sholto Douglas and David Lyndsay as Diana Dods, *Letters of Mary Shelley*, II:7 n8.

8. *Letters of Mary Shelley*, ed. Betty T. Bennett, II:256; dated October 12, 1835.

9. *Letters of Mary Shelley*, ed. Betty T. Bennett, I:379, 385, dated September 9 and 18, 1823.

10. Mary Shelley's Journal, Abinger Dep. d. 311/4: f 68. On Mary Shelley's frustrated craving for a father's love, see also William Veeder, "The Negative Oedipus: Father, *Frankenstein*, and the Shelleys," *Critical Inquiry* 12 (1986): 365–90.

11. *Letters of Mary Shelley*, ed. Betty T. Bennett, II:139; dated June 14, 1831.

12. Mary Shelley's Journal, Abinger Dep. d. 311-4: f 82. In her review of Jane Dunn's *Moon in Eclipse—A Life of Mary Shelley*, Emily Sunstein plausibly conjectures that Mary Shelley was in love with Aubrey Beauclerk after his wife's death in 1834, *Keats-Shelley Journal* 29 (1980): 224.

13. Mary Shelley's Journal, Abinger Dep. d. 311/4: ff 43, 3.

14. Mary Shelley's Journal, Abinger, Dep. d. 311/5: ff 105–6.

15. Mary Shelley's Journal, Abinger Dep. d. 311/5: f 27.

16. Mary Shelley's Journal, Abinger Dep. d. 311/4: ff 52, 67–68; 311/5: ff 4, 10, 22, 50–51, 103–4.

17. Mary Shelley, *Lodore*, 3 vols. (London: Richard Bentley, 1835), I:37. All further citations of this novel will appear in the text.

18. Rousseau, *Emile*, trans. Barbara Foxley (New York: Dutton—Everyman's Library, 1911; repr. 1963), p. 333. After quoting this passage in her *A Vindication of the Rights of Woman*, Mary Wollstonecraft responds, "The being who patiently endures injustice, and silently bears insults, will soon become unjust, or unable to discern right from wrong" (ed. Carol H. Poston [New York: W. W. Norton, 1975], p. 83).

19. For a detailed discussion of the concept of the proper lady in Mary Shelley's fiction, see Mary Poovey, *The Proper Lady and the Woman Writer—Ideology as Style in the Works of Mary Wollstonecraft, Mary Shelley and Jane Austen* (Chicago and London: University of Chicago Press, 1984), Chaps. 4–5.

20. *Letters of Mary Shelley*, ed. Betty T. Bennett, II:185, dated January 31, 1833.

21. *Letters of Mary Shelley*, ed. Betty T. Bennett, II:185, dated January 31, 1833.

22. Mary Shelley's insistence that men as well as women must commit themselves to the selfless maintenance of the family welfare has led William Veeder in *Mary Shelley & Frankenstein—The Fate of Androgyny* (Chicago: University of Chicago Press, 1986) to describe her work as endorsing the concept of androgyny.

23. Mary Wollstonecraft Shelley, *Falkner*, 3 vols. (London: Saunders and Otley, 1837), I:125. All further citations of this novel will appear in the text.

24. *Letters of Mary Shelley*, ed. Betty T. Bennett, II:160, dated November 8, 1835.

25. The unpublished manuscript of "Cecil" is in the Abinger Collection of the Bodleian Library, Abinger Dep. e. 229.

26. For particularly insightful analyses of Milton's Eve from a feminist perspective, see Christine Froula, "When Eve Reads Milton: Undoing the Canonical Economy," *Critical Inquiry* 10 (December 1983), 321–47; and Sandra Gilbert and Susan Gubar, *The Madwoman in the Attic* (New Haven: Yale University Press, 1979), Chap. 1.

27. Mary Shelley finished copying *Mathilda* on September 12, 1819; made a few final revisions and dated the manuscript at Florence on November 9, 1819; and sent her fair copy to her father, William Godwin, by her friend Maria Gisborne, who sailed to London on May 2, 1820. Godwin told Maria Gisborne that he thought highly of parts of the story, although he found the subject "disgusting and detestable" (*Maria Gisborne and Edward E. Williams, Shelley's Friends: Their Journals and Letters*, ed. Frederick L. Jones [Norman, Oklahoma: University of Oklahoma Press, 1951], p. 44). Godwin was asked repeatedly by both Mary and Maria Gisborne either to revise and publish the manuscript or to return it to Mary Shelley; he did neither. Probably he perceived, beneath the surface story of incest, his daughter's portrait of his own equally horrendous failure as a loving, supportive parent, as Bonnie Rayford Neumann has suggested in *The Lonely Muse—A Critical Biography of Mary Wollstonecraft Shelley* (Salzburg, Austria: Salzburg Studies in English Literature, Vol. 85, 1979), pp. 112–13. The manuscript was hidden among Godwin's papers and finally deposited by Shelley's heirs in the Bodleian Library. The first and only publication of *Mathilda*, now out of print, is that edited by Elizabeth Nitchie. This edition includes Mary Shelley's first draft of the opening chapter, tentatively entitled "The Fields of Fancy," an allusion both to Plato's cave in *The Republic* and to Mary Wollstonecraft's *The Cave of Fancy*, an unfinished tale in which a soul confined to the center of the earth to purify herself from the dross of earthly experience tells the story of her ill-fated love for a man she hopes to rejoin after her purgation is completed.

28. Mathilda here quotes Dante's *Purgatorio*, Canto 28, lines 31–33: "—bruna, bruna, / Sotto l'ombra perpetua, che mai / Raggiar non lascia sole ivi, nè Luna" (*Mathilda*, ed. Elizabeth Nitchie [Chapel Hill: University of North Carolina Press, 1959], p. 74). I have cited the translation by Percy Shelley which, according to Thomas Medwin, had been completed by the summer of 1819: see Medwin's *The Life of Percy Bysshe Shelley*, ed. H. Buxton Forman (London: Oxford University Press, 1913), pp. 248–49. This translation is also published in *The Complete Poetical Works of Percy Bysshe Shelley*, ed. Thomas Hutchinson, with Notes by Mary Shelley (London: Oxford University Press, 1905, repr. 1960), pp. 727–29.

29. Elizabeth Nitchie has drawn attention to the biographical elements of *Mathilda*, in "Mary Shelley's *Mathilda*: An Unpublished Story and Its Biographical Significance", *Studies in Philology* XL (July 1943): 447–62; and in her Introduction to *Mathilda*, ed. Nitchie, pp. vii–xv. See also William Walling, *Mary Shelley* (New York: Twayne, 1972), pp. 110–12.

30. Godwin's letter to Hull Godwin was published in C. Kegan Paul, *William Godwin, His Friends and Contemporaries* (London: Henry S. King & Co., repr. New York: AMS Press, 1970), II:246.

31. Don Locke, *A Fantasy of Reason—The Life and Thought of William Godwin* (London: Routledge & Kegan Paul, 1980), p. 276.

32. For Godwin's repeated financial demands on Shelley and Shelley's generous response, see Richard Holmes, *Shelley—The Pursuit* (New York: E. P. Dutton, 1975), pp. 223–38, 311–15, 603–4, and *passim*.

33. *The Letters of Percy Bysshe Shelley*, ed. Frederick L. Jones (Oxford: The Clarendon Press, 1964), II:109.

34. *Shelley and Mary*, ed. Lady Jane Shelley (London: privately published, 1882), I:410A.

35. *Letters of Mary Shelley*, ed. Betty T. Bennett, I:57.

36. U. C. Knoepflmacher also discusses the passive/aggressive authorial impulses in *Mathilda* in "Thoughts on the Aggression of Daughters," *The Endurance of Frankenstein*, ed. George Levine and U. C. Knoepflmacher (Berkeley and Los Angeles, and London: University of California Press, 1979), pp. 113–16.

37. *Mary Shelley's Journal*, ed. Frederick L. Jones, (Norman, Oklahoma: University of Oklahoma Press, 1947), pp. 116, 123. Jean de Palacio has emphasized the impact of Dante's *Divine Comedy* on *Mathilda*, *Valperga*, and *The Last Man*, although he overstates his case when he concludes that "Toutes les figures féminines de Mary Shelley, on l'a vu, tendent plus ou moins à s'identifier à la Béatrice du *Paradis*" (*Mary Shelley dans son oeuvre*, pp. 36–66; p. 63).

38. Dante, *Purgatorio*, Canto 28, lines 64–75.

39. *Mary Shelley's Journal*, ed. Frederick L. Jones, p. 16.

40. *Mary Shelley's Journal*, ed. Frederick L. Jones, pp. 57–58.

41. Horace Walpole, *The Castle of Otranto*, in *Three Eighteenth Century Romances*, ed. Harrison Steeves (New York: Charles Scribner's Sons, 1931), p. 47.

42. Mary Shelley commented on her "excessive & romantic attachment" to her father during her childhood in a letter to Maria Gisborne on October 30, 1834 (*Letters of Mary Shelley*, ed. Betty T. Bennett, II:215).

43. Mary Shelley, in her Note on *The Cenci* in her edition of Percy Bysshe Shelley's *Poetical Works* (ed. Thomas Hutchinson, p. 335) comments that she encouraged Percy to write this verse tragedy and discussed its composition with him. We can only speculate as to how much impact this drama of a raped daughter's murder of her father had on Mary Shelley's own imagination.

44. On Tuesday, September 22, 1818, Shelley from Padua wrote to Mary at Este: "do you be prepared to bring at least *some* of Mirra translated" (*Letters of Percy Shelley*, ed. Frederick L. Jones, II:39). Frederick L. Jones consistently misidentifies the author of *Mirra* as Ariosto (pp. 39 n4, 468) rather than Alfieri; this error has also been noted by Donald H. Reiman, ed. (with Kenneth Neill Cameron), *Shelley and His Circle 1773–1822* (Cambridge: Harvard University Press, 1961–73), VI:691 n3.

Alfieri's *Mirra* is clearly the source for the confrontation scene between Mathilda and her father. In terms very like those used by Mathilda, Ciniro unwittingly forces his daughter Mirra to confess her secret, incestuous love for him. The germ of the passage on page 30 of *Mathilda* is based on Act V, scene 2, lines 160–86 (*Opere di Vittorio Alfieri* (Asti: Casa D'Alfieri, 1974), XVIII: *Mirra*, pp. 95–97).

Thomas Medwin was under the impression that *Mathilda* was suggested by and even in part a prose version of Alfieri's *Mirra*; see Thomas Medwin, *The Life of Percy Bysshe Shelley*, p. 252.

45. Peter Thorslev, "Incest as Romantic Symbol," *Comparative Literature Studies*, II (1965): 47. On the role of incest and the Gothic tradition in *Mathilda*, see also Jean de Palacio, *Mary Shelley dans son oeuvre*, pp. 125–37.

46. Cynthia Griffin Wolff, "The Radcliffean Gothic Model: A Form for Feminine Sexuality," *Modern Language Studies* 9 (Fall 1979): 101.

47. Horace Walpole, *The Castle of Otranto*, p. 16.

48. Mary Wollstonecraft, *A Vindication of the Rights of Woman*, ed. Carol H. Poston, p. 9.

49. The prevalence of father-daughter incest in America has only recently been acknowledged. David Finkelhor concludes that somewhere in the neighborhood of one million American woman have been involved in incestuous relations with their fathers and that some 16,000 new cases occur each year (*Sexually Victimized Children* [New York: Free Press, 1979], pp. 68–71). Judith Herman notes that these are conservative estimates, and the real incidence of father-daughter incest may well be considerably higher (*Father-Daughter Incest* [Cambridge and London: Harvard University Press, 1981], p. 14; cf. Chap. 1).

On the portrayal of incest in literature and popular culture, see James B. Twitchell, *Forbidden Partners—The Incest Taboo in Modern Culture* (New York: Columbia University Press, 1987). On the role of incest in culture, see W. Arens, *The Original Sin—Incest and Its Meaning* (New York: Oxford University Press, 1986); and Robin Fox, *The Red Lamp of Incest* (New York: Dutton, 1980).

50. Karin C. Meiselman, *Incest: A Psychological Study of Causes and Effects with Treatment Recommendations*, (San Francisco, Washington, London: Jossey-Bass, 1978), documents that the female victims of father-daughter incest are often unable to achieve satisfying sexual relationships in their adult lives (Chap. 6).

51. On the role of the mother in father-daughter incest cases, see Judith Herman, *Father-Daughter Incest*, Chap. 3; and Karin C. Meiselman, *Incest*, Chap. 3.

52. See Karen Horney, "The Problem of Feminine Masochism" (1935) in *Feminine Psychology*, ed. Harold Kelman (London: Routledge & Kegan Paul, 1967).

53. Mary Poovey has also drawn attention to *Falkner*'s concern with punishing the father, *The Proper Lady and the Woman Writer*, pp. 159–70.

54. Mary Shelley's Journal, Abinger Dep. d. 311/4.

55. Maud Brooke Rolleston, *Talks with Lady Shelley* (London: George G. Harrap & Co., 1925), p. 112.

56. Jean de Palacio has analyzed the influence of Machiavelli's *The Prince* upon the behavior of Castruccio (*Mary Shelley dans son oeuvre*, pp. 203–5). See also Betty T. Bennett, "The Political Philosophy of Mary Shelley's Historical Novels: *Valperga* and *Perkin Warbeck*," in *The Evidence of the Imagination*, ed. Donald H. Reiman, Michael C. Jaye, and Betty T. Bennett, pp. 354–71.

57. *Mary Shelley's Journal*, ed. Frederick L. Jones, p. 204.

58. This conversation was first reported by Matthew Arnold in his essay on Shelley published in January, 1888, in *Nineteenth Century*; repr. in *The Works of Matthew Arnold* (London: Macmillan, 1903), IV:151.

CHAPTER ELEVEN   Idealizing the Bourgeois Family

1. Lawrence Stone, *The Family, Sex and Marriage in England 1500–1800* (London: Weidenfeld and Nicolson, 1977), pp. 7–8, passim; Randolph Trumbach, *The Rise of the Egalitarian Family—Aristocratic Kinship and Domestic Relations in Eighteenth-Century England* (New York, San Francisco, London: Academic Press, 1978).

2. Alan MacFarlane, *Love and Marriage in England, Modes of Reproduction 1300–1840* (Oxford: Basil Blackwell, 1986); Linda A. Pollock, *Forgotten Children—Parent-Child Relations from 1500–1900* (Cambridge: Cambridge University Press, 1983).

3. On the cult of domesticity in eighteenth-century English painting, see the forthcoming book of David Solkin. A chapter of this work, "Portraiture in Motion: Edward Penny's *Marquis of Granby* and the Creation of a Public for English Art," appeared in *The Huntington Library Quarterly* 49 (1986): 1–23.

4. On the nontransferability of employer-employee relations to the husband-wife relationship, see Randolph Trumbach, *Rise of the Egalitarian Family*, p. 150. On the patriarchal structure of the English husband-wife relationship, see among others Lee Holcombe, *Wives and Property—Reform of the Married Woman's Property Law in Nineteenth-Century England* (Toronto: University of Toronto Press, 1983), Chap. 2, passim; Steven Mintz, *A Prison of Expectations—The Family in Victorian Culture* (New York and London: New York University Press, 1983), pp. 14, 38–39, passim; John R. Gillis, "Peasant, Plebeian, and Proletarian Marriage in Britain, 1600–1900," in David Levine, ed., *Proletarianization and Family History* (New York and London: Academic Press, 1984), pp. 155–57; and Linda A. Pollock's forthcoming study of family relations in England, 1500–1800.

5. On the more egalitarian gender relationships within the proto-industrial family in England in the eighteenth century, see David Levine, "Production, Reproduction, and the Proletarian Family in England, 1500–1851," and John R. Gillis, "Peasant, Plebeian, and Proletarian Marriage in Britain, 1600–1900," both in *Proletarianization and Family History*, ed. David Levine, pp. 98, 138–45.

6. Mary Shelley's Journal, Abinger Dep. d. 311/4: f 92.

7. French feminist theory (I use the terms "French" and "Anglo-American" here as Toril Moi does in *Sexual/Textual Politics—Feminist Literary Theory* [London and New York: Methuen, 1985] to denote not national demarcations but intellectual traditions) has tended to work from a Freudian and Lacanian assumption that the family romance is originary and necessarily reconstituted in the linguistic Nom de Pere. For examples of work within this paradigm, see Julia Kristeva, *Desire in Language*, ed. Leon S. Roudiez (New York: Columbia University Press, 1980); Juliet Mitchell, *Psychoanalysis and Feminism* (London: Allan Lane, 1974); Jane Gallop, *The Daughter's Seduction: Feminism and Psychoanalysis* (Ithaca: Cornell University Press, 1982); Juliet Mitchell and Jacqueline Rose, ed., *Feminine Sexuality—Jacques Lacan & The Ecole ̇Freudienne* (London: Macmillan, 1982); and the essays in *In Dora's Case: Freud-Hysteria-Feminism*, ed. Charles Bernheimer and Claire Kahane (New York: Columbia University Press, 1985). The contrasting Anglo-American feminist tradition has tended to argue that the family romance is a product of Western bourgeois capitalist society and that changes in social practice will produce changes in the family dynamic. For work which supports this paradigm, see Nancy Chodorow, *The Reproduction of Mothering—Psychoanalysis and the Sociology of Gender* (Berkeley: University of California Press, 1978); Nancy C. M. Hartsock, *Money, Sex, and Power—Toward a Feminist Historical Materialism* (Boston: Northeastern University Press, 1985); and the essays in *Rethinking the Family*, ed. Barrie Thorne with Marilyn Yalom (New York: Longman, 1982).

WORKS BY MARY WOLLSTONECRAFT SHELLEY

"Cecil," Abinger Shelley Collection, Bodleian Library (Dep. e. 229).

The Choice—A Poem on Shelley's Death, ed. H. Buxton Forman (London: Privately printed, 1876).

Collected Tales and Stories, ed. Charles E. Robinson (Baltimore and London: Johns Hopkins University Press, 1976).

"The English in Italy," *Westminster Review*, October 1826; printed as Appendix A in *The Journal of Claire Clairmont 1814–1827*, ed. Marion Kingston Stocking.

Falkner (London: Saunders and Otley, 1837), 3 Vols.

The Fortunes of Perkin Warbeck (London, 1830; repr. London: Routledge, 1857).

Frankenstein, or the Modern Prometheus (London: Lackington, Hughes, Harding, Mavor and Jones, 1818); repr. *Frankenstein, or The Modern Prometheus* (The 1818 Text), ed. James Rieger (New York: Bobbs-Merrill, 1974; Chicago: University of Chicago Press, 1982).

Frankenstein, or the Modern Prometheus (London: Colburn and Bentley; Standard Novels Edition, 1831); repr. *Frankenstein, or The Modern Prometheus*, ed. M. K. Joseph (Oxford and New York: Oxford University Press, 1969, repr. 1984).

History of A Six Weeks Tour through a part of France, Switzerland, Germany, and Holland, with Letters descriptive of a Sail round the Lake of Geneva, and of the Glaciers of Chamouni (London: T. Hookham, Jr., and C. and J. Ollier, 1817).

Journal, Abinger Shelley Collection, Bodleian Library (Dep. d. 311/1–5).

Mary Shelley's Journal, ed. Frederick L. Jones (Norman, Oklahoma: University of Oklahoma Press, 1947).

The Journals of Mary Shelley 1814–1844, ed. Paula R. Feldman and Diana Scott-Kilvert (Oxford: The Clarendon Press, 1987), 2 Vols.

The Last Man, ed. Hugh J. Luke, Jr. (Lincoln: University of Nebraska Press, 1965).

The Letters of Mary Wollstonecraft Shelley, ed. Betty T. Bennett (Baltimore: Johns Hopkins University Press, 1980, 1983), Vol. I–II.

The Letters of Mary W. Shelley, ed. Frederick L. Jones (Norman, Oklahoma: University of Oklahoma Press, 1944).

"Life of William Godwin." Abinger Shelley Collection, Bodleian Library (Dep. c. 606/1).

Lives of the most Eminent Literary and Scientific Men of France, for The Cabinet Cyclopedia, conducted by Rev. Dionysius Lardner (London: Longman et. al., 1838–39), Vol. II.

Lodore (London: Richard Bentley, 1835), 3 Vols.

Mathilda, ed. Elizabeth Nitchie (Chapel Hill: University of North Carolina Press, 1959).

"Notes" to the *First Collected Edition of the Poems of Percy Bysshe Shelley* (London, 1839); reprinted in *The Complete Poetical Works of Percy Bysshe Shelley*, ed. Thomas Hutchinson (London: Oxford University Press, 1905; repr. 1960).

Rambles in Germany and Italy in 1840, 1842, and 1843 (London: Edward Moxon, 1844).

Valperga: or, The Life and Adventures of Castruccio, Prince of Lucca (London: Whittaker, 1823).

OTHER WORKS CITED

Abbey, Lloyd, *Destroyer and Preserver—Shelley's Poetic Skepticism* (Lincoln, Nebraska and London: University of Nebraska Press, 1979).

Abrams, M. H. *Natural Supernaturalism—Tradition and Revolution in Romantic Literature* (New York: W. W. Norton & Co., 1971).

Aldini, John. *An Account of the Late Improvements in Galvanism, with a series of Curious and Interesting Experiments performed before the Commissioners of the French National Institute and repeated lately in the Anatomical Theatres of London; to which is added, An Appendix, containing the author's Experiments on the Body of a Malefactor executed at New Gate* (London: Cuthell and Martin, and J. Murray, 1803).

Aldiss, Brian W. *Billion Year Spree—The History of Science Fiction* (London: Weidenfeld and Nicolson, 1973).

Alfieri, Vittorio. *Mirra*, in *Opere di Vittorio Alfieri* (Asti: Casa D'Alfieri, 1974), Vol. XVIII.

Arens, W. *The Original Sin—Incest and Its Meaning* (New York: Oxford University Press, 1986).

Arnold, Matthew. "On Shelley," in *Nineteenth Century*; repr. in *The Works of Matthew Arnold* (London: Macmillan, 1903), Vol. IV.

Bacon, Francis. " 'Temporis Partus Masculus': An Untranslated Writing of Francis Bacon," trans. Benjamin Farrington, *Centaurus* I (1951): 193–205.

———. *The Works of Francis Bacon*, ed. J. Spedding, R. L. Ellis, and D. N. Heath (new edn., 1879–90; Facsimile, Stuttgart—Bad Cannstatt: F. Frommann Verl., G. Holzboog, 1962, 7 Vols.

Barrow, Isaac. *The Usefulness of Mathematical Learning Explained and Demonstrated* (London, 1734; repr. Frank Cass, 1970).

Barruel, L'Abbé Augustin. *Memoirs, Illustrating the History of Jacobinism*, trans. Robert Clifford (London, 1797–98).

Bebbington, W. G. *"The Last Man"* in *Notes and Queries* 216 (May 1971): 163–65.

Bernheimer, Charles, and Claire Kahane, ed. *In Dora's Case: Freud-Hysteria-Feminism* (New York: Columbia University Press, 1985).

Bloom, Harold. "Afterword" to a reprint of the 1831 *Frankenstein, or The Modern Prometheus* (New York: New American Library, 1965), pp. 212–23.

Bowerbank, Sylvia. "The Social Order vs. The Wretch: Mary Shelley's Contradictory-Mindedness in *Frankenstein*," *ELH* 46 (1979): 418–31.

Boyle, Robert. *The Works of Robert Boyle*, ed. Thomas Birch (London, 1772).

Burke, Edmund. *A Philosophical Inquiry into the Origin of Our Ideas of the Sublime and the Beautiful* (London, 1757; repr. Philadelphia, 1806).

———. *Letters on the Proposals for Peace with the Regicide Directory of France, Letter I (1796)*, in *The Works and Correspondence of the Right Honourable Edmund Burke* (London, 1852), Vol. V.

———. *Reflections on the Revolution in France*, ed. William B. Todd (New York: Holt, Rinehart and Winston, 1959).

Burr, Aaron. *The Private Journal of Aaran Burr: During his Residence of Four Years in Europe, with Selections from his Correspondence*, ed. Matthew L. Davis (New York: Harper & Brothers, 1858), Vol. II.

Byron, George Gordon, Lord. *The Works of Lord Byron*, ed. Rowland Prothero (London: John Murray, 1904), 11 Vols.

Cameron, Kenneth Neill. *Shelley—The Golden Years* (Cambridge: Harvard University Press, 1974).

———. *The Young Shelley—Genesis of a Radical* (London: Victor Gollancz, 1951).

Cantor, Paul A. *Creature and Creator: Myth-making and English Romanticism* (New York: Cambridge University Press, 1984).

Carpenter, Edward and George Barnefield. *The Psychology of the Poet Shelley* (London: Allen and Unwin, 1925).

Chernaik, Judith. *The Lyrics of Shelley* (Cleveland: Case Western Reserve University Press, 1972).

Chesser, Eustace. *Shelley and Zastrozzi—Self-Revelation of a Neurotic* (London: Gregg/ Archive, 1965).

Chodorow, Nancy. *The Reproduction of Mothering—Psychoanalysis and the Sociology of Gender* (Berkeley: University of California Press, 1978).

Clairmont, Claire. Correspondence with Byron, in *The Works of Lord Byron*, ed. Rowland Prothero (London: John Murray, 1904), Vol. X, Appendix 7.

———. *The Journals of Claire Clairmont 1814–1827*, ed. Marion Kingston Stocking (Cambridge: Harvard University Press, 1968).

———. Letter to Lord Byron, May 6, 1816, the Abinger Shelley Collection, Bodleian Library (MS. Shelley Adds. c. 8).

———. Letter to Fanny Godwin, 28 May 1815, the Abinger Shelley Collection, Bodleian Library (Dep. c. 478).

———. "Reminiscences, Anecdotes, Etc." Ashley Manuscript Collection, British Museum (Ashley 2820).

Clifford, Gay. "*Caleb Williams* and *Frankenstein*: First-Person Narration and Things as They Are," *Genre* 10 (1977): 601–17.

Coleridge, Samuel Taylor. *The Friend* (London: J. Brown, 1809–1810, repr. New York: Free Press, 1971).

Connell, Brian, ed. *Portrait of a Whig Peer, compiled from the papers of the Second Viscount Palmerston, 1739–1802* (London: André Deutsch, 1957).

Creve, Johann Caspar. *Beiträge zu Galvanis versuchen* (Frankfurt and Leipzig, 1793).

Crouch, Laura. "Davy's *A Discourse, Introductory to a Course of Lectures on Chemistry*: A Possible Scientific Source of *Frankenstein*." *Keats-Shelley Journal* 27 (1978): 35–44.

Darwin, Erasmus. *The Botanic Garden* (London: John Johnson, Part I: "The Economy of Vegetation," 1791; Part II: "The Loves of the Plants," 1789).

———. *Phytologia: or the Philosophy of Agriculture and Gardening.* (London: John Johnson, 1800).

———. *The Temple of Nature* (London: John Johnson, 1803).

———. *Zoonomia: or The Laws of Organic Life* (London: John Johnson, 1794; third "Corrected" edition, 1801).

Daly, Mary. *Beyond God the Father: Toward a Philosophy of Women's Liberation* (Boston: Beacon Press, 1973).

Davy, Sir Humphry. *A Discourse, Introductory to A Course of Lectures on Chemistry* (London: John Johnson, 1802).

———. *Elements of Chemical Philosophy* (London, 1812).

Dibdin, Charles. *The Songs of Charles Dibdin* (London: 1848).

Dicks, R. Stanley. "Mary Shelley: An Unprinted Elegy on Her Husband?" *Keats-Shelley Memorial Bulletin* 28 (1977): 36–41.

Dinnerstein, Dorothy. *The Mermaid and the Minotaur—Sexual Arrangements and Human Malaise* (New York: Harper & Row, 1976).

Dryden, John. *The Works of John Dryden*, ed. A. B. Chambers and W. Frost (Berkeley: University of California Press, 1974), Vol. IV.

Dunn, Jane. *Moon in Eclipse—A Life of Mary Shelley* (London: Weidenfeld and Nicolson, 1978).

Dunn, Richard J. "Narrative Distance in *Frankenstein*," *Studies in the Novel* 6 (1974): 408–17.

Easlea, Brian. *Science and Sexual Oppression—Patriarchy's Confrontation with Woman and Nature* (London: Weidenfeld and Nicolson, 1981).

Eiseley, Loren. *Darwin's Century: Evolution and the Men Who Discovered It* (Garden City, New Jersey: Doubleday, 1958).

Elshtain, Jean. *Public Man, Private Woman: Women in Social and Political Thought* (Oxford: Robertson, 1981).

Ferguson, Frances. "Legislating the Sublime," in *Studies in Eighteenth-Century British Art and Aesthetics*, ed. Ralph Cohen (Berkeley: University of California Press, 1985), pp. 128–47.

Finkelhor, David. *Sexually Victimized Children* (New York: Free Press, 1979).

Fleck, P. D. "Mary Shelley's Notes to Shelley's Poems and *Frankenstein*," *Studies in Romanticism* 6 (1966–67): 226–54.

Fleenor, Juliann E., ed. *The Female Gothic* (Montreal and London: Eden Press, 1983).

Flexner, Eleanor. *Mary Wollstonecraft* (New York: Coward, McCann & Geoghegan, 1972).

Foucault, Michel. *Madness and Civilization*, trans. Richard Howard (New York: Vintage Books, 1961).

———. *Discipline and Punish—The Birth of the Prison*, trans. Alan Sheridan (New York: Vintage Books, 1977, 1979).

Fouché, Joseph. "Declaration aux Citoyens de la Departmente de l'Aube," 29 June 1793, *Archives Parlementaires* (Troyes) 68:73; trans. Lynn Hunt.

Fox, Robin. *The Red Lamp of Incest* (New York: Dutton, 1980).

Frank, Frederick S. "Mary Shelley's *Frankenstein*: A Register of Research," *Bulletin of Bibliography* 40 (1983): 163–88.

Freud, Sigmund. *The Complete Psychological Works of Sigmund Freud: The Standard Edition*, trans. James Strachey, in collaboration with Anna Freud, assisted by Alix Strachey and Alan Tyson (London: Hogarth Press and the Institute of Psychoanalysis, 1957), Vol. 14.

Friday, Nancy. *My Mother/My Self—the Daughter's Search for Identity* (New York: Dell, 1977).

Froula, Christine. "When Eve Reads Milton: Undoing the Canonical Economy," *Critical Inquiry* 10 (December 1983): 321–47.

Galvani, Luigi. *De Viribus Electricitatus in Motui Musculari. Commentarius* (Bologna, 1791); *Commentary on the Effects of Electricity on Muscular Motion*, trans. M. G. Foley, with notes and Introduction by I. Bernard Cohen (Norwalk, Conn.: Burndy Library, 1953).

Gallop, Jane. *The Daughter's Seduction: Feminism and Psychoanalysis* (Ithaca: Cornell University Press, 1982).

Gardner, Joseph H. "Mary Shelley's Divine Tragedy," *Essays in Literature* 4 (1977): 182–97.

Gilbert, Sandra and Susan Gubar. *The Madwoman in the Attic* (New Haven: Yale University Press, 1979).

Gilligan, Carol. *In A Different Voice—Psychological Theory and Women's Development* (Cambridge and London: Harvard University Press, 1982).

Gisborne, Maria. *Maria Gisborne and Edward E. Williams, Shelley's Friends: Their Journals and Letters*, ed. Frederick L. Jones (Norman, Oklahoma: University of Oklahoma Press, 1951).

Godwin, William. *An Enquiry Concerning Political Justice* (London: G. G. J. and J. Robinson, 1793).

————. Correspondence with Mary Jane Clairmoint Godwin, Abinger Shelley Collection, Bodleian Library (Dep. c. 523).

————. Diary, Abinger Shelley Collection, Bodleian Library (Dep. e. 196–227, Dep. e. 273, Dep. f. 66).

————. *The Elopement of Percy Bysshe Shelley and Mary Wollstonecraft Godwin, as narrated by William Godwin*, with Commentary by H. Buxton Forman (London: The Bibliophile Society, 1911).

————. *Fleetwood or, The New Man of Feeling* (London, 1805; repr. New York and London: Garland, 1979), 3 Vols.

————. *Memoirs of the Author of A Vindication of the Rights of Woman* (London, 1798), Second Edition corrected.

————. *Memoir of William Godwin, Jr.* Printed as Preface to William Godwin, Jr., *Transfusion* (London: John Macrone, 1835).

————. *St. Leon: A Tale of the Sixteenth Century* (London: G. G. & J. Robinson, 1799).

————. *Thoughts Occasioned by a Perusal of Dr. Parr's Spital Sermon* (London, 1801).

Godwin, William, Jr. *Transfusion* (London: John Macrone, 1835).

Goldstein, Laurence. *Ruins and Empire: The Evolution of a Theme in Augustan and Romantic Literature* (Pittsburgh: University of Pittsburgh Press, 1977).

Grabo, Carl. *A Newton among Poets—Shelley's Use of Science in "Prometheus Unbound"* (Chapel Hill: University of North Carolina Press, 1930).

Grapengieser, C. J. C. *Versuche den Galvanismus* (Berlin, 1801, 1802).

Grylls, R. Glynn. *Claire Clairmont—Mother of Byron's Allegra* (London: John Murray, 1939).

———. *Mary Shelley* (London: Oxford University Press, 1938).

Guillaume, M. J., ed. *Procès-verbaux du Comité d'Instruction publique de la Convention Nationale* 2 (17 brumaire an II) (Paris, 1894).

Hammermayer, Ludwig. "Die letzte Epoche der Universität Ingolstadt: Reformer, Jesuiten, Illuminaten (1746–1800)," in *Ingolstadt: Die Herzogsstadt—Die Universitätsstadt—Die Festung*, ed. Theodore Müller and Wilhelm Reissmüller (Ingolstadt: Verlag Donau Courier, 1974, pp. 299–357).

Harding, D. W. Introduction to *From Blake to Byron*, ed. Boris Ford (London: Pelican Books, 1957).

Hartmann, Heidi. "Capitalism, Patriarchy, and Job Segregation by Sex," in *Capitalist Patriarchy and the Case for Socialist Feminism*, ed. Zillah Eisenstein (New York and London: Monthly Review Press, 1979), 206–47.

Hartley, Sir Harold. *Humphry Davy* (London: Nelson, 1966).

Hartsock, Nancy C. M. *Money, Sex, and Power—Toward a Feminist Historical Materialism* (Boston: Northeastern University Press, 1985).

Harvey, A. D. "*Frankenstein* and *Caleb Williams*," *Keats-Shelley Journal* 29 (1980): 21–27.

Hatlin, Burton. "Milton, Mary Shelley and Patriarchy," in *Rhetoric, Literature, and Interpretation*, ed. Harry R. Garvin (Lewisburg, Pa.: Bucknell University Press, 1983), pp. 19–47.

Hays, Mary. *The Love Letters of Mary Hays (1779–1780)*, ed. A. F. Wedd (London: Methuen, 1925).

Hellerstein, E., L. Hume, and K. Offen, eds. *Victorian Women—A Documentary Account of Women's Lives in Nineteenth-Century England, France, and the United States* (Stanford: Stanford University Press, 1981).

Herman, Judith. *Father-Daughter Incest* (Cambridge and London: Harvard University Press, 1981).

Hill, J. M. "*Frankenstein* and the Physiognomy of Desire," *American Imago* 32 (1975): 335–58.

Hodges, Devon. "*Frankenstein* and the Feminine Subversion of the Novel," *Tulsa Studies in Women's Literature* 2 (Autumn 1983): 155–64.

Hogg, Thomas Jefferson. Letter to Jane Williams. Abinger Shelley Collection, Bodleian Library (Ms. Dep. c. 535).

———. *The Life of Percy Bysshe Shelley* (London: Edward Moxon, 1858).

Hogle, Jerrold E. "Otherness in *Frankenstein*: The Confinement/Autonomy of Fabrication," *Structuralist Review* 2 (1980): 20–48.

Holcombe, Lee. *Wives and Property—Reform of the Married Woman's Property Law in Nineteenth-Century England* (Toronto: University of Toronto Press, 1983).

Holmes, Richard. *Shelley—The Pursuit* (New York: E. P. Dutton, 1975).

Homans, Margaret. *Bearing the Word—Language and Female Experience in Nineteenth-Century Women's Writing* (Chicago: University of Chicago Press, 1986).

Horney, Karen. *Feminine Psychology*, ed. Harold Kelman (London: Routledge & Kegan Paul, 1967).

Hughes, A. M. D. *The Nascent Mind of Shelley* (Oxford: The Clarendon Press, 1947).

Humboldt, F. H. A. *Sur Galvanisme*, trans. J. F. N. Jadelot (Paris, 1799).

Hunt, Lynn. *Politics, Culture, and Class in the French Revolution* (Berkeley: University of California Press, 1984).

Ingpen, Roger. *Shelley in England* (London: Kegan Paul, 1917).

Jacobus, Mary. "Is There a Woman in This Text?" *New Literary History* 14 (1982): 117–41; repr. in *Reading Woman* (New York: Columbia University Press, 1986).

Janson, H. W. "Fuseli's *Nightmare*," *Arts and Sciences* 2 (1963): 23–28.

Johnson, Barbara. "My Monster/My Self," *Diacritics* 12 (1982): 2–10.

Jones, Louisa. Letters to Godwin, Abinger Shelley Collection, Bodleian Library (Dep. c. 508).

Joseph, Gerhard. "Frankenstein's Dream: The Child is Father of the Monster," *Hartford Studies in Literature* 7 (1975): 97–115.

Joseph, M. K. Introduction to the 1831 *Frankenstein, or The Modern Prometheus* (Oxford and New York: Oxford University Press, 1969, repr. 1984).

Kaplan, Temma. "Female Consciousness and Collective Action: The Case of Barcelona, 1910–1918," *Signs* VII (1982): 545–66.

Keller, Evelyn Fox. "Gender and Science," *Psychoanalysis and Contemporary Thought* II (1978): 409–33.

———. *Reflections on Gender and Science* (New Haven and London: Yale University Press, 1985).

Ketterer, David. *Frankenstein's Creation: The Book, the Monster, and the Human Reality* (Victoria, British Columbia: Victoria University Press—English Literature Studies Number 16, 1979).

Kiely, Robert. *The Romantic Novel in England* (Cambridge: Harvard University Press, 1972).

King-Hele, Desmond. *Erasmus Darwin* (London: Macmillan, 1963).

———. *Shelley—His Thought and Work* (London: Macmillan, 1960).

Klein, Melanie. "On the Sense of Loneliness" (1963) in *Envy and Gratitude and Other Works*, ed. Masud R. Khan (London: Hogarth Press, 1980), pp. 300–13.

Koszul, André. "Notes and Corrections to Shelley's 'History of a Six Weeks' Tour' (1817)," *MLR* 2 (October 1906): 61–62.

Kramnick, Isaac. *The Rage of Edmund Burke—Portrait of an Ambivalent Conservative* (New York: Basic Books, 1977).

Kristeva, Julia. *Desire in Language*, ed. Leon S. Roudiez (New York: Columbia University Press, 1980).

Lamb, Charles. *The Letters of Charles Lamb to which are added those of his sister Mary Lamb*, ed. E. V. Lucas (London: J. M. Dent & Sons, 1935).

Lavater, Johann Caspar. *Essays on Physiognomy, Designed to Promote the Knowledge and Love of Mankind*, 4 Vols., trans. Henry Hunter (London, 1789–98).

Levine, David, ed. *Proletarianization and Family History* (New York and London: Academic Press, 1984).

Levine, George, and U. C. Knoepflmacher, eds. *The Endurance of Frankenstein* (Berkeley and Los Angeles, and London: University of California Press, 1979).

Locke, Don. *A Fantasy of Reason—The Life and Thought of William Godwin* (London: Routledge & Kegan Paul, 1980).

Locke, John. *Some Thoughts Concerning Education*, ed. Peter Gay (New York: Bureau of

Publications, Teachers College, Columbia University, 1964).

Lovell, Ernest J., Jr. "Byron and the Byronic Hero in the Novels of Mary Shelley," *Studies in English* 30 (1951): 158–83.

———. "Byron and Mary Shelley," *Keats-Shelley Journal* 2 (1953): 35–49.

Lyles, W. H. *Mary Shelley: An Annotated Bibliography* (New York: Garland, 1975).

MacFarlane, Alan. *Love and Marriage in England, Modes of Reproduction 1300–1840* (Oxford: Basil Blackwell, 1986).

McGann, Jerome J. *The Romantic Ideology—A Critical Investigation* (Chicago: University of Chicago Press, 1983).

McInerney, Peter. "*Frankenstein* and the Godlike Science of Letters," *Genre* 13 (1980): 455–76.

McNiece, Gerald. *Shelley and the Revolutionary Idea* (Cambridge: Harvard University Press, 1969).

Majewski, Henry R. "Grainville's 'Le Dernier Homme'," *Symposium* 17 (1963): 114–22.

Maniquis, Robert M. "The Puzzling *Mimosa*: Sensitivity and Plant Symbols in Romanticism," *Studies in Romanticism* VIII (1969): 129–55.

Marchand, Leslie. *Byron—A Biography* (London: John Murray, 1957).

Marshall, Florence A. *The Life and Letters of Mary Wollstonecraft Shelley* (London: Bentley, 1889).

Marshall, Peter. *William Godwin* (New Haven: Yale University Press, 1984).

Massey, Irving. *The Gaping Pig—Literature and Metamorphosis* (Berkeley and Los Angeles, and London: University of California Press, 1976).

Mathias, Thomas. *The Shade of Alexander Pope* (London, 1799).

Mayr, Ernst. *The Growth of Biological Thought: Diversity, Evolution, and Inheritance* (Cambridge: Belknap Press, 1982).

Medwin, Thomas. *The Life of Percy Bysshe Shelley*, ed. H. Buxton Forman (London: Oxford University Press, 1913).

Meiselman, Karin C. *Incest: A Psychological Study of Causes and Effects with Treatment Recommendations* (San Francisco, Washington, London: Jossey-Bass, 1978).

Meller, Horst. "Prometheus im romantischen Heiligen-Kalender," in *Antike Tradition und Neuere Philologien*, ed. Hans-Joachim Simmermann (Heidelberg: Carl Winter-Universitätsverlag, 1984), pp. 163–69.

Mellor, Anne K. *Blake's Human Form Divine* (Berkeley: University of California Press, 1974).

———. "Coleridge's 'This Lime-Tree Bower My Prison' and the Categories of English Landscape," *Studies in Romanticism* 18 (1979): 253–68.

———. *English Romantic Irony.* (Cambridge: Harvard University Press, 1980).
———. "On Feminist Utopias," *Women's Studies* (1982): 241–62.

Merchant, Caroline. *The Death of Nature: Women, Ecology and the Scientific Revolution* (San Francisco: Harper and Row, 1980).

Millhauser, Milton. "The Noble Savage in Mary Shelley's *Frankenstein*," *Notes and Queries* CXC (1946): 248–50.

Mintz, Steven. *A Prison of Expectations—The Family in Victorian Culture* (New York and London: New York University Press, 1983).

Mitchell, Juliet. *Psychoanalysis and Feminism* (London: Allan Lane, 1974).

Mitchell, Juliet, and Jacqueline Rose, eds. *Feminine Sexuality—Jacques Lacan & The Ecole Freudienne* (London: Macmillan, 1982).

Miyoshi, Masao. *The Divided Self* (New York: New York University Press, 1969).

Modleski, Tania. *Loving with a Vengeance: Mass-produced Fantasies for Women* (New York and London: Archon and Methuen, 1982).

Moers, Ellen. *Literary Women* (Garden City, New Jersey: Doubleday, 1976).

Moi, Toril. *Sexual/Textual Politics—Feminist Literary Theory* (London and New York: Methuen, 1985).

The Monthly Review (London: September-December, 1798).

Moretti, Franco. *Signs Taken for Wonders—Essays in the Sociology of Literary Form*, trans. S. Fischer, D. Forgacs, D. Miller (London: Verso, 1983).

Mottelay, Paul Fleury. *Bibliographical History of Electricity and Magnetism* (London: C. Griffin & Co., Ltd., 1922).

Murray, E. B. "Shelley's Contribution to Mary's *Frankenstein*," *Keats-Shelley Memorial Bulletin* 29 (1978): 50–68.

Neumann, Bonnie Rayford. *The Lonely Muse—A Critical Biography of Mary Wollstonecraft Shelley* (Salzburg, Austria: Salzburg Studies in English Literature, Vol. 85, 1979).

Nitchie, Elizabeth. *Mary Shelley—Author of "Frankenstein"* (New Brunswick, New Jersey: Rutgers University Press, 1953).

———. "Mary Shelley's *Mathilda*: An Unpublished Story and Its Biographical Significance", *Studies in Philology* XL (July 1943): 447–62.

Oldenburg, Henry. *The Correspondence of Henry Oldenburg*, ed. A. R. Hall and M. B. Hall (Madison: University of Wisconsin Press, 1965).

Opie, Iona and Peter, ed. *A Nursery Companion* (Oxford: Oxford University Press, 1980).

Orange, Ursula. "Elise, Nursemaid to the Shelleys," *Keats-Shelley Memorial Bulletin* 6 (1955): 24–34.

Ovid. *Ovid's Metamorphoses*, trans. John Dryden, in *The Works of John Dryden*, ed. A. B. Chambers and W. Frost (Berkeley: University of California Press, 1974), Vol. IV.

Ozolins, Aija. "Dreams and Doctrines: Dual Stands in *Frankenstein*," *Science-Fiction Studies* 6 (1975): 103–112.

Palacio, Jean de. "Mary Shelley and the 'Last Man': A Minor Romantic Theme," *Revue de Littérature Comparée* 42 (1968): 37–49.

———. *Mary Shelley dans son oeuvre* (Paris: Klincksieck, 1969).

Paley, Morton D. *The Apocalyptic Sublime* (New Haven and London: Yale University Press, 1986).

Paul, C. Kegan. *William Godwin, His Friends and Contemporaries* (London: Henry S. King & Co., 1876; repr. New York: AMS Press, 1970).

Paulson, Ronald. "Gothic Fiction and the French Revolution," *ELH* 48 (1981): 545–54.

Peck, Walter E. "The Biographical Element in the Novels of Mary Wollstonecraft Shelley," *PMLA* 38 (1923): 196–219.

Polidori, John William. *The Diary of Dr. John William Polidori*, ed. William Michael Rossetti (London: Elkin Mathews, 1911).

Pollock, Linda A. *Forgotten Children—Parent-Child Relations from 1500–1900* (Cambridge: Cambridge University Press, 1983).

Pollin, Burton. "Philosophical and Literary Sources of *Frankenstein*," *Comparative Literature* 17 (1965): 97–108.

Poovey, Mary. *The Proper Lady and the Woman Writer—Ideology as Style in the Works of Mary Wollstonecraft, Mary Shelley and Jane Austen* (Chicago and London: University of Chicago Press, 1984).

Potniceva, T. B. "Svoeobrazie romantičeskogo metoda v romane M. Šelli *Matil'da* (1819)," *Filologičeskie Nauki* 18:5 (1976): 28–35.

Powers, Katherine Richardson. *The Influence of William Godwin on the Novels of Mary Shelley* (New York: Arno Press, 1980).

Praz, Mario. *The Romantic Agony*, trans. Angus Davidson (1933; trans., New York: Meridian Books, 1956).

Randel, Fred V. "*Frankenstein*, Feminism, and the Intertextuality of Mountains," *Studies in Romanticism* 23 (Winter 1984): 515–33.

Reed, John R. "Will and Fate in *Frankenstein*," *Bulletin of Research in the Humanities* 83 (1980): 319–38.

Reiman, Donald H., Michael C. Jaye, and Betty T. Bennett, eds. *The Evidence of the Imgination* (New York: New York University Press, 1978).

Reiman, Donald H. "Shelley's 'The Triumph of Life': The Biographical Problem," *PMLA* 58 (1963): 536–50.

Rhys, Jean. *Jean Rhys Letters 1931–1966*, ed. Francis Wyndham and Diana Melley (London: André Deutsch, 1984).

Rieger, James. "Dr. Polidori and the Genesis of *Frankenstein*," *Studies in English Literature* 3 (1963): 461–72.

Rolleston, Maud Brooke. *Talks with Lady Shelley* (London: George G. Harrap & Co., 1925).

Rousseau, Jean Jacques. *Emile*, trans. Barbara Foxley (New York: Dutton—Everyman's Library, 1911; repr. 1963).

Rubenstein, Marc A. " 'My Accursed Origin': The Search for the Mother in *Frankenstein*," *Studies in Romanticism* 15 (Spring 1976): 165–94.

Sambrook, A. J. "A Romantic Theme: The Last Man," *Forum for Modern Language Studies* 2 (1966): 25–33.

Schiff, Gert. *Johann Heinrich Füssli* (Zurich: Verlag Berichthaus, 1973).

Scholem, Gershom G. *On the Kabbalah and Its Symbolism*, trans. Ralph Manheim (London: Routledge & Kegan Paul, 1965).

———. "The Golem of Prague and the Golem of Rehovot," in *The Messianic Idea in Judaism* (New York: Schocken Books, 1971).

Scholes, Robert and Eric S. Rabkin. *Science Fiction: History, Science, Vision* (New York: Oxford University Press, 1977).

Schopf, Sue Weaver. " 'Of what a strange nature is knowledge!': Hartleian Psychology and the Creature's Arrested Moral Sense in Mary Shelley's *Frankenstein*," *Romanticism Past and Present* 5 (1981): 33–52.

Sedgwick, Eve Kosofsky. *Between Men—English Literature and Male Homosocial Desire* (New York: Columbia University Press, 1985).

Seward, Anna. *Letters of Anna Seward, written between the years 1784 and 1807*, ed. Archibald Constable (Edinburgh and London, 1811).

Sharrock, Roger. "The Chemist and the Poet: Sir Humphry Davy and the Preface to the *Lyrical Ballads*," *Notes and Records of the Royal Society* 17 (1962): 57.

Shelley, Lady Jane, ed. *Shelley and Mary* (London: privately published, 1882), 4 Vols.

Shelley, Percy Bysshe. *The Complete Poetical Works of Percy Bysshe Shelley*, ed. Thomas Hutchinson, with Notes by Mary Shelley (London: Oxford University Press, 1905; repr. 1960).

———. *The Complete Works of Percy Bysshe Shelley* (The Julian Edition), ed. Roger Ingpen and Walter E. Peck (London: Ernest Benn Limited; New York: Scribner's, 1926–30), 10 Vols.

———. *The Letters of Percy Bysshe Shelley*, ed. Frederick L. Jones (Oxford: The Clarendon Press, 1964).

———. *Shelley's Prose*, ed. David Lee Clark (Albuquerque: University of New Mexico Press, 1954).

———. *Shelley and His Circle 1773–1822*, ed. Kenneth Neill Cameron and Donald H. Reiman (Cambridge: Harvard University Press, 1961–73), 6 Vols.

SHerwin, Paul. "*Frankenstein*: Creation as Catastrophe," *PMLA* 96 (1981): 883–903.

Small, Christopher. *Ariel Like a Harpy: Shelley, Mary and Frankenstein* (London: Gollancz, 1972).

Smith, John Harrington. "Shelley and Claire Clairmont," *PMLA* LIV (September 1939): 785–814.

———. "Shelley and Claire Again," *Studies in Philology* XLI (1944): 94–105.

Snyder, Robert Lane. "Apocalypse and Indeterminacy in Mary Shelley's *The Last Man*," *Studies in Romanticism* 17 (1978): 435–52.

Solkin, David H. "Portraiture in Motion: Edward Penny's *Marquis of Granby* and the Creation of a Public for English Art," *The Huntington Library Quarterly* 49 (1986): 1–23.

Spark, Muriel. *Child of Light—A Reassessment of Mary Wollstonecraft Shelley* (Hadleigh, Essex: Tower Bridge Publications, Ltd., revised and republished as *Mary Shelley—A Biography*, New York: E. P. Dutton, 1987).

Spector, Judith A. "Science Fiction and the Sex War: A Womb of One's Own," *Literature and Psychology* 31 (1981): 21–32.

Spurzheim, Johann Christoph. *The Physiognomical System of Drs. Gall and Spurzheim* (London, 1815).

Steiner, George. *In Bluebeard's Castle: Some Notes towards the Redefinition of Culture* (New Haven: Yale University Press, 1971).

Steinman, Lisa. "Shelley's Skepticism: Allegory in 'Alastor'," *ELH* 45 (1978): 255–69.

Sterrenburg, Lee. "*The Last Man*: Anatomy of Failed Revolutions," *Nineteenth Century Fiction* 33 (1978): 324–47.

Stone, Lawrence. *The Family, Sex and Marriage in England 1500–1800* (London: Weidenfeld and Nicolson, 1977).

Sunstein, Emily. Review of Jane Dunn's *Moon in Eclipse—A Life of Mary Shelley, Keats-Shelley Journal* 29 (1980): 223–24.

Swingle, L. J. "Frankenstein's Monster and Its Romantic Relatives: Problems of Knowledge in English Romanticism," *Texas Studies in Literature and Language* 15 (1973): 51–65.

Thorne, Barrie with Marilyn Yalom. *Rethinking the Family* (New York: Longman, 1982).

Thorslev, Peter. "Incest as Romantic Symbol," *Comparative Literature Studies* II (1965): 41–58.

Tomalin, Claire. *The Life and Death of Mary Wollstonecraft* (New York and London: Harcourt, Brace, Jovanovich, 1974).

Tomory, Peter. *The Life and Art of Henry Fuseli* (London: Thames and Hudson, 1972).

Tropp, Martin. *Mary Shelley's Monster* (Boston: Houghton, 1976).

Trumbach, Randolph. *The Rise of the Egalitarian Family—Aristocratic Kinship and Domestic Relations in Eighteenth-Century England* (New York, San Francisco, London: Academic Press, 1978).

Twitchell, James B. *Forbidden Partners—The Incest Taboo in Modern Culture* (New York: Columbia University Press, 1987).

Vasbinder, Samuel Holmes. "Scientific Attitudes in Mary Shelley's *Frankenstein*: Newtonian Monism as a Base for a Novel," *DAI* 37 (1976): 2842A (Kent State University).

Veeder, William. *Mary Shelley & Frankenstein—The Fate of Androgyny* (Chicago: University of Chicago Press, 1986).

———. "The Negative Oedipus: Father, *Frankenstein*, and the Shelleys," *Critical Inquiry* 12 (1986): 365–90.

Volney, Chasseboeuf de. *The Ruins: or A Survey of the Revolutions of Empires*, trans. (London: John Johnson, 1795; repr. 1796, 1807).

Vlasopolos, Anca. "*Frankenstein*'s Hidden Skeleton: The Psycho-Politics of Oppression," *Science-Fiction Studies* 10 (1983): 125–36.

Walker, Adam. *A System of Familiar Philosophy* (London, 1799).

Walling, William. *Mary Shelley* (New York: Twayne, 1972).

Walpole, Horace. *The Castle of Otranto*, in *Three Eighteenth Century Romances*, ed. Harrison Steeves (New York: Charles Scribner's Sons, 1931).

Wasserman, Earl R. *Shelley—A Critical Reading* (Baltimore: Johns Hopkins University Press, 1971).

Weiskel, Thomas. *The Romantic Sublime* (Baltimore: Johns Hopkins University Press, 1976).

Weissman, Judith. "A Reading of *Frankenstein* as the Complaint of a Political Wife," *Colby Library Quarterly* XII (December 1976): 171–80.

White, Newman Ivey. *Shelley* (London: Secker and Warburg, 1941; revised edition, 1947).

Wilkinson, Charles Henry. *Elements of Galvanism in Theory and Practice* (London, 1804), 2 Vols.

Wolff, Cynthia Griffin. "The Radcliffean Gothic Model: A Form for Feminine Sexuality," *Modern Language Studies* 9 (Fall 1979): 98–113.

Wollstonecraft, Mary. *Posthumous Works of the Author of a Vindication of the Rights of Woman*, ed. William Godwin (London: J. Johnson, 1798), Vols. I–IV.

———. *A Vindication of the Rights of Woman* (London: John Johnson, 1792). Reprint, ed. Carol H. Poston (New York: W. W. Norton, 1975).

Index